Winter Sports Tourism

Working in Winter Wonderlands

Simon Hudson

Louise Hudson

(G) Goodfellow Publishers Ltd

Published by Goodfellow Publishers Limited,
Woodeaton, Oxford, OX3 9TJ
http://www.goodfellowpublishers.com

British Library Cataloguing in Publication Data: a catalogue record for this
title is available from the British Library.

Library of Congress Catalog Card Number: on file.

ISBN: 978-1-910158-39-5

Design and typesetting by P.K. McBride, www.macbride.org.uk

Cover design by Cylinder

Printed by Baker & Taylor, www.baker-taylor.com

Contents

1   **Winter Sport Tourism: An Overview**   1
Spotlight: Charlie Locke, Multi-tasking ski entrepreneur   1
An introduction to winter sport tourism   4
The evolution of winter sport tourism   7
Profile : Patrick Bruchez, Alpine authenticity at the Hotel de Verbier   12
Winter sport tourism today   14
Case study: Winter sports, part of the 'China Dream'   15

2   **The Winter Sport Tourism Product**   21
Spotlight: Ian Hunter, Working in a winter wonderland   21
Winter sport activities   23
Winter sport resorts   28
Profile: The wonders of winter zip-lining   32
Indoor ski resorts   33
Clothing and equipment   35
Case study: The difficult birth of an all-season destination – Sochi, Russia   37

3   **Understanding the Consumer**   41
Spotlight: X-Games takes X-treme sports to X-citing new level   41
Profiling consumers   43
Motivations   46
Profile: Gstaad: Marketing to millennials   51
Constraints   53
Case study: Freeski female style   57

4   **Design and Planning for Winter Sport Resorts**   61
Spotlight: Paul Mathews, World's greatest ski resort designer   61
Design and planning   64
Profile: Creating America's biggest ski area   72
Dealing with seasonality   74
Case study: From humble to hedonistic -- the gentrification of Andermatt   80

5   **Management and Operations**   87
Spotlight: The quintessential ski couple   87
On-mountain operations   89
Profile: Portable ski instructor   93
Off-mountain operations   96
Case study: Powder and property investment in Japan   99

6   Marketing and Intermediaries   **103**
Spotlight: New Mexico True   103
Marketing communications   105
Branding   107
Advertising   109
Direct marketing   114
Profile: Snow Crystal   118
Intermediaries   120
Alliances   123
Case study: Year round dream skiing   125

7   The Importance of Public Relations and Earned Media   **129**
Spotlight: Susie English – Perfect PR   129
Introduction to public relations   131
Public relations techniques   133
Profile: John Brice, Combining PR with R'n'R   142
Measuring the impact of public relations efforts   144
Case study: 007 puts the spotlight on Sölden, Austria   148

8   The Impact of Technology on Winter Sport Tourism   **153**
Spotlight: Powder Matt, Social media maven   153
The impact of technology on marketing communications   155
The new consumer decision journey   158
Social media tools employed by winter sports marketers   161
Profile: Joe Nevin – From Apple to Aspen   165
The new mobile lifestyle   168
The impact of technology on operations   169
The impact of technology on clothing and equipment   171
Case study: Technology woven into the DNA at Vail Resorts   172

9   The Role of Events for Winter Sport Tourism   **177**
Spotlight: Skiing African-American style   177
The growth of events   179
Types of events   181
Profile: Crashed Ice   184
Planning and operating events   186
Marketing events   188
Leveraging events   190
Case study: Planning the South Korea 2018 Winter Olympics   194

10   The Economic, Social and Environmental Impacts   **199**
Spotlight: Dave Butler – A heli of a job   199
Impacts of winter sport tourism   201
Economic impacts   202

Social impacts   205
Profile: Keeping Whistler wild   210
Environmental impacts   212
The impact of climate change on winter sport tourism   215
Case study: Recycling snow 'Down Under'   217

11   Developing a Service Culture   223
Spotlight: Andrew Dunn, From bacon to beluga   223
Why service excellence is so critical   226
Creating a service culture   228
Profile: Customer service 'Kiwi-style'   233
Managing services promises   235
Service recovery   237
Case study: Customer-centric service at Steamboat Springs   243

12   The Future of the Winter Sport Tourism Industry   249
Spotlight: Tina Maze places Slovenia in the limelight   249
The future for the ski industry   251
Profile: From fear to fearlessness – Adaptive skiing   254
Ten consumer trends influencing winter sport tourism   256
Case study: The Locke ladies   264

Index   271

Acknowledgements

We are grateful to the many individuals and organizations that helped to make this book on winter sport tourism a reality. In particular, we would like to thank Tim Goodfellow, Sally North and Mac Bride from Goodfellow Publishers for their professional support throughout the writing process. We also appreciate the help of University of South Carolina Graduate Assistants Yuan Wang, Yuna Hayakumo and Qiuxue Wang. Finally, the book has benefited tremendously from the people in the industry who took the time to talk to us and help bring all the cases to life. These people are too numerous to name individually, but their enthusiasm and passion for snow sports was obvious in all our interviews, and we are indebted to their contribution.

Preface

The ski and snowboard industry has experienced remarkable growth in the last fifty years. It is estimated that today there are some 120 million skiers and snowboarders worldwide, with around 2,000 ski resorts in 80 countries catering to this important market. While established destinations in North America, Western Europe, Japan, New Zealand and Australia are experiencing maturity, new resorts in Asia and Eastern Europe are competing for budding generations of skiers from countries such as China and Russia. Along with these demographic shifts, technology is also having a huge impact on skiing products and services, and how they are experienced. At the same time climate change is posing challenges to ski hills all over the world. Such dramatic changes require a fresh look at this exciting and dynamic industry.

This new text will be of great interest to students, researchers, and practitioners – particularly those working in the ski industry. There are 12 chapters in the book, with each section exploring the theme of 'working in winter wonderlands' – effectively telling the story of the industry through the eyes of those who shape it.

Chapter 1 begins by plotting the evolution of winter sport tourism, from skiing's earliest emergence as a leisure pastime during the mid-nineteenth century in Europe, to the present day industry, characterized by commodification and diversification. Chapter 2 focuses on the winter sport tourism product - the activities, resorts, and supporting industries such as clothing and equipment sectors. Chapter 3 is dedicated to understanding the consumer, and Chapter 4 explores design and planning for winter sports resorts. Chapter 5 looks at management and operations, both on- and off-mountain, and is followed by Chapter 6 which is dedicated to marketing. Chapter 7 emphasizes the importance of public relations and media in the industry, and Chapter 8 focuses on the impact of technology on communications, operations, and clothing and equipment. Chapter 9 concentrates on events in the winter sports industry, looking at growth and different types of events, as well as their planning, marketing and leveraging. Chapter 10 is an important one, covering the economic, social and environmental impacts of winter sport tourism, and is followed by Chapter 11 which discusses customer service and how destinations can develop a service culture. Finally, Chapter 12 looks towards the future for the ski industry, outlining the key consumer trends influencing winter sport tourism.

Each chapter begins with a *Spotlight* featuring the occupation of a frontline individual in the snow sports industry. In these Spotlights, we learn why Charlie Locke has been honored with a trophy for his outstanding contribution to ski tourism for the Americas; how Paul Mathews became the world's top ski resort designer; why marketing for the X Games is heavily weighted towards social media and online advertising; how Sun Peaks in Canada has cornered the market on après ski entertainments; and how Andrew Dunn developed a strong service culture at Ski Scott Dunn. We also get the inside scoop on jobs such as Director of Communications for Ski Utah; Senior Vice President – Marketing, Sales & Resort Experience – for Resorts of the Canadian Rockies; and Director of Sustainability for the world's largest heli-ski operation.

Each chapter also contains a *Profile* on a particular resort, organization or individual, illustrating a specific concept or theoretical principle presented in the chapter. Fascinating Profiles in the book include those of Patrick Bruchez, owner and manager of Verbier's oldest hotel; Joe Nevin, creator of Bumps for Boomers in Aspen; and Darren Turner, developer of an innovative ski instruction app. The book also profiles Crystal Holidays, one of Britain's largest ski operators, Red Bull's sponsoring of Crashed Ice, and the growing importance of adaptive skiing.

At the end of every chapter there is an up-to-date, relevant and detailed *Case Study*, and as a collection, these Case Studies cover a variety of organizations and regions worldwide. Designed to foster critical thinking, the cases highlight actual business scenarios that stress concepts found in the chapters. Case Studies in the book feature women's instruction camps, Vail's development plans in Utah, ski resort infrastructure in Japan, DreamSki Adventures in South America, the EpicMix app in Colorado, the upcoming Olympics in South Korea, and the growing ski scenes in China and Slovenia. All Spotlights, Profiles and Case Studies have been developed following a personal visit or in-depth interviews conducted by the authors, and there is a pervasive international flavor throughout the book.

About the authors

As well as being an accomplished skier, **Dr. Simon Hudson** is an Endowed Chair in Tourism at the University of South Carolina. He has held previous academic positions at universities in Canada and England, and has worked as a visiting professor in Austria, Switzerland, Spain, Fiji, New Zealand, the United States, and Australia. Prior to working in academia, Dr. Hudson spent several years working in the ski industry in Europe. Dr. Hudson has written six books. His first, written in 2000 and called *Snow Business*, was the first book to be written about the international ski industry, and *Sports and Adventure Tourism* was published by Haworth in 2003. His third book, *Marketing for Tourism and Hospitality: A Canadian Perspective*, has sold over 8,000 copies, and is in its second edition. *Tourism and Hospitality Marketing: A Global Perspective* was published by Sage in 2008, and *Golf Tourism* and *Customer Service for Hospitality & Tourism* were both published by Goodfellow in 2010 and 2013 respectively. He is frequently invited to international tourism conferences as a keynote speaker.

Louise Hudson, who introduced Dr. Hudson to skiing, is a freelance journalist living in South Carolina. She co-wrote *Golf Tourism* and *Customer Service for Hospitality & Tourism*. Originally trained in journalism in England, she writes about skiing for many publications including *Ski Canada Magazine, LA Times, The Dallas Morning News Travel, Houston Chronicle, Canada's Globe and Mail, Dreamscapes Magazine, Calgary Sun, Calgary Herald, Edmonton Sun, Vancouver Sun, Ottawa Citizen, Canada's MORE magazine, Eat Drink Travel, Opulence, Alberta Parent, Calgary's Child, Travel Alberta, Fresh Tracks, Alberta Hospitality magazine* and several U.K. publications. A committed ski bum, Louise has skied every season for the past 42 years all over Europe and North America. She is also a prolific ski blogger on http://www.onetwoski.blogspot.com and a ski tweeter @skiblogger.

Winter Sport Tourism: An Overview

Charlie Locke

In 2014 Lake Louise was named Canada's Best Ski Resort at The World Ski Awards in Kitzbühel, Austria for the second year running. At the same time, owner Charlie Locke was honoured with the trophy for Outstanding Contribution to Ski Tourism for the Americas, the winter sports' Oscar. "This is the high point of my career," says Locke, "I was thrilled we won Best Ski Resort in Canada again, but this personal recognition in front of esteemed peers in an industry so dear to me – just an amazing surprise. I am feeling extremely grateful and honoured."

Known worldwide through the Winterstart World Cup, which kicks off the professional down-hill ski racing season, Lake Louise is a first-class resort with one of the longest ski seasons – stretching from early November into May. The natural beauty of the UNESCO world heritage site is matched by the alpine architectural perfection of its sumptuously rustic lodges.

Unlike many other world-class resorts which are part of corporations or conglomerates, Lake Louise is family-run by Charlie Locke, his wife Louise and daughters Robin and Kimberley. Each has a pivotal executive role and they also muck in at peak periods helping with frontline customer service to ensure the perfect experience for their international clientele. "On very busy days, I have been known to do everything from parking cars to helping in guest relations, to checking lift tickets and assisting with line control and minimization," says Locke.

In winter, he spends four days a week at Lake Louise Ski Resort and three days in the accounting/marketing office in Calgary. "My daily job is to oversee all things to do with the resort, including, but not limited to, personnel issues, costs, pricing, revenues, marketing arrangements, insurance, finance, capital, banking, maintenance, cost control, customer service, grooming and snowmaking, legal, miscellaneous corporate requirements in terms of dealing with the governments (including Parks Canada) and long term planning," Locke explains. His multi-tasking background in cattle farming has been pivotal to his success, he adds, as well as years spent as a mountain guide. He also runs several producing oil wells.

With snow being crucial to the success of a ski resort, Locke's typical day starts with a review of the snow report, the grooming report and the run-open report. "It ends with reviewing the skier count for the day and comparing it, and the year to date numbers, with budgets," Locke adds. He also takes time to compare the Lake Louise reports with those disseminated by Ski Banff Lake Louise and occasionally suggests amendments: "For example, this morning I noted that the report said 20 cm of snow in the last 48 hours, when in reality, there was 20 cm in the last 36 hours. This minor change could make the difference of 100 skiers or so and all of the incremental revenue flows to the bottom line."

Throughout the winter season Locke tours the base as well as the ski area of the 4200 acre resort on the lookout for elements of the grooming, snow control and customer experience which could be improved. "I walk through the lodge, including all the men's washrooms, on a regular basis, talk to managers, supervisors, front-liners and customers, and consistently pick up paper and tidy public spaces and washrooms," he adds. Locke passes suggestions on to area managers who refer his ideas down the command chain to relevant managers and supervisors. "I do this so there is no confusion as to who their day-to-day supervisors/bosses are," Locke explains. Other tasks include fielding around 60 emails per day, signing checks and reviewing the daily bank report. For Locke, this is all a labor of love: "My hobby is my job, and my job is my hobby. I cannot really retire as I have never had a job."

Locke's connection to the ski industry stretches back to the 1970s when he first helped fund the ski lifts at Lake Louise. In the 1990s he founded Resorts of the Canadian Rockies (RCR), encompassing eight ski resorts across Alberta and British Columbia. "Lake Louise was only 15 per cent of the work and, because of its size and ability to hire and retain good managers, created 50 per cent of the profit. Big resorts have the critical mass to do things right," Locke says. He sold RCR in 2003, retaining ownership of Lake Louise.

Over 35 years, Locke has seen dramatic changes in the winter sports world. "These range from IT, to grooming, to snow-making, to lifts, to food service, to difficulties with the environmental lobby, to the way we do our marketing, to the way we distribute our food, rent skis, and teach lessons," he says. Lake Louise has led the way in Canada in many of these respects, anticipating and responding to trends. One particular innovation was the provision of a volunteer ski guiding team, which is available to guide and to orientate customers onhill and at resort base all season. "We initiated the 'ski friend' idea, and copyrighted the name," Locke explains. "Many resorts tried to use that name, including Whistler, but we had to remind them that they had to use another name hence 'snowhosts' at most resorts."

Another front-running initiative was the provision of discount cards for lift tickets. "Originally, at Lake Louise, we called these 'Blue Cards' as a brewery provided us with a sizable contribution to our marketing costs in exchange for naming it after one of their brews. The card later became the Louise Card which I believe is one of the most successful skier incentive cards in North America," Locke says.

The daycare at Lake Louise is the only one in Canada – and one of only a handful in North America - to take babies from 18 *days* old. Despite the permitting and running difficulties and costs, this is pivotal to Locke's commitment to keep families skiing. Most resorts stipulate 18 *months* as the youngest age for childcare. Lake Louise daycare also has its own carpark, an added convenience for parents bearing babies and bags.

The biggest boost to the ski industry, according to Locke, has come from snowboarding, closely followed by the invention of shaped skis. High-speed lifts have also transformed ski hills, resulting in shorter lineups and increased density of skiers on the slopes. "Grooming has resulted in making it easier, and faster, for most to get down the hill and to turn and stop," Locke says. "In the early to late 50s it was unusual to see anyone who could make a parallel turn. Now, of course, even beginners, with the new ski technology, are turning parallel, from their first few days on skis." Easier equipment is one of the factors leading to a general reduction in the amount of ski school lessons required and the gradual demise of the traditional 'ski week'. Destination skiers used to take a whole week of lessons but this has now been reduced, typically, to three or four days of instruction.

Other trends Locke has witnessed include a demand for complementary activities as well as a higher quality of food. Lake Louise now encompasses snowshoeing and a torchlight descent plus dinner dance après ski event as well as a two-lane tube park, a beginner fun zone, a snowcross course, first tracks program, cross country skiing, backcountry ski tours, Podium Club race centre and a substantial terrain park.

Lake Louise has also expanded its restaurants and bar facilities including the renovated Whitehorn Lodge with mountain modern décor, first-rate cuisine, a panoramic patio, and ice bar when conditions permit. Nestled at the base of Larch Mountain, Temple Lodge features an outdoor BBQ, a renovated self-service eatery, a Starbucks coffee, cookies and cake café and, Sawyer's Nook, a cozy, table-service restaurant. Back at base, the Northface Bistro serves bountiful breakfast and lunch buffets and Powderkeg Lounge is famous for its massive nacho platters and succulent pizzas.

Over the past decade all of these culinary facilities – and adjoining restrooms – have been renovated and expanded with customer comfort and changing needs in mind. Another outcome of technological improvements in skiing, according to Locke, is an increased emphasis on ski lodge facilities. "In today's ski world, because of high-speed lifts and shorter lineups, people tend to spend more time in the lodges. In my youth, we never went in for lunch as that was the time when the lineups were shorter," Locke recalls. The expense of constantly updating amenities can be the death knell for smaller resorts, he maintains. "The smaller community-run and single proprietor resorts which do less than, say, 120,000 annual skier visits, have a great deal of difficulty generating sufficient capital to maintain their lodges or replace their aging equipment. So, a number of these smaller resorts have closed which is going to impact the number of skiers in the future," Locke explains. "Generally, our sustaining capital budget allows us to maintain our lodges, staff housing, and other buildings and equipment fairly well, upgrading washrooms and food and beverage distribution systems regularly, always looking for ways to improve the customer experience."

Other modern day requirements include technology, good access roads, good grooming, snowmaking and avalanche control, all of which have been addressed at Lake Louise in recent years. The twinning of the TransCanada highway between Banff and Lake Louise has made a considerable difference to traffic flow, travel time and also safety. Over the past two seasons the resort has added improved water lines for snowmaking and six new snow cats for enhanced grooming.

IT-wise, there are cellphone-recharging stations, computer terminals, ATMs and Wi-Fi in the main lodge. Lake Louise has its own blog and is active on Facebook, Twitter, Pinterest, YouTube, Google+ and Instagram. And, in 2014, Lake Louise became the first Canadian ski resort on Snapchat (with daily posts download-able to smartphones), employing a social media maven to keep the resort's social media presence ahead of the game. The Internet, though, has created another rival for the ski industry, luring youth away from outdoor recreation. "The percentage of the population who ski has dropped in recent years as the youth can now get free entertainment on the Internet, and are more digitally, as opposed to experientially, driven in general, and there have been fewer opportunities to learn skiing through the school system," Locke explains. "The key thing the industry has to learn is how to generate more skiers and keep 'first timers' in the sport. The retention rate for people learning to ski is reportedly only about 15 per cent."

Sources: Interview with Charlie Locke, January 2015

An introduction to winter sport tourism

Winter sport tourism falls under the umbrella of sport tourism, one of the fastest growth sectors of the tourism industry. Although sport tourism is a relatively new concept in contemporary vernacular, its scope of activity is far from a recent phenomenon. The notion of people traveling to participate in and watch sport dates back to the ancient Olympic Games, and the practice of stimulating tourism through sport has existed for over a century. Within the last few decades however, destinations have begun to recognize the significant potential of sport tourism, and they are now aggressively pursuing this attractive market niche.

Sport tourism has also gained strong academic interest in recent years. This is evident in the publication of numerous textbooks related to sport tourism (e.g. Hinch & Higham, 2011; Standeven & De Knopp, 1999; Hudson, 2003; Weed & Bull, 2004; Higham, 2005; Gibson, 2006), as well as the development of the *Journal of Sport Tourism* and a number of special journal issues devoted to sport tourism. Much of this work focuses on describing and defining the concept of sport travel, but broadly defined, sport tourism includes travel away from a person's primary residence to participate in a sporting activity for recreation or competition; travel to observe sport at the grass roots or elite level; and travel to visit a sport attraction such as a sports' hall of fame or a water park, for example.

Robinson and Gammon (2004) differentiate between 'sport tourism' and 'tourism sport' and suggest that that there can be a hard and a soft definition for each. Sport tourists actively participate in competitive or recreational sport, whilst traveling to and/or staying in places outside their usual environment. The difference between the hard and the soft sport tourist is that the hard sport tourist actively or passively participates at a competitive sporting event. Tourism sport on the other hand consists of persons traveling to and/or staying in places outside their usual environment and participating in, actively or passively, a competitive or recreational sport as a secondary activity. The holiday or visit is their primary motive for travel. The hard definition of tourism sport includes holidaymakers who use sport as a secondary enrichment to their holiday whilst a soft definition of tourism sport involves visitors who, as a minor part of their trip, engage in some form of sport on a purely incidental basis. Figure 1.1 applies this framework to winter sport tourism.

Winter Sport and Tourism

Winter Sport Tourism		Winter Tourism Sport	
Hard definition	Soft definition	Hard definition	Soft definition
Passive or active participation at a competitive sporting event.	Primarily active recreational participation in sport.	Visitors who engage in some minor form of sport or leisure; their participation is purely incidental.	Tourists who as a secondary reinforcement passively or actively participate in sport.
Winter Olympics Paralympic games World Championships X-Games Crashed Ice	Ski holidays Ski resorts Ski schools Ski clinics	This category is open to interpretation and includes all ski-related facilities that tourists encounter during their stay, though they wouldn't necessarily consider using them	Winter sport resorts Hotels near ski resorts Mountain holidays with ski resorts nearby Holiday villa complexes with ski hills Visitor Attractions

Figure 1.1: Application of the sport tourism and tourism sport framework to winter sport tourism (Source: Adapted from Robinson & Gammon, p. 229)

Winter sport tourism itself has also been defined in a number of ways, and theoretically could include any type of sport tourism undertaken during the winter. However, for the purposes of this book, winter sport tourism is simply defined as travel away from home to participate in or observe winter sports on the snow, or to visit attractions associated with snow-based winter sports. Furthermore, the focus of this book is the ski and snowboard industry, an industry supported by 115 million participants worldwide who travel to about 2,000 ski resorts in 80 countries. However, winter sport tourism has numerous other facets and these will be considered in Chapters 2 and 3 of the book. In fact Mintel (2012) classifies winter sports into four segments: downhill skiing; snowboarding; cross-country skiing (including skating); and ski touring. While alpine skiing and snowboarding are mass participation sports, cross-country and ski touring remain niche activities.

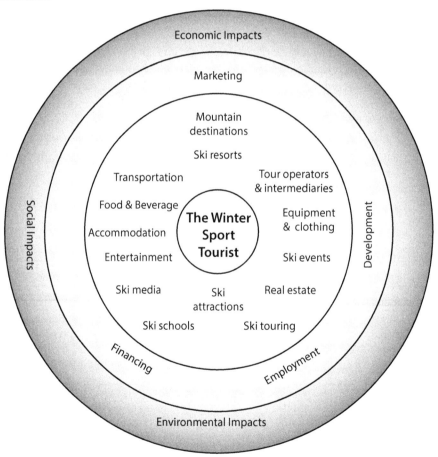

Figure 1.2: The business of winter sport tourism

Figure 1.2 is a representation of the business of winter sport tourism. The figure shows the winter sport tourists in the middle and they can be divided into three basic categories:

1 Tourists who go on holiday principally to participate in winter sports;

2 Tourists who participate in winter sports as a secondary activity whilst on holiday or on a business trip; and

3 Those who attend winter sports events as spectators, or visit winter sports attractions.

Chapter 3 expands on the segmentation of winter sport tourists. They in turn are served by a number of different sectors. These include the ski resorts themselves (Chapters 2, 5 and 9), intermediaries (Chapter 6), marketing specialists (Chapter 6 and 8), and the media (Chapter 7). In turn, these stakeholders have to make important decisions regarding planning and development, marketing, technology, financing and human resource development (Chapters 5, 8 and 11). Finally, the industry has a number of economic, social and environmental impacts, and these are addressed in Chapter 10 of the book.

Skiing is no longer the strenuous climb to risky terrain and untouched nature, but a mass touristic undertaking in a highly mechanized ski arena (Hudson, 2000). How snow sports have developed into such an important part of the tourism industry is described in the next section.

The evolution of winter sport tourism

The origins of skiing are open to debate. In the Altay Mountains of China, a handful of petroglyphs have been discovered depicting archaic skiing scenes, including one of a human figure on skis chasing an ibex. But since petroglyphs are notoriously hard to date, it remains a controversial clue in the debate over where skiing was born (Jenkins, 2013). Chinese archaeologists contend it was carved 5,000 years ago, but others say it is probably only 3,000 years old. The oldest written record that alludes to skiing, a Chinese text, also points to the Altay, but dates to the Western Han dynasty, which began in 206 B.C. Norwegian archaeologists have also found ski petroglyphs and, in Russia, what appears to be a ski tip, carbon-dated to 8,000 years ago, was recently excavated from a peat bog. Each country stakes its own claim to the first skiers. What is widely accepted, however, is that whoever first strapped on a pair of skis, likely did so to hunt animals (Jenkins, 2013).

Documentation of skiing's earliest emergence as a leisure pastime associated with tourism dates back to the mid-nineteenth century in Europe. There are references in 1868 to Norwegians traveling on skis from Telemark to Christiana (now Oslo) primarily for social purposes. Almost two decades later (1890), recreational skiing emerged in North America (Scharff, 1974), and soon after, socially-focused skiing clubs began to develop across Europe and North America, facilitating the creation of more and better ski facilities (Batchelor et al., 1937).

It is believed that winter mountain holidays started after 1866, when an hotelier in St. Moritz, Switzerland, invited a small group of British summer guests to visit his property during the winter months (Cockerell, 1988). On their return, this group enthused so much about their trip that it soon became fashionable among the British upper classes to take a winter holiday in Switzerland. In those days there were no lifts, so considerable time was spent walking and climbing mountains but, in the winter of 1910-11, Sir Henry Lunn managed to persuade the local authorities in Mürren to open the Lauterbrunnen-Mürren railway line. The Lauberhorn drag-lift opened the following year. Lunn was then responsible for organizing the first-ever downhill race in Montana, Switzerland in 1911. Meanwhile the 1905 Olympic Games had included skiing in its program of activities, despite skiing not being a recognized Olympic sport. At this time, not only was there a growing interest in skiing as a participant sport, but there was a desire on the part of destination managers and developers to keep resorts operational for an entire winter season. In the process of developing this strategy, the concept of a broader set of physical facilities and a more sustainable market base for skiing development is believed to have originated (Williams, 1993).

By the beginning of the First World War in 1914, there were at least as many German skiers in Switzerland as there were British, and these two countries today still provide a large proportion of outbound winter tourists. In 1924, skiing was introduced as a formal event at the Olympic Games in Chamonix, France, and was highlighted again in the 1932 Olympic Winter Games in Lake Placid, U.S. These two events helped place skiing at the forefront of winter recreational activity in both Europe and North America and gave a further push to its development as a major contributor to winter-based tourism (Liebers, 1963).

In 1929, the first mechanically-propelled uphill lift designed solely for skiers was installed in Canada, and within a few years most ski slopes of any significance in North America and Europe had one or more such lifts in place. Snow-trains transporting thousands of skiers to the slopes became commonplace throughout North America in the 1930s, and then in 1936 Union Pacific developed the first tourism-oriented ski resort in Sun Valley, Idaho. The resort became the prototype for world-class ski areas in North America. In Europe, the first real mountain ski resort was Megève in the Haute Savoie region of France, its development coinciding with the first ski lift in France in 1933. The Winter Olympic Games of 1936 held in Garmisch-Partenkirchen in Bavaria, Germany included both downhill and slalom races, and further raised the profile of the sport.

The growth of skiing was dampened by the Second World War but, after the war, skiing in a mass tourism context began to emerge. Inspired by the military role that skiing played in northern combat areas (my own father learned to ski in the army), skiing was introduced to thousands of returning troops as a form of winter recreation. Meanwhile better access to ski destinations was brought on by the development of family automobiles and rising standards of living, and rapid improvements resulted in safer and more comfortable ski equipment. By the late 1940s and early 1950s, the second phase of ski resort development took place in France with the opening of resorts such as Courchevel, Méribel and Tignes. Off-slope amenities for skiers began to emerge, with lodging, culinary experiences and entertainment becoming important components of a ski vacation (Tanler, 1966). The invention of snowmaking in the 1950s gave a further impetus to the growth of ski facilities, a technological development that not only lengthened the duration of a ski season, but also made the sport possible in areas where natural snowfall was less than abundant.

The 1960s saw the start of the great ski boom. Europe witnessed the creation of a new generation of fully integrated ski stations, while in North America, larger resorts in New England, Colorado, California, the Canadian Rockies and the Eastern townships of Quebec emerged to meet the growing demand for winter vacations. Wooden skis and leather boots were slowly phased out and replaced by metal and fibre glass skis and plastic boots. While the 1970s were a period of massive market and product expansion, the 1980s presented a decade characterized by industry consolidation and product management (Williams, 1993). Influenced by changing demographics, ski markets began to mature. By the mid-1980s ski facility supply had in many regions outstripped demand, and many poorly managed ski destinations were experiencing financial difficulties (Kottke, 1990). In response, destinations were forced to address both product and market issues in a more business-like fashion, and a more tourism-focused approach to ski area development commenced. Larger ski centers with tourist, rather than resident, ski markets continued to grow, while many small centers faltered. Consequently, between 1980 and 1990 the number of ski areas dropped by 18 per cent in North America. Counteracting this trend, ski area capacity expanded by approximately 50 per cent during the same period.

In the 1990s the greatest impact on the ski industry came from the snowboarding boom. One of the disadvantages of skiing is that it is technically demanding at a high level of performance. Unless they start at a very young age, the average recreational skiers taking an annual week's ski holiday cannot develop the skills necessary to ski steep, fast runs, big bumps and deep powder snow. However, a snowboarder can learn to stay upright and turn after one morning, and tackle powder within a week. Such a high learning curve led many skiers to cross over to snowboarding, with over 60 per cent of snowboarders in North America in the 90s having skied before they adopted boarding (Spring, 1997). Snowboarders now represent around 30 per cent of the market for most ski resorts.

The arrival of 'shaped' skis on the market was another big influence on the industry in the 1990s. Deep sidecuts to help skis carve short, clean turns had been sneaking up on the industry for a century, but in 1991 Elan came out with a Sidecut Extreme (SCX) ski that had a 22.25mm sidecut, three times what most racers were using for slalom at the time. The ski performed extremely well on the race circuit, and then in 1993 Elan sent out the prototype SCX to ski instructors in American resorts and the reaction was extremely positive. The instructors couldn't believe what a fabulous teaching tool the new skis were – beginners and intermediate skiers were able to carve turns almost immediately after trying shaped skis. Atomic, Fischer and Head joined Elan a few years later and began to design sidecut skis of their own, and by 1997 shapes had proliferated in all directions. It was possible to buy deep shapes, moderate shapes, race shapes, carver shapes, powder shapes, expert shapes, learn-to-carve shapes and learn-to-ski shapes (see Patrick Bruchez's comments in the Profile below). In fact, shapes were so radical by the turn of the century that the International Ski Federation had to impose limits on the size of sidecuts used in ski races.

The 2000s witnessed a general maturity of the industry and Figure 1.3, which shows the evolution of skier visits per region, confirms this trend. Total skier visits fluctuated around the 400 million mark during this decade, with the 2006/07 season characterized by particularly weak demand due to unusually warm weather in the Alps. Visits were steady as major mature markets (like the U.S., Canada and the Alpine countries) stagnated or declined, as was the case of Japan, while other markets were emerging, such as China and Korea.

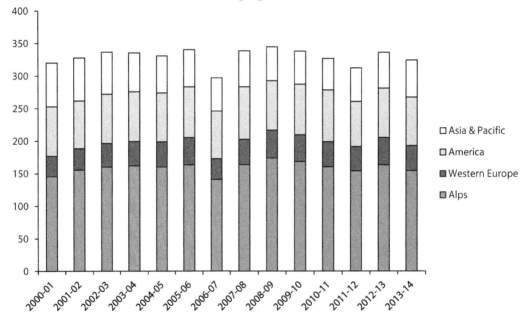

Figure 1.3: Evolution of skier visits per region (Vanat, 2015, p. 14)

The 2000s were also characterized by diversification in the industry. An increasing proportion of those taking winter sports holidays on a regular basis were not skiing at all. Secondly, as Charlie Locke explains in the opening Spotlight, even avid skiers were typically skiing less. On average they were somewhat older, and new high-speed lifts enabled skiers to attain their physical stamina quotient much more quickly. So winter resorts realized that they had to offer more activities than just skiing and boarding, both on- and off-snow. The more progressive resorts began to expand the range of activities they offered, such as ice-skating, snow-scooting, sledging and dog-sledding, ice-driving, paragliding, snowmobiling, and tubing (the increasingly popular activity of sliding down the slope on the inner-tube of a truck tire). Many resorts – Verbier in Switzerland is one example and Lake Louise another (see opening Spotlight) – also looked to enhance the efficiency, quality and profitability of their restaurants and shops. The market for in-destination services in general is vast. According to Euromonitor International (2014), it accounted for almost $2,000 billion globally in 2013 (see Figure 1.4) – significantly larger than the transportation and travel accommodation markets – and it is expected to record a strong eight per cent CAGR (compound annual growth rate) in the 2013-2018 period, to reach $2,800 billion.

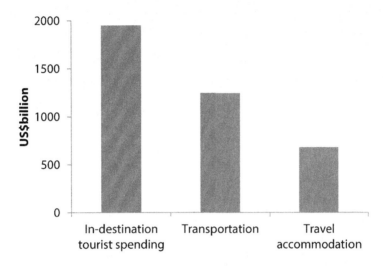

Figure 1.4: Global travel and tourism sales by category 2013 (Source: Adapted from Euromonitor International, 2014).

In addition to diversifying their product offerings, destinations are also positioning themselves as more than a place to visit, attempting to expand economic development by attracting new businesses and new residents. Stowe in Vermont, for example, is currently regarded as one of the most tech-friendly towns in the U.S., according to Google. In its second annual award program, Google named Stowe as the 2014 eCity for the State of Vermont. The eCity Awards recognize the strongest online business communities in all fifty states, communities that are embracing the web to find new customers, connect with existing clients and fueling their local economies. Stowe is now home to a robust array of businesses that have created growth and advanced the digital economy in the state. Stowe's recognition as Vermont's eCity is also built upon the many small businesses that are participating in e-commerce and the technology industry throughout the community.

Profile : Patrick Bruchez, Alpine authenticity at the Hotel de Verbier

Hotel de Verbier, photo courtesy of Inghams

The Hotel de Verbier is the quintessential, authentic Alpine hotel in Switzerland's trendiest ski resort. Set on the main square just 400m from the slopes, it is at the epicenter of après ski, commerce, retail and, on December 31, one of the biggest New Year's celebrations in the Alps.

Known for its Royal chalet girl (Sarah Ferguson worked in Verbier in her youth), for its celebrated hotelier (Richard Branson owns the 18-bed, mega-expensive Verbier Lodge) and also for its focus on all-night partying (at the 40-year-old Farm Club for example), Verbier has always been hip. Nearby Zermatt appeals to the more mature, affluent crowd, but Verbier has always attracted a young, trendy mix of ski bums, jetsetters, regular holidaymakers and entrepreneurs. Every March the world holds its breath, watching top freeriders plummet from vertiginous slopes on the Mont Fort glacier during the Swatch Xtreme Verbier competition.

Patrick Bruchez inherited what is now Verbier's oldest hotel from his father, who built it back in 1948. Bruchez has owned and managed the 31 room, boutique operation since 1981. "Due to the size of the hotel, I am involved in all fields of the operation," he says. "Human resources, marketing, finance, maintenance, front desk, back office, general manager, housekeeping manager etc."

The hotel was the resort headquarters for the Ski Club of Great Britain, an organization which provides free on and off-piste ski guiding for members, with reps stationed around the Alps. Bruchez hosted the Ski Club reps all season and combined daily "office hours" with happy hour in the Hotel de Verbier bar.

The hotel has relied heavily on the British ski market during winter and for many seasons Bruchez was the smiling face at the front desk, ensuring customer satisfaction in the après ski bar and restaurant. "The perks of the job include being your own boss," he says. "But at the same time it is often trying and heavy duty. There is a direct return from both dissatisfied customers and good clients."

Service can often mean a shoulder to cry on, according to Bruchez. "One lady came in crying, telling me that it was the third time that day that she was losing her husband and she was sure he wanted to get rid of her." With its extensive network of around 90 interlinked lifts spanning four resorts (Verbier, Veysonnaz, Thyon and Nendaz) and 412km of skiable terrain, it is not surprising that many guests get lost while skiing. "So, I have the long story of people skiing the Four Valleys and missing the return lift, explaining their adventure getting back by bus, train, taxi, etc," says Bruchez. His powers of diplomacy, however, were more severely tested by the guest who told him that the last time he was in Switzerland there were no mountains. "He must have traveled in the Swiss plains on a foggy day," Bruchez quips.

In order to stay current, Bruchez has traveled extensively, observing trends in other ski resorts and hotels and avidly reading papers and magazines dedicated to the trade. This, however, has revealed an inequity in pricing between Switzerland and other Alpine ski areas which is always a challenge to address: "There are less and less hotels in Verbier, and the new hotels built are of much higher rating, so not really direct competition. My competition comes more from other resorts such as Zermatt, St Moritz, and Austria, where the standards of the same category of hotel are higher, and people who come to Verbier are surprised to have to pay more here than there for the same product but of less quality."

In recent years Bruchez has noticed a trend towards faster pace operations. "Last minute booking, shorter stays, more competition, and the difficulty of maintaining your property up to the standards that change rapidly," he says. Daily work involves interaction with his own staff, local authorities and the Verbier tourist office as well as ski tour operators and others specializing in hiking, music and the arts.

Customer turnover has also changed, meaning fewer regular returnees. This has led to Bruchez reaching out to British tour operator, Inghams to help fill rooms. The 80-year-old company, part of the Swiss travel organization, Hotelplan, now runs the hotel during the winter season, November - April: "You need to be more and more aggressive when it comes to marketing your product; with Inghams, for instance, the hotel is full from day one to the last," he explains. Inghams provides its own ski guides, so the Ski Club of Great Britain is no longer based at the hotel but continues to operate the same service based from the T-Bar, also in Verbier's Place Centrale.

Other trends emerging during Bruchez's career include technological changes which have significantly enhanced the sport: "Carving skis, free ride, more fun skiing, cheap flights, better groomed slopes which makes skiing more accessible to everyone," says Bruchez. He feels snowboarding has enhanced the industry, with its spirit of fun and freedom infusing the whole world of alpine skiing.

Over the years the Hotel de Verbier has attracted many ski celebs including British journalist Alistair Scott, who dubbed Verbier 'the Aspen of the Alps' - and particularly praised the Hotel de Verbier's famous homemade happy hour chips. Top skiers, such as Pirmin Zurbriggen, musical stars including Youssou N'Dour and British racing driver, Damon Hill have all stayed at the Hotel de Verbier. But, like many service-centric hoteliers, Bruchez has been reluctant to make mileage out of celebrities who value their privacy.

Sources: Interview with Patrick Bruchez, September 2014

Winter sport tourism today

The current ski and snowboard market is estimated at some 120 million world-wide (Vanat, 2015). Europe accounts for approximately 30 per cent of skiers and boarders, the U.S. and Canada about 20 per cent, and Asia and Pacific 20 per cent. The majority of these participants are domestic, although skiing is truly global, with about 80 countries around the world hosting either outdoor or indoor skiing facilities. Around 2,000 ski resorts have been identified, with the U.S., Japan and France having the most resorts, more than 200 each. Austria and France have the greatest number of large ski resorts which register one million or more skier visits annually. Besides the major destinations of Europe and North America, there are a number of smaller destinations where skiing has been an industry for a long time or is currently developing (Vanat, 2015). These include Eastern Europe, China, New Zealand and Australia.

Today, there is clearly a trend towards stagnation in attendance in major markets (Vanat, 2015). Figure 1.5 shows the trends in skier visits over the last 10 years in Europe and North America.

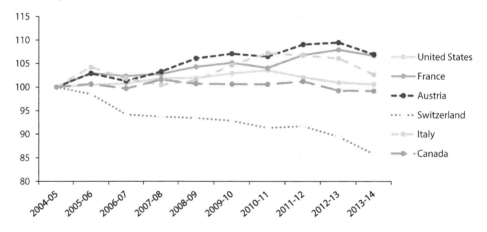

Figure 1.5: Average skier visits over the last 10 years in Europe and North America on a 100 base for season 2004/05 (Source: Vanat, 2015, p. 10)

The industry also continues to undergo consolidation, particularly in North America, as large operators buy up individual ski resorts or send small operators out of business. The industry is highly competitive and the recession hurt some of the smaller operators, who have less access to capital than well-funded operators such as Vail Resorts and Intrawest. IBISWorld estimates that technological advances and rising infrastructure costs are the primary reason for increasing concentration in the industry, and further consolidation is possible as smaller regional resorts are acquired by larger resort operators with more sophisticated management capability (IBISWorld, 2013). At the end of the 2015 season, one characterized by poor snow conditions in western North America, CNL Lifestyle

Properties, decided to sell off its portfolio of 16 ski resorts, collectively worth hundreds of millions of dollars. If sold to a single buyer, it would be the biggest ski resort purchase in history. The 16 properties include Crested Butte in Colorado, Brighton in Utah, Northstar-at-Tahoe and Sierra-at-Tahoe in California, and Sunday River and Sugarloaf in Maine.

The ski industry is highly vulnerable not only to spending patterns, but also to climate change, which can have a devastating economic impact on ski resorts. A recent study by the American Natural Resources Defense Council (NRDC) found that the ski industry in the U.S. lost over $1 billion in aggregate revenue because of poor snow seasons between 2000 and 2010 (NRDC, 2012). Predictions, though, are that the industry in that country will return to stable growth over the next five years, with consumers anxious to return to their previous spending patterns and vacationing habits. Elsewhere, the regions of Eastern Europe and Asia and Pacific represent the future growth potential of the market. Vanat (2015) suggests that they may end up reaching the weight equivalent of the other major regions in terms of skier visits by the year 2020. If this growth occurs without affecting skier visits at western resorts, worldwide skier visits may then increase to over 420 million by this date. The final case study focuses on one of those countries that could have a major impact on the future of winter sport tourism – China.

Case study: Winter sports, part of the 'China Dream'

Wanlong Ski Resort, China

Over the past 20 years, the Chinese have become increasingly fascinated by skiing which is quickly ousting golf as the favored sport of top earners. During its bid for the 2022 Winter Olympics, Beijing hoped to establish China among the world's top winter sport countries. As part of the bidding procedure, the International Olympic Committee carried out a five-day inspection of Beijing, which was slated for the skating sports, and nearby ski areas. They also checked out the Nordic skiing potential in the county of Chongli – located in the mountains near the Great Wall – as well as Genting Resort, China's largest ski area, which would potentially host the snowboarding and freestyle events. Also on the itinerary was the ski resort at Yanqing where bobsled, skeleton, luge and other Alpine events were planned. Just before the IOC arrived, billboards were erected along the route, depicting skiers and snowboarders "Sharing the China Dream".

With such a huge population spread over a massive variety of terrain, relatively few Chinese have ever been to the ski resorts, let alone put on skis or a snowboard. The 2012 China Ski Study, Desk Research Report produced by the Canadian Tourism Commission (CTC) claims there were 70 ski resorts in China by 2012, a leap from just three in 1980. "Older resorts are upgrading their facilities while new resorts appear on the scene every year," the report states. "In China, skiing is a luxury trend driven by beginners with money to spend." Because of the predominant number of newbies to winter sports, equipment rental statistics that year were high, estimated at around 90 per cent of visitors, it said. And, along with shopping, dining and sightseeing, skiing was gaining popularity as a family activity.

Already business conferences are being located at ski resorts in China. The China Entrepreneurs Conference, for example, is held at Yabuli in northeastern Heilongjiang province, bringing together over 700 businessmen in 2012. Ski & Style – dubbed China's Ultimate Winter Lifestyle Show – is an industry trade show, run by China Rendez Vous and sponsored by the Beijing Park Hyatt. It has been held annually since 2014 in Beijing in November and also at the Park Hyatt in Changbaishan ski area in January. Booths are run by companies such as the luxury skiwear brand, Bogner, as well as national tourism authorities from Switzerland, Iceland and around the world. The Changbaishan event includes skiing, dogsledding, moto skis, sledging, horse-carriage rides, themed nights and an ice sculpture exhibition.

Winter 2014-2015 was the best season on record for Chinese ski resorts. "Attendance at Wanda Changbaishan Resort in northern Jilin province jumped to 240,000 this year from 150,000 last year for the season. During the peak Lunar New Year holiday week, demand was so high that ski rentals were limited to only half a day so others could have a chance to rent the gear," said journalist, Wei Gu in an article for the *Wall Street Journal*.

Around the world, countries such as Japan and Canada, in particular, are benefitting from the new Chinese obsession with winter sports. Both Hokkaido in Japan and Whistler Blackcomb in Canada have seen an increase in Chinese visitors enjoying their beginner trails, private lessons and rental and retail outlets. "We are noticing many beginner Chinese skiers coming to Whistler Blackcomb and are looking at new lessons and programs to better address this market," said Ian Jenkins, General Manager of Sales for Whistler Blackcomb. "We do currently have several Chinese-speaking instructors but are actively recruiting more. We are also building ski packages with select tour companies in China and in conjunction with Canadian Tourism Commission, Destination BC and Tourism Whistler." The resort sent instructors over to Chinese resorts during the 2013/14 and 2014/15 seasons with the intention of promoting Whistler

Blackcomb as well as improving their instruction techniques. "This has been well received and we will continue to do so," said Jenkins. "This year we had four instructors and visited nine resorts throughout the Northeast of China."

Although all surveys are agreed that Chinese ski participation is on the rise, there is considerable confusion as to the exact numbers involved. According to statistics from the China Ski Association, around 10 million Chinese, one per cent of the population, skied by 2015. The luxury-retail website Jing Daily claimed 20 million. Rapid growth in the Chinese ski industry was documented in the 2012 CTC Study, which reported an increase from 10,000 skiers in 1996 to "around a reported five million" in 2010. Whichever figure is correct, what is certain is that numbers are increasing: Figure 1.6 shows the evolution of skier visits in China according to Laurent Vanat's latest international ski report. And officials hoped that the media spotlight from the Winter Olympics bid could encourage many more to get out on to the slopes.

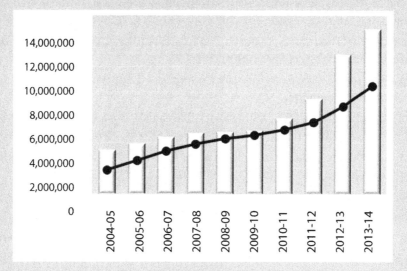

Figure 1.6: Evolution of skier visits in China (Source: Vanat, 2015, p. 124)

The CTC report also points out that "China is the third largest outbound tourist market in the world, and it is still growing." The CTC thinks that Canada is well-positioned to take advantage of the growth in Chinese ski tourism due to high awareness created by the Vancouver Olympics as well as targeted marketing efforts emanating from Canadian resorts. "It is also essential for those marketing Canada's ski destinations to recognize that Chinese tourists see skiing/snowboarding as a potential vacation activity, but are unlikely to plan an entire vacation around skiing/snowboarding. At this point in time the best way to bring these travelers to Canadian slopes is to include skiing/snowboarding outings in vacation packages with other activities," it recommends.

Sources: Interview with Ian Jenkins, General Manager of Sales for Whistler Blackcomb April 2015; Gu (2015); Levin (2015); Canadian Tourism Commission (2012); Vanat (2015)

References

Batchelor, D.E., Brewster, F., Carscallen, A.N., Douglas, H.P., Hall, F.A., McCorbey, A.A. and Mortureaux, C.E. (1937) 'Skiing in Canada', *Canadian Geographical Journal*, **14**(2), 57.

Canadian Tourism Commission (2012) *2012 China Ski Study, Desk Research Report*, April.

Cockerell, N. (1988) 'Skiing in Europe – potential and problems', *EIU Travel and Tourism Analyst*, **5**, 66-81.

Euromonitor International (2014) 'Trends shaping online travel', accessed 9/12/2014 from http://www.genesysdownload.co.uk/TTI/1403_conference/Caroline_Bremner_Euromonitor.pdf

Gibson, H. (2006) *Sport Tourism: Concepts and Theories*, New York: Routledge.

Gu, W. (2015) 'Skiing is the latest obsession for China's wealthy', *The Wall Street Journal*, 26 March, accessed 3/25/2015 from http://www.wsj.com/articles/skiing-is-the-latest-obsession-for-chinas-wealthy-1427357462?mod=e2tw

Heineman (1986) 'The future of sports: Challenges for the science of sport', *International Review for the Sociology of Sport*, **24**(4), 271-285.

Higham, J.E.S. (ed.) (2005) *Sport Tourism Destinations*, London: Elsevier Butterworth-Heinemann.

Hinch, T.D. and Higham, J.E.S. (2011) *Sport Tourism Development* (2nd edn.), Bristol: Channel View Publications.

Hudson, S. (2000) *Snow Business: A Study of the International Ski Industry*, London: The Continuum International Publishing Group.

Hudson, S. (ed.) (2003) *Sport and Adventure Tourism*, Oxford: Haworth.

IBISWorld (2013) *Ski & Snowboard Resorts in the US*, IBISWorld, December.

Jenkins, M. (2013) 'On the trail with the first skiers', *National Geographic*, December, 85-101.

Kottke, M. (1990) 'Growth trends: Going both ways at one,' *Ski Area Management*, **29**(1), 63-4, 96-7.

Levin, D. (2015) 'Shortage of snow aside, China jumps into bid for 2022 Winter Games', *The New York Times*, 16 February, accessed 4/5/2015 from http://www.nytimes.com/2015/02/17/world/shortage-of-snow-aside-china-jumps-into-bid-for-2022-winter-games.html?_r=0

Liebers, A. (1963) *The Complete Book of Winter Sports*, New York: Coward-McCann.

Mintel (2012) *Sport Tourism Worldwide*, London: Mintel Group Ltd.

Natural Resources Defense Council (2012) *Climate Impacts on the Winter Tourism Economy in the United States*. Elizabeth Burrows and Matthew Magnusson: New York: Natural Resources Defense Council.

Robinson, T. and Gammon, S. (2004) *Sports Tourism: An Introduction*, London: Thompson Learning.

Scharff, R. (ed.) (1974) *Ski Magazine's Encyclopaedia of Skiing*, New York: Universal.

Spring, J. (1997) 'Crossovers fuel boarding', *Ski Area Management*, **36**(3), 55-56.

Standeven, J. and De Knopp, P. (1999) *Sport Tourism*, Windsor, Ontario: Human Kinetics.

Tanler, B. (1966) 'A decade of growth', *Ski Area Management*, **5**(4), 10-14.

Vanat, L. (2015) '*2015 International Report on Snow & Mountain Tourism*', Geneva, Switzerland, April.

Weed, M. and Bull, C. (2004) *Sport Tourism: Participants, Policy and Providers*, Oxford: Elsevier Butterworth-Heinemann.

Williams, P.W. (1993) 'The evolution of the skiing industry', in Khan, M.A., Olsen, M.D., and van Var, T. (eds.) *VNR's Encyclopaedia of Hospitality and Tourism*, 926-33, New York: Nostrand Reinhold.

1

2 The Winter Sport Tourism Product

Spotlight: Ian Hunter, Working in a winter wonderland

Ian Hunter

Ski rep, Ian Hunter has been in the ski sales business since 1979. He started his career working in ski retail for three years before moving to an in-house position with Norvinca Inc – at that time, the Canadian distributor for Nordica, LOOK and Dynastar. After nine years he left Norvinca to form his own sales agency in order to maximize income by representing multiple brands.

In 1990 Hunter signed with Group Rossignol Canada Ltd and is still in the same role today although he has also represented many other lines during this period. "I'm responsible for sales into retail and rental markets, as well as sell-through from retail markets which can involve co-op advertising, staff training, promotion through athletes and ski professionals," Hunter explains.

Over the past 35 years or so, trends in ski gear have evolved considerably, driven partly by the advent of snowboarding. "Ski designs changed radically, starting in the mid 90s," says Hunter. "Shaped skis started a period of tremendous growth in the ski industry which was suffering at that time due to the popularity of snowboarding."

In order to compete with the popularity and growth in the snowboard industry, ski manufacturers put considerable resources into designing more user-friendly, higher performing skis to try to regain the 'cool factor'. Hunter says that snowboarding's success, particularly with the younger generation, caused ski manufacturers to re-think their approach to the sport. "It accelerated the development of recreational skis to make skiing more fun, easier to learn, and to provide more performance," he says.

With skiers increasingly seeking equipment to enhance fatigue-free skiing, it is new technology that is driving sales in ski equipment today. "Wide skis brought skiers into the powder fields allowing intermediate skiers to go where previously only snowboarders and expert skiers could go," Hunter explains. "Twin tip skis brought the youth back into the sport as freestyle, slope style and half pipe gained popularity."

Retail staff has a significant impact on what products the consumer chooses, so Hunter works closely with the Rossignol retail network. "Staff training sessions, demo days and casual conversations with the staff are all key components of grass roots marketing," he explains. He also runs popular consumer demo days but says these tend to be "a bit of a shotgun approach". Private demo days can be very effective but are cumbersome to orchestrate.

Like many people working in the ski industry, Hunter's job is synonymous with his passion for the winter sports' lifestyle. "I get to get out of bed every day and talk about something I love: snow sports and related equipment," says Hunter. "I have been fortunate to ski with current, past and future world class skiers. I have been to ski, boot, binding and pole factories. I have seen the evolution of equipment from prototypes to finished products and have been lucky to be, in a small way, a part of that process. I have skied in a number of countries and many resorts, all under the guise of working."

Hunter's core business remains alpine, Nordic and snowboard hard goods, although he has also represented companies which specialize in goggles, helmets, sunglasses, bikes, cycle clothing, technical outerwear and layering systems. These days a job in his field would require experience in retail as well as wholesale sales. "Experience selling as an agent for smaller brands would be good training in preparation for selling a major brand," he advises.

His prognosis for the future of skiing is a bright one: "Ski manufacturers like Rossignol will continue to test new designs and materials to expand the performance and ease of use envelopes. Boots will continue to become warmer and more comfortable and bindings will also evolve or perhaps radically change to offer even greater protection."

Source: Interview with Ian Hunter, November 2014

Winter sport activities

As mentioned in Chapter 1, the focus of this book is on the winter sports of skiing and snowboarding, and as previously noted, there are approximately 120 million ski and snowboarders worldwide, with nearly a third of those coming from Western Europe. Figure 2.1 shows the distribution of skiers and boarders by region of origin. The share of international visitors is less than one sixth of participants, with the international flow of skiers and boarders primarily restricted to Europe. Overseas visitors in the U.S., for example, represented just 3.8 per cent of total skier visits in 2012/13. Although some countries have very few ski areas, they are still, like the Netherlands and the U.K., significant outbound markets, sending around one million skiers and boarders each to the mountains every winter.

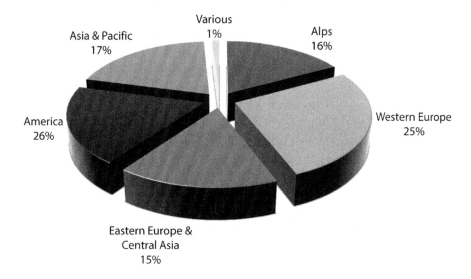

Figure 2.1: Distribution of skiers and snowboarders by region of origin (Source: Vanat, 2015)

France, Germany, Japan and the U.S. have the biggest domestic ski and snowboard markets, each numbering between 11.5 and 13 million people. In terms of inbound visits, Austria leads the way, with over 34 million, followed by France with 15 million and Switzerland with 13.8 million. Meanwhile, countries with a high level of participation rates amongst domestic populations include Switzerland (37%), Austria (36%), Norway (25%), and Finland (24%). Interestingly, only 4.3 per cent of the population in the U.S. takes to the mountains each winter. Table 2.1 lists the countries that receive over one million skier visits, along with participation rates as a percentage of their population.

Other variations on downhill skiing include heli-skiing, where skiers are flown by helicopter to virgin slopes where they can ski on pristine powder snow. The sport has shown a marked increase over the last few decades. Approximately 95 per cent of all heli-skiing in the world occurs in British Columbia, Canada where, collectively, the industry accounts for about 100,000 skier days with gross revenues exceeding $100 million annually. Hans Gmoser, an Austrian mountain guide, had a major pioneering role in heli-skiing in the 1960s and was the founder of Canadian Mountain Holidays (CMH). Mike Wiegele was also a leader in the industry, with his operation commencing in 1970. The profile of heli-skiing has continued to increase, in part due to the exposure in Warren Miller movies that show extreme skiers making the most of the enviable conditions.

Country	Number of ski areas	Skier visits (SV)	National partici-pation rate (in % population)	Number of skiers (national)	Proportion foreign skiers (%)
Andorra	3	2,184,806	20.00	17,059	92.00
Argentina	22	1,500,000	2.50	1,065,275	25.00
Australia	10	2,082,600	2.00	445,250	1.50
Austria	254	53,155,600	36.00	2959,793	66.00
Bulgaria	32	1,200,000	5.00	349,082	25.00
Canada	288	18,700,400	12.50	4,307,199	12.00
Chile	21	1,250,000	3.00	516,508	15.00
China	350	6,880,000	0.40	5,128,426	0.50
Czech Republic	176	8,700,000	20.00	2,032,584	35.00
Finland	76	2,846,000	24.00	1,263,867	17.00
France	325	56,226,000	13.00	8,573,709	32.00
Germany	498	14,922,000	18.00	14,606,508	10.00
Italy	349	28,100,000	8.00	4,918,584	15.00
Japan	547	34,432,389	9.00	11,452,777	3.00
Korea, South	18	6,531,832	6.00	2,937,312	10.00
New Zealand	25	1,413,552	7.00	305,558	36.00
Norway	213	6,390,000	25.00	1,180,675	8.00
Poland	182	5,000,000	13.00	4,989,895	10.00
Romania	45	1,200,000	3.00	653,714	5.00
Russia	220	3,653,870	2.50	3,562,512	2.00
Slovakia	91	5,000,000	18.00	987,901	25.00
Slovenia	44	1,357,128	15.00	298,904	17.00
Spain	34	5,677,571	5.00	2,368,527	10.00
Sweden	228	8,070,800	20.00	1,823,885	8.00
Switzerland	240	26,538,264	37.00	2,958,530	50.00
Turkey	43	1,200,000	1.00	806,945	15.00
Ukraine	54	1,400,000	2.50	1,114,330	5.00
United States	481	57,092,127	4.30	13,616,748	5.60

Table 2.1: Skiers visits along with participation rates as a percentage of the population (Source: Adapted from Vanat, 2014)

The industry has continued to evolve from its first inception, when pilots would shuttle eager skiers, one at a time, to mountain tops via helicopter. As time progressed, due to increasing popularity in the sport, helicopters carrying 12 skiers were used to facilitate the ever-increasing demand. Many companies still operate with the large capacity helicopters; however, newer heli-ski operators have begun what is now called Small Group Heli-Skiing (Whitfield, 2013). Heli-skiing safety has also increased in the form of advancements in technology and equipment (Whitfield, 2013). Helicopters and personal safety equipment, in addition to top-level guiding practices, have all continued to evolve. Avalanche hazards are being mitigated by heli-ski guides with ever increasing levels of certification in safety training and risk awareness.

A variation on heli-skiing is 'snowcat' skiing (also known as cat-skiing). Snowcats are large, trucklike vehicles which run on tracks instead of wheels and, like helicopters, they carry powder enthusiasts to high mountain areas that do not have lifts or groomed trails. The first snowcat operation in Canada was opened in British Columbia (B.C.) by Ontario native Allan Drury. While working in Aspen, Drury noticed that snowcats were being used to shuttle skiers up an unfinished ski area whose lifts weren't yet running. With a vision of starting his own wilderness snowcat operation, Drury moved to B.C. in 1975 with his wife Brenda and opened Selkirk Wilderness Skiing. In 1979, friend and fellow cat-ski pioneer, Brent McCorquodale, opened British Columbia's second snowcat operation, Great Northern Snowcat Skiing, in the historic mining town of Trout Lake. Cat Powder in Revelstoke, and Island Lake Catskiing near Fernie, were soon to follow. Over 30 years later, there are snowcat skiing operations scattered throughout B.C. The combination of abundant snowfall, cool temperatures and regular breaks in weather systems, as well as massive networks of forestry roads leading deep into the mountains, make B.C. ideal for cat-skiing and snowboarding.

Cross-country skiing is another popular winter sport and used to be considered the poor cousin of alpine skiing (Loverseed, 2000), but evolution in ski equipment, snow making, waxes, and track setting has contributed to the continued success of the sport. The most notable change has been in technique. Made popular by American Olympic silver medal winner, Bill Koch in the early 1980s, skate skiing, or the free technique, has given cross-country skiing a facelift (Rolfe, 2001). Telemarking, the first type of downhill skiing introduced by the Norwegians, also appears to be experiencing some growth. The telemark turn, designed to be executed in a loose-heeled binding, worn with light-weight boots and skis that are comfortable walking uphill and on the flat, has come into its own again. Alpine touring skiing, a cross between cross-country and telemark, has been on the increase for some time, with an eight per cent growth in the market during the 2013/14 season.

Snowshoeing is similarly a mode of transport used originally by native people but 'adopted' by the winter sports tourism industry. Pre-dating skis by many centuries, traditional 'snowshoes' resembled giant tennis rackets and were made from flexible ash wood and laced to moccasins with caribou or deer hide. New lightweight shoes made with aluminum frames are now more common. They are easy to use and no special skill is required to take off into the wilderness. According to Loverseed (2000), the activity burns between 400-900 calories per hour but does not put a strain on the joints in the same way as skiing or snowboarding.

Over the years, mountain resorts have made significant capital investments in providing alternative activities to the major ones profiled above. These activities range from the high-energy (like ice skating and snowtubing) to the more passive (like moonlit snowmobiling). Resort websites now provide detailed information about facilities such as snow rafting, skating rinks, tobogganing, curling and hot-air ballooning. Table 2.2 lists the more traditional winter sports along with those that are gaining popularity in the 21st century. The Profile in this chapter focuses on winter zip lining.

Traditional winter sports activities	Contemporary winter sports activities
Skiing	Snowboarding
Cross-country skiing	Snowmobiling
Telemarking	Snowshoeing
Cat-skiing	Heli-skiing
Ice skating	Dog sledging
Horse-drawn sleigh	Tubing
Curling	Snowcycling/ Fat biking
Toboganning	Ice-climbing
	Ice-driving
	Ice sculpting
	Snowskating

Table 2.2: The diversification of winter sport activities

Two factors are driving this diversification of winter sports. Firstly, winter resorts are losing customers. An analysis of market trends suggests that an increasing proportion of those who take winter sport holidays on a regular basis do not ski at all. Secondly, even avid skiers are typically skiing less. On average, they are somewhat older, and new high-speed lifts enable a skier to attain his/her physical stamina quotient much more quickly. As a result, winter resorts, as well as the hotels operating within them, realized that they had to offer more activities than just skiing, both on-snow and off-snow. A good example of a hotel promoting much more than skiing and snowboarding is Washington School House in Park City Utah, one of the town's newest luxury boutique hotels. Figure 2.2 shows the various winter sports offered on the hotel's website.

The **Alpine Coaster** takes you on a ride in one- or two-person toboggans through the aspen glades on the coaster's elevated track as it winds through nearly 4,000 feet of breathtaking curves, bends and loops

Bobsled Rides on "The Comet" at Utah Olympic Park exhilarate as you ride with a trained pilot through 15 curves, reaching speeds up to 80 mph, and pulling close to 5Gs of force over the equivalent of a 40-story vertical drop

Cross country ski though Park City's gorgeous tracks for one of the best workouts of your life – all skill levels welcome

Dogsledding offers a unique experience for you to play with the pups, learn how to drive the sled and spend the day experiencing an interactive family adventure

Fly fish on the Provo River, Weber River or other area streams and creeks on a custom, guided trip

Flying Eagle Zipline at the Park City Mountain Resort allows you to soar to new heights all winter long on this two-person ride full of fun for both kids and adults

Heli-skiing takes the advanced skier and snowboarder to new heights. Head into the mountain areas where you can ski and board in untouched snow, cutting through deep, fluffy, Utah powder

Historic Mountain Tours take you through Park City's intriguing mining town past with a complementary guided, historic, on-mountain tour of the Park City Mountain Resort

The Homestead Crater is a 55-foot tall, beehive-shaped limestone rock that nature has hollowed out and filled with 90-96°F water. Swim, scuba dive, snorkel or enjoy a therapeutic soak

Horseback ride through breathtaking scenery as you traverse through the pristine mountain terrain of Park City

Hot air ballooning is a thrilling experience that takes you a mile up in the sky for amazing views of Park City, the beautiful Wasatch and Uinta Mountains and Salt Lake City

Ice Skate at one of Park City's two skating venues – a great way to enjoy time together off the slopes

Sleigh Rides offer a unique winter excursion and can be combined with special dinner experiences, even in a Viking Yurt, where the thrill of being the only ones dining on the top of the mountain is breathtaking

Snowmobile through pines and aspens to experience unsurpassed views, unmatched scenery, the best snowmobiles, and a professional guides committed to excellent experiences and your safety

Snowshoe through the absolute stillness of the winter woods, whether you are looking for a scenic aerobic experience or just a peaceful escape

Tubing is a downhill blast for the whole family, with lift-served tubing lanes and snowy play areas for the little ones

Utah Olympic Park invites you to explore the place where Olympic dreams came true in 2002 and are still motivating today's aspiring Olympians

Yoga Adventures offers a one-of-a-kind adventure off the ski hills, yoga paddleboarding or a yoga and snowshoeing trek is sure to entertain your adventurous spirit

Figure 2.2: Winter sport activities at Washington School House in Park City, Utah (Source: Washingtonschoolhouse.com)

Winter sport resorts

As mentioned in Chapter 1, there are approximately 2,000 ski areas in 80 countries. The U.S., Japan and France have the most ski resorts with more than 200 each. Only Austria and France have more than 10 resorts that generate over one million skier visits per season. The relative importance of the major destinations is shown in Figure 2.3. The European Alps are the largest destination capturing 44 per cent of skier visits, with America the second biggest, accounting for 21 per cent of skier visits worldwide.

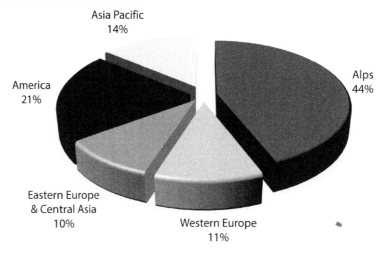

Figure 2.3: Skier visits worldwide (Source: Vanat, 2015, p. 15)

Ski resorts can be broken into three categories. First, there are national resorts that attract people generally from within a state, province, or region within a country. Second, there are regional resorts, those that skiers will travel several hundreds of miles to reach. In Europe, these resorts will entice skiers across one, or several countries. Examples are skiers traveling from the U.K. to Austria, or from New York to the Canadian Rockies. Lastly, there are top-class international destination resorts (three to four hundred in total) that attract skiers from all over the world, such as Whistler in Canada, Vail in Colorado, and Zermatt in Switzerland. In the first few decades of ski area development, most people did not ski beyond their own ski hills. But that has changed as people travel more and as ski companies become multinationals. Thousands of North Americans now flood the European Alps every year, with an even greater influx of Europeans to North America. In fact, without European skiers, Canadian resorts would be showing negative growth.

The products and services offered by ski resorts tend to vary depending on their size, but they usually include skiing facilities, accommodation, food and beverages, ski schools, and equipment rental and merchandise. Figure 2.4 shows the products and services offered by U.S. resorts and the percentage of revenue that they each generated in 2013. The total revenue that year was $2.6 billion.

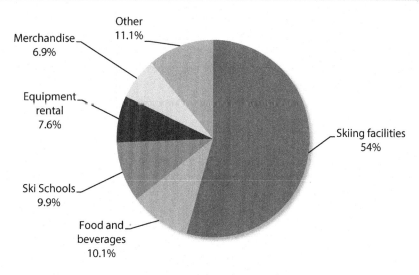

Figure 2.4: Ski resort products and services (Source: Adapted from IBISWorld.com, 2013)

The skiing facilities are the primary product provided by resorts, and operators offer general lift tickets and season passes to customers wanting to use those facilities. Most resorts in North America own and/or operate a large proportion of the accommodation, and, to a greater extent, food and beverage operations (this is different in Europe where the industry is more fragmented). They typically offer a variety of restaurants, bars, cafés and cafeterias, in order to capture more guest spending. In 2013, food and beverage operations were estimated to account for 10.1 per cent of revenue. Ski resorts also tend to operate ski and snowboard schools to provide instruction to customers, offering a wide variety of development programs for all ages. This business segment is estimated to generate 9.9 per cent of revenue for resorts. Many resorts also own retail and ski rental shops that sell ski equipment and accessories, and, in 2013, merchandise represented 6.9 per cent of resort revenue while equipment rental accounted for 7.6 per cent. Other products include summer activities and private events. These might include mountain biking or gondola rides for weddings. These other products account for about 11.1 per cent of revenue for resorts.

Of course, the demand for ski resort services is seasonal and highly dependent on weather conditions. Resorts earn 85-100 per cent of their income between November and April with a large proportion of earnings coming over the Christmas break and other major holidays. Adverse weather conditions during these periods can jeopardize annual revenues and cause visitor numbers to fall in subsequent years. Typically, ski resorts categorize their guests as local visitors and destination visitors with the latter being out-of-state or international visitors. In 2013, destination visitors accounted for about 56 per cent of revenue for U.S. ski resorts (see Figure 2.5). Resort operators are increasingly banking on destination visitors to fill hotels, townhouses and condominiums in the valleys below the slopes. Destination skiers tend to spend more, and it has been suggested that

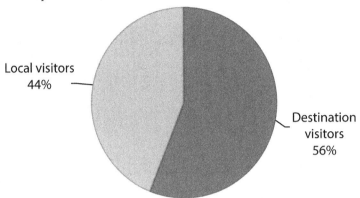

to defeat seasonality, destinations should focus on yield, rather than volume. In the Banff region of Canada, for example, the ski areas have been aggressively targeting European skiers over the last few decades. Although these destination skiers represent only 50 per cent of the market, they account for nearly 80 per cent of tourism expenditures.

Figure 2.5: Major markets for ski resorts (Source: Adapted from IBISWorld.com, 2013)

In the U.S. the largest ski resort operator, with about a third of the market share, is Vail Resorts Inc. which operates resorts in both the U.S. and Canada. Vail has a real estate and a lodging segment in addition to the mountain segment which includes the six ski resorts of Vail, Beaver Creek, Breckenridge, Keystone, Northstar at Tahoe and Heavenly. In 2014, Vail added Park City Mountain Resort in Utah to its portfolio, and then in 2015 expanded outside of North America by acquiring Perisher in Australia. Other major players in the U.S. include Intrawest Corporation which operates Snowshoe, Steamboat, Stratton and Winter Park Resorts, and Boyne Resorts, a Michigan-based company that operates 10 ski resorts in North America. POWDR Corporation is based in Park City, Utah and owns nine resorts in the U.S. including Copper Mountain and Killington in Colorado. Figure 2.6 shows the major players in the U.S. along with their market shares.

Successful winter sport resorts appear to have followed one or more of three strategies to enhance the service experience: product diversification, product improvement, and product differentiation. Product diversification has already been alluded to, but mountain resorts also have to evolve continually and improve to meet the new demands of the consumer. The ski runs and related lift systems clearly represent a prime attraction of resorts and therefore have long been the object of continuous improvements (see the Case Study below on the development of Olympic ski runs at Rosa Khutor, Russia). The process of linking ski areas has now become commonplace in France, for example, following the initial lead given by resorts such as Tignes and Val d'Isere, which combined to form 'Espace Killy', and Courchevel, Meribel, Les Menuires and Val Thorens, which created the 'Trois Vallees'. Along with these changes, skiing areas have been expanded to higher altitudes, giving better snow conditions, increasing resorts' capacities and extending their season. The customer service experience can also be enhanced by the training of instructors and guides, and by offering authentic and natural experiences.

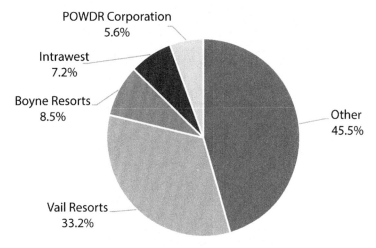

Figure 2.6: Major players in winter sport tourism (Source: IBISWorld.com, 2013, p. 25)

A third strategy taken by ski areas to enhance the service experience is differentiation. Despite the trend towards large resort alpine villages, there is a future for the small, independently-owned resorts with comparatively shallow pockets. Some local hills are often more accessible, making them perfect for day trips, especially when they are close to large urban areas. Others can differentiate themselves from the large alpine resorts and gain a competitive advantage. Lake Louise and Sunshine in Alberta, Canada, for example, are based in a National Park and cannot offer all the amenities of a bustling alpine village. However, the relative tranquility and beauty of the preserved environment sets them apart from other more developed resorts. Smaller resorts can also differentiate on other aspects such as customer service as mentioned above. Crested Butte in Colorado, for example, is attempting to differentiate on customer service, and believes its small size is a selling point. "You don't have to be a huge mega resort to offer a good ski vacation," says Tim Mueller, the resort owner. Tamarack, also in Colorado, is positioning itself as a 'boutique' resort limiting the number of skiers and boarders to 3,500 a day, despite capacity to accommodate 7,000. The idea is to create a private resort, with a focus on yield rather than volume, catering for a more discerning customer.

Profile: The wonders of winter zip-lining

Jori Kirk

It's all about the rush, the sense of flying through the towering treetop canopy, with a bald eagle's view of the immense whiteness of a winter wonderland. Winter zip lining started spreading around North American ski resorts in the mid-2000s, adding yet another activity-based après ski alternative.

This was part of the ski industry's push to diversify, appealing to a wider demographic, keeping visitors on the hill longer into the evening, and providing a menu of non-skiing options. Zip lining also adds a significant cool factor and helps provide all-season appeal for ski areas.

One of the early pioneers of zip lining in Canada is Jori Kirk, who started Cypress Hills Eco-Adventures Ltd in 2010 after graduating from the Haskayne School of Business at the University of Calgary. "If I'm not mistaken, the first commercial canopy tour in the U.S. was built in 2005 in mainland Ketchikan, AK," says Kirk. The first in Canada was at Grouse Mountain, Whistler.

Since the early days, there has been some confusion in terminology between canopy tours and zip line tours. "Canopy tours are guided, with a series of zips and suspension bridges through the natural canopy of trees," Kirk explains. Zip line tours, on the other hand, take participants through a series of manmade structures. However, even the industry has used the terms interchangeably.

The wide appeal of zip lining, says Kirk, is the "storytelling factor" as well as the social aspect: it can be enjoyed by any age-group, both genders, and in relatively large groups of family or friends. "It is also very inclusive as it takes very little expertise to conquer a zip line tour," Kirk adds. Although most winter zip lines were originally summer structures, it is relatively cheap and easy to winterize them and keep them running year round. "People are already there, the zip line course is there, staff are there. Close it down or make incremental revenues? I would choose the latter 10 times out of 10," says Kirk. "I don't believe the places that do this are expecting to operate at full capacity, but it is a great way of offering another option for guests."

Zip lines vary considerably from resort to resort – some have seats, some dangle participants from ropes and hooks, some are single, others double lines, and some have more of an assault course set up with climbs and platforms. Copper Mountain's 'Alpine Rush' is a village experience with dual zip lines strung 30 ft above West Lake, enabling tandem riders to traverse the ice rink between condos, shops and restaurants. The Guided Canopy Tour at Crested Butte Mountain Resort has five lines ranging from 120 - 400 feet long, connected by three wooden suspension bridges and massive platforms designed for winter use with tough grips and snow grates. "It's about a two hour tour, with two guides, that make it fun and interactive," says Director of Innovations, Erica Mueller. "It is something different for people to do on a day off from skiing or after skiing and really attracts all age groups," she adds, although participation is limited to those weighing between 70 and 250 lbs. It is open summer, fall and winter, with some weather-friendly modifications in the colder months.

Vail's all-season, four-line, 1,200 foot-long zip line provides another après ski experience, next to the tubing hill at Adventure Ridge. The Purgatory Plunge at Purgatory Durango Mountain Resort drops zippers on two lines off a massive tower, offering vertical as well as horizontal plummeting. Gunstock Mountain, New Hampshire has five zip lines, the longest 1.5 miles, with speed control and opportunities to stop and appreciate the scenery and wildlife. The longest zip line in Utah is at Canyons Resort with two different routes over mid-mountain pine trees. The Flying Eagle Zip Line at Park City, Utah is a two-person circuit, 110 feet above the resort, starting and finishing at the same spot. Two companies operate zip lines at Whistler Blackcomb, Canada. Ziptrek Ecotours runs a network above Fitzsimmons Creek between the two resorts offering Twilight Tours in winter. And the Adventure Group has multiple side-by-side Super Fly Ziplines connected by trails and boardwalks at Cougar Mountain.

So is zip lining here to stay? "I really do not know. I don't seeing it going away any time soon," says Kirk. "There will likely be less development of new tours and closures of poorly managed ones as the profitable ones rise above the rest. If the current zip line companies place their focus on providing a great experience, it is doubtful that they will disappear from the scene." Kirk's company was named the 2014 Canadian Tourism Small to Medium-Sized Business of the Year.

Source: Interview with Jori Kirk, November 2014

Indoor ski resorts

Skiing and snowboarding on indoor plastic slopes, or dry slopes as they are called, has become increasingly popular worldwide. Around 80 have been built in approximately 30 countries over the past 25 years, and around 50 are still in operation (Vanat, 2014). A few of them are dedicated to cross-country skiing. Between them they total around 20 million yearly skier visits. Although earlier versions date back to the 1920s in Berlin and Vienna, the longest established and still operational *real snow* indoor snow facility is Tamworth Snowdome in the U.K., which opened in 1993. The first indoor slopes like Tamworth were straightforward up-and-down runs, but as they became used more and more for teaching and training, and then for recreational activities, they became bigger and more ambitious.

The best artificial slopes are those that attempt to simulate mountain conditions by varying the slopes and gradients; by having adequate nursery areas (bunny runs) that are not too steep to frighten beginners; and that have long run-out areas at the bottom of the slope. In the U.S., Hard Rock International is partnering with Grand Alps Resort DFW, Inc. to build a $215 million, 350,000 square foot indoor ski facility in conjunction with a Four-Diamond Hard Rock Hotel, just north of I-30 in the Dallas/Fort Worth market area. Preliminary plans call for 300 rooms, 48,000 square feet of meeting space, two restaurants, fitness and spa facilities, a rooftop pool complex and a year-round snow dome with a 300-foot high, 1,200 foot-long ski slope, an indoor ice climbing wall, a luge track and a 'winter wonderland' play area. The scheduled opening is early 2018.

Much of the development in indoor ski centers, however, seems to be occurring in developing countries. Ski Dubai in the United Arab Emirates, for example, opened in 2005, and, at 25 stories high, it is billed as the world's third largest interior slope. The slope ticket of about $20 includes both equipment and apparel – gloves, pants, jacket, and even disposable socks, because winter clothing is not often in the wardrobe of those who live in 100-degree heat. Arabs, who wear long, flowing dishdashas, can rent knee-length coats to stay warm, as skiing in traditional robes is prohibited. Brazil has also recently opened an indoor center in Gramado, in the Serra Gaucha region. Snowland, as it is called, incorporates an indoor ski slope to accommodate more than 30 sliding activities including skiing, snowboarding, airboarding, tubing and sledging. The facility also includes an indoor ice rink and an Alpine-themed street of shops and restaurants. Brazil has no real conventional ski area but the burgeoning Brazilian population, including a rapidly expanding middle class, is a major market for Argentinean and Chilean ski areas.

Finally, construction work is reported to have begun on the world's largest indoor ski slope due to open in Harbin in North Eastern China, in 2017. The $3.3 billion 'Cultural Tourism City' will be the first indoor slope to offer a 100m vertical, and will have six separate slopes. The Wanda group, a large Chinese corporation, is behind the project. Wanda is one of the world's biggest companies and already runs conventional ski areas in China. Other details so far published include a figure of 1,500 slope users at any one time with a 50,000 capacity for the entire complex, which will also include an Olympic sized ice rink, theatre, shopping mall, four and five star hotels, restaurants and cinema facilities. Harbin has a population of 10 million people and attracts a further 20 million tourists every year.

Clothing and equipment

2

As suggested in Chapter 1, the evolution of winter sports is closely tied to the evolution of skiing and snowboarding equipment. Downhill ski shape and design has morphed in every direction imaginable (see opening Spotlight), with skis designed for women, kids, powder, hardpack, off-piste, big mountain, pipe and park, alpine touring, freeride, and racing. Many skiers are using twin-tip skis designed for riding both directions, as skiers have adopted and adapted many of snowboarding's moves (Knight, 2013). While skis, boards and boots have improved considerably over time, accessories have also become more and more important. Following horrific ski accidents in 1997 involving Sonny Bono and Michael Kennedy, helmets became de rigueur as a skiing accessory. Now skiers and snowboarders tend to stick out if they fail to wear a helmet. The growth of extreme skiing has made helmets even more important.

With ski clothing, fashion is just as important as function these days, and there is something for everyone – from heated gloves and technical parkas that are designed for sub-zero temperatures, to form-fitting four-way-stretch jackets, that are both warm and fashionable. Today's modern ski wear is made from such materials as Goretex, a breathable, water-proof material, and under-layers are often polypropylene, which draws sweat away from the skin, promoting consistent warmth on cold days. Thinsulate is another modern material used in ski gear to keep the ski enthusiast warm.

In the U.S. in 2013-14, the sales of clothing and equipment were worth $3.6 billion according to Snowsports Industries America (SIA, 2014). This was up seven per cent in dollar sales and up four per cent in unit sales on the previous year, despite the drought in California. Some highlights from that season included the fact that more girls bought snowboard equipment. Junior girls snowboarding equipment sales in particular grew 37 per cent. Alpine insulated tops sales were also up 13 per cent in dollars sold to $529 million and sales of women's specific cross country equipment increased 32 per cent in units sold and 28 per cent in dollars sold to over $6 million. Sales of action cameras were also up 10 per cent in units sold to 121,000 cameras and up 20 per cent in dollars sold to $41 million. But sales of skis themselves have fallen over the last few years. Figure 2.7 shows the alpine ski equipment sales in the U.S. for the last four seasons, indicating a drop in ski sales, but an increase in boot sales.

Apparel accessories include gloves, baselayers, headwear, and neck gaiters, and all these showed an increase of seven per cent in units sold and 11 per cent in dollars sold to $664 million. Safety technology in helmets continues to improve as riders grow bolder in terrain parks and backcountry. Brands are increasingly using technology like MIPS Brain Protection System, as well as their own proprietary technology systems. Figure 2.8 shows the accessories product mix versus dollars for the 2013-14 season.

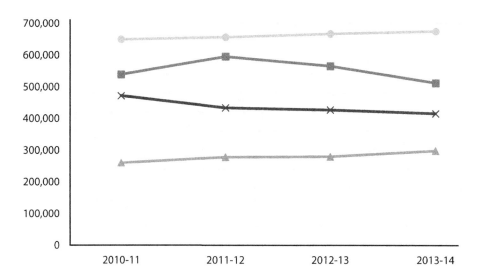

Figure 2.7: Alpine ski equipment sales in the U.S. Source: Adapted from Snowsports Industries America (2014)

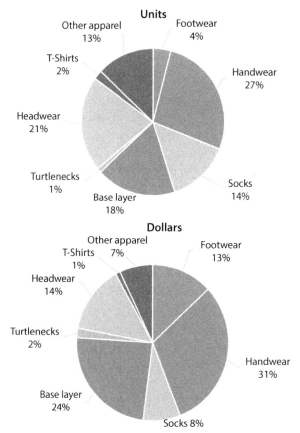

Figure 2.8: Apparel accessories sales in the U.S. 2013-14. Source: Adapted from Snowsports Industries America (2014)

One of the largest growing sectors in winter sports sales over the past few years has been backcountry equipment (Hjorleifson, 2012). Figure 2.9 shows the backcountry equipment sales in the U.S. over the last four seasons. While many parts of the ski industry such as skier visits and the sales of ski equipment are influenced greatly by the amount of snowfall in the region, backcountry equipment and trips have changed the trends and have actually increased. The backcountry ski industry is now worth over $33 million, but is still only one per cent of the snow sports industry. With more mainstream brands reaching into the backcountry industry such as K2, Lange and Burton, it is evident that the backcountry industry is now becoming a mainstream part of the ski industry (Hjorleifson, 2012), with backcountry equipment increasingly seen on the slopes. Sales of alpine touring boots, for example, were up 27 per cent in 2013-14. Their non-slip, rockered soles, improved walkability, relative lightness and comfort are making them a popular choice among skiers.

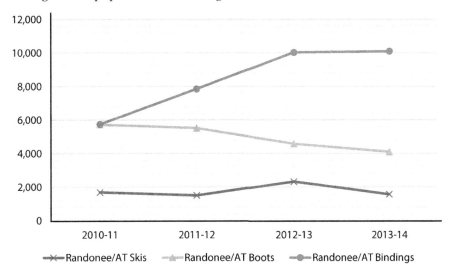

Figure 2.9: Backcountry equipment sales in the U.S. Source: Adapted from Snowsports Industries America (2014)

Case study: The difficult birth of an all-season destination – Sochi, Russia

As mentioned earlier in the chapter, most mountain resorts have made significant capital investments to provide alternative activities to winter sports – diversifying their offerings to cope with seasonality and to attract visitors in the summer months. The strategy for Sochi in Russia, host of the 2014 Winter Olympic Games, has been exactly the opposite. Until Vladimir Putin fell in love with Sochi, the summer resort was best known for the packs of Soviets who used to sun themselves on the rocky shore of the Black Sea. However, seven years of frantic construction for the Olympics has turned the resort into an all-year around destination – but such a transformation has not been without its hiccups.

Rosa Khutor Ski Area

It was ski resort designer, Paul Mathews, who was initially brought in to study the tourism potential in the North Caucasus for the Russian Federation. "Once we identified Rosa Khutor and the Gazprom Laura projects, we designed them for commercial ventures and then later we were asked if these resorts could host Olympic Winter Games," he says. Mathews' company Ecosign Mountain Resort Planners then went on to create a venue master plan which they presented first to the Russian Olympic Committee and then to the International Olympic Committee in February 2007. "Sochi won the right to host the 2014 Olympic Winter Games in July 2007," says Mathews. "And we were immediately hired to redesign the Rosa Khutor Ski Area to host the Games."

This was the beginning of a succession of difficulties for Ecosign. "Once Russia had the Olympics, all hell broke loose in the Sochi region with everyone claiming they owned the lands where the competition venues were planned," says Mathews. This led to a freeze being put in place by Putin who eventually claimed all the disputed lands for the Federal Government, Mathews explains: "Even Interros, our customer, lost our rights to the lease that we had signed to develop Rosa Khutor. The project went on hold for a good fourteen to sixteen months which was very precious time to waste considering all of the new design and construction which had to be done."

Despite these setbacks, Ecosign continued to work on the huge project throughout 2011. Once major construction was started, however, they came up against another problem. "We did not know how to play the Russian game of 'kickbacks' and so we were replaced by other Russian companies," Mathews says. "Ultimately, these companies made a real mess of the Rosa Khutor mountain site with unprofessional practices."

During fall 2013, the *Wall Street Journal* reported that hotel delays were imperiling the Games. With the focus firmly on the sports venues, the International Olympic Committee (IOC) had overlooked the progress of urgently needed accommodation. Jean-Claude Killy, the IOC's chief supervisor for the 2014 Olympics (and winner of three Olympic golds for France) had to declare a 'red alert', expanding the work force and encouraging round-the-clock, seven day working weeks from September 2013 in order to finish building by February 2014.

These behind-the-scenes glitches, however, did not do long-term damage to the project. "Sochi hosted a pretty decent Olympic Winter Games and Rosa Khutor is enjoying good business and visits during its first year of commercial operation so time will tell how the project lasts into the future," Mathews concludes.

Although Sochi has been a popular tourism destination for Russians since before the fall of the Soviet Union, many people have questioned the value of spending so much money on the area in order to make a massive media impression during the Games. Over $50 billion was reportedly invested into the sports venues, massive network of ski lifts, luxurious resorts, upmarket hotels and general infrastructure of the area – but was it worth it for the long term?

Critics have said that the area lacks a targeted marketing effort which would be necessary to capitalize on the international exposure provided by the Games. An article in *Medical Tourism Magazine* says "the legacy of an international sporting event is the measure of a host nation's success" but also points out that this can also be a burden on the host country's economy for many years.

 Short term, Sochi saw a reduction in tourism numbers during the construction period before the Games. In 2012 1.3 million visitors came to the city whereas a year later, during peak construction, only 900,000 were recorded. Another problem for the area is that holidays in Turkey, Egypt or Thailand cost less for Russians and foreigners than Sochi which now flaunts five-star hotels and other high quality facilities.

With its sub-tropical climate, the long term plan for Sochi is to turn it into an all-season destination, with a winter ski season followed by a focus on year round outdoor sports and activities both for athletes in training and holidaymakers. It's one of the few places in the world where visitors can swim in the sea and ski on the mountains during the same day. The spectacular sporting venues built for the Winter Games were intended to attract more high profile events: for example, the Fisht Stadium for the 2018 FIFA World Cup, Formula 1 races and the G8 Summit.

The Sochi Games also put the Russian Winter Olympic Team back on the world sports map. After a paltry three gold medals in the Vancouver Olympics, they were back on form in 2014, winning the most golds and also the most medals overall.

Good press, bad press – at the end of the day, the Games kept Russia in the news for several years. Very few international skiers would have considered a Russian ski vacation when Sochi boasted a mere handful of antiquated ski lifts. Now, with over 50 high-speed chairlifts and gondolas, Russian skiing has gone from the background to the spotlight because of the Games and many keen skiers and snowboarders all over the world have Rosa Khutor on their bucket lists.

Sources: Interview with Paul Mathews Feb 2015; *Medical Tourism Magazine* (2014); Conway (2014); Futterman and White (2014); Bachman (2014)

References

Bachman, R. (2014) 'The dangling future of Sochi's ski gondolas', *The Wall Street Journal*, 24 February, B10.

Conway, R. (2014) 'Sochi 2014: Does Sochi success signal a new Russia?' *BBC Sport Winter Olympics*, 22 February, accessed 3/21/2015 from http://www.bbc.com/sport/0/winter-olympics/26316456?print=true

Futterman, M. and White, G.L. (2014) 'IOC: Hotel delays imperiled Games', *The Wall Street Journal*, 18 February, D5.

Hjorleifson, E. (2012) 'Future changes in the skiing industry', accessed 12/09/2014 from http://amerryweather.wordpress.com/2012/12/03/future-change-in-the-ski-industry/

IBISWorld (2013) *Ski & Snowboard Resorts in the US*. IBISWorld, December.

Knight, P. (2013) 'The evolution of ski equipment', *Distinctly Montana*, 12 December, accessed 12/09/2014 from http://www.distinctlymontana.com/outdoor/history-ski-equipment

Loverseed, H. (2000) 'Winter sports in North America', *Marketing Intelligence,* **6**, 45-62

Medical Tourism Magazine (2014) 'Let the Games begin: Is there life after Olympics for resort city?' 17 February, accessed 3/21/2015 from http://www.medicaltourismmag.com/let-games-begin-life-sochi-olympics/

Snowsports Industries America (2014) *Snow Sports Participation Report*, accessed 08/27/2014 from http://www.snowsports.org/Retailers/Research/SIASnowSportsParticipationReport

Vanat, L. (2014) '*2014 International Report on Snow & Mountain Tourism*', Geneva, Switzerland, April.

Vanat, L. (2015) '*2015 International Report on Snow & Mountain Tourism*', Geneva, Switzerland, April.

Whitfield, A. (2013) 'Heli skiing the new revolution,' accessed 12/09/2014 from http://www.biglines.com/articles/heli-skiing-new-revolution

3 Understanding the Consumer

Spotlight: X-Games takes X-treme sports to X-citing new level

Launched in 1995 in Newport, Rhode Island, the X Games is an extreme sports competition encompassing skateboarding and motocross and (since 1997) winter sports – including snowboarding, skiing and snowmobiling. It acts as an incubator for the latest, hip sports both for summer and winter. Targeting Generations X and Y, the annual X Games competitions are put on by American sports broadcaster ESPN and also shown on ABC Sports network. Since 2002, the winter event has been held at Aspen's Buttermilk ski hill. The Summer X Games moved from Los Angeles to Austin, Texas in 2014.

Chris Schuster, President & Founder of the Association of Freeskiing Professionals (AFP), provides the management team for X Games under his company Event Production Specialists (EPS Events). Based in North Lake Tahoe, Andrew Gauthier is AFP's Marketing & World Tour Manager. "As a member of the EPS team, we manage all sports and competition at X-Games. We are responsible for coordinating between ESPN Live TV, the athletes, the judges, hospitality, medical, and the course builders," says Gauthier. "As a crucial pivot point for these events to occur, we ensure that the timing, the safety, the competition process are all aligned. Furthermore, we also are responsible for coordinating athlete practices for each discipline."

Andrew Gauthier

Executive Director for AFP, Eric Zerrenner, was originally looking for a couple of interns from Sierra Nevada College to do the work that Gauthier now does. At the time Gauthier was evaluating different marketing coordinator roles, going through interviews at various resorts such as Sugar Bowl, Kirkwood, Squaw Valley, and Northstar while finishing his MBA. When he saw the request for interns for AFP he came up with a novel idea. "The job description was extensive, but I thought two or three internships could potentially add up to one job," Gauthier explains. After some negotiations, Gauthier's new role was created.

Marketing and sales are his chief areas, with a wide involvement in sponsorships and partnerships, social media strategy, event promotion, athlete membership drives, and also basic video editing for exclusive AFP content. The AFP World Tour is another of his responsibilities. "I accept and review all event sanctioning applications, update athlete rankings with new event results and manage the AFP judging program," he explains. This includes procurement, education and scheduling for all AFP Certified Judges. Alongside Jeff Schmuck (Managing Editor of @SBCSkier Mag), he also manages event media and content on afpworldtour.com and is responsible for athlete communications. Gauthier creates and distributes all formal AFP documentation, manages the inventory logistics including banners, signage, cameras, equipment etc. And he distributes and analyzes post-season surveys to both athletes and event organizers. Ironically, he also gets to manage new interns from Sierra Nevada College. Despite this taxing tally of tasks, Gauthier thrives on the scope, the deadlines and the competitive nature of his work. And, it's a pretty glamorous job. Traveling to the premier North American ski resorts, he meets the world's top freeskiing and snowboarding athletes. "It is difficult to pinpoint one star struck moment," he says. "However, I believe when I finished my last powder run at Whistler at the 2013/14 AFP World Championships, myself, Mike Atkinson, and Chris Schuster (ski sport organizer for Winter X Games) popped out of our bindings and there was none other than Mike Douglas. Basically, he was the leader of the Canadian Air Force, creator of the D-Spin and just a huge freeski star. We had lunch soon after with the AFP team, Mike, and Jeff Schmuck. What a day that was!" The position comes with other perks, too, particularly living the winter sports lifestyle. "I did not grow up a skier, racer, or competitor. It was the environment, community and the people that attracted me to the winter industry. My love for skiing and snowboarding came later," Gauthier says.

When it comes to marketing, AFP and the X Games are heavily weighted towards social media and online advertising. "In the past, many marketing campaigns have focused on product. Today we see many brands moving away from product-focused content and more towards entertainment and building a personality of their brand," Gauthier explains. "See Salomon Freeski TV, The North Face's *The Rise*, and Atomic's recent video series, all live on You Tube. In addition, you find many brands have a dedicated online theater, if you will, to present this content. What's particularly interesting here is that this is the most difficult type of campaign to track back to the bottom line, yet companies continue to invest."

Gauthier's boss, Eric Zerrenner, says content is king these days: "Brands – both hard goods and soft goods – are looking to create their own, unique content. Typically this has resulted in brands looking to their sponsored athletes to provide them with this content – whether it's action footage at a comp, lifestyle footage from the offseason, training, or travels or general free skiing content. Because of social media, and the scope and immediate reach via those channels, brands are able to tap into an athlete's audience to help them get their brand/marketing message out to a relevant and receptive audience."

Media, both traditional and especially social media are paramount, says Zerrenner: "As the main source for competitive freeskiing, we want to be as informative as possible about the competitions, courses, athletes and results. If we're not able to be at an event - or even at every competition at an event - social media provides instant access. We rely on this information to keeps us informed and current on what's happening within our sport and culture."

Sources: Personal interviews with Andrew Gauthier, Nov 2014, and Eric Zerrenner, Dec 2014

Profiling consumers

As a recent White Paper on skiers stated, "adults who take ski trips, quite simply, are a distinct and special bunch" (PhocusWright, 2013, p.8). The report found that, in the U.S., a higher proportion of ski travelers are male, younger and more affluent, compared to the general traveler population. Downhill skiing is the most common form of the sport, but many skiers participate in more than one type of skiing. Figure 3.1 shows participation rates for a five-year period in six winter sports activities.

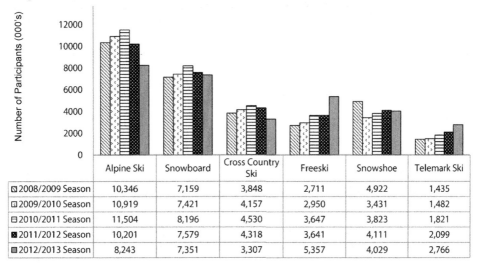

	Alpine Ski	Snowboard	Cross Country Ski	Freeski	Snowshoe	Telemark Ski
2008/2009 Season	10,346	7,159	3,848	2,711	4,922	1,435
2009/2010 Season	10,919	7,421	4,157	2,950	3,431	1,482
2010/2011 Season	11,504	8,196	4,530	3,647	3,823	1,821
2011/2012 Season	10,201	7,579	4,318	3,641	4,111	2,099
2012/2013 Season	8,243	7,351	3,307	5,357	4,029	2,766

Figure 3.1: Winter sports participation rates in the U.S. 2008-2013 (Source: Adapted from Snowsports Industries America, 2014a)

According to PhocusWright, downhill skiers make up about 58 per cent of participants on the slopes and snowboarders 25 per cent (the remainder both ski and snowboard). Whereas general U.S. travelers are evenly split between male and female – with women frequently taking a lead in travel planning and therefore attracting considerable attention from travel marketers – this is not the case with skiers and boarders. About two thirds of them are male, under 45, and, perhaps of most importance to travel marketers, high earners. Nearly half report an annual household income of at least $100,000, compared to a quarter of general U.S. travelers (see Table 3.1). Methods of attracting more women into skiing are explored in the Case Study below.

	U.S. tourists	Winter sport tourists
Male	50%	66%
Ages 18-44	54%	63%
>$100,000 annual income	24%	49%

Table 3.1: Winter sport tourists versus regular travelers in the U.S. (Source: Adapted from PhocusWright, 2013)

Not surprisingly, snowboarding appeals to a younger demographic, a population that is also less affluent, travels less, and spends less on a ski vacation. Figure 3.2 shows the demographic differences between the two groups.

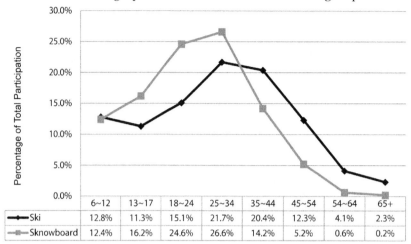

	6~12	13~17	18~24	25~34	35~44	45~54	54~64	65+
Ski	12.8%	11.3%	15.1%	21.7%	20.4%	12.3%	4.1%	2.3%
Sknowboard	12.4%	16.2%	24.6%	26.6%	14.2%	5.2%	0.6%	0.2%

Figure 3.2: Age demographics – skiers versus snowboarders (Source: Adapted from Snowsports Industries America, 2014a)

A recent report from Snowsports Industries America (2014b) digs deeper into generational differences of winter sports participants. Table 3.2 shows those differences. There has actually been little change in the pattern of age distribution over the last 15 years, as snowboarding has gained a critical mass of participants. Fifteen years ago, the values of Generation X (born 1965 to circa 1980) dominated the participant base, particularly in the snowboard category sports base that had nothing but youthful participants in the 1990s. The Baby Boomers (born 1945 to circa 1964) still held their claim on the values of downhill skiing 15 years ago, but that has shifted to a more mature Generation X and the children of the Baby Boomer generation, the prolific Generation Y or Millennials (born 1981 to circa 2001) – see the Gstaad Profile below for more information. Now Generation Z (under 18) is taking its place in the snow sports base and future research will determine what characteristic mark they will make on snow sports. As the opening Spotlight outlined, the annual winter X Games events held in Aspen specifically target both Gen X and Y.

Interestingly, there are a significant number (16%) of snow sports participants that both ski and snowboard, and members of this group are more likely to characterize themselves as luxury travelers, spending more on shopping and dining during trips (PhocusWright, 2013). They are an interesting group, skiing more than other groups, taking more vacations with paid lodging, are more skilled, and much more likely to hold a season pass (see Figure 3.3). They are more passionate about their winter sports, caring more about having the best gear and looking good on the slopes, and seem to have made skiing/snowboarding an important part of their lifestyle. For ski marketers, this unique set has considerable potential to be a major influencer within the ski traveler population (PhocusWright, 2013).

Total Participants	Snowboard	Alpine	Freeski
Total Participants (all ages) 1+ times	7,351,000	8,243,000	5,368,000
Baby Boomers (55+) 1+ times	1%	6%	3%
Gen X (35 to 54) 1+ times	19%	33%	24%
Gen Y (18 to 34) 1+ times	51%	37%	50%
Gen Z (under 18) 1+ times	29%	24%	23%
Female Participants			
Total Participants (all ages) 1+ times	2,396,000	3,305,000	1,945,000
Baby Boomers (55+) 1+ times	0%	3%	2%
Gen X (35 to 54) 1+ times	17%	27%	20%
Gen Y (18 to 34) 1+ times	60%	40%	55%
Gen Z (under 18) 1+ times	23%	30%	24%
Male Participants			
Total Participants (all ages) 1+ times	4,955,000	4,938,000	3,423,000
Baby Boomers (55+) 1+ times	1%	9%	3%
Gen X (35 to 54) 1+ times	20%	36%	26%
Gen Y (18 to 34) 1+ times	47%	35%	47%
Gen Z (under 18) 1+ times	32%	20%	23%

Table 3.2: Generational differences in skiing and snowboarding (Source: Adapted from Snowsports Industries America, 2014b)

A special set: Ski + Snowboarders				
• The Ski + Snowboarder Set		**Skiers**	**Snow-boarders**	**Ski +Snow-boarders**
• Represent one in five ski travelers				
• Take the most trips	Spend on travel	$874	$765	$990
• Are mouch moreadvanced/expert on slopes				
• Are more likely to stay in an upscale/luxury resort	Spend on shopping/ dining	$344	$355	$435
• Are younger: 60% are under 35				

Figure 3.3: Profiling participants who both ski and snowboard (Source: Adapted from PhocusWright, 2013).

The PhocusWright (2013) study of American skiers also looked at information sources used by skiers for comparing and choosing their ski trips. Online sources – including websites and apps – dominate the ski shopping process, with seven out of 10 ski trips planned via websites. Recommendations from family and friends are the second most important source, with ski travelers relying on personal connections for nearly four out of 10 ski trips. This is consistent with general U.S. travel, where information from family and friends also exerts significant influence. Beyond friends and family, however, the influence of other offline sources of information in ski travel planning and shopping drops off considerably.

In Europe, snow sports holidays remain a relatively exclusive market with a high financial barrier to entry. A recent Mintel (2014) report on British skiers found that university graduates, higher earners and people who describe their finances as healthy are the most likely to have taken, or have any future interest in taking, a snow sports holiday. Less-affluent people have struggled to gain entry, and the penetration of snow sports holidays is lowest among people who describe their financial situation as tight or struggling. Table 3.3 shows holiday behavior for a sample of snow sports participants from the Mintel report, and for 27 per cent of them, their last snow sports vacation was their first. A quarter of the sample booked their vacation as a package and 20 per cent traveled with their school or university.

	%
This trip was my first snowsports holiday	27
I booked the holiday as a package (eg includes travel and accommodation)	25
This trip was organized by my school/university	20
I booked transport and accommodation separately	17
I paid a for ski/snowboard school	17
I took advantage of a deal or special offer	17
I travelled outside of peak season to save money	16
I paid for private ski/snowboard instructor lessons	15
I brought my own skis or snowboard from the UK	13
I tried another activity aside from skiing/snowboarding (eg ice climbing, dogsledding, tobogganing, paragliding, snowshoeing) during my trip	12
A holiday rep/ski host escorted me around the slopes for free	11

Table 3.3: Last snow sports holiday behavior (Source: Adapted from Mintel, 2014)

Motivations

Winter sport tourists, in general, are passionate about their sport. Some four in five ski travelers view skiing as an important part of their lifestyle, and skiing is overwhelmingly the central driver of travel where the sport is involved. The significance of this stands out when compared to other activities travelers take part in on leisure trips. A 2011 study of more than 20 types of in-destination activities, tours, events and attractions found that winter sports score higher in relative importance to a trip than all other trip activities (see Figure 3.4).

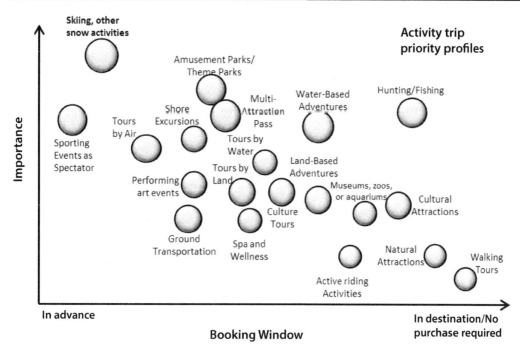

Figure 3.4: Relative importance of skiing compared to other activities (Source: Adapted from PhocusWright, 2011)

Over the years, many researchers have sought to understand what drives this passion. One of the early studies was conducted by Mills (1985), who tried to determine whether or not the empirical structure of motivation for participating in skiing corresponded to Maslow's theory of motivation. He found that in order to have a successful skiing experience, skiers are seeking to satisfy four needs: safety, affiliation, esteem and self-actualization. Boon (1994), on the other hand, found there were certain 'push' factors involved in the decision to go skiing including the desire to 'get away from the usual demands of office life'. He found differences in skiers depending on their ability. For example, beginners placed a significantly higher amount of importance on 'being near others who could help' than other groups. Benefits such as 'experiencing excitement' and 'leading other people' were more important to advanced skiers than they were to other groups, whereas intermediate skiers placed greater importance on benefits such as 'being with other people who enjoy the same things we do.'

Tikalsky and Lahren (1988), in reviewing motivational research for risk-taking sports, suggested a few hypotheses that could help explain skier behavior. Firstly, recreational activities often function as a form of social release, in which participants can temporarily behave in a way not constrained by usual customs and protocol. Secondly, many skiers are involved in the sport for non-athletic reasons, since the social benefits may be more powerful primary motivators. Thirdly, for many non-athletic people, skiing often functions metaphorically in that one can claim to be a vigorous mountain person coming to grips with risk and danger.

Finally, a high percentage of skiers are more concerned with safety and ambience than athletic challenge or risk. The authors conclude that the motivations for skiing are multiple, and that dangerous skiing is a complex social phenomenon.

A decade later, research conducted by Williams and Dossa (1995) suggested that people ski for personal achievement, social reasons, enjoyment of nature, escape and thrill, and, even today, the primary drivers of destination selection for ski trips are all connected to the ski experience (PhocusWright, 2013). Easily the most important factor for skiers/snowboarders is the quality of snow conditions, with more than eight in 10 skiers indicating that this is extremely important or important to them in terms of destination selection (see Figure 3.5). Another influential factor in destination choice is the distance between the slopes and lodging options. The number of lifts and advanced trails also rank highly as a driver of destination choice.

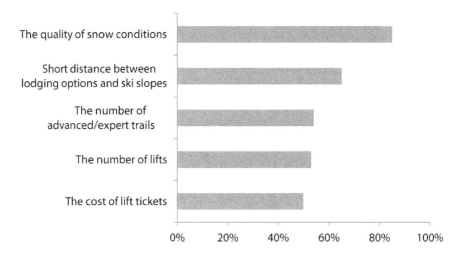

Figure 3.5: Factors driving ski destination selection (Source: Adapted from PhocusWright, 2013)

In fact, early season snow conditions and skier perception of these conditions greatly influence the momentum and success of the overall season (IBISWorld, 2013). According to a recent report on the 2013/14 winter season by Crystal Ski Holidays, Italy's market share of British skiers increased (from 15.2% to 15.7%) over the previous season because of excellent snow conditions throughout the winter, whereas France's market share decreased (from 34.8% to 33.5%) because of poor early snow (see Figure 3.6).

In terms of loyalty, research has shown that older skiers are more likely to return to a particular ski resort. Resort-marketing firm Ryan Solutions collected three seasons of lodging data from 10 resorts across North America, finding that the older the skier, the more likely they are to be loyal – which fits nicely with other research showing older skiers stay longer and spend more each day (Ski Canada, 2014).

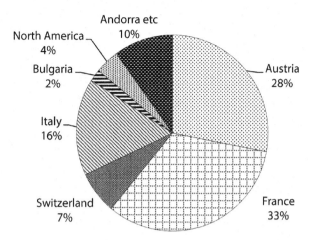

Figure 3.6: Where British skiers traveled in 2013/14 (Source: Adapted from Crystal Ski Holidays, 2014)

As for the ingredients that contribute towards the ultimate winter sports experience, a recent German study suggested safety, comfort, hedonism and relaxation were key influences (Hallmann et al., 2012). The researchers found that a combination of some winter sport activities (alpine and sledging, for example) had a positive impact on the perceived experience, and they therefore recommended that resorts promote the range of activities they have available in their promotional material. They did note, however, that different segments of the market appreciate different experiences, the same conclusion drawn by Konu, Laukkanen and Komppula (2011), who identified six different customer segments in Finland using the cluster-factor method: passive tourists, cross-country skiers, want-it-all, all-but-downhill skiing, sports seekers, and relaxation seekers.

A study of British skiers found three key motivations for participation in winter sports: sport motivations, where desire to participate in the sport is strongest; social motivations, where intention to socialize is integral to both motivation for travel and activities participated in; and finally vacation motivations, where desire to relax precedes all other interests (Phillips & Brunt, 2013). The results also demonstrated disparities between skiers and snowboarders in their use of terrain, equipment buying behavior, demographic profile, group type, destinations visited and motivations for participating. Destination choice determinants, including cost, terrain variety and accommodation, were also shown to vary.

Social motivations are clearly important, and Snowsports Industries America (SIA) (2014) suggests that being with family and friends is more important today than ever before for winter sports participants. In their 1999 study of consumers, the desire for freedom and getting away from it all was the most appealing aspect of a snow sports holiday for skiers and boarders, whereas in 2011 this had changed to being with family and friends. SIA suggests that this may be a result of economic issues that have forced many to reassess the way they allocate their resources including their time and their money. They did say, however, that advanced participants value the thrill and excitement of snow sports more than other proficiency groups, and beginners and intermediates most enjoy being with their families and friends on snow.

A recent study of British skiers by Mintel (2014) found that half of people interested in taking a snow sports holiday say they find the natural landscape appealing (see Table 3.4). A large percentage (29%) are attracted by the physical challenge of a snow sports vacation, and 31% would prefer to visit a resort that offered a range of winter sports activities. Another key influencer is concern over adequate snow cover: 28% of people interested in taking a snow sports holiday say they would only travel to a resort with guaranteed snow cover. Nearly a third say they would practice/learn on an artificial/indoor slope in the U.K. before a snow sports holiday, indicating the importance of indoor ski slopes.

	%
The natural landscape of a snowsports holiday appeals to me	49
I would prefer to visit a resort that offered a range of other activities (eg ice climbing, dogsledding, tobogganing, paragliding, snowshoeing)	31
I would practice/learn on an artificial/indoor slope in the UK before a snowsports holiday	31
The physical challenge of a snowsports holiday appeals to me	29
I would only travel to a resort with guaranteed snow cover	28
I would only go to a well-known ski destination	26
I would travel to an emerging ski destination (eg Bulgaria) to save money	23
I would hesitate to take a snowsports holiday that did not include a rep/ski host	15
I am concerned about the environmental impact of snowsports	8
None of these	4

Table 3.4: Attitudes towards snow sports holidays (Source: Adapted from Mintel, 2014)

Finally, in a segmentation study in Canada, Joppe, Elliot and Durand (2013) discovered, through cluster analysis, seven distinct skier profiles on the slopes of Quebec.

1   Isabelle represents a timid beginner who wants easy slopes, lessons and good service.

2   Mathieu (the party animal) is a skier seeking après ski entertainment, and

3   Phil (the extreme) wants snow jumps and night skiing.

4   Marc (the demanding professional) wants quality facilities, from chalets to lifts.

5   Yvonne (the familiar veteran) is looking for groomed trails and competent staff.

6   Cluster 6 (Eric, the passionate) is a skier seeking difficult slopes without crowds.

7   Annie (the beginner/saver) is value seeking and price sensitive.

Profile: Gstaad: Marketing to millennials

Millennials enjoying a fondue lunch at Gstaad's Restaurant Eggli - Copyright: Gstaad Saanenland Tourismus

A click of a mouse, the scroll of a finger, the press of a button – this is how Millennials have grown up and how they now conduct business, reservations, purchasing, communication and social transactions. Increasingly, marketers have been turning their attention away from Baby Boomers and towards gratifying the instantaneous needs of the Now Generation.

There are currently around 79 million Millennials in North America – that's three million more than Baby Boomers, who are predicted to dwindle to just 58 million by 2030. Otherwise known as Generation Y, they were born between 1980 and 1999, children of the Digital Age. While the younger component is still financially dependent on parents, older Millennials are at peak purchasing power and an ideal target market for ski resorts. So what are the keys to attracting, satisfying and retaining this demanding demographic?

Here are a few Mountain Must-Haves for Millennials:

- Free Wi-Fi throughout ski hill
- Social and wired areas in lodges and in ski hotel lobbies
- High tech, cellphone-friendly websites
- Apps to replace traditional ski maps, ski info
- Real time reporting and responding
- Trustworthy peer reviews
- Automated check in/out at ski accommodation and automated bill paying
- Automated, smart card lift passes for ease of purchase and use
- Smart technology and plentiful power outlets in lodges, hotels, bedrooms

- Cool factor at the hill – unique, emotional component, age-appropriate freebies
- Social responsibility programs at hill, après ski venues and hotels
- Pod hotels – reducing hotel costs in order to have a larger budget for more active vacation experiences

Social media, online reviewing and apps are mainstays of Millennial choice-making. Around 40 per cent of Millennials are likely to share travel experiences during their trip and 34 per cent will disperse details via social media on their return. Likewise, they use peer reviews, checking on average 10.2 sources, before booking. This is a vast resource of feedback that hotels and destinations can harness for their own marketing purposes.

One Swiss resort which has responded to this high tech trend is Gstaad, particularly in regard to apps. Visitors can benefit from up to date information from many different sources including iGstaad App for Android, iSKI Swiss, Skiresort.de, Snocountry, Skitude, myswitzerland, Skiline, Schee & Mehr. Gstaad's piste map is interactive and Pistenbericht gives a daily updated snow report, slope report, weather and web cams.

Gstaad is also active on social media. Its Facebook tagged "Gstaad – come up, slow down" is updated daily and the resort has a strong presence on Instagram and Twitter. Gstaad incorporated a responsive design into its website - www.gstaad.ch - which is compatible with every gadget, smartphone and computer. They are also able to track users. "During last year (2014) 64.02 per cent of the users were desktop-users, 19.15 per cent mobile users and 16.83 per cent tablet-users," says Antje Buchs, Project Manager Public Relations for Gstaad Saanenland Tourismus. "Thanks to the responsive design, it is also possible to book hotels and apartments with smartphones."

Despite their reliance on online communication, Millennials are actually more sociable offline than previous generations – so long as technology is close at hand. With such constant access to images of social activity, they are subject to the FOMO (Fear of Missing Out) phenomenon. Around 58 per cent prefer to travel with friends: that's 20 per cent more than other demographic groups. Free Wi-Fi around the slopes of Gstaad in social spots such as the Eggli, Rellerli, Saanerslochgrat and Wispile mountain restaurants means that digital devotees can relax in between runs and socialize while still keeping in touch online.

Wow factors for Gstaad include the chance to visit the world's first peak-to-peak suspension bridge, Peak Walk. Spanning 107m, with spectacular mountain views, the bridge starts at the top of View Point on Glacier 3000 and finishes at Scex Rouge peak. Glacier 300 also gives Gstaad the longest ski season in the area.

While every Alpine resort offers fondue evenings, Gstaad has gone a step further with Fondueland. Here guests enjoy fondue while sitting in one of two giant wooden fondue-pots which each seat up to eight people. The specially designated huts are open year round and accessible by foot, bike, sledge or snowshoes. Catering to Millennial music mania, Gstaad's Ride on Music is a three-day festival with a mix of hiphop, street, rock and folk music, with satellite events on the slopes by day and in town by night.

The Superpass satisfies another 'Millennial Must-Have': value for money. It covers three ski areas with one ticket, encompassing 188 lifts and 630km of skiing. Although Gstaad is by no means a cheap ski resort, it prides itself on making skiing accessible to youth and families. And youth lift ticket rates have been extended up to the age of 23. The resort also has several affordable lodging options including Saanewald Lodge, Spitzhorn, Hamilton Lodge and a new youth hostel in the nearby community of Saanen which was incidentally dubbed by actress, Julie Andrews as "the last paradise in a crazy world."

Environmental sustainability is an important issue for Millennials, who have grown up with recycling and the notion of reducing environmental footprints. In this respect, Sustainable Gstaad has various ongoing ecological projects including traditional alpine farming, hydro-electric power stations, a central hotel laundry, and green fuel for piste equipment.

Sources: Personal interviews with Kerstin Sonnekalb for Gstaad Saanenland Tourismus January 2015, and with Antje Buchs, Project Manager Public Relations for Gstaad Saanenland Tourismus February 2015; http://expediablog.co.uk/wp-content/uploads/2013/10/Future-of-Travel-Report1.pdf

3

Constraints

Given maturing ski markets in the western world, interest in why skiers quit has grown over the years, as has the interest in identifying potential markets that might be persuaded to ski. Williams and Basford (1992) studied the non-skier population and found that the two major deterrents preventing respondents from participating in skiing were perceptions of the activity's dangers and costs. Following on from this study, Williams and Lattey (1994) focused specifically on constraints facing women, concluding that the reasons women are not more involved in the sport arise from their interpretation of what constitutes satisfying leisure, and the types of constraints they associate with the skiing experience. Many women perceive skiing to be a physically challenging sport beyond their athletic capabilities, and they place greater emphasis on enhancing the emotional and social dimensions of skiing, as opposed to valuing the physical benefits (see the Case Study below for more information on female constraints).

Gilbert and Hudson (2000) operationalized a contemporary model of leisure constraints in order to examine the constraints to skiing for both participants and non-participants. A qualitative approach was used to develop a questionnaire that could measure perceptions of intrapersonal, interpersonal and structural constraints. A list of 30 constraints was developed directly from the results of in-depth interviews and focus groups (see Figure 3.7).

An instrument was then developed to measure these constraints, and tested on members of a sports club. The results indicated that economic factors were the major constraints for both skiers and non-skiers. The 10 highest scoring constraints are listed in Table 3.5. The fact that ski clothing and equipment are too expensive is the number one deterrent, with 64 per cent of respondents agreeing with this statement. Hudson also compared skiers to non-skiers finding that 24 out of 30 constraints were rated significantly higher by non-skiers than skiers. The only constraint that concerned skiers more than non-skiers was the worry about lack of snow. This confirms the findings of previous researchers who found snow conditions to be the key variable for existing skiers when making destination choices.

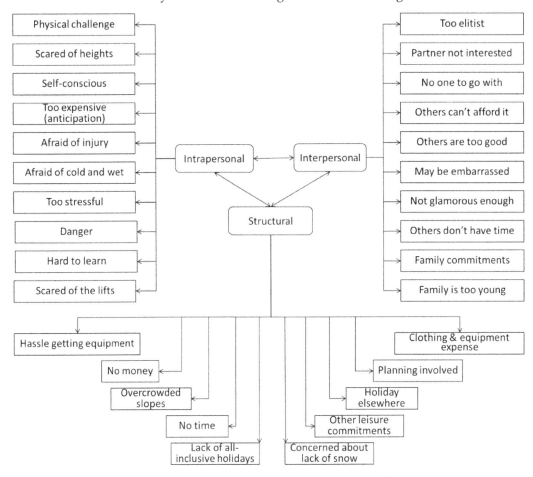

Figure 3.7: Constraints to skiing participation (Source: Adapted from Gilbert & Hudson, 2000)

Constraint	Mean Value
Clothing and equipment are too expensive	3.75
Anticipation of expense	3.55
Lack of low-cost all-inclusive holidays	3.48
Prefer to take a holiday elsewhere	3.16
Do not have enough money	3.14
Others do not have the money to go with me	2.89
The slopes are too crowded	2.79
Concern about the lack of snow	2.76
Too much hassle buying or renting equipment	2.63
Too much planning involved	2.57

Table 3.5: Perceived constraints to skiing (Source: Adapted from Gilbert & Hudson, 2000)

In a 2011 study of American non-skiers by Snowsports Industries America (SIA) (2014c), increased family commitments (26%), no one to go with (23%), and increased work commitments (18%), were the top three reasons for not participating in snow sports during the 2009/2010 season. Interestingly, expense did not make the list of top 15 constraints for lapsed participants. Mintel (2014), on the other hand, found that British non-skiers and boarders preferred warmer and more relaxing vacations. Lack of previous experience was also one of the primary reasons cited for not wanting to take a snow sports holiday, and Mintel speculates that beginner packages offered by snow sports brands are therefore failing to appeal to the first-timer demographic.

A more recent study by Hudson et al. (2013) in Canada, examined the effects of ethnicity on constraints to downhill skiing/snowboarding. The goal was to gain a better understanding of the constraints facing existing and potential skiers/boarders, especially those from minority ethnic backgrounds who increasingly form a larger percentage of the Canadian population. The minority market has incredible potential as it represents one third of the millennium generation in North America (age 12 to 17) and 45 per cent of those aged five and younger are a member of a racial or ethnic minority. However, despite the growth in Chinese-Canadian skiers in Canada, only about 10 per cent of Chinese-Canadians have tried the sport, compared to 15 per cent of Canadians in general. Thus, from an industry perspective, the ski industry would benefit from a better understanding of the constraints facing existing and potential skiers/boarders, especially those from minority ethnic backgrounds.

A new leisure constraints model guided the study, a framework that recognizes the importance of macro- (i.e., ethnicity) and micro-level (i.e., participation, self-construal) variables on the traditional concepts of intrapersonal, interpersonal, and structural constraints (see Figure 3.8). To address the research questions, a survey was developed based on previous literature and the results from an in-depth qualitative study. The qualitative research showed that Anglo-Canadians were more constrained by structural constraints (time and money) whereas the Chinese-Canadian respondents were constrained by the lack of friends to ski with, a lack of information on the sport, language barriers, and a higher priority for non-leisure activities such as studying. This supports previous research suggesting that Chinese people place a greater emphasis on higher education and a strong work ethic than on leisure. However, they did express a desire to 'experience the Canadian lifestyle' and would therefore like to participate if only to 'fit in' with the Canadian lifestyle.

From the survey, structural constraints were reported as the highest barriers to participation, followed by intrapersonal and then interpersonal constraints. Not surprisingly, participants reported significantly lower levels of all three types of constraint compared with non-participants. Expense was consistently reported as an important structural constraint across groups. Ethnicity was found to play a significant role regardless of whether the person did or did not ski; manifesting in Chinese-Canadians reporting significantly higher levels of all three types of constraint compared with Anglo-Canadians. Apart from the expense, Chinese-Canadian non-participants were highly constrained by a fear of personal injury and concern that skiing is a dangerous sport. They were also notably constrained by perceived language barriers that they might encounter, and by difficulties in finding others to participate with. In general, and comparatively to Anglo-Canadian non-participants, Chinese-Canadian non-participants felt that they lacked information about how to go skiing, and held perceptions that skiing would be a difficult sport to learn and that much work is involved in planning to go skiing.

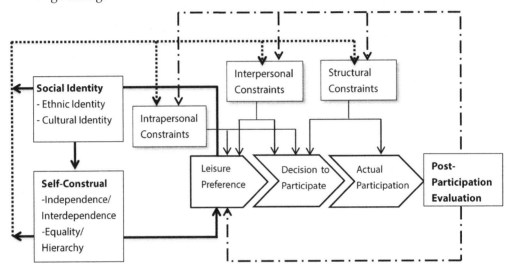

Figure 3.8: Leisure constraints model used as framework (Source: Adapted from Hudson et al., 2013)

The results of the study offer a number of important practical implications, particularly providing unique insight into what is constraining Chinese-Canadians from participating in skiing and snowboarding. The growing ethnic population poses a challenge for North American winter resorts, which have not traditionally succeeded in appealing to minority markets. Chinese-Canadians may be persuaded to participate if marketing emphasis was placed on the provision of a safe, comfortable learning environment with few language barriers. Canadian ski areas may wish to follow the example of some Colorado resorts that have increased their frontline minority hiring. Employing Chinese-speaking ski instructors, for instance, would alleviate some of the concerns of non-participants of Chinese origin. Similarly, having information and education materials (brochures, maps, etc.) available in Chinese would also be helpful to address the perceived lack of information available about the sports and perceived difficulty in planning to go skiing. Finally, given the importance of friends for Chinese-Canadians trying to negotiate constraints, special introductory 'buddy' rates (for example, two-for-one specials) may be worth considering as an incentive to try the sport.

In summary, according to a new report by Snowsports Industries America (2014b), the barriers to participating in snow sports have not changed much over the years. Past and recent research indicates that major barriers to growth of the sport include lack of access to snow sports due to expense, proximity of resorts, lack of knowledge about how to get started, nobody to ski or snowboard with, and opportunity costs (so many things to do, so little time). The report concludes that while most of these barriers have been addressed one way or another by traditional programs that do bring some new participants into the market, and have brought some lapsed participants back, they have not brought them in droves.

3

Case study: Freeski female style

Despite the fact that around two-thirds of skiers and boarders are male, there's a growing number of ski school programs devoted to promoting advanced skiing for women. Just as females generally respond better to group instruction at fitness centers, they also prefer a women-only group format for winter sports. Resorts have recognized that many women are intimidated by mixed gender groups, are more likely to sign up for same sex instruction and also more likely to stay in skiing if they have females among their ski friends.

Jackson Hole has been running Elevate Women's Ski Camp since 2000. The concept is to raise the bar on women's ski progression by day, and to facilitate socialization and relaxation in the luxury of Teton Mountain Lodge & Spa by night. A stone's throw from the resort's gondola and aerial tram, this four-star hotel is the après ski hub of the camp, offering 25 per cent discount on lodging to campers. Evening events are held in conference rooms, in the Spur Bar & Restaurant – a very lively après ski spot - and in the K-Bar, a more intimate lounge bar in the hotel lobby. Although the women separate off into small groups for ski tuition, they mix and mingle at organized lunches and receptions, impromptu dinners and at the final banquet.

Designed for intermediate and advanced skiers, the camp runs in January and March and has seen so many repeat attendees that it inaugurated a 10-timer award in 2015 to help encourage and reward repeaters. "After 15 years of involvement with the Women's Camp, I am still amazed at the improvement, camaraderie, and the stark enthusiasm of the campers," says Lexey Wauters, camp coach and coordinator. "Campers come from all over the country with widely varied ski backgrounds; they all slide away better, happier, more confident skiers."

Participants - mostly from the USA but also from as far away as Great Britain and Australia - numbered in the 50s at the January camp by the 2013/14 season and in the 60s by 2014/15. As well as providing a vast array of female instructors, one of the camp's cachets is having three professional freeskiers to help coach. These are Kim Havell, Jess McMillan and Crystal Wright, all cast members of the groundbreaking all-female extreme ski movie, *Pretty Faces*. As well as trouble-shooting each four or five person ski group with tips and techniques for tackling tough slopes, they contribute motivational presentations during après ski sessions.

"Having three of the top female freeskiers in the industry here in Jackson Hole is a testament to the fact that this is an ideal mountain for women of any ability to cultivate their interests in skiing, thrive with support and keep taking it to the next level," says Jackson Hole Mountain Resort Communications Manager, Anna Cole. "Increasing popularity of the camp year after year only underscores the importance of embracing this strong female demographic and giving them what they need to elevate."

During camps, ski fitness advice is offered by Crystal Wright, a professional big-mountain skier, Jackson Hole gym owner and fitness trainer. "Ski preparation, maintenance and strength are so, so important. The stronger the skiers are, the less likely they are to become injured," says Wright. "They also will enjoy themselves so much more because they will be able to ski until the end of the day without feeling like they might hurt themselves. Also, recovery after a hard day will be quicker."

Crystal Wright

As well as providing the blueprint for fitness and stretching at an evening exercise class, Wright rotates around the ski groups adding her tactics for skiing tricky terrain. It's all about instilling confidence in the women and in their skiing ability, she maintains: "We all look at ski runs and lines differently so I try to relate to them how I push myself through something that is intimidating. The women are better skiers than they think they are, so I try to give them some helpful cues they can think of when skiing a run that they are uncomfortable with." The key to progress is pushing comfort zones in the company of other like-minded women, Wright concludes. Video analysis enables instructors and skiers to dissect skiing stance as a very visual means of instilling new techniques. And highlights from the videos are put together with matching music to create a lively show at the end of camp banquet.

Attending the January 2015 Elevate Camp, Tenessa Singleton transformed ski apathy into renewed ski fervor. "Until I did this camp, I was so frustrated with skiing that I was going to take up snowboarding," she says. "I really enjoyed being with women from all over who have a passion for skiing," she adds. "I have spent the last several winters in Jackson Hole but our amazing instructor introduced us to parts of the mountain I have never seen, secret little powder stashes and tree skiing galore. Besides confidence building and technical skiing, I made some great friends. And the highlight of the camp had to be skiing with three of the best pro skiers in the world."

During her January 2015 Elevate presentation, Jess McMillan explained how the female pro skiers at Jackson Hole have pushed the boundaries not only on female skiing instruction but also on how female athletes are perceived by the ski industry. "Kim, Crystal, Lindsey Dyer, me and a few others got together four years ago and changed the profile of women in skiing," said McMillan to the rapt audience. "Before then there was just one token woman in ski movies and in advertising, which meant all the female freeskiers were fighting for the one spot all the time. But we got together and we said enough, we're going to work together from now on."

One of the results of this collaboration was the movie, *Pretty Faces*. This has been a springboard for many female freeskiing careers, including McMillan's. She was next asked to star in Warren Miller's 65th feature film, *No Turning Back*, with carte blanche to choose a co-star. She picked a personal idol, Ingrid Backstrom. "All it took was us to start supporting each other and it changed the entire ski industry," McMillan added. With women buying 60 per cent of the ski gear sold, manufacturers are gradually realizing that they need female skiers to advertise their products, said McMillan, who helps design ski suits for Spyder.

Another revolutionary aspect of *No Turning Back* was that, for the first time in 20 years, the advertising poster featured a woman. The first three skiers depicted in the movie are also female, with McMillan the first woman on skis. As well as two female heli-ski guides, Kim Grant and Chris Anthony, the film also casts women throughout the various scenes, including Heather Paul, Sierra Quitiquit, Kaylin Richardson, Julia Mancuso, and Mikaela Shiffrin.

Sources: Attendee at Elevate Women's Ski Camp January 2015; personal interviews with Crystal Wright January 2015, Anna Cole January 2015, and Tenessa Singleton January 2015.

References

Boon, M.A. (1984) 'Understanding skier behavior', *Society and Leisure*, **7**(2), 397-406.

Crystal Ski Holidays (2014) *Ski Industry Report 2014*, Crystal Ski Holidays, September, accessed 1/11/2014 from http://mag.digitalpc.co.uk/fvx/crystal/sir2014/

Gilbert, D. and Hudson, S. (2000) 'Tourism demand constraints: A skiing participation', *Annals of Tourism Research*, **27**(4), 906-925.

Hallmann, K., Feiler, S., Muller, S. and Breuer, C. (2012) 'The interrelationship between sport activities and the perceived winter sport experience', *Journal of Sport & Tourism*, **17**(2), 145-163.

Hudson, S., Walker, G. J., Hinch, T. and Simpson, B. (2013) 'The influence of ethnicity and self-construal on leisure constraints', *Leisure Sciences*, 35(2), 145-166.

IBISWorld (2013) *Ski & Snowboard Resorts in the US*, IBISWorld, December.

Joppe, M., Elliot, S. and Durand, L. (2013) 'From ski market to ski traveler: A multidimensional approach', *Anatolia: An International Journal of Tourism and hospitality Research*, **24**(1), 40-51.

Konu, H., Laukkanen, T. and Komppula, R. (2011) 'Using ski destination choice criteria to segment Finnish ski resort customers', *Tourism Management*, **32**, 1096-1105.

Mills, A. (1985) 'Participation motivations for outdoor recreation: A test of Maslow's theory', *Journal of Leisure Research*, **17**(3), 184-199.

Mintel (2014) '*Snowsports – UK*', London: Mintel Group Ltd.

Phillips, J. and Brunt, P. (2013) 'Tourist differentiation: Developing a typology for the winter sports market', *Tourism*, **61**(3), 219-243.

PhocusWright (2011) *When They Get There, and Why They Go: In-Destination Activities*, New York: PhoCusWright Inc.

PhocusWright (2013) *Ski Traveler Snapshot. U.S. Skier and Ski Traveler Report*, New York: PhoCusWright Inc.

Ski Canada (2014) 'Loyalty Program', *Ski Canada Magazine, Buyer's Guide 2015*, 10.

Snowsports Industries America (2014a) *Snow Sports Participation Report*, accessed 8/27/2014 from http://www.snowsports.org/Retailers/Research/ SIASnowSportsParticipationReport

Snowsports Industries America (2014b) *2014 SIA Downhill Consumer Intelligence Report. Phase I – The Discovery Phase*, accessed 7/11/2014 from *http://www.snowsports.org/ SuppliersServiceProviders/ResearchSurveys/DownhillConsumerIntelligenceProject*

Snowsports Industries America (2014c) *Revisiting Growing the Snow Sports Industry*, accessed 9/12/2014 from http://www.snowsports.org/portals/0/documents/ Revisiting%20Growing%20the%20Snow%20Sports%20Industry.pdf

Tikalsky, F.T. and Lahren, S.L. (1988) 'Why people ski', *Ski Area Management*, **27**(3), 68-114.

Williams, P.W. and Basford, R. (1992) 'Segmenting downhill skiing's latent demand markets', *American Behavioral Scientist*, **36**(2), 222-235.

Williams, P.W. and Dossa, K.B. (1995) 'Canada's skiing markets', *Ski Area Management*, **34**(5), 62-63.

Williams, P.W. and Lattey, C. (1994) 'Skiing constraints for women', *Journal of Travel Research*, **33**(2), 21-25.

4 Design and Planning for Winter Sport Resorts

Paul Mathews

Since 1975 Paul Mathews has been designing ski resorts all over the world, numbering in the 400s by 2015. In the course of his work he has met many world leaders including the Prime Minister of the Russian Federation, President of Montenegro and the King of Spain, Juan Carlos, who offered to trade jobs with him for a winter season. "I declined saying that being a King was really too hard work; shaking hands and smiling at people you did not know and did not particularly care for," says Mathews. "To which he laughed and said my job was definitely better than his."

Having grown up skiing in Colorado, early in his career he designed a brand new resort on Vancouver Island, Mount Washington Ski Resort, which opened in 1978. With his academic background in forest ecology and landscape architecture, he was able to satisfy environmental prerequisites at Mount Washington, preserving soil, water and forests while creating a viable resort. "It was critically acclaimed and it quickly became the second most visited ski resort in British Columbia," says Mathews. "Word of mouth led to jobs down in Washington, Idaho, Montana and Oregon."

In 1975 Mathews became Chairman of the initial Resort Municipality of Whistler Planning Commission with some oversight of the design of the new Whistler Village. He also commenced planning for Whistler Mountain ski area with responsibility for the extensive system of lifts and slopes. From his Whistler-based company, Ecosign, Mathews has gone on to design over 400 resorts in 38 countries, always with an eye to creating an Alpine flavor, looking at the resort as a holistic picture, and centralizing services. This is not an easy task, but Ecosign has researched how far the average skier will willingly walk around a resort and how much uphill walking they will tolerate. Moreover, Mathews does not allow stairs in an Ecosign resort, favoring ramps instead. Slope capacity is also taken into account as well as the difficulty level of runs and the carrying capacity of lifts. Ecosign is now able to use a software program detecting the best snow on the mountain and the warmest spots to construct restaurant patios.

With annual revenues around $3 million, Ecosign remains a relatively small company with 20 employees. Their modus operandi is to identify terrain for the ski area and base village, bearing in mind climate – especially snowfall, sun and wind. Next they map out the best slopes and send in foresters and surveyors to fine-tune the layout to match the natural topography. Lifts, ski runs, and base areas are then penciled in. "A greenfield project could take four years," says Mathews. "An addition or renovation to an existing project could perhaps take just one year." The team travels extensively, dealing with different cultures, languages and international media and attends trade shows in America, Canada, Europe and China on an annual basis.

The name Ecosign is actually a contraction of 'ecological design', a new concept back in the 1970s. "Needless to say, I was very optimistic when I started Ecosign and frankly, would have been happy just working in British Columbia and Alberta in western Canada and indeed I did start with Whistler Mountain and Hemlock Valley in British Columbia," says Mathews. Forty years later, the forward-thinking company has become a worldwide reputable brand for international mountain resort design.

Mathews' innovative ideas were honed by negative experiences in his youth, skiing at badly executed ski areas in Washington State: "That led to interest later in life to undertake university studies in forest ecology and landscape architecture at the University of Washington in Seattle as the educational foundation needed to design good mountain resorts."

Ecosign was responsible for identifying possible sites in readiness for the 1988 Calgary Winter Olympics. This job was a big break for the company, launching it into Olympic limelight, and also giving employment to the staff for several years during an economic downturn. "We ended up identifying seventeen different potential areas, narrowed that down to approximately three and, finally, the Government of Alberta chose development of Nakiska at Mount Allan to host the Olympic Alpine Skiing events, the legacy training site and a commercially viable recreational ski area," Mathews explains. "Nakiska at Mount Allan filled all of those goals and was built for $23 million and continues to host about 200,000 skier visits annually." This work led the Austrian lift company, Doppelmayr to recommend to Nippon Cable, Japan that they hire 'Olympic Planners' which resulted in Ecosign's first job in Mount Zao, Japan in 1984. "We have since made plans for 34 areas in Japan including 13 new greenfield projects," Mathews adds.

Next followed work preparing master plans for Swiss resorts in Laax, Arosa and Savognin which in turn led to assignments in Austria, Spain and France. "The company's reputation and breadth of projects just grew organically, averaging about ten new projects per year plus of course taking care of a lot of existing customers," says Mathews.

A career coup was getting the contract in 2010 to re-design the ski lift system at Courchevel, one of France's ritziest resorts. The same year Mathews redesigned Canyons Resort in Park City, Utah. He was also responsible for choosing the location and designing the resort of Rosa Khutor as well as mapping out the competitive courses for the 2014 Sochi Winter Olympics. This job proved to be one of the most difficult of his career. It began as a project for the Russian Federation looking at tourism potential in the North Caucasus. "Once we identified Rosa Khutor and the Gazprom Laura projects we designed them for commercial ventures and then later we were asked if these resorts could host Olympic Winter Games," Mathews explains. "We put the snow cluster venue Master Plan together for the Russian Olympic Committee and I personally presented the venues to the International Olympic Committee in February 2007." When Sochi won the right to host the 2014 Olympic Winter Games in July 2007, Ecosign was immediately hired to re-design the Rosa Khutor Ski Area.

After this high profile endeavor, Ecosign was chosen to plan PyeongChang, Korea for the Free-style Skiing and Snowboarding venues for the 2018 Winter Olympics. The company also won an international competition to design the Snow Cluster competition venues for the Beijing bid to host the Olympic Winter Games in 2022.

During Mathews' long career he has noticed three important technological improvements which have assisted ski area planning. "Detachable grip chairlifts, snowmaking systems and winch cats for grooming ski slopes have very substantially changed how we design ski resorts," he explains. "In fact, I was considered the first 'early adopter' in seeing the tremendous potential benefits of detachable grip chairlifts and gondolas. Given rope speeds two to three times faster than conventional fixed grip lifts allows us to go two or three times longer distances for equivalent travel times and due to the carrier spacing allows us to go much higher verticals up to 800 or even 1,000 meters with existing wire rope construction methods. Winch cats allow grooming of steep slopes and snowmaking has improved tenfold from when I started in the business, in efficiency and quality and quantity of snow."

And the future for Ecosign when Mathews retires? There's a transition plan in place whereby several senior VPs will team up with Mathews' son and daughter to continue the lasting legacy.

Sources: Interview with Paul Mathews February 2015; Ebner (2010)

Design and planning

As mentioned already in this book, the ski industry has experienced considerable consolidation in the last few decades, particularly in North America, as larger operators buy up individual ski resorts or send small operators out of business. The industry is also highly vulnerable to climate change, which can have a devastating economic impact on ski resorts, requiring them to diversify their products and services and focus on alleviating the negative consequences of seasonality. If we factor in demographic shifts which are also dramatically affecting the ski industry landscape, then we have an environment of increasing uncertainty – where ski resort planning and development takes on a greater significance.

The key stages in the design of ski resorts are gaining development approval, analyzing site feasibility, deciding on design guidelines, and choosing development styles. Each of these is examined in turn.

Development approval

After the initial concept has been created, general design guidelines are established and the ski and base area capacities are determined. The ski runs will dictate the layout and size of the ski lift network, which will, in turn, influence the layout of the base area. Usually an environmental statement is then drafted, a profitability or pro-forma analysis made, and final design approval sought. This approval can sometimes take many years. The final approval for the Jumbo Glacier Resort in British Columbia, Canada, for example, completed an unprecedented 21-year long approval process that included four major public reviews of the proposal.

Many ski areas in North America are partially or completely located on public lands; over 90 per cent of ski areas in the Rocky Mountains and Pacific West, for example, operate under U.S. Forest Service permits. In addition to a use fee, ski areas are asked to prepare Master Development Plans (MDPs) that identify the existing and desired conditions for the ski area and the proposed improvements on the National Forest System lands within the permit boundary. These plans help the ski areas articulate their long-range vision for the use of public lands, and they help the Forest Service anticipate future use. A similar system is in place within the National Parks of Canada. Ski resorts will often employ specialist consultants to create such master plans, companies like International Alpine Design (IAD), Brent Harley & Associates (BHA), and Ecosign (profiled in this chapter).

Development approval is different in other parts of the world. In France, the Environmental Protection Act of 1976 requires an impact study to be conducted for any project where the costs exceed six million francs (updated to 12 million in 1993). In Germany, the political acceptability of the project is a major factor in determining whether or not it will be approved. Politics was clearly the driver at Sochi, home of the 2014 Winter Olympics. Russian President, Vladimir Putin pushed development of the mountain area near Sochi with two agendas: to prepare for the Olympics and to foster in Russia the kind of world-class ski area available in other parts of Europe (Bachman, 2014). A long-term plan to expand ski facilities kicked off in 2007 when Sochi won the bid for the Games. Organizers built a train that takes visitors from the Sochi Airport to Rosa Khutor, the largest of the region's ski areas, and then accelerated lift construction. In total, 21.6 kilometers (13 miles) of cable-car routes were built for the Games. One gondola took people to a peak near the start of the Olympic cross-country skiing and biathlon events. It is the world's longest and fastest detachable-car ropeway, traveling at up to 8.5 meters per second.

Site feasibility

Naturally a key component of the planning process is site feasibility. As has often been said, the three most important factors necessary to ensure a successful business are 'location, location, location.' This old adage definitely applies to alpine ski resorts, particularly regarding the influence that location, elevation and relief have on reliable snow cover. The location, elevation, skiable area and configuration of a resort's slopes and physical environment are particularly crucial in its success (Martinelli, 1976). In addition to its ability to make snow, a ski resort's success entails the melding of key geographical factors such as continentality, relief, climate and microclimate, elevation of the base and summit, elevation of the seasonal snowline, slope aspect and reliable natural snow cover. These and other geographical factors may significantly influence how a resort's location influences the degree of its vulnerability to the long-term effects of warming temperatures.

The location for Jumbo Glacier Resort, referred to earlier, was chosen for its optimal snow conditions and high elevations. The resort will provide lift-serviced access to four nearby glaciers at an elevation of up to 11,217 feet (3,419 meters). In winter, the ski area will offer 5,627 feet of vertical, and in summer, up to 2,300 feet of natural snow vertical will be available on the glaciers. The resort is planned in three phases and will ultimately include 5,500 bed-units (plus 750 beds for staff accommodations) in a 110-hectare resort base area. At build-out, the resort will see up to 2,000 to 3,000 visitors per day in high season (see Figure 4.1).

Accessibility is also a critical component of site feasibility. For most winter sports enthusiasts, travel time and cost are critical variables when deciding to head to the mountains. In the U.S., for example, 67 per cent of resort areas are within 74 miles – or easy commuting distance – of major metropolitan areas. A high proportion of weekend resort areas require two or more hours of driving time, while vacation destinations are typically in more remote locations where snow conditions are more consistent. Because of the need for snow, appropriate terrain and climate, resort areas tend to be clustered, offering skiers several choices when they reach the mountains. This is the case in Canada, where most of the ski area facilities are clustered around the eastern, most populated provinces, Ontario and Quebec, which are close to the American border. However, the most popular resorts, particularly among overseas visitors, are in Western Canada. About half of all international visitors head for British Columbia or Alberta.

Figure 4.1: Proposed Jumbo Glacier Resort (Courtesy of Oberti Resort Design)

In Europe vacation skiers from the northern countries such as Germany, the Benelux countries, the U.K. and Scandinavia, represent half the skier market for the European Alpine countries. Austria is in the top position for the European winter vacation market with nearly half of European winter sports enthusiasts traveling to Austria (largely from Germany and the U.K.) About 14 per cent travel to France (mainly from the U.K.) and about 11 per cent visit Switzerland and Italy. Accessibility to the latter two countries has improved with a new Eurostar Swiss service, complementing its existing French one, and the opening of a new international airport at Turin in Italy. However, the British skiers are increasingly favoring France as a destination using low-cost airlines and high-speed rail and road links via the Channel Tunnel. Andorra, located between France and Spain, has benefited from easy access from Barcelona. With over 2.3 million skier visits per year, the main problem now is finding road space and lodging to fit everyone in. Large numbers of Russians travel to Andorra each winter, attracted as much by the low prices in the retail shops as for the skiing.

Outside of Europe and North America, access is similarly an important consideration in ski area development. In China, for example, where skiing is growing faster than anywhere else in the world (see Case Study in Chapter 1), numerous studies have been made to determine the best locations within easy reach of the major populated cities. To date, the best option for the Chinese capital, Beijing is Saibei, a rather basic resort created within 170 miles (272kms) of the capital. Alongside Jilin province, Heilongjiang in the North Eastern corner of China appears to be the country's major boom area for resort development, especially around the city of Harbin which has seen heavy investment in a modern airport and road network. The Provincial Government has announced plans to open up 250 new ski centers in that province alone in the next decade. It would join

Austria's Tyrol and Canada's Quebec as one of the few 'regions' in the world to boast in excess of 100 ski centers.

Some resorts have been quite innovative in recent years in order to improve their accessibility for skiers and boarders. In 2013, Aspen Skiing Company successfully lobbied for taxpayer-funded incentives to be offered to Delta to lure the airline back to Aspen airport. The incentive reportedly cost a total of $350,000 and resulted in Delta launching a daily route to and from Atlanta and Saturday-only flights from Minneapolis. The same year, Jay Peak in Northern Vermont applied to join a pilot program that would allow for the supplemental funding of border-cross services. Jay Peak attracts more than half of its customers from Canada, so was keen to cut down on border crossing times and make the trip more appealing to customers.

4

Design guidelines

Certain design guideline principles provide an umbrella for the specifics of site planning and these include avoiding land conflicts, designing access roads based on expected peak traffic, and considering the varied abilities of skiers and snowboarders (Mill, 2012). Ski slopes should offer a range of slopes to attract a variety of skiers. Sibley (1982) suggested some time ago that novice slopes should be under 20 degrees, intermediate slopes 20-45 degrees, and advanced slopes 45 degrees or steeper. Experienced skiers and boarders will also look at the variety of runs available and the total vertical drop. Considerable care must be taken in locating both the base and uphill facilities in order to avoid avalanche paths.

It also helps if there is a certain amount of flat, stable land close by to provide adequate building sites. Ski areas are increasingly using land development as a way of boosting profits. Vail Resorts' recent acquisition of Park City Mountain Resort, for example, was heavily influenced by the real estate opportunities. Vail planned to link Park City to neighboring Canyons Resort where there were already over 90 acres of undeveloped land (see Profile below). At Park City there were another 15 acres of developable land within and around existing parking lots. Another example of property development driving the growth of ski areas comes from the Niseko United ski area of Japan, where in the last decade over 7,000 new beds have been developed and an estimated US$800 million has been invested (see Case Study in Chapter 5).

Resorts also have to consider the needs of snowboarders, by including terrain parks, and also the needs of non-skiers, by considering other activities such as skateboard parks and zip-lines. In fact winter zip-lining is spreading around North American ski resorts, adding yet another activity-based après ski alternative. The Canopy Tour at Crested Butte Mountain Resort, for example, has five lines ranging from 120 - 400 feet long, connected by three wooden suspension bridges and massive platforms designed for winter use with tough grips and snow grates. "It's about a two-hour tour, with two guides, that make it fun and interactive," says Director of Innovations, Erica Mueller. "It is something different for people to do on a day off from skiing or after skiing and really attracts all age groups," she adds, although participation is limited to those weighing between 70 and 250 lbs (see Profile in Chapter 2).

Resorts need to identify capacity of the area when planning, the usual process being to use the amount of skiable area for each skier classification, which in turn is used to determine the necessary ski lift and base area facilities. The capacity of the ski lifts to bring skiers up the mountain must be balanced against the capacity of the ski trails to take them down. The goal is to spread the skiers and snowboarders over the mountain while ensuring that the time spent in line is not too uncomfortable. Experts believe that the ideal lift system covers 1,000 to 2,000 vertical feet over a slope length of 4,000 to 5,000 feet. From an economic point of view, the earning potential of the lift increases as the length increases while cost per foot decreases. However, some resorts prefer to put a cap on the number of skiers on the hill. Deer Valley in Utah, for example, has a cap of 7,500 skiers, even though the ski hill has the capacity to hold many more. The thinking behind this cap is that the visitor experience will be much more pleasant if there are limited lift lines and fewer skiers on the slopes. Of course, there is always a price to pay for such extra comforts – the daily lift ticket price at Deer Valley in the 2014-15 season was $114.

Linking smaller resorts together can help with capacity problems and make an area more attractive to skiers and snowboarders. For example, in Switzerland, Grimentz and Zinal and also Arosa and Lenzerheide have recently linked up; and in Austria, Lech and Warth have joined together with new lifts. Earl Knudsen, partner at Alpine Partners, believes that these kinds of collaborations make smaller resorts more attractive to customers: "The link between Grimentz and Zinal will provide skiers with some of the best off-piste in Switzerland, while the Lech and Warth connection will offer 50 per cent more terrain," he says (Chomé, 2013). On a larger scale in the U.S., some stakeholders in the Utah ski industry are pushing to interconnect up to seven resorts in the future – including Snowbird, Alta, Solitude, Brighton, Canyons, Deer Valley and Park City – believing that such interconnection could be vital to Utah's ability to compete both nationally and internationally.

A good example of a ski resort Master Plan addressing capacity issues is the one produced by Brent Harley & Associates (BHA) for Big White in British Columbia, Canada (see Figure 4.2). The Master Plan describes the proposed transformation of the ski resort into a major all-season world-class destination. The ski area was analyzed in terms of slope, elevation, aspect, and fall-line in order to gain an understanding of the alpine skiing development potential and its capability to support, physically and environmentally, additional four-season recreation activities. The plan suggested that at build-out, the facilities could accommodate a comfortable carrying capacity of 24,240 skiers and snowboarders per day. One of Big White's distinguishing features is the 'ski in-ski out' resort residential offering. Direct linkages to and from the base areas and the resort residential development areas are established by return ski trails, the pedestrian trail network and gondola lift.

Figure 4.2: Master Plan for Big White in British Columbia (Courtesy of Brent Harley & Associates)

Big White's ambition is to create a resort experience similar to that found in Europe, whereby skiers can spend their day exploring – traveling on snow from one end of the resort to the other. Certainly ski resorts have an advantage if they link to other resorts, and the Europeans are champions in this respect. One of the largest collaborations is in France called Paradiski, and combines two resorts, La Plagne and Les Arcs, plus the smaller Peisey-Vallandry. The results is 15 villages, 133 lifts and more than 250 miles of trails. It also has two glaciers for reliable skiing in almost any conditions. Even bigger is the nearby Les Trois Vallées, combining Courchevel, Méribel, Val Thorens and four other stations into one enormous resort with nearly 400 miles of trails linked by 170 lifts. At almost 26,000 skiable acres, Les Trois Vallées claims to be larger than the five biggest U.S. resorts combined. Further north, a ticket to Les Portes du Soleil combines more than a dozen interconnected resorts across France and Switzerland into one giant resort with around 200 lifts and over 400 miles of trails. Combining resorts like this can be a big draw for skiers, and as mentioned earlier, Vail Resorts is hoping to attract more skiers to Utah by linking recently purchased Park City Mountain Resort to its Canyons Resort (see Profile below). The connection will make it the largest resort in America with over 7,300 acres of skiable terrain.

Finally, ski resorts need to be sensitive to environmental limitations, such as the presence of wildlife habitats that are home to endangered species, the existence of special cultural or archaeological sites deemed worthy of preservation, and a scarcity of natural resources such as water for snowmaking. As Smith (2013) has commented, one of the biggest changes in the past twenty years has been the need for ski resorts to embrace environmentally-friendly practices, from recycling waste and implementing public transportation systems, to adopting energy-saving strategies and constructing LEED-certified buildings. Sixty per cent of the world's 250 leading ski resorts are now using at least some renewable energy and a third are using 100 per cent renewable energy (Thorne, 2014).

Development styles

The literature on ski resort development is heavily oriented to studies from the European Alps. Preau (1970), for example, suggested that development had occurred in France in two different ways. In the first, tourists discovered the attractions of the Alpine environment, and local society adapted to this demand by providing accommodations and services. Urban developers from outside the area played only a gradual and complementary role, providing, for example, hotels or capital for a mountain railway. He profiles Chamonix as an example of such development. In the second type of development, such as Les Belleville, the process begins with the image of a functional resort conceived by urban promoters. It is no longer the mountains that are presented to tourists, but the developed facilities such as apartments and lifts. The mountain is reduced to a technical analysis of its characteristics – capacity of the ski runs, construction possibilities, ease of access, etc. The only demands made on the local community are for its land and labor. Figure 4.3 depicts these two different types of development.

Barker (1982) has similarly found clear variances in development style, identifying differences in scale, intensity and form of tourist development between the Western Alps (France and western Switzerland) and the Eastern Alps (eastern Switzerland, northern Italy, Austria and Bavaria). In the west, large integrated ski resorts were built in the sub-Alpine zone long after the local population had retreated to the main valley where agriculture, forestry and manufacturing provided employment. In these resorts, the main thrust for development came from distant urban capital. In contrast, tourism in the eastern Alps coexists with a strong pastoral economy. The impetus for development has come from within robust rural communities with a tradition of local autonomy in planning, and this has favored community-based investment initiatives.

Smith (2013) has explored the evolution of ski resorts in America from a design and architectural perspective. She traces this evolution of resorts from modest beginnings as rustic cabins and unpretentious lodges in the 1930s; to second homes for the newly upwardly-mobile middle class pursuing the good life in the postwar period when skiing exploded in popularity; and, finally, to supersized postmodern vacation homes and corporate-owned, carefully planned mountain villages offering a total vacation experience in the 1980s. Vancouver-based Intrawest would be a good example of a company involved in this latter phase of development. Operating seven North American ski resorts, Intrawest invests heavily in real estate developments and tourism infrastructure, adding retail, lodging and restaurants to attract people to the resort and keep them there. Intrawest has developed a business model consisting of four distinct 'waves'. Wave 1 is the starting point when the company first becomes involved in a resort and Wave 2 is characterized by increasing development and longer staying guests. In Wave 3, the village is well established and there is a dramatic increase in the number of destination visitors. Finally, in Wave 4, the resort is transformed and destination visitors are visiting year-round, maximizing the use of shops, hotels, convention facilities, and restaurants. Intrawest also owns Canadian Mountain Holidays (CMH), the largest heli-skiing operation in the world. CMH is profiled in Chapter 10.

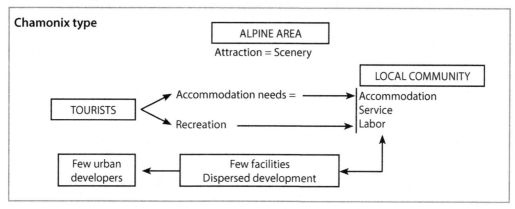

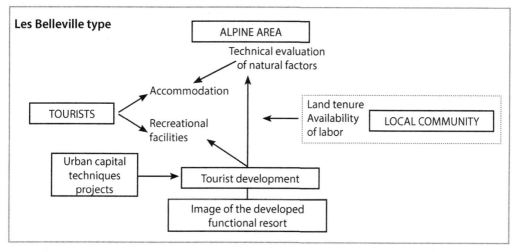

Figure 4.3: Preau's two scenarios of Alpine tourist development (Adapted from Preau, 1970)

An edited book by Clark, Gill and Hartmann (2006) contains several good chapters that examine planning issues and problems of resort development in North America. One section by Dorward (2006) discusses the appeal of the village concept for the design of mountain resorts but argues in favour of regional planning strategies that are more typical of urban regions and that support the growth of healthy resort communities. Another by Hartmann (2006) takes a critical look at the sprawling resort landscapes of the Colorado High Country and the loss of community in the original resort areas. He discusses an expanding new entity – the 'down valley' in current mountain resort areas. Finally, Johnson et al. (2006) look at the important subject of regional transportation and focus on a rapidly changing rural area near Jackson Hole/Yellowstone Park that has seen a considerable influx of amenity migration. The authors conclude that future research should include better cost accounting of rural residential development that results from changes to the local transportation infrastructure as well as ecological and qualitative amenity accounting for rural residents.

Profile: Creating America's biggest ski area

Author Simon Hudson pictured next to a billboard in Park City advertising the new expansion

Vail Resorts always thinks big and its acquisition of Park City and Canyons Resort in Utah is no exception. Less than two years into its first foray into Utah, the huge ski resort development and management company announced its $50 million plan to merge the two areas into America's largest ski resort.

Vail Resorts intended to complete the ambitious renovation over the summer and fall 2015, to be launched for the 2015/2016 ski season. By connecting Park City Mountain Resort to neighboring Canyons Resort, they would link more than 7,300 acres of skiable terrain, creating the USA's biggest ski resort. A brand new interconnect gondola (the first for Park City since 1983) was planned to facilitate the merger as well as upgrades to other lifts, runs, snowmaking facilities, and maintenance areas. A new eatery to be constructed near the gondola, as well as expansions to other mountain restaurants and lodges, would create enough lunchtime seating for the anticipated rush of voracious visitors. The two resorts were already linked by road via free public transit.

"This comprehensive capital plan for Park City and Canyons is one of the most ambitious and impactful plans undertaken at any resort in industry history, transforming the experience at both resorts and creating the largest single ski resort in the U.S.," said Blaise Carrig, president of the Mountain division for Vail Resorts. He added: "The improvements offer skiers and riders more terrain and upgraded lifts to enhance the guest experience and reduce crowding and lift lines, new and upgraded restaurants, more snowmaking and an overall 'touching up' of all aspects of the resorts. The plan was based on feedback from guests and the local community as well as discussions with the senior operating teams at the two resorts. We look forward to continuing to work with the county and the city and are hopeful we can bring this plan to life for the 2015-2016 ski season."

For the 2015-2016 season, the company intended to operate the two resorts as one unified branded experience under the name 'Park City Mountain Resort'. The Canyons base area, home to the only Waldorf Astoria on a ski slope, was to be renamed 'Canyons at Park City'. The company planned to maintain the unique history and atmosphere of the two different base areas with differentiated marketing for the diverse hotel and hospitality experiences offered.

The ambitious development was scheduled for completion for the beginning of the 2015/16 ski season. "Just one of the improvements would be big news but we're doing all of them in a few months," said Park City Mountain Resort's Communications Manager, Andy Miller. "If Vail says it can be done, it will be done." With regular press releases, media familiarisation trips and billboards strategically placed all over the slopes, the project attracted massive media, local and visitor attention during the 2015/16 season.

The 'Vailification' of Park City and Canyons meant cheaper skiing for locals via the Epic Local Pass which went on sale from March 10 2015 at $579 per adult for the whole season with multiple benefits at sister resorts. The Epic Local Pass offered unlimited days of skiing (with 11 holiday restrictions) in Park City and also included unlimited access to Breckenridge, Keystone and Arapahoe Basin in Colorado, with limited restrictions at Heavenly, Northstar and Kirkwood at Lake Tahoe. A total of 10 days at Vail and Beaver Creek were also included (with holiday restrictions). "There truly is no better ski or snowboard value being offered in the state of Utah," said Bill Rock, Park City's Chief Operating Officer, who previously oversaw a $30 million refurbishment at Kirkwood. "When you consider the acreage and the variety of terrain, and then add in $50 million dollars of improvements that will completely transform the ski experience and the additional access to Colorado and Tahoe, there is no pass in this market that compares with the Epic Local Pass." To put this price into perspective, compare the Deer Valley, Utah adult season pass at the earlybird discount price of $1,985 for the 2014/15 season.

Bent on attracting newcomers to winter sports, Vail Resorts also introduced new cut-price kids' passes for local residents including the Park City Youth Pass which features unlimited, unrestricted access to Park City for $289 for children (ages 5-12), $309 for teens (ages 13-18) and $399 for college students. Another innovation for the Utah resorts was the Vail Resorts Season Pass Auto Renewal Program whereby the next year's pass is guaranteed at the lowest price for a $49 automatic credit card down payment each spring.

Caitlin Martz, Senior Communications Specialist for Canyons Resort, said that the community response to the merger, infrastructure upgrades and investment in the local economy was very positive. "It is a great thing for the town," she added. "How can you argue about some-body coming in and investing $50 million? It is also very obvious that Vail Resorts cares about the area."

Sources: Interviews with Caitlin Martz, Senior Communications Specialist for Canyons Resort, and Andy Miller, Communications Manager for Park City Mountain Resort February 2015; Vail Resorts Press Release February 2015

Dealing with seasonality

The issue of seasonality in winter sport destinations is a critical one, as in many parts of the world the ski industry has stagnated, leaving some resorts facing severe financial difficulties. One could argue that the industry is witnessing the onset of a mature phase of development, as envisaged by Butler (1980) in the tourist area lifecycle. If resorts are not to face inevitable decline, adaptation is essential. Coping with seasonality is an important part of that adaptation. Figure 4.4 suggests that tourism seasonality at winter sport tourism destinations can be attributed to many factors, caused by both generating and receiving areas. The cause common to both, and probably the key reason for seasonality, is a natural factor – climate. Climate and weather conditions have led to the appearance of distinct seasonal variations in sport tourism visitation in a significant number of mountain destination areas across the globe. Sporting activities specifically relating to snow, such as skiing, snowboarding and snowmobiling, have clear seasonal patterns due to the weather. In fact, a major challenge to future develop-ment of such sports is global warming. Most scientists tend to agree that winters will be shorter and warmer, meaning the economic viability of many winter sport destinations will be in doubt (see Chapter 10 for further discussion on this issue).

The remaining causes of seasonality tend to be classified as *institutional* fac-tors (BarOn, 1975), and from the generating area include customs and holidays, (Frechtling, 1996), social pressures or fashion, and inertia (Butler, 1994). The scheduling of school and statutory holidays are common forms of institutional-ized seasonality, and have a significant impact on the winter tourism season. In Europe, for example, holidays are taken primarily in the summer months, so that the skiing trip is seen as a 'second' and even 'luxury' holiday. Social pressure or fashion can also cause institutionalized seasonality. In the past, in many societies the privileged elite frequently divided their year into specific 'seasons' during each of which it was considered socially necessary to participate in selected activities and visit certain locations. For example, late in the nineteenth century, the British upper classes made skiing into a fashionable winter pursuit, with the first winter mountain holidays starting in St Moritz, Switzerland (Hudson, 2000). Inertia or tradition can also cause seasonality. Many people take holidays at peak seasons because they have always done so, and such habits are hard to break.

Consequences

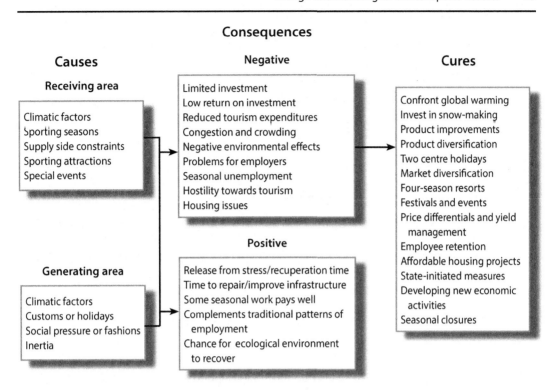

Causes

Negative

Cures

Receiving area

Climatic factors
Sporting seasons
Supply side constraints
Sporting attractions
Special events

Limited investment
Low return on investment
Reduced tourism expenditures
Congestion and crowding
Negative environmental effects
Problems for employers
Seasonal unemployment
Hostility towards tourism
Housing issues

Confront global warming
Invest in snow-making
Product improvements
Product diversification
Two centre holidays
Market diversification
Four-season resorts
Festivals and events
Price differentials and yield
    management
Employee retention
Affordable housing projects
State-initiated measures
Developing new economic
    activities
Seasonal closures

Positive

Generating area

Climatic factors
Customs or holidays
Social pressure or fashions
Inertia

Release from stress/recuperation time
Time to repair/improve infrastructure
Some seasonal work pays well
Complements traditional patterns of
    employment
Chance for ecological environment
    to recover

4

Figure 4.4: Seasonality at winter sports destinations: causes, consequences and cures (Source: Adapted from Hudson & Cross, 2005)

Institutional factors at work in the receiving area include sporting seasons (Butler, 1994), supply side constraints (Baum & Hagen, 1999), and special events and sporting attractions (Butler, 2001). Sporting activities related to snow are clearly confined to distinct seasons in mountain regions. The supply side is also a potential cause of seasonality: for example, where constraints in labor availability, the restriction of services, or the alternative uses of facilities lead to closures or altered target markets. In Europe, for instance, many tour operators from the U.K. do not package skiing holidays in April even though snow conditions are often very good. This is because the airplanes that they have been chartering all winter are also used for the summer season which starts at the beginning of April. The types of sporting attractions are also likely to impact seasonality for winter sport destinations. The most specialized destinations are the most seasonal (World Tourism Organization, 1999). Finally, special events can lead to seasonality in winter sports destinations. Such events may have long traditions, like the Inferno Cup first held in 1928 in Mürren, Switzerland, or they may be more contemporary, such as the World Ski and Snowboard Festival in Whistler.

Figure 4.4 lists the negative consequences of seasonality applicable to winter sport destinations, but it also reflects the notion that there may well be economic or social benefits that flow from seasonality, and these are listed as positive consequences. BarOn (1975, p. 45) coined the term 'seasonal loss' to refer to costs which may be attributed to the negative effects of seasonality. The viewpoint that seasonality is a problem is primarily taken from an economic position, and reflects concerns with the difficulty of ensuring efficient utilization of resources. The seasonal nature of the tourism industry is often blamed for limited investment and low returns on investment, and a key reason that winter sports destinations attract limited investment is that they are perceived as operating a strictly seasonal business. Linked to these impacts is reduced tourism expenditures off-season. Congestion and crowding are also closely associated with issues of seasonality. The threshold or saturation level of visitor use of a destination usually is reached only during the peak periods of use and not during the low season or on an annual average basis. Therefore peak tourist demand must be considered in calculating carrying capacities. There has also been much discussion about the environmental effects of seasonality, focusing on the intensity of pressure on often fragile environments because of crowding and overuse during the peak season. It is often suggested that the seasonal nature of tourism presents problems for employers, making it difficult to recruit full-time staff and to retain them (Mathieson & Wall, 1982). A consequence of not being able to attract qualified staff is the variable quality of product and service delivery. In addition, Mill and Morrison (1985) have argued that seasonal work is less meaningful, and that this will have a negative impact on productivity. Seasonal unemployment is also often cited as a negative consequence of seasonality, and it is frequently implied that unemployment in the off-season is an involuntary state in which seasonal workers are regarded as victims.

Jafari (1974) has linked seasonal fluctuations to the hostility towards tourism that is sometimes generated within local communities. More specifically, several studies have noted the association between tourism and crime. The late Jost Krippendorf (1994) blamed mass tourism in the Swiss Alps for the resident hostility towards tourists, particularly among the younger generation. Krippendorf also linked the seasonality of tourism with negative impacts on the housing market in mountain resorts. He referred to the 'unpaid social costs' for the host population associated with tourism development in the mountains (p. 49).

Murphy (1985) suggests that seasonality is not necessarily bad for everyone, and for some communities, the end of the tourist season is looked forward to. This is because individuals need release from stress and some populations would not be capable of, or at least content to, experience the strain of catering for tourists throughout the year. The off-season may represent the only time that the local population can operate in what to it is a 'normal' manner and engage in traditional social and cultural activities (Butler, 2001). Krippendorf (1994) points to evidence in the Swiss mountains that shows residents are glad when the season is over. "They need the intervening time between each invasion of holidaymakers to recuperate from the last lot" (p. 46). Finally, destinations might welcome a period of rest so that infrastructure can be repaired or improved (Twining-Ward and Twining-Ward, 1996). Ski lifts, for example, are usually repaired, replaced or upgraded in the summer months.

Others have argued that many employees choose seasonal tourism employment because it pays better than alternative work that is available, and also because it allows those who wish to pursue other activities during the off-season to do so (Mourdoukoutas, 1988). Flognfeldt (1988) found evidence that employment in the tourism industry, particularly in remote and small communities, may complement traditional patterns of employment rather than compete with them. Ball (1989) has raised the possibility of the development of long-term 'symbiotic' relations between areas that have contrasting periodic demands for labor. This certainly exists in France, where the demand for seasonal labor is high during the winter for winter sport destinations, and correspondingly high during the summer months in the coastal resorts. Finally, Hartmann (1986) has argued that a dormant period for the environment is the only chance for an ecological environment to fully recover. While areas may experience heavy use in peak seasons, a lengthy rest period may allow almost complete recovery, or at least a new level of stability, to be achieved.

The complexity of factors that give rise to seasonal impacts are not easily addressed by tourism destinations, and many attempts to reduce seasonality fail (Butler, 2001). But some winter sport tourism destinations around the world have attempted to cure, or alleviate the problems associated with seasonality. The first strategy is to confront global warming. The main cause of seasonality – climate – is a major challenge. In the past few years ski area operations have begun to acknowledge their vulnerability and the need to confront global warming. The National Ski Areas Association's (NSAA) "Keep Winter Cool" program coalesced several ski areas in 2003 into explaining their efforts to reduce greenhouse gases as well as other environmental accomplishments. NSAA's campaign seeks to strike a balance between raising awareness of global warming and raising alarms about the possibly detrimental effects on snow conditions.

A second strategy has been investing heavily in snowmaking. The invention of snowmaking in the 1950s actually gave an impetus to the growth of ski facilities, a technological development that not only lengthened the ski season in the snowbelt states, but made the sport possible in areas where natural snowfall was less than abundant. These days, operators are investing heavily in snowmaking equipment just to survive, but it is an expensive investment for many resorts (Bender, 2000). Buying the machinery and accessing the water, a process than can require protracted negotiations with state authorities and installing dozens of wells and miles of pipes, can cost tens of millions of dollars (see the Case Study about recycled snow in Chapter 10). In addition, low altitude resorts do not always receive low enough temperatures in order to make snow.

Product improvements can also help alleviate the problems caused by seasonality. The ski runs and related lift systems clearly represent a prime attraction of resorts and therefore have long been the object of continuous improvements. For example, the process of linking ski areas has now become commonplace in France, following the initial lead given by resorts such as Tignes and Val d'Isere, which combined to form 'Espace Killy', and Courchevel, Méribel, Les Menuires and Val Thorens, which created the 'Trois Vallées'. With these changes, skiing areas have been expanded to higher altitudes, giving better snow conditions, increasing resorts' capacities and extending their season. As mentioned in Chapter 2, another commonly advocated strategy for the achievement of a more balanced flow of trade is product diversification (BarOn, 1975; Manning & Powers, 1984). Many ski resorts have started to attract summer tourists by developing a wide range of sports and activities. A sub-variety of this approach to counter seasonality, developed by several tour companies, has been the 'two-center' holiday. This attracts the customer to a well-established resort with an accepted reputation, which may be suffering from excessive demand, but links a part of the holiday spent there to a less well-used resort, or one with different types of attractions. In the Spanish Pyrenees, for example, Sierra Nevada – the most southerly ski resort in Europe – appeals to tourists in search of both skiing and the beaches of the Costa del Sol.

Market diversification is a further strategy used by resorts to counteract seasonality. Understanding market segmentation and differing demand motives permits recognition of those segments that are less tied to traditional vacation structures and are, therefore, more likely to travel during the shoulder and off season. Such groups, widely recognized in the tourism industry, include senior travelers, conference delegates, incentive travelers, 'empty nesters', affinity groups and special interest groups (CEC, 1993). In the ski areas of Canada, resorts have achieved reasonable success targeting ski clubs to build visitor volumes during the 'off-peak' periods of the winter season (Williams & Dossa, 1998), and other resorts like Whistler have been successful attracting conference business in the shoulder season. Some resorts with glaciers attract skiers in the summer, although the popularity of glacier summer skiing has been falling – especially in Europe (Falk, 2015).

It has been suggested that to defeat seasonality, the destinations should focus on yield, rather than volume (Getz & Nilsson, 2003). In the Banff region of Canada, for example, the ski areas have been aggressively targeting European skiers over the last few decades. They are known as 'destination skiers' - the longer stay tourists. Although they represent only 50 per cent of the market, non-resident skiers account for 77 per cent of tourism expenditures. Other resorts are taking a more targeted approach to development (Forstenzer, 2003). Tamarack Resort in Idaho, for example, is limiting the number of skiers and boarders to 3,500 a day, despite capacity to accommodate 7,000. The idea is to create a 'boutique' resort, with a private club, with a focus on yield rather than volume. As mentioned above, Deer Valley, Utah also limits the number of skiers on the slopes focusing on yield as opposed to volume.

One strategy for coping with seasonality in winter sports destinations, is the development of four-season resorts - in which skiing is not the only activity – where sporting and entertainment facilities are open throughout the year, rather than just in the winter months. It is not just in North America that mountain areas are seeking to develop year-round resorts. In Australia, mountain resorts have traditionally been promoted as winter destinations, but a state government directive to resort management boards at Victoria's mountains initiated an investigation into the promotion of year-round tourism (Russell & Thomas, 2004). Alpine resorts in Europe have also been investing heavily in developing all-year attractions. The provision of purpose-built conference facilities in resorts like Val d'Isere and Alpe d'Huez is attracting a very different clientele from normal and not necessarily during the peak season. The Case Study below documents how one Swiss town, Andermatt, has begun its metamorphosis into a four-season resort.

Festivals and events are often introduced to cope with seasonality and boost tourism receipts during typically quiet times of the year. Nearly two decades ago, Whistler in British Columbia held its first World Ski and Snowboard Festival (WSSF) in April in order to increase occupancy rates in its quietest week at the end of the winter season. Now the event is North America's largest snow sport and music event, and attracts thousands of young enthusiasts from all over the world. An Economic Impact Assessment conducted during the 2006 event found that the WSSF generated $37.7 million in economic activity for the province of British Columbia, with visitor spending and operational expenditure injecting more than $15.7 million into the Whistler economy. Over 28,000 hotel room nights were sold during the Festival, with 86 per cent being directly driven by WSSF.

The use of price differentials as stimuli to the market in periods outside the main season might be considered an obvious corrective to disproportionate seasonal concentration, but pricing has not been excessively examined in relation to seasonality (Allcock, 1989). Pricing may work in two directions in relation to seasonal congestion. Price reductions can attract visitors during the low season, and higher prices can discourage trade during the peak season. Yield management is the practice of developing strategies to maximize opportunities for the sale of an organization's perishable products such as airline seats, hotel rooms, and tour seats, and therefore improving its long-term viability. It was initiated by the airline industry in the 1980s as a way to increase revenue from existing routes and aircraft, and the practice of yield management is now common in other sectors of tourism, from hotels to ski resorts. Perdue (2002) found that the use of yield management for setting season pass prices in Colorado ski resorts significantly influenced skier loyalty to the respective resorts.

Retaining employees can help with some of the problems for employers caused by seasonality, and can reduce seasonal unemployment. A study of ski industry employees in Colorado and New Mexico, by Ismert and Petrick (2003), found that satisfaction with money and job challenge were best at predicting intention to return, while satisfaction with management attitude, level of camaraderie and job challenge were the best predictors of seasonal employee's overall job satisfaction. Providing reasonable housing options, be it rental units or home ownership, for those who live and work in mountain resorts, has been the most challenging issue facing many communities over the last few decades. Affordable housing projects have emerged as a solution to the problems of employees unable to rent or purchase property in winter sports destinations. In North America (more than Europe) there are many mountain communities that have made efforts to address resident housing, including the Banff Housing Corporation, Aspen/Pitkin County Housing Authority, Town of Vail Housing Division, and Mountainlands Community Trust in Utah.

Considerable effort has been applied, especially in European countries, to influence the pattern of seasonal concentration through various state-initiated measures directed at its institutional roots. For example, attention was applied systematically in the francophone countries during the 1980s to the possibility of staggering the main school and industrial holidays over a longer period. In fact, winter rather than summer holidays are staggered in France, as the popularity of skiing holidays has caused substantial peaking problems. A new law just passed in Japan may result in increased participation in winter sports. In 2014 parliament passed a law mandating a new national day off – Mountain Day! The government is actually trying to get its white-collar workers to leave the office more often, as long hours and infrequent vacations remain the norm for Japanese workers.

More recently there have been certain resort level strategies to offset seasonality that focus on developing new economic activities to encourage people to relocate. These people will move into mountain communities, often for lifestyle reasons, but they will generate income (often using new technologies) from sources that have nothing to do with tourism. Chapter 1 referred to Stowe in Vermont, that has positioned itself as one of the most tech-friendly towns in the U.S. Stowe is now not only a popular ski resort, but is also home to a robust array of businesses that have created growth and advanced the digital economy in the state.

Finally, seasonal closures might sometimes be the most appropriate strategy to deal with seasonality. Flognfeldt (2001) suggested that some destinations must learn how to live with strong seasonality, and his idea is to fit different types of tourism production into the seasonal patterns of other production activities, including an adjustment of some public services. He noted a number of business strategies in place in Norway, such as mixing employment (tourism and agriculture), using student and migrant workers, or just taking long holidays.

Andermatt, Switzerland

SkiArena Andermatt-Sedrun

Village Center Andermatt

The Chedi Andermatt

Train Station

Golf Clubhouse

Golf Course

Gotthard Residences
Radisson Blu Hotel

Chalets

House Biber   House Hirsch
House Gemse   House Steinadler

Andermatt. Courtesy Andermatt Swiss Alps

Competing with glitzy St Moritz and Zermatt, Egyptian-born billionaire developer, Samih Sawiris hatched a daring plan to transform humble Andermatt into a year-round resort. After a helicopter tour of the central Swiss mountainous area in 2005, he mapped out ski hill improvements as well as a blueprint for 25 topnotch chalets, six hotels, an indoor pool, an 18-hole golf course, and a chain of 490 condominiums across 42 buildings.

With a dwindling population of around 1400, the former army town had been struggling economically, with many younger residents migrating elsewhere for job opportunities. Swiss Tourism figures recorded around 60,600 overnight hotel stays for 2012 whereas rival resort, St Moritz clocked up 692,000 and Zermatt almost 1.3 million.

Sawiris's global real-estate company, Orascom Development Holding AG kick started the $2 billion gentrification project by purchasing around 345 acres of developable land, on which his Swiss company, Andermatt Swiss Alps AG, is now realizing the project. Already popular with off-piste skiers, the pretty village was surrounded by a varied and challenging ski area on the 2,961-meter Gemsstock Mountain. While these predominantly Dutch, Scandinavian and local expert skiers were content to hike to fresh snow, much of the new ski infrastructure development would focus on improving the inbounds ski area, opening up the appeal to every level of skier and snowboarder. "The SkiArena Andermatt-Sedrun project will see six new lifts linking Andermatt with the high plateau at Oberalp and the Sedrun ski area by the

2017/18 season, creating the largest ski area in central Switzerland," said Will Hide in an article for *The Guardian Travel* in November 2014.

Ecosign was responsible for the ski hill structure plan with stakeholders, Andermatt Gotthard Sportbahnen, the Sedrun Bergbahnen, the Matterhorn-Gotthard-Bahn and Andermatt Swiss Alps all working closely together. Plans included construction of a gondola from Andermatt to Nätschen and Guetsch; a six-seater chairlift from Oberalp to Calmut; an improved connection between Nätschen and the Matterhorn Gotthard Bahn; a six-seater chairlift on the Gurschen; the covering of the valley descent from Gurschen to Andermatt with artificial snow; plus the continuous connection of the Ursern Valley with Sedrun through mountain infrastructure. In addition, there would be extensive snowmaking installations as well as new resort restaurants. Ground breaking for this - the largest Swiss ski resort development at the time - was scheduled for summer 2015 with the first two chairlifts (Oberalp Calmut and Gurschen) opening for the 2015/16 ski season.

In any resort development, community collaboration is key and this is where Sawiris excelled. At a town gathering, he got locals on board by presenting (in fluent German) his plans to bring hundreds of jobs to the area, with sketches and also pamphlets about his successful regeneration of a Red Sea desert resort at El Gouna. He worked with local farmers and town-dwellers in decision-making forums, listening to and adopting some of their ideas for traffic re-routing, building heights, land use and financial compensation. The village voted overwhelmingly for the project in March 2007 (96 per cent of Andermatt residents and 88 per cent from neighboring Hospental). The company also produced a comprehensive FAQ document, prepared especially for the community and potential investors. It answered questions ranging from why Sawiris identified the area in the first place, to environmental concerns, affordable housing, critical mass worries, new ski infrastructure plans right down to the minutiae of second home furnishings.

Breaking ground on Sept 26 2009, the blueprints called for a modern design to blend with Andermatt's traditional cobblestone alleys and rustic wooden chalets. Financing for the development came from pre-sales, Orascom and a $160 million personal investment by Sawiris, said Marta Falconi in a 2013 article for the *Wall Street Journal*. Falconi said it was a "risky venture". Competition was coming from other developments around Switzerland including nearby Lake Lucerne. "The developer struggled 1 ½ years ago to keep up the project's timetable and cash flows, prompting some investors to swoop in," said Falconi. "One of them, Hans-Peter Bauer, a co-founder of the Swiss Finance & Property AG real-estate firm, bought 72 units for about $135 million." Bauer, who now sits on the board of Andermatt Swiss Alps, has been responsible for pitching the resort to overseas investors in Singapore, Hong Kong and Russia. Unlike most Swiss resorts - which are subject to the Lex Koller law which drastically limits foreign investment – the Sawiris project in Andermatt is exempt and is targeting markets in Switzerland, Germany, England, Italy and overseas. The FAQ document explains that although the global economic recession coincided with the timing of the project, Sawiris was confident that the project would be implemented as planned, although over a longer time scale than originally anticipated.

Alongside ski lift redevelopment, Andermatt Swiss Alps focused on real estate development and – together with local authorities – planned improvements in water systems, roads and a train station facelift. No extra retail or restaurant facilities were planned at the initial stages, although future phases would allow this. Most of the resort was designed to be car-free, facilitated by new underground parking structures.

One of the major town center improvements was the five-star, deluxe flagship, The Chedi Andermatt Hotel, launched in time for the 2013-2014 ski season. Offering private ownership as well as overnight stays in 48 rooms, the high-end hotel combines "traditional region values so uniquely with the vision of a luxury, state-of-the-art holiday destination". The design motif chosen was 'Alpine Traditional' with added luxury details such as soapstone fireplaces, oak parquet flooring, and built-in wine closets. As well as 107 apartments for sale, The Chedi development included 12 penthouses and two suites. Around 10 per cent of units were pre-sold with only 30 per cent left on the market by April 2015. "In time for winter season 2014/15 the condominiums of the first two apartment houses of the new resort were handed over to their owners and put on the rental market," said Markus Berger, Head of Communications for Andermatt Swiss Alps. "Whenever the owners are not using the condos for themselves, they will be let to vacationers."

By the following ski season, a total of almost 70 apartments would be available to skiers in the new Andermatt resort. Three or four further condo buildings as well as a second hotel were scheduled for completion by 2017, said Berger. "In summer 2016 the brand new championship standard golf course – 18 holes, par 72 – will see its official opening after having been played in two pre-opening seasons by hundreds of enthusiastic golfers," he added.

By transforming Andermatt into a highly competitive, all-season destination, Sawiris planned to create a stable, growing local community. "This project brought new life to this place," confirmed Andermatt Mayor, Roger Nager in an article for the *Wall Street Journal* in 2013.

Sources: Communications with Markus Berger, Head Communication for Andermatt Swiss Alps AG; Falconi (2013); Hide (2014).

References

Allcock, J.B. (1989) 'Seasonality,' in S.F. Witt and L. Moutinho, *Tourism Marketing and Management Handbook*, Englewood-Cliffs, NJ: Prentice-Hall, pp. 387-392.

Bachman, R. (2014) 'The dangling future of Sochi's ski gondolas', *The Wall Street Journal*, 24 February, B10.

Ball, R.M. (1989) 'Some aspects of tourism, seasonality and local labour markets,' *Area*, **21**(1), 35-45.

Barker, M.L. (1982) 'Traditional landscape and mass tourism in the Alps,' *Geographical Review*, **72**(4), 395-415.

BarOn, R.R.V. (1975) *Seasonality in Tourism: A Guide to the Analysis of Seasonality and Trends for Policy Making*, London, England: Economist Intelligence Unit, Technical Series No. 2, London.

Baum, T. and Hagen, L. (1999) 'Responses to seasonality: The experiences of peripheral destinations', *The International Journal of Tourism Research*, **1**(5), 299-312.

Bender, C. (2000) 'Snowmaking Survey', *Ski Area Management*, **39**(6), 52.

Butler, R.W. (1980) 'The concept of a tourist area life cycle of evolution: Implications for management of resources', *Canadian Geographer*, **XXIV**(1), 5.

Butler, R.W. (1994) 'Seasonality in tourism: issues and problems', in A.V. Seaton, C.L. Jenkins, R.C. Wood, P.U.C. Dieke, M.M. Bennett, R. MacLellau, and R. Smith (Eds.), *Tourism: The State of the Art*. Chichester: Wiley, pp. 332-339.

Butler, R.W. (2001) 'Seasonality in tourism: Issues and implications', in T. Baum and S. Lundtorp (Eds.), *Seasonality in Tourism*, New York: Pergamon, pp. 5-22.

CEC (1993) *All-season Tourism: Analysis of Experience, Suitable Products and Clientele*, Brussels: Commission of the European Communities and Fitzpatrick Associates.

Chomé, L. (2013) 'Ski holiday trends,' *TourismLink*, accessed 12/3/2014 from http://www.tourismlink.eu/2013/12/ski-holiday-trends-20132014/

Clark, T., Gill. A. and Hartmann, R. (Eds.) (2006) '*Mountain Resort Planning and Development in an Era of Globalization*', New York: Cognizant Communication Corporation

Dorward, S. (2006) 'The evolution of village form and its relevance as a model for resort design and development,' in T. Clark, A. Gill and R. Hartmann (Eds.) '*Mountain Resort Planning and Development in an Era of Globalization*', New York: Cognizant Communication Corporation, pp. 253-277.

Ebner, D. (2010) 'Canada's ski resort designer to the world', *The Globe and Mail*, 13 October.

Falconi, M. (2013) 'Swiss Valley Aims for Peak of Luxury', *Wall Street Journal*, 23 August, M1 and M6.

Falk, M. (2015) 'The stagnation of summer glacier skiing', paper presented at the Tourism Intelligence Forum, Naples, 4-7 May.

Flognfeldt, T. (1988) 'The employment paradox of seasonal tourism,' chapter presented at Pre-Congress meeting of International Geographical Union, Christchurch, New Zealand, 13-20 August.

Flognfeldt, T. (2001) 'Long-term positive adjustments to seasonality: consequences of summer tourism in the Jotunheimen area, Norway', in T. Baum and S. Lundtorp (Eds.), *Seasonality in Tourism,* New York: Permagon, pp. 109-117.

Forstenzer, M. (2003) 'Solving the resort puzzle', *Ski*, **68**(4), 45-48.

Frechtling, D.C. (1996) *Practical Tourism Forecasting,* Oxford: Butterworth-Heinemann.

Getz, D. and Nilsson, P.A. (2003) 'Responses of family businesses to extreme seasonality in demand: the case of Bornholm, Denmark', *Tourism Management*, **25**(1), 17-30.

Hartmann, R. (1986) 'Tourism, seasonality and social change,' *Leisure Studies,* **5**(1), 25-33.

Hartmann, R. (2006) 'Downstream and down-valley: Essential components and directions of growth and change in the sprawling resort landscapes of the Ricky Mountain West,' in T. Clark, A. Gill and R. Hartmann (Eds.) *'Mountain Resort Planning and Development in an Era of Globalization'*, New York: Cognizant Communication Corporation, pp. 278-293.

Hide, W. (2014) 'Skiing in Andermatt: Changes afoot to a resort with awesome off-piste', *The Guardian Travel*, 8 November, accessed 3/25/2015 from http://www.theguardian.com/travel/2014/nov/08/andermatt-skiing-switzerland alpe oedrun

Hudson, S. (2000) *Snow Business: A Study of the International Ski Industry*, London: The Continuum International Publishing Group.

Hudson, S. and Cross, P. (2005) 'Winter sports destinations: Dealing with seasonality, in Higham, J., and Hinch, T. (Eds.) *Sport Tourism Destinations: Issues, Opportunities and Analysis*. Oxford: Butterworth Heinemann, pp. 188-204.

Ismert, M. and Petrick, J.F. (2003) *Indicators and Standards of Quality Related to Seasonal Employment in the Ski Industry*. Proceedings of the 34th Annual Conference of the Travel and Tourism Research Association, St. Louis, MO.

Jafari, J. (1974) 'The socio-economic costs of tourism to developing countrie', *Annals of Tourism Research*, **1**, 227-59.

Johnson, J., Maxwell, B., Brelsford, M. and Dougher, F. (2006) 'Transportation and rural sprawl in amenity communities,' in T. Clark, A. Gill and R. Hartmann (Eds.) *'Mountain Resort Planning and Development in an Era of Globalization'*, New York: Cognizant Communication Corporation, pp. 294-320.

Krippendorf, J. (1987) *The Holidaymakers*, London: Heinemann.

Manning, R.E. and Powers, L.A. (1984) 'Peak and off-peak use: redistributing the outdoor recreation/tourism load', *Journal of Travel Research*, **23**(2), 25-31.

Martinelli, M. (1976) 'Meteorology and ski area development and operation,' in Proceedings of the Fourth National Conference on Fire and Forest Meteorology, USDA, RM-52.

Mathieson, A. and Wall, G. (1982) *Tourism: Economic, Physical and Social Impacts,* Harlow: Longman.

Mill, R.C. (2012) *'Resorts: Management and Operation,* (3rd edition),' Hoboken, NJ: John Wiley & Sons Inc.

Mill, R.C. and Morrison, A.M. (1985) *The Tourism System: An Introductory Text,* Upper Saddle River, New Jersey: Prentice-Hall.

Mourdoukoutas, P. (1988) 'Seasonal employment, seasonal unemployment and unemployment compensation: The case fro the tourist industry of the Greek Islands,' *American Journal of Economics and Sociology*, **47**(3), 314-329.

Murphy, P.E. (1985) *Tourism: A Community Approach*, New York: Methuen.

Preau, P. (1970) 'Principe d'analyse des sites en montagne,' *Urbanisme*, **116**, 21-25.

National Resources Defense Council (2012) *'Climate impacts on the winter tourism economy in the United States'*, Elizabeth Burrows and Matthew Magnusson: New York: Natural Resources Defense Council.

Perdue, R.R. (2002) 'Perishability, yield management, and cross-product elasticity: A case study of deep discount season passes in the Colorado ski industry', *Journal of Travel Research*, **41**, 15-22.

Perla, R. and Glenne, B. (1981) 'Skiing', in D.M. Gray and D.H. Male, (Eds.). *Handbook of Snow: Principles, Processes, Management and Use*, Toronto: Pergamon.

Preau, P. (1970) 'Principe d'analyse des sites en montagne,' *Urbanisme*, **116**, 21-25.

Russell, R. and Thomas, P. (2004) 'Destination image: Victorian mountain parks and resorts in the summer', in M. Hall & S. Boyd, *Nature-based Tourism in Peripheral Areas: Development or Disaster.*

Sibley, R.G. (1982) 'Ski resort planning and development', Foundation for the technical Advancement of Local Government Engineering in Victoria, Melbourne.

Smith, M.S. (2013) *American Ski Resort. Architecture, Style, Experience*, Norman, OK: Oklahoma University Press.

Thorne, P. (2014) 'What are ski resorts doing to combat climate change?' accessed 11/12/2014 from http://www.snowcarbon.co.uk/ski-resorts/what-are-ski-resorts-doing-combat-climate-change

Twining-Ward, L. and Twining-Ward, T. (1996) *Tourism Destination Development: The Case of Bornholm and Gotland*, Research Centre of Bornholm, Denmark. Report 7/1996.

Williams, P.W. and Dossa, K.B. (1998) 'Ski channel users: A discrimination perspective', *Journal of Travel and Tourism Marketing*, **7**(2), 1-29.

World Tourism Organization, (1999) *World Tourism Statistics.* Madrid: WTO.

5 Management and Operations

Al Raine and Nancy Greene

Al Raine, a former ski racer, coach and resort hotel entrepreneur, has been Mayor of Sun Peaks Resort, near Kamloops, British Columbia since 2010. And yet back in his gung-ho ski racing youth his parents were anxious that he might never find a 'real job'.

His introduction to skiing was in his preteen years at Mt Seymour in North Vancouver and he went on to ski at Mt Baker where his childhood mentors were Al Menzies and Franz Gabl. During the 1960s, Al lived and ski raced in Badgastein, Austria where he learned German. A trilingual coach, Al rose rapidly through the ranks from club level, to division and, ultimately, to the national team. He was Head Coach and Program Director for the Canadian ski team from 1968-73.

In 1974 he turned to the ski industry, working first as B.C.'s Provincial Ski Coordinator where he authored B.C.'s successful Commercial Ski Alpine Policy and served as the provincially appointed councillor on Whistler's Municipal Council between 1975 and 80. He went on to become the Executive Director for the Whistler Resort Association from 1980-82. Winter wanderlust sent him on sabbatical to Switzerland with his family from 1983-85. And, on his return to Canada, he brought progressive European inspirations to hotel projects he developed and managed, first in Whistler and then in Sun Peaks between 1985 and 2010. In 1988 Raine was inducted into the Canadian Ski Hall of Fame.

During his phenomenal fifty-year career he has noticed major changes in the focus and infrastructure of the ski industry. "From 1950 to the 1960s skiing was a small family of people, smaller ski areas and everyone knew everybody who skied," Raine recounts. By the 1970s Canadian skiing had become "chic", he says, with more expensive, bigger and more commodious resorts: "By the 80s and 90s, resorts were full service and skiers were no longer hard core 'mountain people' except for the minority." This is when resorts started to focus on a wider range of facilities and amenities to make skiing a comfortable winter vacation for everyone. Raine says resorts began to improve access, lifts, grooming, and ski equipment to reflect this softer trend.

Nowadays, as Mayor of Sun Peaks, Raine is committed to providing a positive experience for everyone in town. "We do what is necessary to improve the resort for those who live, work, and visit Sun Peaks," he explains. Ironically, the resort he moved from is Sun Peaks' main rival in attracting destination skiers. "The major competition for Sun Peaks is Whistler in the long haul markets and regional Okanagan ski areas in the regional market. But we focus mainly on improving our product and service and not on what the other resorts are doing," says Raine.

His format for a great ski vacation follows the '6, 8 and 10 rule': "Winter sports today cater to the masses and it is much more than just the sport, we are in the entertainment business and there are only six hours of skiing, eight hours of sleeping and rest and 10 hours - or the biggest part of the day - is spent eating, socializing, relaxing, enjoying friends etc. These 10 hours of fun with friends and family are a very important part of our business today."

And Sun Peaks has certainly cornered the market on après ski entertainments. As well as having lovely, alpine architecture and décor throughout the easily walkable resort, it has a full menu of activities including bungee trampoline, cat trax groomer rides, dog sled tours, horse drawn sleigh rides, fondue dinner with torchlight descent, snow limo, snowmobile tours, snowshoeing, tube park, pro-photographer shoots, first tracks breakfast, resort transit, a wide array of accommodation and eateries and spas, as well as the more traditional ice skating and ice hockey. "In the old days, skiing and ice skating were about the only activities happening in winter," says Raine. "Today there is a ton of competition for the entertainment activities, indoor tennis, fitness halls, basketball, volleyball, professional sports watching, badminton, squash etc., mostly easy and relatively inexpensive to access."

These kinds of amenities also facilitate four-seasons' functionality which Raine considers vital for the future success of Sun Peaks, and ski resorts in general. "Resorts must diversify during the winter months and for the off season," says Raine. "The best resorts in the future will be those that have strong winter and summer seasons, better value for money and better staff and services. The economics of resort operations change when you have year-round revenues and stable committed year-round staff."

His love of skiing is reflected by his career path but, when asked what the perks of his job are, he says "I met my partner for life." This is Nancy Greene Raine who as Nancy Greene is known to millions of ski fans for her illustrious career in ski racing. She was top racer for Canada throughout the 1960s, winning Olympic gold and silver in 1968 and notching up 13 World Cup victories (still a record), and 17 Canadian Championship titles. She then went on to become the mother of team ski racing for children all over Canada when the Nancy Greene Ski League spread across the country on the tailcoats of her 1968 successes. Interestingly, Al Raine, then the Southern Ontario Coach, proposed the League and asked Nancy to endorse it the year prior to her Olympic medals. Greene is still Honorary Chairman of the League and in 1999 she was named Canada's female athlete of the century.

Nowadays, her roles include Director of Skiing at Sun Peaks, past Chancellor of Thompson Rivers University and also, since Jan 2009, Senator for British Columbia in the Government of Canada. And she still finds time to guide people around the mountain, working for the Sun Peaks Resort Corporation as well as Tourism Sun Peaks. "My situation is pretty unique, and I am very much part of a team," she says. "I've never considered what I do as a 'job' - certainly I don't have a job description. I just use my initiative to promote Sun Peaks as best I can, and to be out on the slopes connecting with our guests every chance I get."

As well as her value in celebrity endorsement, her interaction with tourists helps garner valuable feedback to resort management. And being able to ski with Nancy Greene is an added "wow factor" for visiting media and travel industry personnel as well as tourists at the resort as Nancy skis with guests daily when she is in Sun Peaks. For many years she partnered with Raine in the building and running of Nancy Greene's Cahilty Lodge at Sun Peaks. "We have sold the hotel management company to former staff, but still assist with hosting," she says. "Everything I have been able to do in ski tourism has been alongside Al." The two were married a year after Greene retired from ski racing at the age of 24.

Sources: Interviews with Al Raine and Nancy Greene Raine, November 2014

On-mountain operations

Ski lift operations

The network of lifts at a ski resort can be arranged in several patterns depending on the size and topography of the area. A common pattern is where several lifts run outwardly from a common base area to top stations along surrounding peaks and ridges. Lifts might also run inwardly from several base stations to a common summit area. Ski areas located along the face of a long ridge may simply have numerous lifts running roughly parallel, and high-traffic areas may have two or more lifts in parallel for increased capacity. A small percentage of ski areas have lifts which cross one another, usually with an aerial lift crossing above a surface lift, and some have lifts connecting two mountains; the PEAK 2 PEAK Gondola connecting Whistler and Blackcomb mountains is a good example of such a lift.

Needless to say, operating ski lifts is an important element of ski area operations. In the U.S. alone, there are approximately 3,500 lifts, the vast majority being
traditional double, triple and quad chair lifts (both fixed and detachable), as
well as gondolas, surface lifts, rope tows and aerial tramways. Ski areas tend to
adhere to rigorous and exacting inspections procedures for their lifts, and they
tend to have an excellent safety record (NSAA, 2012). Ski area employees conduct
their own individual inspection to their lifts on a daily, weekly, monthly, and
annual basis. This maintenance regime is conducted pursuant to state agencies,
lift manufacturer requirements, federal regulations, national safety standards
and other inspection entities. It is not unusual for a ski area to close a lift due to
adverse weather conditions and the decision to close lifts is usually determined
by a select group of ski area managers, which may include the general manager,
ski patrol director, the risk manager, and/or the manager of the lifts department.

Ski areas tend to invest heavily in new and upgraded lifts. In the U.S., capital
expenditures on new and upgraded lifts is well over $1 billion going back to
the 1996/97 ski season, with an average investment at more than $69 million on
lifts at resorts each year (NSAA, 2012). In addition, ski area expenditures on lift
maintenance and repair has increased overall by 92 per cent in the last decade,
representing an ongoing financial commitment to effective and safe lift operations
at ski areas across the country.

Snowmaking

As was mentioned in Chapter 3, early season snow cover is critical for ski resorts,
as demand is often the greatest at this time (over the New Year period in particular). Skier perceptions of early conditions greatly influence the momentum and
success of the overall season (IBISWorld, 2013). If the temperature is low enough,
most resorts now have the snowmaking capability to put down a base at the start
of the season if natural snow has not arrived. The quality of snow cover is also
important, with skiing performance and enjoyment being related to the following
parameters: density, temperature, liquid water, hardness and texture (Perla &
Glenne, 1981).

Snowmaking requires extremely large amounts of water – about 140,000 gallons for an acre-foot of snow. A typical ski run, 200 feet wide with a drop of
1,500 feet would take three acre-feet of water (55 tanker truck loads) to cover it
with one foot of snow (Mill, 2012). Most resorts pump water from one or more
reservoirs located in low-lying areas. The run-off water from the slopes feeds back
into these reservoirs, so the resort can use the same water over and over again.
Capital costs for snowmaking can run from $10,000 to $20,000 for each acre to be
covered, but the big expense is power consumption. If a slope uses compressed
air in its snow guns, it needs to provide a large amount of energy to run the large
air-compressing pumps. It also requires a pump system to provide the water to
the snowmakers. Airless snow guns consume a lot less energy for every foot of
snow they produce, but they are still major power draws. Snowmakers have to

take many variables into account to cover a slope with ideal skiing snow. Many snowmakers describe the job as a challenging marriage of science and art - the basic elements are precise weather measurements and expensive machinery, but instinct, improvisation and creativity are needed to get it exactly right.

Ski resort grooming

Ski resort grooming is part snow science, part instinct, and part caffeine (Hicks, 2012), given that the majority of grooming takes place overnight in a resort. Most ski resorts will use snowcats for grooming and pushing around snow. These machines, which can cost up to $450,000, are basically composed of a climate-controlled cab, tracks made of rubber and metal, and an engine. Typically, a ski resort snowcat has what is called a pusher on the front that moves snow and a tiller on the back that first churns and then presses snow into corduroy. Some modern snowcats have winches, and these are used to groom a resort's steepest ski slopes. Winch cats attach the cable of their winch to a post at the top of a ski slope, then use the winch to lower and raise themselves on the slope for grooming.

In the U.S., Steve Bradley is generally credited as the father of snow grooming. Bradley assumed management of Winter Park in June of 1950 and immediately began working with Ed Taylor on ideas for stabilizing and smoothing the snow surface. Taylor, a member of the Winter Park board of directors, was a former chairman of the National Ski Patrol and had a special interest in snow physics, based on his work controlling avalanches. Bradley and Taylor appear to be the first experimenters to focus on the problem of smoothing out moguls (previously done manually). The pair tried a number of devices to automate this process, beginning with their own version of Cranmore's Magic Carpet, a six-foot length of chain-link fencing they pulled down the slope while skiing. These ideas evolved into the modern powered snowcat technology in use today.

Most resorts will have a fleet of snowcats nowadays. Deer Valley Resort in Utah, for example, has 13 snowcats, including two Prinoth Beasts, which are larger and more powerful snowcat models than anything else on the snowcat market. The Prinoth Beast weighs 25,000 pounds, lies down a 24-foot corduroy pass and has a 13-liter diesel engine. 'Regular' Prinoth snowcats, in comparison, weigh about 20,000 pounds, lay an 18-foot pass, and have a nine-liter diesel engine. Most snowcats are in operation for 14 to 15 hours each night over two work shifts, and cost roughly $100 an hour to operate, including labor, gas, and other expenses (Hicks, 2012).

Mountain safety

Although skiing and snowboarding are less dangerous than many other high-energy participation sports, they are still challenging and require physical skills that are only learned over time with practice. According to Dr. Jasper Shealy, who has studied ski-related injuries for more than 30 years, the number of collision accidents with other skiers or snowboarders accounts for only 6.4 per cent of reported accidents. Alpine skiers are also three times more likely to be involved in a collision with other people than snowboarders. However, snowboarders are more likely to get injured on the slopes. In the last 10 years the rate of ski injuries has remained about the same, with 2.63 reported injuries per 1,000 skier visits. But the rate of injury for snowboarders has increased to 6.97 from 3.37 per 1,000 visits.

Freestyle terrain is becoming more popular at resorts, encouraged in part by the popularity of the X Games (see Spotlight in Chapter 3) and other sporting events where participants regularly perform risky tricks on skis and snowboards. Unfortunately, many young people, eager for an adrenaline rush, are trying to copy extreme sports' idols without the proper training, thereby putting themselves at terrible risk. A twelve-year study (2000-2012) of injuries attributable to extreme sports found a steady increase in such injuries (Brody, 2014). In response, the NSAA and Burton Snowboards have developed a "Smart Style" Freestyle Terrain Safety initiative, a cooperative effort to continue the proper use and progression of freestyle terrain at mountain resorts, while also delivering a unified message that is clear, concise and effective.

Ski areas have undertaken several programs to increase safety. Those programs range from establishing family ski areas to increasing the number of monitors on the slopes. Programs are largely based on the Heads Up safety initiative and the Responsibility Code, two programs that support ski area safety education efforts and provide a unified platform in which to reach skiers and snowboarders proactively with timely slope safety information. January is National Safety Month in the U.S. and resorts nationwide host special safety-related programs and activities all month long to raise awareness and demonstrate the many ways they work to keep the slopes safe every day. Safety activities at the resorts include ski patrols conducting a wide array of hands-on demonstrations such as bringing guests on patrol sweeps at the end of the day, training exercises, and many more interactive safety experiences. Additionally at some resorts, highly-trained avalanche dogs will show off their impressive skills in avalanche response simulations, an annual favorite for guests.

Instruction

Models of skier visitation suggest that sustainable long-term growth in the industry is strongly tied to retaining entry-level skiers and snowboarders, largely through improved and upgraded lessons (Mill, 2012). The President of the National Ski Areas Association (NSAA), Michael Berry, is adamant that ski resort operators need to get intimately involved in the long-range success of their ski and snowboard instruction programs. "For the decision makers at ski areas across the country, this has got to be priority number one" (Kray, 2011). Results tend to be much better when management, snowsports schools and even grooming and equipment staff have teamed up to create a better beginner product. Massachusetts' Jiminy Peaks, Vermont's Stowe, Indiana's Perfect North Slopes,

Alaska's Eaglecreast, California's Northstar-at-Tahoe, and Utah's Park City, to name just a few, have all reaped the rewards of putting proven experienced people in charge of their beginner programs (Kray, 2011). Incentives, including cash bonuses for instructors who generate return visits and discounted tickets and rentals for visitors taking a second or third lesson, are the norm in successful beginner operations.

Snow Time Inc., owner of three ski area operations in Pennsylvania Liberty Mountain Resort, Roundtop Mountain Resort, and Whitetail Resort – won NSAA's first annual Conversion Cup Challenge in 2011, an award that recognizes efforts to create lifelong skiers and riders. Snow Time's ski destinations are primarily day ski areas drawing their guests from the local metropolitan areas of Washington D.C., Baltimore, MD, and Harrisburg and York, PA. "Snow sports are not part of the culture of the region so developing strong programs to attract and retain new guests is very important to our success," said Chris Dudding, Roundtop Mountain Marketing Director (Hawks, 2011). Snow Time breaks down its approach to converting guests into lifelong enthusiasts into four palpable actions: 1) Promote the ease and affordability of learning; 2) Offer guests a program that makes continuation easy and affordable; 3) Track the success of guests that arrive at the mountain; and 4) Follow up with guests as they progress. Winners of the Conversion Cup since have been Mt. Bachelor, Oregon (2012), New Jersey's Mountain Creek Resort (2013), and Camelback Mountain Resort in Tannersville, Pennsylvania (2014).

More recently, instruction apps for smartphones have helped reinforce tuition tips for beginner skiers and snowboarders. One of the early adopters of this is Darren Turner, featured in the Profile below.

Profile: Portable ski instructor

Students of skiing often say they wish they could take their instructor out with them all the time. Just like golfers, skiers perform better under class situations and when left to their own devices often revert to old bad habits. But now with ski instruction apps it is possible to have that familiar trusted voice reinforcing lessons, encouraging skiers down difficult slopes and guiding them into new techniques.

One of the pioneers of the instructional ski app is Darren Turner, a ski instructor from Serre Chevalier in France. Turner started skiing on artificial slopes in Britain and progressed to racing by the age of 14. At 16 he began instructor training and later worked in France. Transferring to the British BASI system, he went on to get the highest level 4 ISTD qualifications which enable him to work anywhere in the world, including France.

Now in his 20th season teaching and skiing the 102 pistes of Serre Chevalier Vallée, Turner says he actually ended up living there by accident. He had visited at the age of 15 when competing in the British Ski Championships but his first work experience in the mountains was at Alpe d'Huez where he worked as a barman for a winter season: "The dream job for a young ski

enthusiast as it gave me all day every day to spend up the mountain," he says. He was transferred by his employers to their hotel bar in Serre Chevalier. "I loved the down-to-earth feel
of the place and made friendship bonds with people whom I still call my best friends," Turner
recounts. "It's a close knit community where everyone has a common bond: i.e. a love of the
mountains."

Darren Turner

Like many itinerant ski fans, he followed this experience with seasonal travel and work, taking
in South Africa, Switzerland, Sweden and Egypt before returning to settle in Serre Chevalier
to work as an independent instructor. "Originally my client base was mainly British but it has
evolved into a truly international spectrum with people coming from as far as Australia and
America," he says. He teaches all age and ability levels but finds that many long-term skiers
reach a plateau. In order to help with this, Turner teamed up with Elate Media run by New
Zealand pro skier, Andrew Gowans to produce a series of ski technique videos. Having watched
many poorly produced versions, he wanted to make video instruction more user-friendly. "Our
focus was on simplifying and keeping things as clear as possible," he explains. "After discussing
ideas for filming there was a bit of a 'eureka moment' - rather than just film and make a DVD,
an app seemed like a much more versatile platform." It could be easily updated whenever
necessary and wouldn't involve stock or shipping issues. "Most importantly the user can use
the information whenever needed," Turner points out. "I have never seen anyone on a chairlift
reviewing a DVD!"

Targeting skiers of all levels, the Ski School Apps first launched in 2010, are available
from iTunes, Android Play and Windows app stores. With future plans to expand into Instagram,
skiers can link to the app via Facebook and Twitter. "Both feature frequent posts - pretty much
anything technique and ski-related," he says

As with all new technological breakthroughs, there are people who jump to the conclusion
that the ski app could adversely affect ski instructor jobs. But Turner finds this ludicrous
and thinks it could actually do the opposite – give newcomers to the sport a head start and

improve every skier's awareness of how lessons can actually help them. "Also, if the app can help increase the amount of people who try this sport for the first time and have a positive fun experience through understanding, then the chances are they will participate in the sport for longer and fall in love with it like I have," he concludes.

The team closely monitors feedback, finding enhanced confidence and goal-setting to be the main comments. The skier analysis feature is particularly successful as it enables the user to take a video of a skier and, using split screen technology, compare it directly with Turner's demonstration. "Or you could also compare yourself to a previous video of yourself or your friend, the options are endless," he says. Users can take notes and store ski videos on the app to keep a history of progression and share images by email or social media.

With the expert level Ski School App about to be launched, Turner is convinced that ski apps are the way of the future: "I am confident that it is a useful tool for all recreational skiers. We have had a lot of positive feedback from first time skiers all the way up to fellow ski instructors and coaches."

Sources: Interview with Darren Turner, November 2014; http://skischoolapp.com/, http://www.serre-chevalier.com/, http://www.insightski.com

5

Mountain hosts

Many resorts in North America also offer a free mountain host service. For more experienced skiers and snowboarders at a resort for the first time, following a local guide takes the worry out of weather and snow conditions, links, drop offs and cliffs, leaving them free to enjoy themselves while safely learning the lie of the land. Lake Louise in Canada launched its signature ski friend program 30 years ago with the wives of ski patrollers helping visitors find their way to the best snow (see the Spotlight on Charlie Locke in Chapter 1). Today, yellow-jacketed, cheery hosts of both genders greet visitors, guide them on twice daily tours and direct skiers at the top of the front-face lifts. Announcements are made in the Lodge of the Ten Peaks about the 10 a.m. and 1:15 p.m. groups and meeting signs are just outside the lodge above the Glacier Express Quad.

At Lake Louise, hosts are chosen firstly through a telephone or face-to-face suitability screening interview. Personality and mountain know-how are tested, followed by a one-day or two-evening training session in Calgary. A full day on-hill training session in early December completes the process. Hosts pay $60 annually to belong to the association and have to commit to a minimum of 12 days resort duty. In return they receive their Helly Hansen uniform, $10 food vouchers each day they host, and gain credits for 12 free lift passes for the following season. If they clock up 18 hosting days, they are eligible for a free season's pass so long as they continue volunteering.

In Europe, however, free ski hosts are the exception rather than the rule, and even overseas tour operators are often unable to provide their own guides for clients. In France, there has been a fair amount of controversy over the banning of ski hosts. In 2012 an employee of a British ski company was even arrested on the slopes for guiding his clients, and the company was then prosecuted for compromising safety. The French insist that all hosts must be fully qualified ski instructors certified by the notoriously tough French examining system. One British ski holiday company is leading an appeal against a ban on ski hosting in the French Alps. Yorkshire-based Le Ski has joined forces with 12 other British tour operators to argue that the decision is in breach of European law. But in 2014, an appeal court in Chambéry upheld the ban on ski hosting. Le Ski was expected to appeal against the decision to the Supreme Court in Paris.

Off-mountain operations

Access

Accessibility was discussed in Chapter 3, but the importance of access is crucial to mountain operations in terms of getting visitors in and out of a resort. Skiers tend to arrive at the base area either by foot or skis from accommodation, private car, charter bus, public transportation or shuttle bus. The proportion of skiers arriving by each of these methods must be estimated to determine the acreage required for parking and access. Patterns of arrival and departure must also be considered in order to provide safety and avoid congestion. The size and number of elements at the base area of a ski hill is determined by the number and type of skiers on the slopes, but at minimum, a base area should have equipment rental and sales, a first aid section, a ski patrol office, ski school, and food and beverage services (Mill, 2012).

Property

While lift tickets usually provide the foundation of 'ski-nomics', a resort that offers only skiing is a risky business model and many resorts have devised and refined a business strategy that keeps income as constant as the weather is variable. This comes down to two smart hedging strategies: own the skiers and own the mountain (Thompson, 2012). Vail and Whistler, for example, are more profitable than most resorts around the world, because they own the mountain, and therefore make at least half of their money from lodging, rentals, ski schools and food (see Table 5.1).

As mentioned in Chapter 4, ski areas are increasingly using land development and real estate sales as a way of boosting profits. Intrawest, for example, has accommodation in seven four-season mountain resorts, and owns over 1,150 acres of mountainside development parcels. Its Club Intrawest timeshare division has over 22,000 memberships, nine locations and over 3,000 affiliated locations. The company also has a real estate brokerage called Playground, and a development sales business. Table 5.2 shows Intrawest's real estate holdings in five different resorts.

	Vail Resorts	Whistler/Blackcomb
Tickets	46%	50%
Retail/Rental	23%	16%
Ski school	11%	11%
Dining	9%	13%
Other	11%	10%

Table 5.1: Resort income at Vail (U.S.) and Whistler (Canada) (Source: Adapted from Thompson, 2012)

Resort	Parcels	Acres	Entitled Units	Value (m)
Steamboat	5	27	640	$51.0
Tremblant	15	509	2,242	$48.6
Winter Park	21	95	962	$23.5
Snowshoe	n/a	359	1,464	$18.0
Stratton	7	161	200	$9.2
Total core real estate holdings $150.3 m				

Table 5.2: Intrawest real estate holdings in 2014 (Source: Adapted from Intrawest, 2014)

The average price of ski homes around the world increased 4.6 per cent in 2013, outperforming luxury homes in many primary and second home locations. Ski homes in South Lake Tahoe (U.S.) and Queenstown, New Zealand, recorded the strongest rates of price growth, jumping 20.9 per cent and 18.9 per cent respectively. Fractional ownership developments and private residence clubs suffered significantly during the recession with sales down 78 per cent since the peak 2007 period. But timeshare fared much better, with sales totalling $7.6 billion in 2013, representing an increase of 11 per cent over 2012 and a 20.6 per cent increase over 2009 (Bowden, 2014). The most common types of timeshare ownership structure are based on the number of weeks of access (74%) and points (62%). The emergence of the point system as an alternative to use periods has affected a significant improvement in the marketability of timeshare products.

In Japan, property development in The Niseko United ski area has been burgeoning since 2003 – see the Case Study below for more on the 'Aspen of Asia'.

Restaurants

Restaurants are also an important component of a resort's service offering, and in most parts of the world, they tend to be independently owned and operated. Sun Peaks, in Canada, for example (featured in the opening Spotlight), boasts several owner-operated eateries including Bolacco's, Mayor Al Raine's favorite café. Elsewhere in North America however, vertically integrated resort operators like Vail and Whistler own most of the restaurants, and even smaller resorts in the U.S. will often own and operate food and beverage outlets. Sundance in Utah, for example, has long been a bastion of sustainable dining. Reflecting the tastes of owner, Robert Redford, the Tree Room is rustic but rarefied with a menu of fresh, organic local ingredients served in a candlelight environment surrounded by beautiful Native American art. As well as being a Forbes Travel Guide Four Star Restaurant, the Tree Room won Utah's 2014 Best of State award for fine dining and the Wine Spectator Award of Excellence 2014. And the sustainable, fresh food philosophy extends to Sundance's other eateries including the more casual cowboy-themed Owl Bar which serves tasty treats by the fireside. And its biggest claim to fame is the fact that it is the original bar dating back to 1890 frequented by the Hole in the Wall Gang. Robert Redford bought it, dismantled it and recreated it at Sundance. The resort also owns The Foundry in the village and Bearclaw Cabin perched at the summit with 360-degree panoramic views over Mt Timpanogos – and famous for its chili and oatmeal molasses cookies. Sundance also owns Zoom in Park City, Utah, located at the bottom of historic Main Street.

Chefs are a vital part of any ski holiday, providing the sustenance required after a hard day's skiing and the convivial cuisine which is such an integral part of après ski. It is not uncommon that ski resort chefs ski or snowboard in their spare time, and usually a passion for the sport is what has brought them to the mountains to pursue their culinary career. However, it is most unusual for guests in a resort to get to ski with their chef. One hotel, though, offers just that service. During the 2014/15 season, guests at the Viceroy Snowmass in Colorado could take to the slopes with Executive Chef Will Nolan as their personal guide. It was part of a unique program in which Nolan skied with hotel clients all day and then returned to the resort to teach the group how to prepare the ultimate après ski cuisine. It was a ski in/out culinary experience which could be customized to suit individual food and beverage preferences. And the chef also offered advice on cocktail, beer and wine pairings.

Staffing

Wages are one of the largest costs for ski resorts, as many employees are required to run operations. Staff are required for marketing, customer service, instruction, managing lifts, grooming slopes and conducting many other facility maintenance jobs. A study of the 2009/2010 season in the U.S. found that winter sports activities support the employment of over 200,000 people and generate more than $7 billion in wages (NRDC, 2012). Ski resort operations contributed the most to winter tourism employment and value added to the overall economy, with 75,900 employed (36% of total winter tourism employment) and $2.8 billion in added economic value (23% of total economic value added) (see Table 5.3). Dining (bars and restaurants) was the second greatest contributor to the winter sports economy, with 31,600 employed (15% of the total) and $940 million in added economic value (8% of total). Colorado was the state that benefited most from winter sport tourism, with 37,800 employed, generating $2.2 billion in total economic value added. California had the next highest level of economic activity, with 24,000 employed and $1.4 billion in economic value.

Industry	Winter Tourism Employment (thousands)	Labor Income ($ millions)	Value Added ($ millions)
Resort operations	75.9	$1,495.80	$2,851.50
Dining (bars and restaurants)	31.6	$612.60	$941.50
Accommodations	17.6	$558.90	$1,035.10
Professional services	8.4	$659.00	$779.80
Administrative support services	8	$257.80	$296.10
Food & beverage stores	5.2	$148.70	$214.70
Government	4.6	$307.90	$358.70
General merchandise stores	4.3	$113.30	$176.50
Real estate	4.2	$74.30	$1,157.30
Health care	3.6	$239.80	$255.60

Table 5.3: Impact of winter sports in the U.S. (Source: Adapted from NRDC, 2012)

Ski industry employment is seasonal, with operations hiring most workers for the length of the winter season. Panorama in British Columbia, for example, employs about 450 employees in the winter time. Of these 150 are full-time (year-round) employees, and of the seasonal workers, about 120 return every year so they are re-hiring about 180 each winter. Employees are often students or young adults who are willing to work for low wages in exchange for discounted accommodation and skiing. As a result, the average wage for the industry – especially in North America – is very low (just below $10,000 in 2013). Employment is fairly transient, and resorts will hire staff each year through job fairs and other arrangements prior to the winter season. In North American ski resorts, many of these workers can come from as far as Australia. According to the Australian Department of Foreign Affairs, there are about one million Aussies living and working overseas at any one time. Whistler in Canada has actually been dubbed 'Australia's best ski resort' due to the volume of expats in the British Columbian village. Since 2006, Australians traveling to Canada have been able to acquire two-year visas which are relatively easy to renew.

Case study: Powder and property investment in Japan

Unlike development in many of Japan's smaller ski areas, winter sports' infrastructure and tourism is on the rise in Hokkaido, Japan's most northerly island. Australia and New Zealand have traditionally been the strongest ski holiday markets and they continue to grow year on year. While interest in ski resort investment has declined from the Aussie market, demand for both ski vacations and also for investment in ski property in Japan is increasingly coming from Hong Kong and the Chinese mainland. There are also significant numbers from other parts of Asia, including Singapore and Malaysia, as well as growing visitation from Europe and North America.

Niseko, Japan, photo courtesy of Explore Niseko

Since hosting the 1972 Winter Olympics in Sapporo, Hokkaido's ski industry has blossomed with dramatic development over the past 20 years. According to the Japanese National Tourism Organization, there are around 600 mostly small, local ski resorts dotted all over the mountainsides of Japan. But, on Hokkaido there are a number of premier resorts, notably Niseko, dubbed the 'Aspen of Asia'.

Greg Hough, Director of Marketing for the Niseko Promotion Board, says that Niseko – and Japan in general – is firmly on the map now as a global ski destination. Although many smaller ski resorts are suffering due to declining domestic visitation, Niseko is blossoming. "Overall the domestic ski industry in Japan remains in decline with many ski resorts having to close each year," says Hough. "In recent years there has been an increased awareness of some resorts (including Niseko) because of the inbound growth and interest from foreign investors. There has been a flood of general media interest - mainly international - and most of the major ski and snowboard production companies have been, and are still coming, to Niseko and Japan each year including Warren Miller, Sweetgrass Productions, Matchstick etc." This continues to heighten awareness from the hardcore powder skier perspective.

Around 100 km south of Sapporo, The Niseko United encompasses four resorts (like Aspen's Power of Four) on one mountain, the 1,308 meter-high Niseko Annupuri. Renowned for dry light powder and consistent abundance of snow, the mountain is open for winter sports from late November into May with slight variations at each resort. Here, visitor numbers jumped 103 per cent over the 2011/12 season, according to the Niseko Tourism Board, including more overseas visitors than other Japanese ski areas.

"The Niseko ski area has a 50-plus year history but the most recent boom started in 2003 and was driven largely by the Australian market and a few opportunistic developers," says Hough, who also owns and directs Explore Niseko KK. "Since the start of this development boom over 7,000 new beds have been developed and an estimated US$800 million has been invested including the sale and re-purchase of two of the adjoining resorts - Niseko Village and Hanazono - as well as some infrastructure upgrade projects." The key driver up until this point, he adds, has been property development and although the lift network has seen some upgrades, for the most part it remains unchanged. Niseko's primary target markets for attracting investment are Hong Kong, Singapore and Malaysia.

International awareness of Japan's ski industry has been heightened over the years largely by media and social media. "There has been very limited investment in marketing by the resort and much of this has been left to the individual businesses," says Hough, who has worked in travel and tourism since 1998. "Over the past 10 years most of our growth has happened organically and we have relied heavily on word of mouth marketing. The quality of the snow and a renewed interest in Japan as a ski destination has driven much of the growth."

The Niseko United is an all-season resort with a skiing/snowboarding focus in winter and golf, cycling and food in summer. One of the big benefits for Hong Kong visitors is the small time difference (Niseko is just one hour ahead of H.K.) and a four-hour flight – both big pluses compared with traveling to Europe or North America. Other advantages include a network of 38 lifts accessing 48km of terrain with a substantial snow record (up to six or seven meters according to Japanese National Tourism Organization figures) - and the possibility of very light powder particularly between January and mid-March. Niseko also has many *onsens* throughout the area – natural hot springs ideal for après ski soaking – with a shuttle-bus link to all four base stations. And there are rapidly developing facilities for other winter activities, including snowshoeing tours, snowmobiling, heli and catskiing, backcountry tours and a focus on developing other off mountain infrastructure and retail.

Sources: Interview with Greg Hough, February 2015; http://www.nisekotourism.com/niseko; www.scmp.com/property/international/article/1237630/resort-interest-hot-japan

References

Bowden, R.S. (2014) '*Bowden's market barometer*', Volume **XXIII**(4), November/December.

Brody, J.E. (2014) 'With the thrills come extreme risks', *New York Times*, 31 March, accessed 1/26/15 from well.blogs.nytimes.com/2014/03/31/with-the-thrills-come-extreme-risks

Hawks, T. (2011) 'Snow Time Inc. takes home 2011 Conversion Cup, accessed 1/26/15 from https://www.nsaa.org/media/22311/SnowTime.pdf

Hicks, M. (2012) 'Making corduroy – the life of a ski groomer', *Utah Adventure Travel*, 21 February, accessed 11/26/14 from http://utahadvjournal.com/index.php/making-corduroy-the-life-of-a-ski-groomer

IBISWorld (2013) *Ski & Snowboard Resorts in the US*, IBISWorld, December.

Intrawest (2014) '*Intrawest investor presentation*', July.

Kray, P. (2011) 'Fresh start" Is this the new golden age of snowsports instruction?' *32 Degrees*, Winter, 26-34.

Mill, R.C. (2012) *'Resorts: Management and Operation*, (3rd edition),' Hoboken, NJ: John Wiley & Sons Inc.

Natural Resources Defense Council (2012) *'Climate impacts on the winter tourism economy in the United States'*, Elizabeth Burrows and Matthew Magnusson: New York: Natural Resources Defense Council.

NSAA (2012) 'National Ski Areas Association ski lift safety fact sheet', accessed 12/2/2014 from www.nsaa.org/media/68048/NSAA-Ski-Lift-Safety-Fact-Sheet-10-1-2012.pdf

Perla, R. and Glenne, B. (1981) 'Skiing', in D.M. Gray and D.H. Male, (Eds.). *Handbook of Snow: Principles, Processes, Management and Use*, Toronto: Pergamon.

Thompson, D. (2012) 'No business like snow business: the economics of big ski resorts', *The Atlantic*, 7 February, accessed 11/23/2014 from http://www.theatlantic.com/business/archive/2012/02/no-business-like-snow-business-the-economics-of-big-ski-resorts/252180/

6 Marketing and Intermediaries

Spotlight: New Mexico True

When a country or state is best known for its dry climate, desert flora and long, laid back summers, it's pretty difficult to imagine it in winter, covered in snow with skiers and snowboarders merrily zooming down groomed runs, slaloming through glades and pounding the powder.

But New Mexico, which has this extreme variation in climate, has managed to change people's perception recently and open their eyes to a new winter sports wonderland, doused in around 300 inches of snow annually. This has been achieved via the New Mexico True campaign launched by the New Mexico Tourism Department (NMTD) in November 2013.

"Last year (2013) was the first year we did a designated winter campaign," says Rebecca Latham, NMTD Cabinet Secretary. "The perception was that New Mexico is a dry and arid state and we wanted to dispel those misconceptions." New Mexico True summer advertising shows lush greenery and water with mountain backdrops and this has been extended to winter, with a heavy focus on the ski industry. "We are showing that New Mexico has snow and also an abundant offering of skiing and snowboarding as well as snowshoeing, sleigh rides and snowmobiling," Latham explains.

The creative campaign is being disseminated via multi media: "We're using a little bit of everything, really targeting print in AFAR, Food Network magazine, Texas Monthly, Southwest, Outside mag. So we have some really targeted messages based on what the appeal of the publication is. We also do broadcasts, 30-second TV commercials, and also cinema advertising in our main target markets. In New York City and Chicago we do transit advertising, on subway trains and taxi cabs. And we have beautiful, larger than life dioramas in the airports. And closer to home we have billboards within the state of New Mexico," Latham explains. This is backed up with a wide scale social media presence on Facebook, Twitter, Instagram and Pinterest plus 15-second digital ads on targeted websites.

The aim is to enhance awareness of New Mexico's snow and dedicated program of winter recreation which includes eight alpine and three Nordic ski resorts. Probably the most famous alpine area is Taos Ski Valley, but there are also Apache, Angel Fire, Sipapu, Red River, Ski Santa Fe, Pajarito Mountain and Sandia Peak. "It is a general promotion message rather than pinpointing specific resorts," says Latham but she says that all the resorts are very pleased that NMTD is fronting a winter campaign and they are already seeing the trickledown benefits of it. "As well as showing our skiing, we are also showcasing our culture - for example, people having a bowl of green chili stew at the end of their ski run, adventures that you can't have anywhere else," Latham describes.

New Mexico print ad in Outside Magazine>

This kind of promotion doesn't come cheaply. "We don't necessarily have the breakdown of our total marketing budget for winter versus summer, but $8.6 million in total is our annual budget," says Latham. "And that's what we'll be spending in the budget cycle from July up to June 2016."

Is it worth it? Definitely, says Latham, when you look at the return on investment (ROI). "Shortly after New Mexico True campaign launched, we did an ROI study and saw that for every $1 spent, $3 was returned on the tax base level, so we know we have a 3:1 ROI. We now have a new study with results coming at the beginning of 2016. We look at the money that's being spent while people are vacationing here and the taxes that are coming back to us as a result of the dollars being spent. Let's say if someone saw a New Mexico True ad and then traveled here as a result of the advertising and let's say they spent $200 while here, it's the percentage of that that goes back into the state tax level."

Total visitor spending since 2010 has also increased by 24 per cent and the amount of overnight leisure trips has gone up 37.5 per cent: "That is three times the national average," says Latham. The change in perception – and resulting leisure travel increase - has emanated from New Mexico's target "fly markets": Dallas, Houston, Denver, Phoenix, San Diego, Chicago and New York City. "We know that the past two years we have seen record-breaking tourism growth as a result of the New Mexico True campaign," she adds.

So what does Latham envisage for the future? "We don't see the idea of New Mexico True changing at all. But I think there are things that we can do differently and ways we can expand on the message," she says. "However, we don't see it as your traditional ad campaign but more like a standard within the industry in New Mexico. The whole idea of New Mexico True is promoting everything that separates us from our neighbors. That adventure culture we don't see changing."

Sources: Interview with Rebecca Latham, February 2015; nmtourism.org/nm-true-brand/

6

Marketing communications

Effective communication with target customers is carried out by a variety of methods, referred to as 'marketing communications', and the Spotlight above highlighted the importance of an integrated marketing communications campaign. In many people's perception, marketing is promotion, for promotion is the highly visible, public face of marketing. However, promotion is only one element of the marketing mix, its role being to convince potential customers of the benefits of purchasing or using the products and services of a particular organization. Promotions decisions will be determined by the overall marketing plan, as illustrated in Figure 6.1. Marketing objectives are derived from the strategic tools of targeting and positioning. The marketing mix is then used to achieve these objectives, and promotions are just one part of this marketing mix.

Figure 6.1: The role of promotions in the marketing strategy

The blend of promotional elements outlined in Table 6.1 is known as the promotional mix, and promotional management involves coordinating all the elements, setting objectives and budgets, designing programs, evaluating performance, and taking corrective action. Advertising and sales promotion are covered in this chapter, whereas the remaining elements are discussed in other chapters of the book.

Promotional tool	Winter sport tourism application
Advertising	Television, newspapers, magazines, billboards, Internet, brochures, guidebooks
Sales promotion	Short-term incentives to induce purchase. Aimed at salespeople, distributors such as travel agents, and consumers. Can be joint promotions. Includes merchandising and familiarization trips.
Public relations	All non-paid media exposure appearing as editorial coverage. Includes sponsorship of events and causes.
Personal selling	Meetings and workshops for intermediaries; telephone contact and travel agents for consumers
Word of mouth	Promotion by previous consumers to their social and professional contacts.
Direct marketing	Direct mail, telemarketing, and travel exhibitions
Internet marketing	Direct e-mail marketing, Internet advertising, social media, customer service, selling, and market research

Table 6.1: The promotional mix used in winter sport tourism

Promotion can be a short-term activity, but considered at a strategic level it is a mid- and long-term investment aimed at building up a consistent and credible corporate or destination identity. Promotion, when used effectively, builds and creates an identity for the product or the organization. Brochures, websites, advertisements, sales promotions, and so on, create the identity of the company in the mind of the consumer, and all aspects of the promotional effort should therefore project the same image to the consumer.

Perhaps one of the most important advances in marketing in recent decades has been the rise of integrated marketing communications (IMC): the unification of all marketing communications tools, as well as corporate and brand messages, so they send a consistent, persuasive message to target audiences. This approach recognizes that advertising can no longer be crafted and executed in isolation from other promotional mix elements. An IMC campaign includes traditional marketing communication tools, such as advertising or sales promotion, but recognizes that other areas of the marketing mix, like the Internet, are also used in communications. Planning and managing these elements so they work together helps to build a consistent brand or company image, as was the case for New Mexico in the Spotlight above.

One final factor to consider in the promotional strategy will be the position of the organization in the distribution channel. For example, does a retailer (i.e. the travel agent) carry out its own promotion for the ski package, or does the producer (i.e. the tour operator or destination) have to promote the package in order to bring the public into the travel agency to buy it? This is known as the choice between push and pull promotional strategies. A push strategy calls for using the sales force and trade promotion to push the product through channels; the producer promotes the product to wholesalers, the wholesalers promote to retailers, and the retailers to consumers. In contrast, a pull strategy calls for spending a large amount on advertising and consumer promotion to build up consumer demand; if successful, consumers will ask their retailers for the product, the retailers will ask the wholesalers, and the wholesalers will ask the producers.

Branding

Before advertising is discussed in any detail, it is important to consider the concept of branding and how it applies to ski industry marketing. The subject of destination branding has received increased attention over the last few decades (Ferguson & Bourke, 2013; Garcia, Gomez & Molina, 2012; Pike & Mason, 2011; Zenker & Martin, 2013). In an increasingly competitive global marketplace, the need for ski resorts, in particular, to create a unique identity – to differentiate themselves from competitors – has become more critical than ever. A brand in the modern marketing sense offers the consumer relevant added value, a superior proposition that is distinctive from competitors', and imparts meaning above and beyond the functional aspects.

The process of building a brand should begin with an analysis of the current situation. This stage should consider how contemporary or relevant the brand is to today's consumer and how it compares with key competitors (see the DreamSki

Case Study at the end of the chapter). Once this market investigation is complete, the next stage is to develop the brand identity. Critical to the success of any brand is the extent to which the brand personality interacts with the target market. A brand's personality has both a head and a heart: its 'head' is its logical features, while its 'heart' is its emotional benefits and associations. Brand propositions and communications can be based around either. Local residents and workers have a significant role to play in the development of place brands. Freire (2007), for example, from in-depth interviews with British tourists in Portugal, revealed that local people were often perceived as a strong factor in differentiating the place brand, as far as interviewees were concerned. He concluded that brand construction should strongly focus on the 'local people' factor. Ferguson and Bourke (2013) examined the role that workers in a ski resort setting play in the brand experience, in particular how employees represent and co-create brand experiences with and for consumers. They found that seasonal workers are "evangelical brand ambassadors" (p. 444), who create a sense of unique customer experience within the destination that actually contributes to the meaning of the destination brand itself for their experience and that of the customer. Ferguson and Bourke's and Freire's research illustrates that, not only are the local communities impacted by place branding, but also they can - and should - provide valuable guidance in the place branding process.

The third stage in brand building is to communicate the vision and launch the brand. This may be done through a single announcement or as a part of a huge international advertising campaign. This stage involves translating the brand personality and proposition into deliverable messages. A logotype or brand signature and a design style guide, which ensures consistency of message and approach, should also reinforce the brand values. The vision should be expressed in the brand's core values that are consistently reinforced through the product and in all marketing communications. Every execution in all media contributes to maintaining brand presence. The Spotlight above described how the New Mexico True branding campaign utilized numerous methods to get across the message that the state was open for business in the winter. These included print ads in magazines, 30-second TV commercials, transit advertising, billboards, and a wide scale social media presence.

The final stage is to evaluate the brand's performance in the marketplace. The Spotlight indicated that the New Mexico True campaign had a return on investment (ROI) of 3:1, with a 24 per cent increase in visitor spending and a 37.5 per cent increase in overnight leisure trips. Continuous monitoring and evaluation of the communications is the key here, in conjunction with open-mindedness and a willingness to embrace change on the part of the brand managers. Any change must be managed with the overall consistency of the brand. The secret is to evolve continually and enrich the original brand personality, building on the initial strengths to increase their appeal and broaden the market.

Advertising

Advertising is a key communications tool for winter sport tourism marketers. These marketers often require potential customers to base buying decisions upon mental images of product offerings, since they are not able to sample alternatives physically. As a result, advertising is a critical variable in the marketing mix, and it covers a wide range of activities and agencies. Its role reflects that of promotion in general, which is to influence the attitudes and behavior of audiences in three main ways: confirming and reinforcing, creating new patterns of behaviors, or changing attitudes and behavior. Thus winter sport tourism marketers use images to portray their products in brochures, posters, and media advertising.

The process of developing an advertising program includes six important stages. These are illustrated in Figure 6.2.

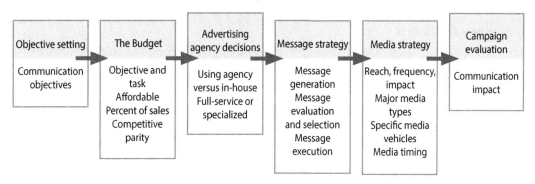

Figure 6.2: The process of developing an advertising program

1) Setting objectives

The first stage is the setting of objectives. An advertising objective can be defined as a specific communication task to be accomplished with a specific target audience during a specific period of time. In general terms, advertising has four major tasks: informing, persuading, reminding, and selling. However, advertising in tourism can have many uses. These might include creating awareness; informing about new products; expanding the market to new buyers; announcing a modification to a service; announcing a price change; making a special offer; educating consumers; challenging competition; reversing negative sales trends; and recruiting staff.

2) The budget

The second stage of an advertising program is establishing the budget, and ideally, the budget should be calculated on the basis of the objectives set in the first stage of the process. The media plan must reach sufficient numbers in the target market to produce the size of response that will achieve the sales target. Several methods can be used to set the advertising budget. The objective and task method involves developing the promotion budget by (1) defining specific objectives, (2) determining the tasks that must be performed to achieve these objectives, and (3) estimating the costs of performing these tasks. Using this method requires considerable experience of response rates and media costs, as well as confidence in the accuracy of predictions. Cautious managers prefer to base the advertising budget on what they know from previous experience they can afford to spend. This is often referred to as the affordable method. The percentage of sales method involves setting the promotion budget at a certain percentage of current or forecasted sales or as a percentage of sales price. In tourism and hospitality, the percentage of gross sales generally set aside for marketing is somewhere between four and 12 per cent, advertising being allocated about a quarter of this amount. Another way of setting the budget is the competitive parity method, which sets the promotion budget at the level needed to achieve parity or 'equal share-of-voice' with competitors.

3) Agency decisions

The third stage of developing an advertising program is to decide whether or not to hire an outside agency. Only very small businesses, such as guesthouses or local visitor attractions, are likely to undertake their own advertising without professional help. There are two main types of advertising agency: the full-service agency and the specialized agency. In advertising, a full-service agency is one that provides the four major staff functions: account management, creative services, media planning and buying, and account planning (which is also known as research). However, winter sports organizations often use the services of a specialized agency. This type of agency will specialize in certain functions (e.g. writing copy, producing art, media buying), audiences (e.g. minority, youth), or industries (e.g. health care, computers, leisure), or in certain marketing communication areas, such as direct marketing, sales promotion, public relations, events and sports marketing, and packaging and point-of-sale.

4) Message strategy

The message strategy is the fourth stage in developing an advertising program and a critical one. Studies have shown that creative advertising messages can be more important than the number of dollars spent on the message. The industry is often criticized for creating advertisements that appeal to a very narrow segment. It was mentioned in Chapter 3 that in the last decade, the most appealing aspect of a snow sports holiday for skiers and boarders has changed. Ten years ago the main motivator was the desire for freedom and to get away from it all, whereas now being with family and friends is more important. However, according to Snowsports Industries America (2014) advertising content has changed little over the years, and is maybe even more skewed toward 'extreme air', 'male' and 'under 30 years of age'. In an in-depth content analysis of advertisements produced by the industry, they found that two critical market segments – women and families – were almost entirely left out of imagery. Since the groundbreaking, female freeski film *Pretty Faces*, however, the industry has started to reflect women's needs in advertising – see the Case Study in Chapter 3.

The intangibility of services does makes advertising difficult for service marketers like ski resorts. Before buying services, consumers have problems understanding them, and after purchase, they have trouble evaluating their service experiences. Various strategies have been proposed to overcome these problems. One is to present vivid information and evoke strong emotions. Advertisers of top-notch resorts, for example, often try to build a mood or image around the resort, such as beauty, love, or serenity, creating an emotional relationship between the resort and potential visitors. Marketers are realizing the importance of touching emotions and getting into the consumer psyche, and have begun to focus on promoting experiences as opposed to physical attributes. The print ad below, from the Stein Eriksen Lodge in Deer Valley Utah, actually uses a mixture of both rational appeals (hotel room features), and emotional appeals (skiers enjoying the après ski). But the emphasis is on the experiences guests can expect at the five-star resort with the tagline 'Experience Legendary'.

Figure 6.3: Print advertisement for Stein Eriksen Lodge in Deer Valley, Utah (Courtesy of Stein Eriksen Lodge)

Employees are also often featured in advertisements in order to promote the promise of good customer service externally and internally. Another hotelier in Deer Valley, Dan Howard, Director of Public Relations at The Montage says: "We try to use images of our associates in all of our public relations messaging." The example below features Bob in Daly's Pub, one of several dining options at the luxury resort.

Figure 6.4: Example of employees featured in communications: Daly's Pub, The Montage Deer Valley (Courtesy of The Montage Deer Valley)

Certainly, ski industry advertisers have to think creatively to grab the attention of the target market. Ski Area Management's 2014 pick for 'most creative messaging' was Ski Utah's 'several text message' print ads (Rufo et al., 2014). Ski Utah promoted the message of "you can put yourself on the greatest snow on earth in just a few hours" in a fun way, and in 25 words or less.

Figure 6.5: One of Ski Utah's creative print advertisements from 2014 (Courtesy of Ski Utah)

5) Media selection

The fifth stage of an advertising program is media selection and includes media objectives (reach and frequency), media strategies (targeting, continuity, and timing), media selection (the specific vehicles), geographic strategies, schedules, and the media budget. The range of advertising media available to today's advertiser is increasingly bewildering and is becoming ever more fragmented. While these changes offer the prospect of greater targeting, they also make the job of the media planner more difficult. All the different media outlets are referred to as the media mix – created by media planners by selecting the best combination of traditional media vehicles (print, broadcast, etc.); non-traditional media (the Internet, cell phones, unexpected places like the floors of stores); and marketing communication tools such as public relations, direct marketing, and sales promotion to reach the targeted stakeholder audiences. Media planners usually select the media that will expose the product to the largest target audience for the lowest possible cost.

Although the Internet is considered to be extremely cost effective, television is still a good way to reach the mass market. Wachusett Mountain in Massachusetts, for example, frequently advertises on television in the Boston market. In the 2012/13 season, the resort changed its advertising frequency and TV spot length in an effort to stand out. While some resorts shoot their TV commercials the season prior, Wachusett committed to same day turnaround with a date stamp on all the spots, in order to showcase snow quality and up-to-date conditions. The commercials were a mixture of 30, 15 and 5 second spots.

6) Campaign evaluation

The final stage of an advertising plan – the campaign evaluation stage – is often the most difficult in the advertising cycle, largely because while it is relatively easy to establish certain advertising measures (such as consumers' awareness of a brand before and after the campaign), it is much harder to establish shifts in consumer attitudes or brand perception. Despite such uncertainties, the evaluation stage is significant not only because it establishes what a campaign has achieved but also because it will provide guidance as to how future campaigns could be improved and developed. There are many evaluative research techniques available to marketers to measure advertising effectiveness. Memory tests are often used and fall into two major groups: recall tests and recognition tests. In a traditional recall test, a commercial is run on television network and the next evening interviewers ask viewers if they remember seeing the commercial. Another method of measuring memory, called a recognition test, involves showing the advertisement to people and asking them whether they remember having seen it before.

Direct marketing

Direct marketing is a marketing system, fully controlled by the marketer that develops products, promotes them directly to the final consumer through a variety of media options, accepts direct orders from customers, and distributes products directly to the consumer. It is rapidly becoming a vital component of the integrated marketing communications mix. Direct marketing has increased in popularity as businesses have come to place more importance on customer satisfaction and repeat purchase. Direct marketing makes use of databases, which allow precision targeting and personalization, thus helping companies to build continuing and enriching relationships with customers.

There are eight key advantages of direct marketing (Hudson, 2008):

1   Precision targeting – direct marketing is aimed at a specific individual. It provides opportunities to target not only general groups of potential buyers but specific buyers individually.

2   Personalization – direct marketing provides an opportunity to personalize messages and build stronger links between the company and the consumer. It enables the sender to use names, and thus to target promotions to the individual.

3   Flexibility – not only can the contents of each direct marketing message be changed to suit the specific requirements of each participant, but the message can also be delivered to specific geographic locations.

4   Privacy – offers made by direct marketing methods are not readily visible to competitors. Direct marketing does not broadcast an organization's competitive strategy as widely as mass communication advertising.

5   Measurability – a major advantage of direct marketing is the ability it gives a company to measure the effectiveness of various response fulfilment packages sent out to prospects, in terms of converting enquiries into sales, costs per booking, response by market segments, and so on.

6   Low cost – direct marketing has the advantage of generally lower costs per transaction than other forms of communication.

7   Detailed knowledge – direct marketing methods allow the gathering of valuable consumer information – not only names and addresses, but also lifestyle information and purchasing behavior.

8   Fast or immediate – because of the format of direct marketing, offers can be made quickly – and can be quickly accepted. This has become more applicable recently with the advent of the Internet.

Direct response advertising is one segment of the direct-marketing industry, and it plays a major role in influencing consumer purchase patterns. It can be defined as advertising through any medium, designed to generate a response by any means that is measurable (e.g. mail, television, telephone, fax, or the Internet). If traditional mass media are used, the message will include a free telephone number, mailing address, or website address where more information can be obtained. The major forms of direct response advertising are direct mail, telemarketing, the Internet, and direct response television (DRTV). Figure 6.6 presents some of the communication strategies of the four main forms of direct response advertising.

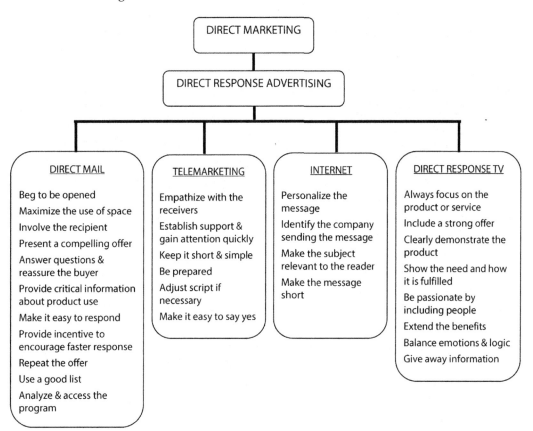

Figure 6.6: Strategic considerations for the major forms of direct response advertising

Two common forms of direct marketing used by the ski industry are direct mail and the Internet. The Internet will be covered in detail in the next chapter, but a good example of an attractive direct mail piece is one received by the authors in October 2014 from Aspen Snowmass, Colorado. The 6x8 brochure (see Figure 6.7) folded out into various sections that advertised lift ticket prices, lessons, and equipment rentals. The front and back covers encouraged readers to purchase in advance, with a 10 per cent additional savings if lift tickets or group lessons were purchased by a certain date (November 6).

Figure 6.7: Copy of direct mail piece sent out by Aspen Snowmass in 2014 (Courtesy of Aspen Snowmass)

Sales promotions

When a marketer increases the value of its product by offering an extra incentive to purchase the product, it is creating a sales promotion. The above direct mail piece from Aspen Snowmass included such an incentive. In most cases, the objective of a sales promotion is to encourage action, although it can also help to build brand identity and awareness. Like advertising, sales promotion is a type of marketing communication. Although advertising is designed to build long-term brand awareness, sales promotions are primarily focused on creating immediate action. Simply put, sales promotions offer an extra incentive for consumers, sales reps, and trade members to act. Although this extra incentive usually takes the form of a price reduction, it may also be additional amounts of the product, cash, prizes and gifts, premiums, special events, and so on. It may also be a fun brand experience (See Snow Crystal Profile below for examples). Furthermore, a sales promotion usually has specified limits, such as an expiration date or a limited quantity of the merchandise.

The use of sales promotion is growing rapidly for many reasons: it offers the manager short-term bottom-line results; it is accountable; it is less expensive than advertising; it speaks to the current needs of the consumer to receive more value from products; and it responds to marketplace changes. Sales promotions can also be extremely flexible. They can be used at any stage in a product's life cycle and can be very useful in supporting other promotional activities. In 2014, seven out of 10 marketers expected their companies to increase spending on social media in response to shrinking television audiences and stale print ads (Sass, 2013).

There has also been an increase in joint promotions, where two or more organizations that have similar target markets combine their resources to their mutual advantage. This collaboration can reduce the cost of the incentives offered, and it may be a one-off joint promotion or a long-term campaign such as a trade association campaign using an 'umbrella' brand name. An example of a joint promotion comes from California where Sugar Bowl Resort partnered with ski and snowboard shops to cut through the clutter with a clever combination of traditional and online media. The target market was ski shops and their fans. Sugar Bowl's 'Rep Your Shop' Facebook contest ran for three weeks in February 2013. The resort's fans voted for their favourite Northern Californian ski and snowboard shops, and one voter was chosen to receive five free tickets and five meal vouchers. The winning shop received 20 lift tickets to reward employees and could also brag about being the most popular shop in the region. Sugar Bowl partnered with its most loyal vendors and reached out to their customers as well as their own visitors, promoting the contest via Facebook, Twitter, e-blasts, newsletters, text messages and radio. The shops themselves promoted the competition in their stores and on Facebook. As a result of the competition, Sugar Bowl's fan base grew more than 13 per cent.

6

Figure 6.8: Sugar Bowl's 'Rep Your Shop' Facebook contest

Profile: Snow Crystal

A Crystal ski rep using an iPad
loaded with custom-built software

In 2013/14 there were just over 900,000 British skiers. The Brits have been skiing en masse since the 1960s when tour operators began organizing packaged winter holidays firstly to the Alps and later across the whole of Europe, Canada and the USA. Skier enthusiasm has been fuelled since 1978 by *Ski Sunday*, the longest-running BBC Sports program, as well as annual Daily Mail Ski & Snowboard Shows in London and Manchester (now sponsored by *The Telegraph*). The Ski Club of Great Britain has also been instrumental in perpetuating the sport with its network of fervent volunteers specializing in off-piste ski guiding in 33 resorts.

Nowadays, one of the foremost tour operators is Crystal Ski Holidays, founded in 1981 to take British skiers to European resorts in winter and to mountain lakes in summer. Crystal's focus has always been on accessibility and affordability and by the 1990s it became the largest ski operator in the U.K. Offering the broadest choice of accommodation of any rival, it now transports over 200,000 Brits annually to ski resorts in Europe and North America.

Debbie Marshall worked for Crystal Holidays for 14 years. "I did a wide range of jobs from 1987 until 2001 – from overseas resort rep to Managing Director and just about everything else in between," she says. "Crystal was a very entrepreneurial business, where we were given a lot of responsibility from an early stage. It was dynamic and fast growing – as well as great fun." Things have changed considerably in the ski industry since Marshall first started at Crystal Holidays. "I saw the advent of snowboard – replacing mono-skiing – and the very early stages of the Internet as well as mobile phones," she recalls. An efficient multi-tasker, her role included interaction with resort staff, chalet and hotel owners, lift pass companies, ski hire facilities, ski schools, supermarkets, suppliers, the home office in London and the media – all without the benefit of the Internet. "I am still not entirely sure how we coped with moving 50,000 clients around the Alps each winter with such limited communications," she says. But the pressure of work was balanced by the joys of spending winters in the mountains and being part of an upbeat and fast-growing organization.

With charismatic 'cuckoo clock' chalets in short supply and great demand, one of Marshall's jobs was to sustain lasting relationships with accommodation owners in resorts: "Inghams were always the main competitors as well as other chalet operators. We had to watch our backs to make sure that our best chalets were not going to get poached!" Over the years ownership at Crystal has changed to Thomson Holidays in 1997 and a merge with First Choice Holidays in 2007 when it became one of the largest brands in the Specialist and Activity sector within TUI Group. As part of a new focus on luxury, Crystal Finest was launched in 2007 but still with an emphasis on affordability.

Espousing the Internet at the turn of the century, Crystal established an online pricing facility – 'what-you-see-is-what-you-pay' – along with Crystal iPack: up-to-date online resort information available to travelers four weeks before their departure. By winter 2010/11 overseas staff were using social media including Twitter to give real time updates to customers. And, by 2014, 700 overseas personnel were equipped with iPads loaded with custom-built software enabling pre-departure video calls as well as online info packs complete with in-depth advice and resort tips. This new technology also facilitates snow reports and advance ski and boot orders to eradicate queuing in rental outlets.

The Crystal Ski Explorer App, designed to maximize online information, can also be used as a location device to find friends and family – as well as resort teams – around the mountains. Tamsin Todd, managing director of Crystal Ski Holidays says this combination of the latest mobile technology and ski expertise of resort staff is giving Crystal's customer service an edge over competitors: "Personalized service direct from the slopes to your mobile means you can worry less and focus on enjoying and getting the most out of your ski holiday."

This investment in technology also means Crystal is better prepared to deal with the unexpected, which in the ski industry can often mean flight and resort transfer delays due to adverse weather. Using a variety of communication tools, from Twitter accounts to text messages and live-chats, Crystal can now keep customers updated. Sustainability side benefits include reduced carbon emissions, by going paperless, as well as a reduction in the amount of travel required by staff, due to Google Hangout and FaceTime.

With a Facebook following of over 62,000 people, Crystal Ski also launched a novel online quiz on its Facebook page in 2014. Dubbed "What Type of Skier are you", the quiz identifies 11 different skier types (from Après Animal to Fairweather Fred) in order to pair potential customers with the most compatible ski resorts.

Although no longer working for Crystal, Marshall keeps a close eye on the ski industry as part of her research for Silver Travel Advisor, an award-winning forum for travel reviews and holiday advice for the Over 50s traveler. "I see the growth of the 'silver' skier and, with the ageing demographic, this will become an increasingly important market for resorts and tour operators," she observes. "Some already seem to be waking up to this and offering senior concessions." And although she has moved out of the tour operator business, Marshall is gratified to see the original companies still flourishing: "Crystal recently won a 'best ski operator' award – and we first won that back in 1997."

Sources: Interview with Debbie Marshall December 2014; http://www.crystalholidays.co.uk/press/crystal-ski-holidays-quiz-uncovers-your-skier-type/; http://www.crystalholidays.co.uk/

Intermediaries

An organization's distribution system is centered on the 'place' aspect of a company's marketing mix. Its purpose is to provide an adequate framework for making a company's product or service available to the consumer. In the tourism industry, distribution systems are often used to move the customer to the product. There are two different types of distribution channels that players in winter sport tourism can use to deliver their products. The first and most simple form of distribution is a direct distribution channel, a channel through which a company delivers its product to the consumer without the outside assistance of any independent intermediaries. In such a case, the service provider is solely responsible for the delivery of its product. Most bed and breakfasts in a resort would use a direct distribution channel to market products to potential customers, and resorts themselves also often go direct to the consumer – the Aspen Snowmass direct mail piece referred to above is an example of that.

The second type of distribution channel used to deliver a product is an indirect channel. In this case, the service provider makes use of independent intermediaries to help facilitate the distribution of its product. Outside intermediaries such as travel agents, tour operators and other tourism specialists assist the supplying company by helping to attract consumers to the product or destination (see reference to Silver Travel Advisor in the Snow Crystal Profile above). Most large ski resorts use both methods of distribution to sell winter sports vacations. They target consumers directly through websites, newsletters, videos and promotional written material, but also use intermediaries – in the form of selected tour operators or travel agents – to attract customers.

Marketing intermediaries are channels of distribution that include travel agents, tour operators, travel specialists and the Internet (discussed at length in Chapter 7). Through the use of channel intermediaries, a company is able to expand the strength of its distribution network and to reach a much larger portion of its target market. As a result, the combined marketing efforts of the entire distribution network will lead to an increase in the number of customers using the service, thus boosting overall revenues.

Travel agents offer the tourism customer a variety of services, including everything from transportation plans and tour packages to insurance services and accommodation. An agency will earn a commission for each sale, the amount depending on the type of product sold. The modern tradition of holiday packages started with the Industrial Revolution and the railways. In July 1841, a Baptist cabinet-maker called Thomas Cook booked a party of 500 on a train from Leicester to a temperance rally in Loughborough. The future travel agent negotiated a price that included entertainment in local private gardens.

Today, the travel agency market is very competitive. Barriers to entry are low and as a result there are many new entrants, which is especially true of the rapidly growing segment of online agents. Independent travel agents are under pressure not only from e-agents but also from direct selling by tour operators. They therefore seek to differentiate themselves, and add value to the product, in order to justify their role in the value chain and retain market share. Despite the benefits that travel agents can provide to a company's distribution system, the emergence of new and cheaper distribution tools such as the Internet has placed the future role of travel agents in doubt. For this reason, a large number of travel agencies are seeking new positioning strategies to maintain their foothold in the tourism market. In the last decade, most airline carriers have eliminated base commissions for travel agents, so many agents are charging service fees to customers. Agents used to earn up to 10 per cent on all airline tickets sold; approximately one-third of agency business came from the sale of scheduled airline tickets. Apart from charging fees to customers, agencies are now looking at other ways to make up for the loss of airline commissions, including selling more package tours and cruises and focusing on selling their expertise. While traditional agents have lost market share to online purchasing, expert advice from travel advisors is likely to remain a vital service in the tourism marketplace. Travel agents are especially valuable to marketers of luxury travel, but also to highly specialized travel, such as the Dreamski ski packages to South America and Japan, profiled in the Case Study below.

Tour operators are organizations that offer packaged vacation tours to the general public, and play a significant role in the winter sports sector, particularly in Europe. The packages they put together can include everything from transportation, accommodation and lift tickets, to entertainment, meals and drinks. Tour operators have the ability to bring in large volumes of customers (see Crystal Profile above). They receive discounted rates from various service providers in exchange for providing a large number of guaranteed visitors. Tour operators make their profits by providing low-margin travel packages to a large number of consumers. In the past, the majority of tour operators distributed their travel packages through travel agencies, but they are increasingly selling their packages direct to customers, cutting out the intermediary, by using their own outlets or web pages. Gerry Winchester from Dreamski, featured below, uses a combination of direct selling and travel agents to promote his ski packages.

The tour operating sector has become increasingly concentrated. In Europe, for example, about 70 per cent of the market is cornered by the five largest companies, which all have their corporate seats in either Germany or the U.K. In the 1990s these tour operators followed a strategy of vertical integration. By controlling the value chain from sales and packaging through to transportation and hotels, tour operators sought to secure their market share strategically and shore up low profit margins in their core business with more profitable activities in downstream areas of the value chain. But a slowing and changing tourism market has exposed the lack of flexibility in this model. The 'de-packaging' of travel – with customers building their own trips piece by piece on Internet platforms – has struck a blow at the heart of traditional tour operator products.

Figure 6.9 shows the make-up of the snow sports market in the U.K. with the number of winter sport tourists in terms of how they book their holidays, whether it is through a tour operator, with a school trip, or independently. The data – from 2007 to 2014 – shows that the tour operator and independent travel segments have remained significantly down against 2007/08. However, despite the winter snow sports market suffering during the recession, the share of the tour operator segment has stayed largely stable at around 57 per cent.

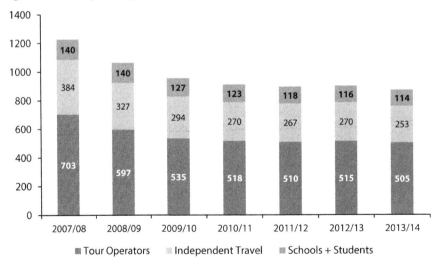

Figure 6.9: U.K. share of the snow sports market by holiday type (Source: Adapted from Mintel, 2014, p. 28)

Just as the tour operating sector in general has become increasingly concentrated, so too has the tour operating sector for winter sports. In the U.K., for example, three operators control about 63 per cent of the market (see Figure 6.10).

In turn, two parent companies dominate the market, with TUI (41% of the market) owning Crystal Ski and Thomson Ski, while Hotelplan (26%) owns Inghams, Esprit and Ski Total. In the 2012/13 season, Crystal Ski held a 34 per cent share of the operator market, doubling sales of the closest rival, Inghams.

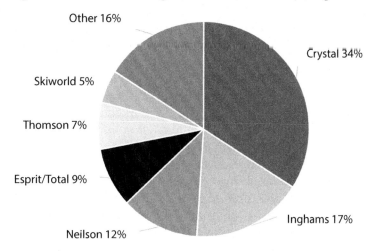

Figure 6.10: Market share of winter sport tour operators by brand, by number of holidaymakers (Source: Adapted from Mintel, 2014, p. 32)

Alliances

Finally, a further form of promoting or distributing the winter sport tourism product is via an alliance. An alliance is a partnership formed when two or more organizations combine resources through a contractual agreement that allows them to overcome their weaknesses by benefiting from each other's strengths. In this form of distribution channel, each organization shares everything from information to resources to strategies, but the key advantage to alliances is increased distribution. Those organizations joined through the alliance will enjoy access to new markets through new and diversified sales locations. Also referred to as clusters (Porter, 1998), alliances involve businesses in one geographical area that work collaboratively to draw customers to their common location, where, as individual rivals, they then compete to draw these customers into their own specific business.

Increasingly, ski resorts are collaborating in order to create a competitive advantage for the region in which they operate. A good example comes from British Columbia, Canada, where in 2006, seven ski resorts came up with the concept of the Powder Highway to showcase snow sports in the entire Kootenay Rockies region. "When we first set out to brand the Powder Highway, we did it to place ourselves as a cohesive region within B.C. that could compete with areas like Banff and Whistler and the big American snow resorts," said Anne Pigeon, vice-president of marketing and director of operations at Whitewater Ski

Resort near Nelson, B.C. at the time. "It's been very successful for the region. As a collective we're able to saturate the market in a way that an individual resort can't do." (Milner, 2013). Ashley Tait, former director of sales and marketing for Revelstoke Mountain Resort, said that though the Kootenay Rockies resorts compete for customers, the Powder Highway brand supports all of them. "It's about identifying our region, so that collectively we promote tourism in our area and across the province," she said. "We market internationally with the Canadian Tourism Commission, nationally with Destination B.C., and regionally with Kootenay Rockies Tourism and the Powder Highway. We're competitive in a supportive environment." Kathy Cooper, CEO of Kootenay Rockies Tourism, said the Internet has been a powerful factor in marketing the Powder Highway. "A shift has taken place from traditional marketing in newspapers, magazines and consumer shows to web-based marketing that has grown significantly even in the last four to five years," Cooper said. "The Powder Highway website is a one-stop shop for information on all the winter activities." The site is a specific landing spot for information about the complete Powder Highway product; it provides snow reports, information about the terrain and the nearby communities, and blog posts from enthusiastic visitors (Milner, 2013).

Resorts are also joining forces to provide passes that allow visits to multiple ski areas at a discount. The Epic Pass in Colorado started the momentum when it connected all of the Vail Resorts under one pass. Since then a number of others have followed suit, including the Powder Alliance Pass, the Mountain Collective Pass, and the White Mountain SuperPass. "From a consumer point of view, you're always looking for the best value, and I think that's why these passes are trending," said Snowbasin Marketing Manager, Jason Dyer (Krichko, 2013). Snowbasin, a Utah resort, joined Stevens Pass (Washington), Crested Butte (Colorado), Bridger Bowl (Montana), and eight other big-name western resorts on the Powder Alliance Pass in 2013. The Alliance had grown to 36 resorts by the 2014/15 season, including Lake Louise featured in Chapter 1. The Pass is available automatically with the purchase of a top-tier season pass at any of the Powder Alliance resorts and includes three days of free skiing at each of the other resorts.

Such alliances started in Canada back in the 1990s. "Resorts of the Canadian Rockies was the first in the Canadian ski industry to introduce multi-resort passes and loyalty cards, providing guests with the greatest benefit in flexibility, savings and variety of terrain," says Matt Mosteller, RCR's Senior VP Marketing & Resort Experience. The group owns Kicking Horse, Fernie, Kimberley and Nakiska, bundled in the Rockies Season Pass. Similarly the Rockies Card covers all four resorts, giving three days skiing at each and discounts at partners, Blacktail Mountain, Canyon Resort, Rabbit Hill and Snow Valley. While this may seem like taking away business from the parent resort, Mosteller thinks it adds wow factor: "Offering guests multi-resort discount cards like the RCR Rockies Card provides them with the most choice, based on snow, ease of access, variety of terrain, flexibility and convenience based on their schedule and time, with the huge benefit of savings or free days."

Ski resorts are also forming alliances with brands for mutual benefit. In January 2015 Whistler Blackcomb announced a three-year retail and marketing alliance with Oakley, manufacturers of men's and women's sunglasses, athletic apparel, goggles, watches and accessories. The agreement put Oakley products on a large number of resort employee ambassadors involved with Whistler Blackcomb Snow School, the retail division and Whistler Heli-Skiing. The partnership also resulted in a variety of Oakley brand and marketing touch points throughout the Whistler Blackcomb Resort, both on the mountain and in Whistler Blackcomb's retail shops in the village. "We are excited to bring Oakley on board as our newest corporate partner," said Stuart Rempel, Senior Vice President of Marketing and Sales at Whistler Blackcomb. "The Oakley brand is synonymous with high performance eyewear which is critical for an optimal guest experience at Whistler Blackcomb whether you are skiing, riding or downhill mountain biking on our mountains." Alexandre Langevin, Oakley Canada Marketing Director said: "It is an honor to be an official partner of Whistler Blackcomb. We are excited to share our passion for winter and summer sports with such an iconic resort. Whistler Blackcomb is key in the development of so many Oakley international athletes. Our objective is to provide the best brand experience to consumers in this sporting mecca." (WhistlerBlackcomb.com, 2015).

6

Case study: Year round dream skiing

Gerry Winchester

Word of mouth, a website presence and a high return rate have been the driving forces behind a North/South American tour operator's success. Gerry Winchester, originally from Alberta, Canada, relocated DreamSki Adventures, his boutique ski guiding business, to Chile in 2010. Established in Banff in 2004, the head office is now in Santiago with tours taking place in the USA, Japan and South America. The company offers all-inclusive guided resort-based tour packages which follow the best snow conditions. "The customers set up their own flights and we look after all the rest from the time we pick them up at the airport until we return them to the airport," says Winchester. "The DreamSki concept is to take small groups on traveling ski tours that go where there is more snow and less people because that's what I like and what they are looking for, too."

Groups of around 10 skiers – average age 40-60 - spend each day with two guides, visiting three to five resorts, based on weather and snow conditions, during their trip. "We're unique as far as the South American market is concerned. My guys are guides as well as high level trained instructors and offer ski improvement throughout the tour," he explains. The idea is to blend tuition with practice, while exploring different segments of each resort, until the new movement or feeling becomes an intrinsic part of the skiers' muscle memory. "This method can really change your skiing and you have fun doing it," Winchester adds. "It's instruction with lots of guided mileage because for adults it takes a lot of repetition for new messages to stick, as opposed to the younger mind."

During northern hemisphere winter, DreamSki runs tours to Utah, Southwest Colorado, Montana and Wyoming and to Chile and Argentina in southern winter/northern summer. Since 2010 Japan has been added to the January schedule in the eternal quest for more powder, less people. "Japan has only just started to come into North American consciousness," Winchester says, but he started researching the Japanese ski areas back in 2008 just as the economic crisis hit the West. He found that Australian skiers had been exploring Japan since around 2000, particularly Hokkaido due to a substantial snow record.

Winchester started out as a professional engineer in oil rich Alberta. During that time he indulged his passion for skiing by teaching part time during evenings. "I finally pulled the plug on my engineering and went to the mountains for a season in Banff to teach for Club Ski, a three-day instructing and guiding program for tourists," he says. He went on to combine working winters in Banff, with launching his fledgling company initially in Chile during Canadian summers. Later on, he added his own tours in Canada during the winter due to the popularity of the DreamSki format in Chile. "I was going back and forth for around six or seven years, swapping hemispheres," says Winchester.

His experiences working for Club Ski at Ski Big 3 resorts – Lake Louise, Sunshine and Mt Norquay – were the basis for DreamSki Adventures. "Club Ski's a very popular program, with around 99 per cent Brits," he says. "And so, using that data base, I started my own business and from there it spread by word of mouth." He also promoted DreamSki at ski shows in London, Birmingham, Calgary and Toronto in 2006 and 2007 to give the business a kickstart. "Since then we have had a high rate of return clients, and success with word of mouth and our web presence," he adds.

DreamSki customers are generally empty nesters, child-free couples or single travelers. "They tend to be working professionals who aren't encumbered by growing families and, as they are signing up for a group program, everybody tends to be very likeminded and sociable," says Winchester. This social element of the skiing makes the program easier to implement and more enjoyable for the clients and for the guides. But it is primarily adventure and new frontiers that both customers and guides are seeking. "It's something different that we are all after. Our destinations are unique," Winchester explains. "Japan has other guided tours but our ski improvement and combination with powder skiing and travel and the experience element make us different."

The tours are not just about the skiing, however. There is also an emphasis on the unique nature of each location. "Chile's great: wine is a big part of the culture," says Winchester. "We travel to the central valley to visit vineyards and have wine tastings. We show some of the culture while getting in lots of ski days."

DreamSki mainly attracts experienced skiers varying in ability level from intermediate to advanced and expert. The intermediates, mostly British and Australian, can join tours rated for them in the hope of improving sufficiently to enjoy the powder on that tour and subsequent trips. "We have one lady who is about to set the record at nine tours with us," says Winchester. "Her feedback from her first one – the Chile tour – was that it reinvigorated her interest in skiing as she improved her technique to the point where she was enjoying the sport in an entirely new way." Occasionally a snowboarder will book a trip but the majority of clients are dedicated skiers. DreamSki's edge, says Winchester, is having guides who really enjoy working with people. "Other companies often employ guides who are former patrollers, lone wolf types, who don't offer the same social aspect or that extra support on the hill. We're student-centered rather than teacher-centered like European models."

In terms of marketing, social media is a new priority for DreamSki Adventures. Blogging has been a useful tool, with new content, rather than interaction, being the main thrust. "It's hard to track results from the blog but basically it's for Google. We're still working on a wider social media presence but haven't put a lot of effort into that yet because we concentrate so much on word of mouth publicizing."

Winchester also employs agents, one web-based in Australia and others in the U.K. where his original customer pool was situated. "That's where 90 per cent of my market was and it was a fun market to work with," he reflects. "Those guys are great in groups but, of course, after the 08/09 banking crisis, things backed off on the U.K. market a little bit and it's been up and down since then to the point that it's now the smaller portion of our clientele." Nowadays the bulk of his clientele comes from Australia and Canada where the economies have been more stable.

Working with hotels in a variety of countries can be a challenge due to the small group sizes of 10 per tour. DreamSki endeavors to operate with hotels as a wholesaler but relationships differ from country to country and resort to resort. Chilean ski resorts are amenable to smaller groups but other destinations require a larger commitment for accommodation and lift passes. "In some places we actually buy tickets at the window, and other places we have wholesale contracts," Winchester explains. The USA is the most accommodating in this respect.

Competition for DreamSki is limited due to the niche nature of the business. There are just two other rival companies in Chile whose focus is more backcountry skiing than resort-based guiding. Winchester does not trawl websites to keep his pricing and marketing competitive as he finds his product sells itself: "It's been all kind of serendipitous. Because we're so small and boutique, I just do my own thing and people seem to find me. That's the benefit of the Internet."

In terms of the future, Winchester doesn't anticipate much growth in the North American ski industry, mainly due to prohibitive costs. "It's becoming too elitist," he maintains. "I grew up in Alberta where families just went skiing as a recreational thing. Now it's much more expensive and the average family can't introduce it to their kids as easily." He's also dismayed by the trend for corporate culture to take over from individual and independent management in ski areas throughout North America and, more recently, in South America. With Japan now fully discovered by Australian skiers and Chile and Argentina engulfed by the Brazilian market, Winchester sees the future for growth in skiing in places like Russia and Kashmir.

Sources: Interview with Gerry Winchester, September 2014; www.dreamskiadventures.com

References

Ferguson, S. and Bourke, A. (2013) 'Living the brand', The evangelical experiences of snowsport workers, in S. McCabe (Ed.), *Handbook of tourism marketing* (pp. 435-446). London UK: Routledge.

Freire, J.R. (2007) ''Local People' a critical dimension for place brands', *Brand Management, 16*(7), 420-438.

Garcia, J.A., Gomez, M. and Molina, A. (2012). A destination-branding model: An empirical analysis based on stakeholders. *Tourism Management, 33*(3), 646-661.

Hudson, S. (2008) *Tourism and Hospitality Marketing: A Global Perspective*, Sage: London.

Krichko, K. (2013) 'Combination Ski Passes are Sweeping the Ski World,'*MtnAdvisor.com*, 29 August, accessed 12/24/214 from http://www.mtnadvisor.com

Milner, M. (2013) 'Powder Highway welcomes the world', *Kootenay Business*, November, accessed 12/24/2014 from http://kootenaybiz.com/tourism/article/powder_highway_welcomes_the_world

Mintel (2014) '*Snowsports – UK*', London: Mintel Group Ltd.

Pike, S., & Mason, R. (2011). Destination competitiveness through the lens of brand positioning: The case of Australia's Sunshine Coast. *Current Issues in Tourism, 14*(2), 169-182.

Rufo, S., Blanchard, G., Grasso, M., Kahl, R. and Rowan, J. (2014) 'Best/worst marketing 2013/14', *Ski Area Management, 50*(3), 50, accessed 12/14/2014 from http://www.saminfo.com/article/bestworst-marketing-2013-14

Sass, E. (2013) 'Most marketers will spend more on social media in 2014', MediaPost Publications, accessed 11/24/2013 from http://www.mediapost.com/publications/article/213850/most-marketers-will-spend-more-on-social-media-in.html.

Snowsports Industries America (2014) 'Revisiting Growing the Snow Sports Industry', accessed 12/09/2014 from http://www.snowsports.org/portals/0/documents/Revisiting%20Growing%20the%20Snow%20Sports%20Industry.pdf

WhistlerBlackcomb.com (2015) 'Whistler Blackcomb and Oakley today announce three-year strategic alliance, 6 January, accessed 1/6/2015 from http://www.whistlerblackcomb.com/about-us/news-releases/jan-6-2015.aspx

Zenker, S. and Martin, N. (2013). Measuring success in place marketing and branding. *Place Branding and Public Diplomacy, 7*(1), 32-41.

7 The Importance of Public Relations and Earned Media

Spotlight: Susie English – Perfect PR

Skiing is in the genes for Susie English who grew up in Park City, Utah, home of the U.S. Ski and Snowboard Team. Her father, Chuck English is Director of Mountain Operations at Deer Valley Resort where he has been since 1985 when she was two years old. Following in his footsteps, English went on to work as Director of Communications for Ski Utah, representing and working with all 15 ski resorts in the state.

English went to school and skied with many future Olympians including two-time gold medalist, Ted Ligety. She was a soccer teammate of Julia Mancuso, a lifelong friend of Tanner Hall and ski buddies with silver medalist Jeret "Speedy" Peterson. "It was an amazing place to grow up and I've been so lucky to know a lot of amazing ski athletes because of it," she says. "It's pretty fun watching the Olympics when you know the athletes personally."

Susie English

After majoring in Marketing and Finance at the University of Denver, she returned to Utah to work as marketing manager for Rossignol Ski Company where she stayed for eight years before moving on to Ski Utah. "Working for Rossignol was a great start to my career and I was able to learn so much, ski all over the world and live back in Utah," she says. At Ski Utah, her responsibilities included outbound media events, local media relations, hosting inbound media trips and pitching media nationwide. "My job is to create brand awareness and demand for the Utah winter sports product through earned media placements," she explains. "Being back on the tourism side of the ski industry is great. I'm passionate about Utah skiing both personally and professionally!"

The job was a perfect fit, she says, and what better person to promote a ski area than a bona fide local who has grown up skiing there, with a family history on the administrative side of the ski tourism industry. So what does the job of Director of Communications entail? On a day-to-day basis English liaised with the Utah Office of Tourism, Visit Salt Lake, Park City Chamber and Visit Ogden. "Ski Utah is a membership organization so I also work with members that help me host media including ski shops, restaurants and attractions," she explains.

Another important facet of her job was working with international media interested in writing about or filming in various Utah destinations. This can have its challenges, particularly with tight deadlines and the increasing need for journalists to do extreme activities in order to create headlines. "I've had interesting requests from 'I don't eat anything that is red', to 'I don't ski' (and they are on a Ski Utah press trip). It's always exciting in PR and keeps you on your toes," says English. Ski Utah uses Cision Point to monitor media coverage. "I also work closely with our public relations firm (Mfa) to pre-approve press trip attendees and then to monitor coverage after the trip. We don't expect immediate coverage but hope to see something within two years of the trip," English explains.

Like everything else in the ski industry, public relations has changed over the years, particularly with the advent of social media. "PR professionals have had to change their pitching methods from sending mass press releases to more targeted, focused outreach," English explains. "Many media members now get many of their story ideas from social media, especially Twitter, so keeping up on all of the trends is more and more important." Out of a total of 10 employees, Ski Utah has a team of three people managing online content and social media channels.

Another focus for a communications director is to keep abreast – and ahead – of the competition. In Utah's case this is Colorado, California and other areas competing for out-of-state winter visitation. "We definitely watch what other states and ski resorts are doing across the country for ideas and trends," says English. "We also work with other states on specific programs, including Learn to Ski and Snowboard Month and the Bring a Friend Initiative."

So, what are pre-requisites for a career in winter sports PR? Firstly experience and understanding of the tourism industry, English says. In order to gain hands-on experience of the area, she recommends internships at resorts or with ski companies or state tourism agencies. "Ski Utah has a fabulous internship program and past interns have gone on to work at Visit Salt Lake, US Ski Team, Petzl, Ski Utah and more," she says.

And the perks of a PR ski job: plenty of skiing and living in a beautiful mountain environment within a likeminded community. "I'll get 70-100 days on skis each year, mostly for work," says English. "The people I work with, at Ski Utah and the resorts, are really amazingly, talented individuals. We are not just co-workers but friends who ski, ride bikes, and BBQ together." She also travels extensively throughout the USA, meeting with intriguing, unique media, all snow sports focused. "It is so much fun to create new relationships with media, hear about all of their amazing travel adventures and ski with them in Utah," she concludes

When it comes to the winter sports product, English thinks that family appeal is one of the biggest factors that will ensure longevity for skiing. "Utah's resorts, specifically Alta, see generation after generation coming out for the same week every year for their annual family ski vacation," she explains. "It is pretty fun to see family grow up coming to Utah and introduce the next generation to the tradition." She also thinks that enjoyment at every level – from beginner, through intermediate, to advanced – will ensure that snow sports perpetuate as a way to have outdoor fun in a beautiful, wintry setting.

One of the things Ski Utah has been addressing recently has been flat skier days and participation following the 2008 financial crisis. "Many of the participants are aging, so it is a big focus for Ski Utah to introduce young skiers and snowboarders to the sports," English says. "The 5th and 6th Grade Passport is a wonderful program that Ski Utah has been doing for over 10 years to help make the sports more accessible for kids. We also have a 4th grade program where a staff member educates the kids on health benefits, costs and more related to skiing and riding and then takes them for a lesson. All of Utah's resorts have school programs as well."

Despite the fact that Utah encompasses two of the three ski resorts which do not allow snowboarding, English thinks snowboarding has been a plus for the industry: "It opened up the options and brought more young people into the sport. Snowboarding numbers have been decreasing in recent years, but a lot of those people are still on the mountain, just on skis." And she says that Alta and Deer Valley re-evaluate their anti-snowboarding policy on a yearly basis.

For the future, English envisions an increase in joint, reciprocal or multi-resort ski passes. "With Vail Resorts Epic Pass program many other resorts are now offering additional benefits for their pass holders," she explains. "It was been an interesting trend to watch and many of the Utah resorts are following suite. Utah's resorts are part of passes like the Epic Pass, Mountain Collective, Powder Alliance and Wasatch Benefit."

Sources: Interview with Susie English November 2014

Introduction to public relations

The field of public relations (PR) is growing. In the U.S. alone, the PR industry is comprised of more than 7,000 companies bringing in estimated annual revenues of $11 billion, and offering a diverse range of services from media relations to event management (Pozin, 2014). There are many types of media available to PR specialists, and these fit into three broad categories: owned, paid, and earned media. Owned media is defined as communication channels that are within the organization's control, such as websites, blogs, or email; while paid media refers mostly to traditional advertising, discussed in Chapter 6. Earned media, on the other hand, is generated when content receives recognition and a following outside of traditional paid advertising, often from publicity gained through editorial influence. Critically, earned media cannot be bought or owned, it can only be gained organically, hence the term 'earned'. Since most of this earned media is gained through PR activities, this chapter will mainly focus on PR and its various techniques. PR is broader in scope than publicity, its goal being for an organization to achieve positive relationships with various audiences (publics) in order to manage effectively the organization's image and reputation. Its publics may be external (customers, news media, the investment community, general public, government bodies) and internal (shareholders, employees).

The three most important roles of PR and publicity in tourism and hospitality are maintaining a positive public presence, handling negative publicity, and enhancing the effectiveness of other promotional mix elements (Morrison, 2002). In this third role, PR paves the way for advertising, sales promotions, and personal selling by making customers more receptive to the persuasive messages of these elements. Ultimately, the difference between advertising and public relations is that public relations takes a longer, broader view of the importance of image and reputation as a corporate competitive asset and addresses more target audiences.

A variety of PR techniques are available to tourism and hospitality organizations. Those applicable to marketers in the winter sport tourism industry are highlighted in Figure 7.1 and discussed below.

Figure 7.1: Selected public relations techniques available to marketers

Public relations techniques

Press releases and press conferences

A press release or news release is a short article about an organization or an event that is written in an attempt to attract media attention, which will then hopefully lead to media coverage. Preparing press releases is probably the most popular and widespread public relations activity. To be effective, the release must be as carefully targeted as an advertising media schedule. It should be sent to the right publications and be written in a style that those publications would use. The headline should give a clear idea of the subject. The release should then open with a paragraph that summarizes the main points of the news story by stating who did what, when, why, and where. The style should be that of a news report, and the story must be genuinely interesting to the publication's readers. Ideally, it should tell them something new that is happening and should contain a strong human angle. Other useful contents of a press release include a photograph and quotations, and it is essential to provide a contact name and telephone number in case journalists require further information.

PR specialists should be routinely pitching stories to journalists, and this is certainly the case at Utah's Office of Tourism (UOT). In 2013, their office conducted 84 international media and trade FAM trips with 213 participants, generating 382 TV, radio and print articles in France, Germany and Japan. Domestically, they hosted 279 journalists on 82 FAM trips and generated 624 articles. According to UOT, this earned media coverage provided $26,372,182 advertising value equivalent (AVE) to the state (UOT, 2014).

FAM trips

A familiarization trip, often referred to as a FAM trip, is a tour offered to media on behalf of an organization to get the media familiar with their destination and services. A FAM trip is a great way for the organization to get positive publicity and for the media to have an opportunity to write a story about an organization they *fully* understand and have experienced. Such FAM trips can be targeted towards certain publications/journalists, or specific regions or countries. Lake Tahoe Visitors Authority (LVTA), for example, hosted three FAM trips in the 2012-13 season for Australians – not just writers, but also key travel agents representing Travel Scene, Harveys World Travel, Navigator Travel, Campas Tara Travel, and Travel 2. These visits resulted in exposure worth $620,000 in the Sun Herald, Sydney Morning Herald, The Age, and Women's Health Magazine, with an additional exposure valued at $1,600,000.

Lutz (2014) suggests that the key to organizing a successful press trip is to make sure that all aspects of the trip are planned properly to the last detail. She offers a checklist to keep in mind when thinking of putting a FAM trip together (see Table 7.1).

Checklist	Explanation
Plan ahead	There is never a great time to give comp rooms or ski passes etc., but most destinations are seasonal and factor in the cost of FAM trips to their overall marketing and public relations budget. So if you can, pick a relatively low occupancy week.
Gather media lists	Work out who is a priority to invite and why. Be strategic about every invitation. Established and trusted travel writers make great guests, because they could write stories on your destination which may be picked up by two or more publications.
Seek help from your local CVB	The local visitors' bureau is a great resource for media lists, verifying reporters' backgrounds, and other information. They may also help you with providing fillers, such as access to city sites and venues, or partnering restaurants, which will make your press trip a full experience. CVBs can also assist with transportation contacts and more.
Decide what expenses to cover	Research the norm for your area by asking your CVB, and then make your decision. Naturally, room, tax and breakfast should be included for everyone, as well as access to amenities. Your itinerary should include airport transfers for those flying, and parking passes for those who are driving.
Create an interesting itinerary	Most journalists will want to have a variety of memorable experiences to write about. You should welcome this opportunity to "sell" your destination. Be creative and informative in your descriptions.
Send the invitations	Send out invitations 6-8 months in advance and track the RSVPs. Online invitations are effective and acceptable these days. Once the media RSVP, you can send a more detailed itinerary about the press trip.
Block the right rooms	You must be willing to give up several VIP guestrooms to accommodate the press. The media are used to being wowed and you need to provide that extra touch, to make their stay at your property unforgettable. The good ones get numerous offers and only have a finite amount of time. So be grateful that they want to spend time with you.
Establish goals of FAM trip	Discuss with your team what you are looking to accomplish from this expense. Once you strategically determine the goals of the trip, it will be easier to track its success and consider repeating another one in the future.
Research media	There are several online sources where you can research the arriving guests. Information is crucial to understanding more about them, and you can customize their stay accordingly. For instance, if you read in a writer's profile that s/he is a vegetarian, let the Chef know in advance. These are the things that your guests will remember.
Welcome gifts	These can make quite an impact so put some thought into these gifts. Make sure you provide a welcome letter, a press kit with contact information, along with any CVB materials, such as lift tickets, free passes, etc. in a separate gift bag.
Dedicate one PR Professional as the main contact	The PR specialist will be the best and most informed contact for the press to ask questions and give tours. The PR contact also has experience in suggesting angles and pointing out special features to the media. The PR contact is also the most appropriate for any media follow-up questions after the FAM trip, as well as facilitating requests for photos and setting up interviews.
Continue to nurture the relationship	Finally, after the FAM trip is over, the publication date of each article may vary depending on editorial calendars, but make sure to maintain the relationship with each writer. These are opinion leaders of the travel industry and the more reason you give them to talk about your destination, the more vacations you will eventually sell, and the better your image will become through editorial endorsement.

Table 7.1: A checklist for putting a FAM trip together (Source: Adapted from Lutz, 2014)

Not all journalists will be visiting on an organized FAM trip, and there is nothing stopping an individual operator from being proactive in terms of earning media. The Profile in Chapter 8 on Joe Nevin from Bumps for Boomers describes Nevin's media strategy. When approached by media, he works with the resort to arrange complementary accommodation and ski passes. "Then in advance of them coming, we'll brief them on what we think are the key elements of the program. What's new and different, interesting story angles, something of interest," Nevin explains. "We have pre-arrival telephone conversations to find out their objectives, send out written material, and encourage them to go to the website to read about our techniques, demographics and the results of our customer service surveys." He can also provide photos or help them with staging them during their stay. "We try to deliver things on a silver platter to make their job and role very successful." He finds topnotch accommodation adjacent to the Bumps for Boomers meeting place for them, wines and dines them at Aspen's finest eateries, furnishes everything needed for a positive story and involves them in the propagation of his philosophy. He has an extensive media room accessible via the website. His greatest success came when an article on Bumps for Boomers was published in the New York Times. He saw an immediate spike in website hits having tracked the response through Google, which resulted in an increase in business.

Travel exhibitions and road shows

Many ski resorts and other industry organizations attend travel trade shows, exhibitions, or conventions. Generally, these occasions bring all parts of the ski industry (suppliers, carriers, intermediaries, and destination marketing organizations) together. Exhibiting at a trade show is similar to putting together a small promotional mix. Some exhibitors send out direct mail pieces (advertising) to intermediaries, inviting them to visit their booths. The booth displays (merchandising) portray the available services and may be tied in with recent advertising campaigns. Representatives working the booth hand out brochures and business cards and try to develop sales leads (personal selling). They may also give away free samples or vouchers (sales promotions). When the trade show is over, exhibitors often follow up with personalized mailings (direct mail) or telephone calls (telemarketing).

In the U.S., the largest industry trade show is the SnowSports Industries America's (SIA) Snow Show. The event brings together nearly 20,000 attendees from the industry. During the four-day trade show, over 1,000 brands present their collections for the following year. Representing over a $3.6 billion industry, more than 80 per cent of the industry's retail buying power attends to see product collections for the following snow sports season. The 2015 show also included 20 educational seminars covering five core tracks – State of the Industry, Production and Protection, The Challenges and Opportunities of the One Season Business, Social Media, and the Wealthy Retailer. In addition to the trade show, the event includes a two-day On-Snow Demo/Ski-Ride Fest, where the industry gathers to ski and ride while retailers and media test the gear and accessories they saw at the Show, including ski, snowboard , backcountry and cross country products. The 2015 On-Snow Demo/Ski-Ride Fest was held at Copper Mountain Resort.

The big trade show in the U.K. is the Telegraph Ski and Snowboard Show in London held in October every year. The show features live freestyle demonstrations, fashion shows, lessons for all abilities, après bars, live music, Olympic athletes and over 250 top brands, tour operators and chalet companies showcasing their wares. The show also includes a Mountain Talks Theatre sponsored by Kia Motors where in 2014 experts and celebrities - including former Olympic skier Martin Bell, Warren Smith, the coach from Channel 4's *The Jump*, and Winter Olympic slopestyle snowboarder Aimee Fuller - shared their advice and experiences. Visitors can also drop into the 'realtime video analysis booth', for a one-to-one consultation with a Warren Smith Ski Academy pro instructor. The instructors conduct a video analysis of technique on a ski training machine and give pointers on how to improve, all in real time. Visitors can see video overlays comparing their skiing with that of one of the pro team, demonstrating what they need to work on.

Hosting and sponsoring events

Ski resorts can also draw attention to themselves by arranging or sponsoring special events. This is discussed in detail in Chapter 9, but a good example of a ski region supporting a winter sports event is at the Winter Alpenglow Mountain Festival. The event takes place in North Lake Tahoe, normally in February, and includes clinics, presentations, films and equipment demos. Promoted as a community-focused event, participants also have the opportunity to Nordic ski, backcountry ski, snowshoe and enjoy natural history excursions. The festival is geared toward beginner and intermediate winter recreation enthusiasts, but offers a range of activities for all interests and ability levels, with most of the events being free. At the other end of the spectrum are the 'big-mountain' contests, such as the Extreme Freeskiing Championships. Some have argued that although such events do bring media attention, they appeal only to expert skiers, but the consensus seems to be that hosting these events is still a good PR opportunity. Crested Butte, Colorado was the first ski area in the U.S. to put on a big-mountain contest, and Scott Clarkson, the resort's vice president of sales and marketing says: "Hosting the Extremes gives you street cred with the core set. The event generates buzz that the core audience is receptive to; buzz that is largely benign to the destination vacationer. We can host a world-class event seamlessly for one audience while operating a world-class resort for the other" (Michelson, 2012).

Event sponsorship is the financial support of an event (e.g. a car race, a theatre performance, or a marathon road race) in return for advertising privileges associated with it. Sponsorships are usually offered by the organizer of the event on a tiered basis, which means that a lead sponsor pays a maximum amount and receives maximum privileges, whereas other sponsors pay less and receive fewer privileges. Investment in sponsorships is mainly divided among three areas: sports, entertainment, and cultural events. Sporting events attract the lion's share of sponsorship revenue. For example, the London 2012 Olympics attracted over £100 million from just the top four to six main sponsors. The sponsorship of events is an effective way of gaining publicity, as it allows the sponsor to invite and host suppliers, journalists, distributors and customers, as well as bring repeated attention to the company's name and products.

Cause-related marketing

Cause-related marketing (CRM), said to be corporate philanthropy organized to increase the bottom line (Barnes & Fitzgibbons, 1991), is a rapidly expanding trend in marketing communications, and is growing at a time when the public is increasingly cynical about big business. It is basically a marketing program that strives to achieve two objectives – improve corporate performance and help worthy causes – by linking fundraising for the benefit of a cause to the purchase of the firm's products and/or services. Companies use CRM to contribute to the well-being of society and to associate themselves with a respected cause that will reflect positively on their corporate image. Companies, and their brands, can benefit from strategic alignments with causes or with not-for-profit organizations. It is hoped the emotional attributes associated with cause-linked brands differentiate them from their rivals (sometimes referred to as 'cause branding').

CRM efforts can be categorized into autonomously branded, co-branded, house branded, and industry branded approaches (Hudson, 2008), the distinctive features of each being summarized in Table 7.2. Autonomously branded philanthropic collaborations are characterized by an arm's length relationship between the corporate sponsor's brand and the brand of the charity/cause that it supports. These are the quickest and easiest kind of relationships to arrange and are the dominant form of philanthropic activity. Mt. Bachelor in Oregon, for example, has Charity Ski Weeks whereby lift ticket vouchers are provided to several Charity Week partners that can be redeemed for $25 full day lift tickets. This offers a great deal for local skiers and riders while generating cash contributions with 100 per cent of the proceeds donated directly to the issuing non-profit organization.

7

Features	Autonomously branded	Co-branded	House branded	Industry branded
Charity reputation	Established/ independent of company	Tied to company and charity	Company dependent	Established/ independent of industry
Company's involvement in charity administration	None	Partial to jointly administered	Company controlled	None
Company control over charity use of funds raised by CRM Program	Limited	Some influence	Complete	Limited
Strategic opportunity	Leverage external brand	Leverage brand congruence	Support existing company/ product brand	Leverage industry brand
CRM promotional objective	Demonstrate firm-charity congruence where not obvious	Demonstrate firm-charity brand congruence	Promote firm's commitment	Promote industry's commitment

Table 7.2: Branding approaches to CRM (Source: Adapted from Hudson, 2008)

In co-branded collaborations, the company and the charity form a new brand co-sponsored and marketed by both organizations. An example of this type of branding approach is Avon's sponsorship of the *Race for the Cure* in partnership with the Breast Cancer Coalition. Collaborations of this type are more strategic than autonomously branded programs because the company can differentiate itself by becoming the sole sponsor of an event or cause, and because co-ownership implies increased commitment and effort. An example within the ski industry comes from New England, where Stowe Mountain Resort Ski and Snowboard School partners with Friends of Stowe Adaptive Sports, to put on an annual event called the Adaptive Ski Bash. Friends of Stowe is a non-profit organization that supports access to sports and recreational opportunities for people living with permanent disabilities.

With the house branded approach, the firm takes ownership of a cause and develops an entirely new organization to deliver benefits associated with the cause (Hoeffler & Keller, 2002). Similar to private label products, house branded charities are by definition differentiated from other charities, and in the increasingly crowded marketplace for philanthropic program partners, the firm has unfettered access to its own charity. Vail Resorts has its own house branded charity, setting up Vail Resort Echo in 2008 to bring a more focused approach to local charitable giving. Local leaders representing each division of the company are part of Giving Councils in each of the communities in which Vail operates. Together, these Councils work to identify key local organizations that are implementing successful programs that will change the lives of children and protect the resources that make the resort towns unique. The Giving Councils award cash grants and in-kind donations once a year through a grant application process.

Finally, industry branded initiatives are those that involve contributions to a cause from the industry as a whole, rather than separate corporations. As with house branded CRM initiatives, few examples exist in tourism, but the Travel Foundation in the U.K. fits this typology. The Travel Foundation was established in 2004 as a partnership between government, NGOs and the travel industry to acknowledge that tour operators have a responsibility to help protect the places that tourists visit and ensure that the benefits of tourism reach the local communities. The Travel Foundation is largely funded by the industry including a number of winter sport tourism operators.

Social media

Social media is discussed in detail in the next chapter, but platforms such as Facebook, YouTube and Twitter have emerged as important channels for generating earned media. As Susie English said in the opening Spotlight, media members now get many of their story ideas from social media, especially Twitter. Certainly, as consumers spend more time on social networks, decisions about what to purchase often reflect interactions with friends and other influencers. Ski travelers, in particular, are more inclined than other travelers to share their travel experiences via social media, especially those under 35 years of age.

Publications

Companies rely extensively on communication materials to reach and influence their target markets. Publications such as annual reports, brochures, and company newsletters and magazines can draw attention to a company and its products, and can help build the company's image and convey important news to target markets. Canadian Mountain Holidays, for example (see Spotlight in Chapter 10) published the first ever sustainability report for the heli-skiing sector in 2004 as a way of sharing successes and challenges and to increase accountability to staff, guests and other stakeholders. The report was updated with Volume 2 in 2007, and Volume 3 in 2010.

Audio-visual materials, such as films and DVDs, are also often used as promotion tools. Many destination marketing organizations use videos to promote their destinations (see Chapter 8), and some send promotional videos directly to consumers as well as to members of the travel trade. An example of such a promotional DVD is the one produced by Travel Alberta to promote the ski resorts in Banff National Park. Every year, a number of Hollywood celebrities gather in the Canadian Rockies for the Fairmont Banff Springs Sports Invitational, an annual fundraiser in support of the Waterkeeper's Alliance. Travel Alberta used the opportunity a few years ago to produce a DVD with the celebrities endorsing the ski areas. The video featured interviews with Robert F. Kennedy Jr., Alec Baldwin, Martin Sheen, and many others, all extoling the virtues of the skiing in Banff National Park.

Winning or sponsoring awards

In many industries, such as the car industry, it has become common practice for companies to promote their achievements. Automotive awards presented in magazines such as *Motor Trends* have long been known to carry clout with potential car buyers. The winning of awards has become increasingly important in tourism and hospitality sectors as well. For individual operators, the winning of an award is a campaign opportunity, a fact recognized by award winning ski resorts. Most of the awards in the ski industry promote best performance and are often an indication of quality. Winning organizations can therefore use the third-party endorsements in their advertising to build credibility and attract customers. They can therefore provide excellent publicity for winners. The case study in Chapter 11 on Scott Dunn Travel refers to the numerous awards that the company has won, including the Condé Nast Traveller Readers' Travel Award for Favorite Specialist Tour Operator in 2011 and 2104. Founder Andrew Dunn says awards give the company 'collateral for the next 12 months or so' for marketing, advertising and online clout.

In 1993, the National Ski Areas Association, the trade association for ski area owners and operators, established the Golden Eagle Awards for Environmental Excellence. These are the highest honors bestowed on a resort for environmental performance. *SKI* Magazine currently sponsors these awards and, in judging applications, the magazine places special emphasis on projects and initiatives that resonate with resort visitors such as green buildings, farm to table dining initiatives, and similar programs that are visible and tangible to guests during their visit. In 2014, *SKI* created a new award category called 'Hero of Sustainability'. A Hero of Sustainability is a ski area employee who goes the extra mile and makes an impact – big or small – that influences company policy, employee action, or resort guest action toward improved sustainability. The winner of the first award was Maura Olivos from Alta Ski Area in Utah, and the resort promoted the winning of this award on its Discover Alta website, Facebook page and via Twitter, amongst other communication channels. Alta's General Manager, Onno Wieringa said "through her persistent efforts, Maura has raised the bar on bringing environmental care into Alta's operations and serving as a valuable model for all departments of the ski area" (NSAA, 2014).

Maura Olivos

Celebrity endorsement

Encouraging celebrities to use or endorse tourism and hospitality products can result in considerable media coverage, and can therefore help to promote that particular product. Richard Branson built Virgin Atlantic Airways with the help of a strong public relations campaign that included inviting as many rock stars as possible to fly on his airline. Destinations, too, can benefit from celebrity endorsements. Vail Resorts, for example, has a sponsorship deal with Olympic gold medalist and World Alpine Ski Champion Lindsey Vonn. Vonn appears at select consumer events and ski shows in the U.S. and Europe, and promotes the popular Epic Season Pass, which offers skiing and snowboarding at all Vail Resorts. Vonn has also designed Ski Girls Rock, a premium lesson product that is exclusively for girls ages 7 to Teen at Vail Mountain. In 2014 in one PR initiative, Vonn went undercover as an employee at Vail in a video that went viral. With nearly 200,000 views it became the most watched video ever put out by Vail. In the video, Lindsey Vonn worked at the counter in a Vail office selling lift tickets with the entire day captured on hidden cameras.

A recent survey of U.K. social media users showed 33 per cent of all users follow celebrities (Pozin, 2014), but research has shown that celebrity endorsement is even more important in emerging markets, where a celebrity endorsement will strongly affect decisions to buy one brand over another (HSBC, 2010). Chapter 12 discusses how Tina Maze, the most successful female ski racer in Slovenian history, has been a great ambassador for skiing in Slovenia. Maze, who regularly wins on the World Cup circuit, is five-time winner of best Slovenian athlete, a fabulous fashion model and a pop star with Slovenia's most watched You Tube music video.

Product placement and branded entertainment

Product placement is the insertion of brand logos or branded merchandise into movies and television shows, and it is another promotional tactic available to marketers. Branded entertainment, on the other hand, is a relatively new term to describe a more contemporary, sophisticated use of product placement, and has been defined as *"the integration of advertising into entertainment content, whereby brands are embedded into storylines of a film, television program, or other entertainment medium"* (Hudson & Hudson, 2006, p. 492). In the area of tourism marketing, industry practitioners have primarily focused on the traditional use of product placement to reach target markets. Destinations, too, concentrate on product placement as an opportunity to gain exposure, aware that placing a destination in a film or television is the ultimate in tourism product placement (Morgan & Pritchard, 1998). Although tourism marketers have not traditionally incorporated an integrated branded entertainment approach, there are signs that some tourism organizations are moving away from traditional product placement, to strategic branded entertainment in order to attract tourists through the medium of film and television.

A good example of a branded entertainment initiative comes from Las Vegas, where it was no accident that the MGM's Aria Hotel played a central role in the 2013 movie *Last Vegas*. MGM strategically 'engineered' the movie to take place in its new hotel, a marketing ploy that benefited the Aria and the film directors, who both wanted to showcase the 'New Vegas'. The architecture depicted in the film had to feel hip, upscale and beyond the expectations of the four main characters in the movie, played by Robert DeNiro, Michael Douglas, Morgan Freeman and Kevin Kline (Mlife, 2013). More recently, Brand USA, the organization that promotes the U.S. internationally as a premier travel destination, used three media platforms to promote the country, partnering with television, film and digital content producers to present engaging stories that would attract international tourists (Hudson & Tung, 2015). One of those initiatives was a partnership with MacGillivray Freeman Films to produce a documentary film for IMAX and large-screen theatres. The $10 million movie, with the working title *America Wild: U.S. National Parks*, showcased the country's national parks.

Profile: John Brice, Combining PR with R'n'R

After a more traditional career in public relations, John Brice switched to snow sports in 2009 in order to further his personal goals of skiing more and eventually relocating during ski seasons to a ski area. Based in San Diego, California, his company, Snow Sports PR now represents snow sports gear manufacturers, mountain lodges, ski areas, heli-ski companies and snow sports trade associations.

John Brice

"In 2009, after years of doing concert publicity, making the fish taco famous over 17 years as the PR rep for Rubio's 'Home of the Fish Taco,' and even repping AT&T at the Republican National Convention in San Diego, I decided to follow a new passion and now persuade consumers to purchase snow sports gear and to travel to ski areas," says Brice, who has more recently changed the name of his business to Snow Sports PR from Brice & Associates, which he started in 1986.

Since the focus switch, Brice has won 'Best Public Relations Campaign' awards from the Utah Office of Tourism (2011) and Visit California (2009). Brice himself achieved another goal, by skiing 24 days last season. "And I hope to get more in next season - not bad for being San Diego-based," he says. "My family situation keeps me from living at a ski area during the season. When I am able to do that, I plan on tripling my ski days - or more. I love to ski and that is why I shifted the focus of my PR business to snow sports. I also love my Seirus schwag - nice gloves, hats and other accessories!"

But how has he managed this mid-career morph into the world of winter sports? Just like the process of learning to ski, success in the winter sports industry is all about passion and persistence, says Brice. When he started skiing at the age of 18, he tumbled off chairlifts and spent his first season falling over in order to slow his erratic descents. It was only when a friend pointed out the value of carved turning to address speed and stopping that he started to improve. "Now, I strongly recommend everyone start with professional lessons," he says. "It's a wonder I stuck with it - or a testimonial to how much fun skiing can be."

Harnessing his own passion for the sport after 25 years in journalism and PR, he set his sights on the winter sports industry. "I targeted a resort in Southern Utah, because I could drive there - and just kept calling and calling them to get my foot in the door," he explains. "I gave them a good deal and, that first season, delivered publicity ranging from the local paper to the *Washington Post*. I could not have done this out of the gate without my PR experience working for brands like Hyatt, Marriott, Hollywood Bowl and AT&T and as a print journalist."

With the huge influence of the Internet and social media, PR agencies have to work hard to keep up with both the amateur industry chatter and professional competition. "There are many other good PR people that work in snow sports and we don't allow each other to get lazy," says Brice. "I want to make sure I get my info to a journalist before the other PR person and do so as clearly and succinctly as possible. I know the journalists will have many options regarding what 'news' to put in their story."

Research is intrinsic to Brice's success. He uses studies from the National Ski Area Association to understand the demographics and motivations of winter sports participants. "It is a passion driven sport," he says. "Even before fully recovering from a lingering economic recession in the U.S., the nation in 2010/11 saw a record number of skier visits, according to the National Ski Area Association: 60.54 million visits." Although participants may spend less on après ski, they will still pay for lift tickets, Brice contends. And their passion for the sport is fueled by the growing number of multi-resort season passes and advancements in ski equipment, which make it easier to learn to ski and to improve.

The 'Now Generation' – Millenials who expect instant gratification at the press of a button or click of a mouse – is impacting the snow sports industry as well as affecting Brice's *modus operandi*. "The news cycle is now 24/7 – even in snow sports," he points out. "So a snow sports publicist is not just pitching the Sunday travel section or the monthly issue of SKI Magazine. I am constantly pitching opportunities and it seems like every day there is a new app or social media tool that helps me know – and reach – my editorial targets more efficiently. What has remained a constant is that you still need to provide accurate info or you will burn bridges with journalists."

For the future, Brice is concerned about baby boomers aging off the mountain and young replacements being put off by the increasing expense barriers to entry: "Lift tickets, equipment, lessons, travel to the mountain, possibly lodging, and the incredible number of other options for spending one's leisure time."

Meanwhile he is concentrating on publicizing high quality products and companies such as Seirus Innovation, a global leader in winter sports accessories including heated gloves and mittens. It is co-owned by Salt Lake City's Joe Edwards and past chairman of the SnowSports Industries America (and current CBS TV football analyst), Mike Carey. Snow Sport PR also represents Arizona Snowbowl and Ski Lift Lodge, Southern Utah's Eagle Point and Nevada's Ruby Mountains Heli-Experience.

Committed to promoting ski and snowboard education, Brice is also a public relations specialist for the Learn to Ski and Snowboard Month/Bring a Friend Program, the gateway for 500,000 introductions to snow sports over the past six seasons. "This program is supported by both National Ski Area Association and Snowsports Industries America making LSSM/BAF the biggest organized recruiting program in the snow sports industry," he says. At the end of the day, he thinks skiing well is one of the best motivators to stick with the sport.

Sources: Interview with John Brice, September 2014; snowsportspr.com; Brice is on Twitter @ SnowSportScribe

Measuring the impact of public relations efforts

The application of evaluation research remains low in public relations, with practitioners most commonly citing lack of budget and lack of time as the main reasons for not undertaking research. However, Macnamara (1999) suggests that even if adequate budget and time were available, many practitioners would still not be able to undertake either evaluative or formative research, due to lack of knowledge of the research process. He has proposed a Macro Model of PR Evaluation that breaks PR activity into three stages. The model has been adapted in Figure 7.2 to include social media, and suggests that each PR project or program is constructed from a series of inputs; outputs are then produced; and finally outcomes are achieved.

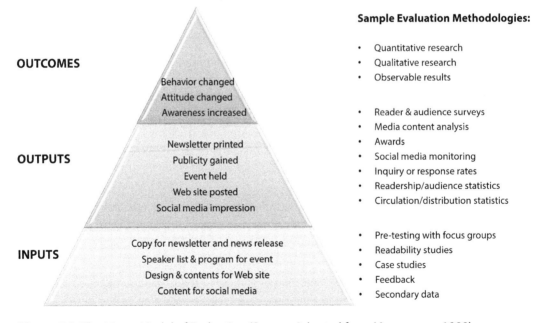

Figure 7.2: The Macro Model of Evaluation (Source: Adapted from Macnamara, 1999)

Inputs include the story list and copy for a newsletter or blog, information for a news release, Tweets, speaker list and program for an event and design and contents for a website. Outputs are the physical communication materials or activities produced such as printed publications, news releases, DVDs, events, or social media activity. Finally, outcomes typically sought in public relations are increased awareness, attitudinal change or behavioral change. The list of evaluation methods shown in Figure 7.2 is far from exhaustive but illustrates that a range of techniques, tools, and research instruments is available to evaluate inputs, outputs and outcomes. The most common is media monitoring, and social media monitoring has recently joined the evaluation of press clippings and media broadcasts under this umbrella. Advertising value equivalency (AVE) is another often used technique to measure PR value, although the method has come under fire in recent years (Likely & Watson, 2013). The Lake Tahoe Visitor's Authority (LVTA) uses such a method to evaluate its PR initiatives. The LVTA retains Weidinger Public Relations (WPR) to execute a comprehensive national and regional media communications plan, and in 2012-13 advertising equivalency reached 5-10 times the LTVA's PR budget investment, translating into $1.5 million value and a circulation of 51 million readers. Table 7.3 below lists some of those PR initiatives and the resulting exposure (LTVA, 2013).

PR initiative	Outcome
Cover story on *Sunset Magazine*'s August "Local's Guide to Lake Tahoe"	Circulation of 1.2M
"Tahoe South Guys/Girls" video that reinforces the brand and various passions	Generated more than 58,200 views via First Track Productions' YouTube Channel
Forbes.com "Greatest sports party on the planet? Celebrity pro athletes think so"	Media exposure value of $67,800 (10M monthly unique visitors)
LTVA hosted a pre-trip for the North American Snowsports Journalist Association with 18 ski writers from across the US	Stories anticipated to run in the following season
GQ Magazine included Harveys, Opal, Red Hut and Tamarack Lodge	Circulation of 824,000
FORE Magazine article on how to ski and golf in the same day "Up the slope and down the fairway"	Circulation of 160,000
Operation Sierra Storm (OSSO) Meteorologist Conference held Jan. 9-12. LTVA and partners hosted 10-12 meteorologists from regional and direct flight markets to conduct live and taped broadcasts from the mountain	Resulted in real-time exposure of early ski season conditions as best in the country while reinforcing the Tahoe South brand. The 2014 OSS event generated Tahoe 48 broadcast stories valued at $2M in media exposure with a potential reach of 45 M national viewers
"Covered in Color" in *Contra Costa Times*; *Harrisburg Magazine* and *Bleecher Report Magazine* - both resulted from Golf the High Sierra Media Tour and South Bay Accent "The New Tahoe" includes Sierra-at-Tahoe, Heavenly and Kirkwood	Circulation of 174,000 for *Contra Costa Times* Circulation of 1.2M for *Harrisburg Magazine* and *Bleecher Report Magazine*
North American Snowsports Journalists Assoc. March 2012 Conference	Circulation 9M; media exposure $165,000+

Table 7.3: Lake Tahoe Visitor's Authority PR initiatives in 2012-13

One problem with both media monitoring and advertising equivalency is that they tend not to measure the quality of coverage. Media content analysis is therefore employed at times to evaluate qualitative criteria such as whether media coverage reaches key target audiences, whether it focuses on the main issues, and whether it contains the organization's message. Often PR specialists will calculate a publicity value as well as advertising value equivalency. Such publicity value is defined in the industry to be a multiplication of three times the advertising value, and may reflect either positive or negative publicity as indicated by Slant. Slant is a subjective evaluation of an article, typically using a table of 10 with 5 as neutral and 1-4 slant trending from 'very negative to 'negative'; and 6-10 trending 'positive' to 'very positive'.

Most practitioners in the industry are aware that return on investment for earned media, although difficult to calculate, is worth the effort. Sandy Best, former Director of Public Relations for Lake Louise in Canada, says: 'It's the most cost-effective form of marketing you can do. If you look at dollar per column length, if I had to buy that, it would be 10 times what it costs to look after the media.' At Lake Louise, he encouraged and conducted numerous media visits as well as travel industry FAM trips every year at the resort. One of his 'party tricks' for visiting journalists was to greet them in their own language. 'I speak reasonable Mandarin so the Chinese are always amazed when I say hello and welcome. I can welcome almost every nationality in their language,' he says.

Measuring the impact of social media campaigns will be discussed further in Chapter 8, but certainly it is a new science. Brands that conduct social media interactions with consumers in a meaningful way are beginning to see a positive return (Cruz & Mendelsohn, 2010), but there are too few research studies that can support this claim. The Profile of John Brice above exemplifies how the social media trend has had impact upon how he conducts his PR business. Figure 7.3 shows the difference between measuring traditional media and social media from a PR perspective according to Ketchum Global Research & Analytics.

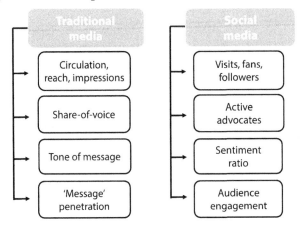

Figure 7.3: Measuring traditional media and social media from a PR perspective (Source: Adapted from Ketchum, 2013)

Troy Thompson, owner and consultant at Travel 2.0 Consulting, refers to a 'trip echo effect' to describe the influence of social media (Thompson, 2010). He suggests that destinations should measure the value of a visitor by social value, not necessarily by economic value. Some visitors may spend more, but have less influence or communication channels to share the experience. A visitor who spends less may communicate more, directly impacting numerous potential visitors. The updates and messages from the engaged visitor create a larger echo within his/her network. Those consumers who are engaged will have a greater influence over a larger number of potential visitors than those who are not.

Some organizations are using tools that show them the influence that online consumers wield with their words. A recent survey of U.S., European, and Asian companies found that 23 per cent used social media analytics tools in order to identify and reward key influencers (Birkner, 2011). Palms Hotel and Casino in Las Vegas, for example, mines online data to give amenities and discounts to customers with the best social media footprint. Quasar Expeditions, a luxury cruise operator, similarly studies its Facebook page to find fans who have posted the most photos and positive comments, and then offers them discounts on future trips. Marketers also use free online tools such as Social Mention to locate brand mentions in social media, and online subscriber services like Klout to find and evaluate individuals based on their value as an online influencer. Klout scores, which range from one to 100, with higher scores representing a wider and stronger sphere of influence, are based on list memberships, message reach, unique Twitter and Facebook mentions and messages re-Tweeted. Influencers are sorted by topic on the Klout site so companies can connect with people who can influence for them.

Finally, how should marketers be measuring the effectiveness of product placement branded entertainment? In a recent study of practitioners' attitudes towards these practices, Um & Kim (2014) found a fair degree of skepticism about the ability to gauge the effect on viewers from a single branded entertainment initiative. For the practice of product placement, academics suggest that message impact should be assessed at recall, persuasion, and behavioral levels (Balasubramanian, 1994). Amongst practitioners, measuring placement's effectiveness is still a rough-and-ready art, but unaided recall and brand recognition are the two most popular means of assessing placements (Karrh, McGee & Pardun, 2003). However, a recent study by Hang (2014) suggests that brand recall/recognition alone may underestimate brand placement impact, and that marketers should use multiple methods to measure branded entertainment effectiveness.

Among the more original measurement tools is that of Rentrak Branded Entertainment, a U.S.-based specialist in branded entertainment measurement. Rentrak's measurement method allows real-time measurement of an integration's effectiveness on the basis of 19 different treatment levels. Rentrak produces a proprietary Media-Q and associated integration value that compares the effectiveness of the integrations to a traditional 30-second advertisement where a

Media-Q of 1.0 is equivalent to the value of a 30-second spot. The evaluation also includes a best-practices qualitative review of the integration and suggestions as to how the integration can be enhanced upon. That being said, there are still some critics who question the high investment that branded entertainment requires, and it is critical that a more formalized measurement model be established to allow accountability (Russell & Belch, 2005; Um & Kim, 2014).

Case study: 007 puts the spotlight on Sölden, Austria

ice Q Restaurant. Photo courtesy of www.skiresort.info

Since 1962 James Bond movies have been introducing viewers to seductive locations all over the world, inspiring travel. The latest of these is Sölden, Austria, which was well placed to become the most famous ski resort in the world when the crew and cast from the 24th James Bond movie, *Spectre*, arrived during the 2014/15 ski season to shoot action scenes.

In a Pinewood Studios press conference in December 2014, the 007 Director, Sam Mendes announced the filming locations which included London, Rome, Mexico City, Tangier and Sölden. "We are bringing Bond back to the Alps, back to the snow – to Sölden in Austria," Mendes said. Since it was way back in 1977 that an Austrian ski chase was featured in the iconic *Spy Who Loved Me* movie, there was considerable media attention focused on Sölden.

This is the largest film production ever to be made in the Tirol, bringing immediate economic gains, long-term media impacts and film-tourism opportunities. Hosting the film meant a production office had to be set up in the quaint town with a team of 500 people involved, including 150 local filmmakers in various capacities, and 22 filming days. Scouts had pinpointed Sölden because of its dramatic scenery and also the deluxe restaurant ice Q. Filming was scheduled for December 2014 to February 2015.

In an article for Cine Tirol (the area's Film Commission Department), it was estimated that the economic impact for the area would be huge: "Taking into account production costs, with accommodation and meals, as well as transportation, accommodation and salaries of the local Tirolean filmmakers it is estimated that 6 million Euros will be spent in Tirol. The impact alone on tourism is incredible: about 26,000 overnight stays will be generated by the film crew in Tirol. Furthermore, the filming of this movie will generate major media attention at an international level and also create future film-tourism opportunities for the Ötztal and lesser-known East Tirol region."

The Grünwald Resort in Sölden jumped on the Bond bandwagon for promotional purposes, advertising holidays during the filming period with a strong emphasis on potential Daniel Craig sightings. The website spiel read: "book your ski holiday now and with any luck you might see the secret agent. The team at Grünwald Resort will be happy to send you a non-binding quote for your stay directly on the ski piste" with a link to the Bond press release and estimated filming times and locations.

One of the reasons Sölden was so perfect for the movie was ice Q restaurant, launched in December 2013 by the Bergbahnen Sölden Lift Company on the Gaislachkogl, the area's premier ski mountain. Linked to the peak by a suspension bridge (ideal for death-defying drama), it features ultra modern glass architecture, constructed from local materials – and, of course, gourmet food. The Sölden website calls ice Q a culinary summit and "a multi-functional and absolute barrier-free gourmet temple at 3,048 meters above sea level". It has a panoramic rooftop terrace as well as glass facades. The website reads: "The entire building seems to be transparent and fits perfectly into its natural surroundings. Together with the top station of the three-rope mountain gondola it ranks among Tirol's undisputed highlights when it comes to architectural masterpieces in ski areas."

Other factors that made the *Spectre* scouts choose Sölden included its unique glacier location and accessibility. "The easy logistics - transport of the material - was crucial for the choice of the location," says Christina Ruhfass, Tourism Marketing Executive for Tirol Werbung GmbH. "Direct access via the glacier road to the glacier ski resort, helicopter landing spot at the glacier ski resort, and big gondolas to the ice Q restaurant."

The Sölden website included an announcement about the film, with an apology for any restricted usages during filming which might have disturbed typical skiing and snowboarding activities. They also posted behind-the-scenes footage of *Spectre* - showing Daniel Craig firing a shot and running towards a burning vehicle in the snow - with links to Facebook, Twitter and Instagram. This teaser – the very first footage released from filming - was also aired on the 007 website along with interviews with Sam Mendes, news about each filming location and a *Spectre* poster available for purchase.

When the 'featurette' was unveiled in February 2015, it sparked a media frenzy with newspapers such as the U.K.'s *Telegraph* raving about the "tantalizing glimpse" of a cable car sequence. The *Telegraph* quotes associate producer, Gregg Wilson as saying: "This is going to be one of the major action sequences of the movie, a jewel in the crown so to speak. It's going to be spectacular and Austria seemed to offer everything that we needed to pull it off." The article also included photos of iconic ice Q restaurant and the cable car.

While information was kept to a minimum during actual filming, the Ötztal Tourism Board planned to position itself as a "James Bond Location" from the following season onwards as well as before, during and after the release of the movie. "They would like to use it for marketing and press activities," says Ruhfass. "It's the aim of the Ötztal Tourism Board, besides an increase of overnights with added value, to use the reputation of the James Bond movie to gain more film projects to the Ötztal valleys in Tirol." Cine Tirol offers free location services to filmmakers.

Spectre was scheduled for release on November 6, 2015, a great pre-season advertisement for Sölden with all the ongoing advantages of being featured so prominently in such a high profile film.

Sources: www.gruenwald-resort.com/news-neuigkeiten-soelden/James-Bond-Soelden/; www.telegraph.co.uk/travel/snowandski/features/11304171/James-Bond-film-locations-Solden-gears-up-for-the-new-007-film.html; www.telegraph.co.uk/culture/film/jamesbond/11407578/Spectre-watch-first-footage-of-new-Bond-film-shot-in-Austria.html; www.smithsonianmag.com/travel/marking-50-years-of-luxurious-travel-with-james-bond-115668572/?no-ist; www.cinetirol.com/en/released/james-bond-in-tirol-2503736.html

References

Balasubramanian, S.K. (1994) 'Beyond advertising and publicity: hybrid messages and public policy issues', *Journal of Advertising*, **23**(4), 29-47.

Barnes, N. G. and Fitzgibbons, D. (1991) 'Is cause-related marketing in your future?' *Business Forum*, **16**(4), 20.

Birkner, C. (2011, March 2) 'Sharing the LOVE', *Marketing News*, 20-21. The American Marketing Association, Chicago, IL.

Cruz, B. and Mendelsohn, J. (2010) 'Why social media matters to your business', Chadwick Martin Bailey, accessed 12/19/2014 from http://www.cmbinfo.com/cmb-cms/wp-content/uploads/2010/04/Why_Social_Media_Matters_2010.pdf

Hang, H. (2014) 'Brand-placement effectiveness and competitive interface in entertainment media', *Journal of Advertising Research*, **54**(2), 192-199.

Hoeffler, S. and Keller, K.L. (2002) 'Building brand equity through corporate societal marketing', *Journal of Public Policy & Marketing*, **21**(1), 84.

HSBC (2010) *Golf's 2020 Vision*. The HSBC Report.

Hudson, S. (2008) *Tourism and Hospitality Marketing: A Global Perspective.* London: Sage.

Hudson, S. and Hudson, D. (2006) 'Branded entertainment: A new advertising technique, or product placement in disguise?' *Journal of Marketing Management*, 22(5-6), 489-504.

Hudson, S. and Tung, V.W.S. (2015) 'Appealing to tourists via branded entertainment. From theory to practice', *Journal of Travel & Tourism Marketing*. Online first: http://dx.doi.org/10.1080/10548408.2015.1008671

Karrh, J.A., McKee, K.B. and Pardun, C.J. (2003) 'Practitioners' evolving views on product placement effectiveness', *Journal of Advertising Research*, **43**(2), 138-49.

Ketchum (2013) 'The principles of PR measurement', presented by Ketchum Global Research & Analytics, accessed 02/07/2015 from http://www.ketchum.com/principles-measurement

Lake Tahoe Visitor's Authority (2013) *Annual Report 2012-13*, accessed 02/04/2015 from http://ltva.org/ltva/docs/LTVA_Annual_Report_2012-2013.pdf

Likely, F. and Watson, T. (2013) 'Measuring the edifice: Public relations measurement and evaluation practices over the course of 40 years', In K. Sriramesh, A. Zerfass and J-N. Kim (Eds.), *Public Relations and Communication Management: Current Trends and Emerging Topics*, (pp. 143-162). New York: Routledge.

Lutz, D. (2014) 'Organizing a Successful Press FamTrip', *Hotel Executive*, accessed 02/02/2015 from http://hotelexecutive.com/business_review/841/organizing-a-successful-press-famtrip

Macnamara, J. R. (1999) 'Research in public relations: A review of the use of evaluation and formative research', *Asia Pacific Public Relations Journal*, **1**(2), 107-134.

Michelson, M. (2012) 'The business of big-mountain contests', *xgames.espn.com*, accessed 02/02/2015 from http://xgames.espn.go.com/skiing/article/7428617/are-big-mountain-contests-good-ski-resort-business

Mlife (2013) Lights! Camera! Aria! *Mlife*, **11**(4), 72-76.

Morgan, N. and Pritchard, A. (1998) *Tourism Promotion and Power – Creating Images, Creating Identities*. Chichester, UK: John Wiley & Sons.

Morrison, A. M. (2002) *Hospitality and Travel Marketing* (3rd ed.). Albany, NY: Delmar Thomson Learning.

Pozin, I. (2014) '5 measurements for PR ROI', Forbes.com, accessed 02/13/2015 from http://www.forbes.com/sites/ilyapozin/2014/05/29/5-measurements-for-pr-roi/

NSAA (2014) 'Ski industry releases annual environmental report',

29 September, accessed 02/02/2015 from http://www.nsaa.org/press/press-releases/ski-industry-releases-annual-environmental-report/

Russell, C.A. and Belch, M. (2005) 'A managerial investigation into the product placement industry', *Journal of Advertising Research*, **45**(1), 73-92.

Thompson, T. (2010, August 5) *A New Destination Marketing Organization Strategy Involving the Tripecho*, accessed 09/06/2011 from http://www.tnooz.com/2010/08/05/news/a-new-destination-marketing-organization-strategy-involving-the-tripecho/

Um, N-H. and Kim, S. (2014) 'Practitioners' perspectives on branded entertainment in the United States', *Journal of Promotion Management*, **20**(2), 164-180.

Utah Office of Tourism (2014) 'UTAH Office of Tourism, 2013 Overview', accessed 02/02/2015 from http://business.utah.gov/publications/utah-office-tourism-2/

8 The Impact of Technology on Winter Sport Tourism

Matt Mosteller

When you think of ski resort personnel, you imagine them skiing into work each day, sitting at their desks in ski gear and zooming off for a powder rather than power lunch. This is not the case, though, for many corporate staff who work for the bigger ski areas. They are often based in major cities like Calgary or Denver, as far away from the action as most of their regional visitors. As Senior Vice President, Marketing, Sales & Resort Experience, for Resorts of the Canadian Rockies, Matt Mosteller – aka Powder Matt – is one of these corporate commuters. "Most of us working here at RCR Calgary office work in a building that was originally a music store," Mosteller says. "Now the only music that is played is the sound-track from the various Dylan Siggers and Kalum Ko videos that are sharing loads of powder skiing and snowboarding eye candy."

Don't feel too sorry for powder lover and ski blogger, Mosteller though – his is a roving position and he gets plenty of time to plough the pow in the six resorts – Nakiska, Fernie, Kimberley, Kicking Horse, Stoneham and Mont Sainte Anne – under the RCR umbrella. To keep fit while at his Calgary desk, he bikes even in winter and sometimes skis to work.

Powder Matt's love affair with skiing started at the age of four when he vowed to enjoy and share the incredible attributes of winter sports throughout his life. These attributes include everything, he says, from "the special bond, to the benefits of spending time outdoors, to the thrill of floating through fluffy weightless and effortless powder on a bluebird day in the Canadian Rockies."

After graduating from the University of Washington in English with a marketing focus, Mosteller majored in ski bumming throughout the mountains of Washington, Idaho, Colorado, Montana and his favorite destination, British Columbia. It was this ski resort internship that refined his philosophy on finding the perfect work/play mix: "Being a ski bum taught me many lessons in life – respect and treat everyone with kindness as you never know when you might need a place to stay or a meal," he says. Lesson two was laugh lots and maintain a positive attitude in all relationships. "Also, build trust into everything you do – heck even ski bums can work at banks and you can't if you make a mistake. Go ahead and give it a try – life is built on learning," he adds. But, most of all, his mantra is to stay healthy, get outdoors as often as possible and experience nature. All these facets are intrinsic to a positive brand, he concludes.

He worked his way up the ski management ladder, starting first as ski school director at White-fish, Montana in 1991, moving on to manager of guest experience and then relocating to Kimberley, BC, Canada to work as VP Marketing in the real estate division of RCR from 1998-2001.

These days he channels his love of the outdoors, humor, positivity and enthusiasm for skiing in his prolific use of social media. "Everything is social now – the critical aspect is being authentic, be creative, and share, share, share," he explains. He warns against the possibility of over-promising and under-delivering, though, and is insistent on listening to and learning from guest experiences. "One of the key changes is the ability to really scan and aggregate the social intelligence and understand more about your brand's klout, the behaviors of your guests and their interests," he says. With RCR Mosteller uses Facebook, Twitter, YouTube and Flickr to disperse information and garner valuable feedback. And, as Powder Matt, he blogs regularly year round on mountain conditions, events, activities and fitness, linking with a veritable menu of social media including Facebook, Twitter, Linkedin, Google+, email, Reddit, Wordpress, Pinterest, Tumblr and StumbleUpon.

Mosteller says that social media is no longer just a simple update on snow reports or sharing web cam images. It has taken on the secondary role of guest relations. "It provides the critical immediate voice of customer which is so important to delivering service excellence," he explains. "As the guest depends on real time updates to decide on where they are skiing, that day, next week or for their annual vacation, it plays a critical role in your communication plan and social media must be integrated into your marketing plan to really turn up the dial on effectiveness – depth, breadth and reach with the market."

In order for social media to be consumed in a meaningful way, it has to be accurate, fun and, above all, an authentic voice. "We started one of the earliest blogs, PowderMatt.com, and it has really taken off both as a communication tool, so your more core guests have a place to get those nuggets of updates on summer capital work, or new trails etc., but also the vacation guests enjoy hearing the real grit and inspiration of real mountain town goings-on," Mosteller explains.

Mosteller's positive philosophy extends to rival resorts which he sees as industry partners, who work together to grow the sport, rather than competition. The real challenges lie, he thinks, in global factors which are beyond the everyday remit of ski resort staff: "Airline capacity, exchange rates, and global unrest and how much things out of your control can have an effect on tourism," he explains.

Mosteller's job has included hosting the Hollywood cast of the blockbuster movie *Inception* at Nakiska Ski Resort where he skied with Leonardo DiCaprio's crew. But he says *all* the wonderful people he gets to ski with are famous to him. For the future he recommends maintaining skiing's original authenticity but at the same time leveraging the energy and innovation of the new people within the industry. Snowboarding has been a dynamic game changer, he says, stimulating ski companies to refine their products and positioning. "Now we see all mountain, freeski, big mountain, and ski touring all on a growth trend," he adds.

Multi-tasking Mosteller is also a ski columnist for Canadian publications, an author - *Adventurer's Guide to Living a Happy Life* – and an outdoor adventurer: "In January 2011 my wife and I competed in what some say is the world's toughest winter adventure race, 'The Yukon Challenge' - over 1600 miles from Whitehorse to Tuktoyaktuk, Northwest Territories, with 10 events including snowshoeing, dog-sledding, running and climbing."

Sources: Interview with Matt Mosteller, November 2014; http://powdermatt.com/; https://www.linkedin.com/profile/view?id=88957432&trk=nav_responsive_tab_profile ; www.skircr.com/

The impact of technology on marketing communications

We are witnessing a rapidly changing communications environment dominated by digital technology. To illustrate how quickly technology is advancing, take the example of Steven Spielberg's sci-fi thriller *Minority Report.* In 1999, the director convened a three-day think tank to gather insights from 23 top futurists for the making of the movie, which depicted the world of 2054. The goal was to create a realistic view of a plausible future 50 years ahead. Projecting out from the present day's marketing and media technologies, Spielberg depicted an advertising-saturated society where billboards call out to passers-by on a first-name basis, cereal boxes broadcast animated commercials, newspapers deliver news instantly over a broadband wireless network, holographic hosts greet customers by name at retail stores, and where biometric retina scans deduct the cost of goods instantly from bank accounts (Mathieson, 2002). The technologies portrayed in the film were far from science fiction, and today many are in use or are in development – an indication of the rapid pace of technological change.

Technology and the Internet have fundamentally altered the way the world interacts and communicates. Traditional approaches to branding that put emphasis on mass media techniques are less and less effective in a marketplace where customers have access to massive amounts of information about brands, product and companies and in which social networks have, in some cases, supplanted brand networks (Keller, 2009). In the new media environment, consumers are increasingly in control. Not only do they have more choices of media to use, they also have a choice about whether and how they want to receive commercial content. In response marketers are employing more varied marketing communications techniques than ever before – see the Powder Matt Snapshot above for examples. Table 1 summarizes some of the interactive marketing communication options that are now available.

Website	Companies must design websites that express their purpose, vision, products and history. A key challenge is to design a site that is attractive enough on first viewing and continue to raise people's interest to repeat visit. Dedicated websites for mobile devices are on the increase.
Mobile Marketing	Mobile marketing will become increasingly important. Particularly, smartphone use is growing amongst travelers.
Social Media	Companies are embracing social media because of its potential for collaboration and engagement with consumers. Social media advertising will yield relatively stronger results due to its ability to tightly target audiences based on social media activity.
Display Ads	Display ads are small, rectangular boxes with text and perhaps a picture that companies pay to place on certain websites. The larger the reader, the more the placement costs.
Internet-Specific Ads and Videos	With user-generated content sites (i.e. YouTube, Google Video, MySpace Video), consumers and marketers can upload ads and videos to be shared virally by millions of people.
E-mail	Email uses only a fraction of the cost of a 'd-mail', or direct mail campaign. Three times more effective in prompting purchases than social media.
Blogs	Blogs are commonly maintained by an individual with regular entries of commentary, description of events, or other material such as graphics or video. Most blogs with high quality are interactive, which allows visitors to leave comments and even message each other.
Microsites	A microsite is a limited area on the web managed and paid for by an external advertiser. A microsite is an Internet web design term referring to an individual web page or a small cluster (around 1 to 7) of pages which are meant to function as a discrete entity within an existing website or to complement an offline activity.
Search Ads	Paid-search or pay-per-click ads, represent 40% of all on-line ads. 35% of all searches are reportedly for products or services. The search terms serve as a proxy for the consumer's consumption interests and trigger relevant links to product or service offerings alongside search results from Google, MSN and Yahoo! Advertisers pay only if people click on the links.
Virtual Reality	Destination marketing using virtual reality is gathering momentum.
Online brand Communities	Many firms sponsor on-line communities whose members communicate via postings, chat discussions and instant messaging about special interest related to the firm's products and brands.

Table 8.1: Digital marketing communications options (Source: Adapted from Keller, 2009, p. 147)

One relatively new method of communication added to this list is virtual reality, computer-generated simulation of an environment that can be interacted with in a seemingly real or physical way by a person using special electronic equipment, such as a helmet with a screen inside or gloves fitted with sensors. Destination marketing using virtual reality is gathering momentum. British Columbia in Canada was one of the first destinations to use virtual reality for tourism marketing, providing trade, media partners and end consumers with a new and unique way to experience the province from their desk chairs. "As the headsets become more widely available to consumers, virtual reality gives them a 360-degree experience – immersing them in the extraordinary travel opportunities that British Columbia offers, from raw wilderness to refined cities," said Marsha Walden, CEO of Destination British Columbia (Rellihan, 2015). While the Destination BC virtual-reality experience was developed for the Oculus Rift headset, it can be transferred to other technologies as they become available. Samsung's virtual-reality headset, Gear VR, is the first virtual reality headset available to consumers; it costs $200.

In a less sophisticated 2013/14 campaign, Monarch Airlines in the U.K. created a 360-degree virtual reality guide to ski resorts served by the airline. As part of a direct marketing campaign by marketing agency WDMP, consumers were 'transported' to a virtual ski slope, with high quality graphics and a 360-degree 'Photosphere' view complete with realistic falling snow and sound. Navigation around the mountain was possible by moving and tilting a smartphone or tablet to travel around and access new areas. By touching icons, consumers could visit each of the ski resorts accessible via Monarch's routes. Users could also watch ski tip videos from the Ski Club of Great Britain, access the latest snow reports, and enter a 'Postcard' competition to win free flights. This encouraged sharing of the campaign by 'posting' a virtual, personalized postcard to friends via social media.

Certainly, to communicate effectively and efficiently, tourism marketers have to go where the consumers are – and this is increasingly online. Skiers, in particular, are much more digitally engaged than U.S. travelers in general (Phocuswright, 2013). The Internet is moving marketers much closer to one-to-one marketing. The web not only offers merchants the ability to communicate instantly with each customer, but it also allows the customer to talk back, and that makes it possible for companies to customize offers and services. The Internet also allows organizations to provide 7-day, 24-hour service response. In fact, the main reason consumers have adopted the Internet is that it enables them to shop 24/7 in the comfort of their home with no time zone worries. Ease of navigation is then the primary reason for variations in purchase decisions between different online products.

8

The new consumer decision journey

The Internet has also upended how consumers engage with brands to the extent that consumers are promiscuous in their brand relationships (Edelman, 2010). They connect with myriad brands through new media channels often beyond the marketer's familiarity or control. In the past, marketing strategies emphasized brand awareness and ultimate purchase. However, after purchase, consumers may remain aggressively engaged, actively promoting or assailing the products they have bought, and collaborating in the brand's development. The touch points when consumers are most open to influence have changed, requiring a major adjustment to realign marketers' strategy and budgets with where consumers are actually spending their time. Court et al. (2009) have developed a new model of consumer decision-making (see Figure 8.1).

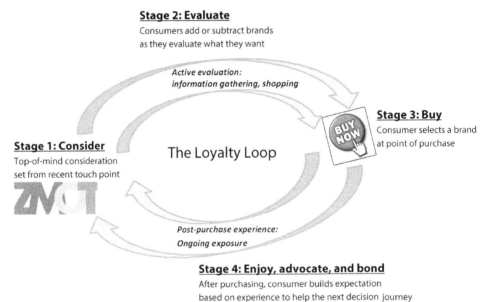

Stage 2: Evaluate
Consumers add or subtract brands
as they evaluate what they want

Active evaluation:
information gathering, shopping

Stage 3: Buy
Consumer selects a brand
at point of purchase

The Loyalty Loop

Stage 1: Consider
Top-of-mind consideration
set from recent touch point

Post-purchase experience:
Ongoing exposure

Stage 4: Enjoy, advocate, and bond
After purchasing, consumer builds expectation
based on experience to help the next decision journey

Figure 8.1: The new consumer decision journey (Source: Adapted from Court et al., 2009)

They developed their model from a study of the purchase decisions of nearly 20,000 consumers across five industries and three continents. Their research revealed that rather than systematically narrowing their choices until they had decided what to buy, consumers add and subtract brands from a group under consideration during an extended evaluation stage. After purchase, they often enter into an open-ended relationship with the brand, sharing their experience with it online through social media.

The four stages of the consumer decision journey are: a) consider; b) evaluate; c) buy; and d) enjoy, advocate and bond. New media make the 'evaluate' and 'advocate' stages increasingly relevant. Consumers' outreach to marketers and other sources of information is much more likely to shape their ensuing choices than marketers' efforts to persuade them. An addition to the original model is the 'Zero Moment of Truth' (ZMOT). Online marketers have coined this term to describe the new reality where marketers have to compete for shoppers' attention online long before a purchase decision is made (Lecinski, 2011).

Ski travelers rely on a range of information sources when comparing and choosing travel products for their ski trips, but online information sources – including websites and apps – dominate the ski travel shopping process (Phocuswright, 2013). Websites via computer are by far the leading source of information for ski trip shopping; seven in 10 ski trips are planned using this channel. Companies must design websites that express their purpose, vision, products and history. A key challenge is to design a site that is attractive enough on first viewing and continues to raise people's interest to repeat visit. Ski resorts will often work with web design specialists to create their websites. In 2014, Ski Vermont worked with both Methodikal, Inc. and Eternity Web to create its new website designed to be easy to use on mobile phones, tablets and desk top computers. The new platform allowed resorts and in-house bloggers to share more stories, videos and photos, and was designed to integrate smoothly with Ski and Ride Vermont's social media platforms. "We are really excited about using local talent at Methodikal, Inc. and Eternity Web to create a fully responsive design that is not only beautiful, but highly functional," said Ski Vermont's Director of Marketing, Kyle Lewis. One feature of the new website was content from Ski Vermont's family ski and ride experts, the All Mountain Mamas (see Figure 8.2).

Figure 8.2: Ski Vermont's All Mountain Mamas web page

Despite the increasing importance of social media, it is important to recognize that at the early stages of the consumer decision journey, email remains a significantly more effective way to acquire customers than social media - nearly 40 times that of Facebook and Twitter combined (see Figure 8.3). According to

McKinsey & Company, this is because 91 per cent of all U.S. consumers still use email daily, and the rate at which emails prompt purchases is not only estimated to be at least three times that of social media, but the average order value is also 17 per cent higher (Aufreiter, Boudet & Weng, 2014). This does not mean marketers should bombard customers with mindless spam. McKinsey's iConsumer survey reported a 20 per cent decline in email usage between 2008 and 2012 as a share of time spent on communications, with the medium surrendering ground to social networks, instant messaging, and mobile-messaging apps. However, McKinsey & Co. suggest that marketers should not be too hasty in shifting budgets away from email - they just need to recognize that: a) email is merely the first click (literally) in a consumer's decision journey; b) every email is an opportunity to learn more about their consumer; and c) emails should be personal and customized (Aufreiter, Boudet & Weng, 2014).

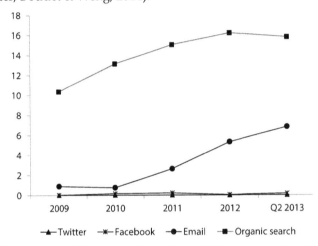

Figure 8.3: U.S. customer-acquisition growth by channel: Percentage of customers acquired (Source: Adapted from Aufreiter, Boudet & Weng, 2014)

After purchase, a deeper connection begins as the consumer interacts with the product and with new online touch points. Vail Resorts has taken advantage of this 'enjoy, advocate and bond' stage with its EpicMix campaign (described in the Case Study below). In decades past, a skier at Vail Colorado would purchase a ski ticket at the hill, enjoy his or her ski day(s), and then have no further contact with the resort (apart from perhaps a direct marketing piece) until the next visit. Now, a skier can purchase a ski ticket online, and have their card (with a built-in chip) delivered to the door. When a skier arrives at Vail, he or she can then engage with Vail's EpicMix social media campaign. The idea of EpicMix is to track activity on and around the mountain via radio frequency scanners installed at the 89 lifts across Vail and also at other Vail Resorts including Beaver Creek, Breckenridge, Keystone and Heavenly. The scanners interact with the RF-enabled chip embedded in lift tickets, listing lift rides, vertical feet skied and days on hill. Special accomplishments – like clocking up 10,000 vertical feet – are recognized with collectible digital pins which can be instantly flaunted on Facebook after downloading the EpicMix app. Users can also create colorful collages, mixing professional photos with their own snapshots, any pins they have won and snow reports or resort stats – effectively designing their own promotional postcard to commemorate their holiday. This gaming option won Vail a Webby award in 2011. The Case Study at the end of this chapter gives more information about the evolution of EpicMix across Vail Resorts' ever-growing portfolio of resorts.

Social media tools employed by winter sports marketers

Social media platforms like those employed by Vail are emerging as a dominant digital communications channel. In 2013, social media advertising increased by 35 per cent over 2012, fueled largely by the growth of mobile (Akhtar, 2014). As consumers spend more time on social networks, decisions about what to purchase often reflect interactions with friends and other influencers. A large percentage of consumers read reviews of hotels, attractions and restaurants prior to vacation, and whilst on vacation over 70 per cent post vacation photos on a social network or update their Facebook status (Lab42, 2012). Ski travelers are more inclined than other travelers to share their travel experiences via social media, especially those under 35 years of age (Phocuswright, 2013).

Many companies, like Vail Resorts, have embraced social media because of its potential for engagement and collaboration with these networked consumers. Through social media, marketers can gain rich, unmediated consumer insights, faster than ever before. Others see the value of social media in its networking. According to Facebook, the average user has 130 friends on the social network, and when people hear about a product or service from a friend, they become a customer at a 15 per cent higher rate than when they find out about it through other means. The growth of social networking is mainly driven by Facebook, which reaches 90 per cent of U.S. social media users and 85 per cent of European users, and is the most popular social networking site (see Table 8.2).

Social networking site	Estimated unique monthly visitors (1,000s)
Facebook	900,000
Twitter	310,000
LinkedIn	255,000
Pinterest	250,000
Google +	120,000
Tumblr	110,000
Instagram	100,000
VK	80,000
Flickr	65,000
Vine	42,000

Table 8.2: 10 most popular social networking sites (Source: Adapted from eBiz, 2014)

Video can be a very effective tool for promoting winter sports, and although not considered as a social networking site by many (including eBiz), YouTube has emerged as the most popular of video sharing sites. Joe Nevin, profiled below, has been using YouTube videos to advertise his innovative ski instruction program since founding BUMPS FOR BOOMERS at Aspen in 2003. An increasing number of resorts have their own YouTube platform, a good example being Aspen Snowmass in Colorado (https://www.youtube.com/user/AspenSnowmass/featured). In addition to videos that promote the resort's hosting of the Winter X-Games (see Spotlight in Chapter 3), marketers at the resort have also created a quality series of six video narratives entitled "Our Story" (http://ourstory.aspensnowmass.com). The YouTube site has links to the company's main website, where amongst other links, there is one to "Aspen/Snowmass LIVE!" a place where visitors can see what is going on at Aspen/Snowmass at that time. The area provides all the latest Tweets, Facebook posts, videos, and photos from the area, delivered in real time from both staff and users alike.

In fact, user generated videos and video contests have become an increasingly popular communication tool for many destinations, which use them to engage consumers and prompt them to become digital ambassadors for their brands. Users are encouraged to submit a personal video to the competition's website, from which they can be selected to win a free dream holiday in a reality TV-like process. In return, the lucky winners are expected to share their impressions on Facebook, Twitter, YouTube, Flicker and blogs, serving as the destination's ambassadors. In 2011, Snowbird in Utah invited contestants from around the world to enter the resort's 'Local Hero POV' (Point Of View) video contest on its Facebook page for a chance to win a ski or snowboard trip to Utah. Snowbird, The North Face, *Powder* magazine, *Snowboarder* magazine and Wasatch Powderbird Guides teamed up to sponsor the video challenge. There were two categories – ski and snowboard – and the winner in each category received a trip for two to Snowbird for five days, a day of helicopter skiing with Wasatch Powderbird Guides, a $500 gift card from The North Face, and two free subscriptions to *Powder* and *Snowboarder* magazines. By giving out an opportunity to win a free vacation, marketers involved with these types of campaigns create excitement, interest and commitment among competitors and hope to raise awareness of their destination by generating free media coverage.

In a different twist on the video-sharing phenomenon, part of Tourism New Zealand's 2014 campaign to target Australian skiers involved a drone (a remote controlled flying camera), traveling around the South Island's ski fields. The drone gave visitors the chance to capture an eight second video of themselves which they could instantly share with their friends on social media using the hashtag #NZDronie. A play on the 'selfie' phenomenon, a 'dronie' is a new trend emerging globally that uses a flying camera to take videos from the sky. The #NZDronie appeared at various New Zealand ski fields including Cardrona, Coronet Peak, Mt Hutt, Mt Cook, as well as Queenstown and Lake Tekapo. Tourism New Zealand's General Manager Australia, Tony Saunders said, "We are excited to be the first country to launch the new #NZDronie on its ski slopes and hope it will add another dimension to the way people share their holiday memories. Word of mouth is an incredibly powerful tool in sharing experiences and the campaign aims to maximize visitors' use of social channels to share the New Zealand winter experience even further" (Scoop, 2014). Skiers and snowboarders were encouraged to share their 'dronies' using social media with daily prizes up for grabs including double ski passes and off mountain winter experiences. Australia is New Zealand's largest international visitor market for ski and snow visitors, with approximately 15 per cent of Australian visitors skiing while on holiday there.

Another type of social media is the online brand community. Brand communities are defined as "specialized, non-geographically bound communities, based on a structured set of social relationships among admirers of a brand" (Bagozzi & Dholakie, 2006, p. 45). The emergence of brand communities has coincided with the growth in consumer empowerment. They are venues where intense brand loyalty is expressed and fostered, and emotional connection with the brand is forged in customers. Research on such communities has found that commitment to a brand can be influenced (positively) by encouraging interactions with groups of like-minded customers and identification with the group in social context offered (and sponsored) by the firm and the brand, but controlled and managed primarily by the consumers themselves.

As use of the Internet becomes more pervasive, so too have online brand communities become effective tools for influencing sales. One study of online brand communities (Adjei, Noble & Noble, 2010) found that the quality of the communication exchanged between customers reduces the level of uncertainty about the company and its products, which relates to increased profits for the company in terms of immediate purchase intentions, and the number of products purchased. It also found that the impact of negative information is not as strong as the benefits of positive information. So maintaining a brand community that lets customers know the company more intimately through peer-to-peer conversations will work in the company's favor, even if negative information is shared.

A challenge in building and managing online brand communities is that consumers can easily associate marketers' efforts with extrinsic motives of profit exploitation and thus become less likely to engage with, and contribute to, such a community (Algesheimer, Dholakia & Herrmann, 2005; Lee, Kim & Kim, 2011). One possible solution is to develop a platform of online brand communities encouraging consumers to share and exchange their ideas voluntarily rather than imposing the organization's own ideas, such as sales coupons or sweepstakes. This implies that marketers should employ a passive role when facilitating brand communities.

A good example of this passive engagement in a brand community came from Vail Resorts, where in 2012 the company launched a partnership with expert family travel writers and created a new website, www.EpicMoms.com. Similar to Ski Vermont's All Mountain Mamas website referred to above, EpicMoms was designed to provide moms (and dads) with thoughtful tips and expert advice on planning the family vacation experiences at Vail's resorts. Vail cleverly set up a 'social lesson' page, to teach moms how to Instagram their trip. Aspen/ Snowmass and Breckenridge in Colorado have also been successful in facilitating online brand communities in order to create value for both consumers and resort marketers (Branislav, 2013).

Because brand community members have a strong interest in the product and in the brand, they can also be a valuable source of innovation. In a study of brand community members, research found that the stronger the identification with the brand, and the higher the brand trust, the more likely a consumer was willing to contribute to open innovation projects initiated by a brand. This activity has been called 'crowdsourcing', a term coined in 2006 by *Wired* magazine Contributing Editor, Jeff Howe (Sullivan, 2010). Crowdsourcing-led innovation means opening the door to allow customers, employees, or the general public at large into the innovation process to help improve products, services or marketing efforts. Consumers get a direct line to the company and the opportunity to steer offerings to reflect their needs better, while companies benefit from getting more insights, opinions and wisdom that can be translated into actionable innovation ideas for less money than a typical R&D initiative.

Club Med used crowdsourcing in 2014 to engage consumers in the development of a ski resort in the French Alps town of Val Thorens. The all-inclusive brand rolled out a seven-phase marketing campaign via Facebook which encouraged fans to contribute to the development process for the Club Med resort. The Facebook campaign had three tracks, one to Discover the Resort, another to Join the Vote and one that outlined available Prizes for participation. Beyond simply marketing the upcoming launch of the resort to the community, the voting functionality allowed fans to select a series of components of the new experience. For example, voters chose 'Val Thorens Sensations' over 'Val Thorens Titanium' for the new brand name, and decided on a climbing wall versus a modern atrium as part of the design.

Club Med offered a seven-day stay at the new resort to participating fans, and the winners were the first two guests to fully experience the resort. In the release supporting the rollout, VP of Marketing for Club Med North America, Jerome Hiquet said: "Club Med welcomed almost 200,000 guests at its Alpine ski resorts last year and has launched this innovative platform in order to engage with discerning travelers and empower them to create their ideal ski resort. We greatly value our guests and want to ensure they are able to take part in this new generation of resorts. With the resort opening in December of this year, it's vital for the brand to get out in front of the opening to ensure a place in consumers' travel budgets and get those rooms booked. Delivering a drip marketing campaign will contribute to significant buzz amongst Club Med evangelists, while also offering up a multi-month marketing campaign to fill up the social media pipeline with compelling, engaging and ultimately shareable content" (tnooz, 2014).

One downside to the proliferation of online social networking for tourism marketers is the loss of control over the consumer evaluation process (Kim & Hardin, 2010). While reasonable criticisms taken from social networking sites could lead to further improvements in services, consumers can easily distribute damaging information using social media, without the opportunity for companies to resolve consumer complaints. However, it is important that marketers embrace social review sites – even to the extent of publishing negative reviews - as they are a major influence in the decision process for visitors. A recent study by Medallia found that hotel properties that actively engage with social media reviews grow occupancy at double the rate of properties that don't (Hertzfeld, 2015). It is encouraging to see an increasing number of ski resorts, like Sugar Bowl Resort in California, add TripAdvisor and Yelp to their website banner links in addition to Facebook, Twitter and YouTube.

Another challenge with social media is measuring the return on investment (ROI) and its impact on the bottom line. Brands that conduct social media interactions with consumers in a meaningful way – for example Joe Nevin's BUMPS FOR BOOMERS profiled below – are beginning to see a positive return (Cruz & Mendelsohn, 2010). But there are too few research studies that can support this claim. If a social media campaign is linked to a specific offer, then it is much easier to measure the ROI. In 2012/13, Squaw Valley/Alpine Meadows in California monetized their Facebook fan base by offering their fans an exclusive Facebook offer – a $25 golf card with purchase of a season pass made available over a three-day period. The offer reached over 18 million people on Facebook and over 2,600 gift certificates were claimed. In addition to getting 2,535 new fans, Squaw Valley/Alpine Meadows were able to get 337% return on investment in marketing dollars, with most of the purchases coming from new season pass holders (Regos, 2013).

8

Profile: Joe Nevin – From Apple to Aspen

When a former Apple executive launches a ski business, he naturally brings some forward-thinking research and technology with him. Joe Nevin, founder of BUMPS FOR BOOMERS ®, first defined his target market back in 2003, deciding to focus on baby boomers (now 50-68 age range) due to sheer numbers. "In 1962 there were four million skier days in the USA Currently there are approximately 60 million skier days," he says. "That growth was fueled entirely by the boomer demographic. These are folks who started skiing when they were young, got married and introduced their families to skiing and now the children of their children are being introduced to the sport. Skiing has become a family theme full of great memories and boomers want to continue skiing into their later years and continue to make memories with their family members."

As those boomer parents become empty nesters, Nevin sees even more of an opportunity: "As family members leave the nest, boomers now have more free time to spend on the sport that they love – but also on continuing family holidays with the extended family. But the challenge is that, metaphorically, boomers are physically starting to 'circle the drain' with undesirable metrics going up – increased weight, higher blood pressure, increased fatigue, more anxiety about possible injury, joint discomfort, etc. – and undesirable metrics going down – eyesight declining, less muscle mass, lower bone density, slowing reflexes, etc. It is a battle of how to ski better versus the realities that come with age. Boomers clearly understand these dynamics and are looking for solutions that enable them to safely ski into their later years."

Joe Nevin

That is where BUMPS FOR BOOMERS becomes very relevant. "It turns out the skills required to ski moguls are the exact same set of skills required for skiing longevity: Better Balance, More Control and Smart Tactics," Nevin elaborates.

He first taught skiing at Alpine Meadows, while working in California for Apple. On retirement in 2003 he moved to Aspen where he set up his unique three and four day clinics backed by the Ski and Snowboard Schools of Aspen: "I worked for Apple for 12 years where the DNA is all about making complexity simple so what I started with was integrating short boards with teaching progressions."

Choosing Aspen was also key: it is one of the most luxurious ski resorts in the world. Outside the BUMPS FOR BOOMERS offices, the sidewalk has underground heating, so no-one has to negotiate icy patches in slippery ski boots. There is a ski valet just up the stairs by the lift station and a kiosk dispensing free coffee nearby. On the slopes there are complementary, ski-in cider and water bars. And the on-mountain lodges feature in-house masseurs along with all the typical cold-weather comfort food.

Having established his market, his resort and his product, Nevin then turned his attention to marketing, choosing the Internet as his vehicle. With his Apple background, he believes firmly in the distribution of free content. "We offer free mogul and powder skiing tips specifically designed for boomer skiers," he explains. "Uniquely, these techniques emphasize controlled skiing, increased efficiency, less fatigue and do not require fast reflexes. These are techniques that will enable boomer skiers to keep up with their grandchildren who want to ski more exciting terrain than boring old groomed runs." As 80 per cent of skiers congregate on the groomed runs, collision – and therefore injury – potential is actually higher than skiing in the off-piste areas.

Other freebies include two ski fitness videos to ensure optimum physical readiness for skiing and help reduce the chance of injury. There is also a Mogul Techniques Learning Center on the website as well as testimonials from participants. After registering for a BUMPS FOR BOOMERS course, Nevin sends prospective pupils free mogul and powder skiing tips by email to give a head start on the learning process.

In the world of instantaneous communication, Nevin is at the forefront of social networking as a tool for business promotion, using blogs, video, website, Facebook, YouTube and Twitter to disperse information about his innovative techniques. Right from the get-go, Nevin knew that social networking was the modern-day 'word of mouth' needed to heighten awareness about his company. His marketing efforts have been reinforced by Virginia-based BCF, a brand communications firm that specializes in marketing products and experiences to baby boomers.

Nevin speaks knowledgeably on subjects such as search engine optimization, database management and anchor texting. He has even produced a summary of how he uses technology for marketing. And he's also media savvy, having hosted a large number of journalists to take part in the program. He finds topnotch accommodation adjacent to the BUMPS FOR BOOMERS meeting place for them, wines and dines them at Aspen's finest eateries, furnishes everything needed for a positive story and involves them in the propagation of his philosophy. He has an extensive media room accessible via the website. His greatest success came when an article on BUMPS FOR BOOMERS was published in the New York Times. He saw an immediate spike in website hits having tracked the response through Google, which resulted in an increase in business.

When approached by media, he works with the resort to arrange complementary accommodation and ski passes. "Then in advance of them coming, we'll brief them on what we think are the key elements of the program. What's new and different, interesting story angles, something of interest," Nevin explains. "We have pre-arrival telephone conversations to find out their objectives, send out written material, and encourage them to go to the website to read about our techniques, demographics and the results of our customer service surveys." He can also provide photos or help them with staging them during their stay. "We try to deliver things on a silver platter to make their job and role very successful."

With its 'Ski For Life' tagline, BUMPS FOR BOOMERS has become one of the most popular specialized instruction programs offered by the Aspen Skiing Company, with skiers flying in from around the country weekly, from the middle of December through March. The original clinics have been joined by a new 'MBA – Master of Bumps Academy' featuring a different mountain for each of the three days of mogul ski lessons, enabling participants to experience the diverse delights of Aspen Highlands, Snowmass and Aspen Mountain.

Sources: Interview with Joe Nevin, October 2014; http://www.bumpsforboomers.com/; http://www.aspensnowmass.com/; http://www.bcfagency.com/; http://www.bumpsforboomers.com/mba-program-master-bumps-academy

The new mobile lifestyle

The latest evolution on the consumer technology front is the widespread use of smartphones. The pervasiveness of mobile technology is creating what MTN, the South African-based telecommunications and mobile finance brand, calls a whole mobile lifestyle (Roberti, 2011). Providing accessibility to banking and credit facilities, travel itineraries, insurance, utilities services, as well as voice and Internet connectivity, is revolutionizing where, when, and how we communicate personally and with businesses.

Certainly smartphone use is growing amongst travelers; nearly two thirds of U.S. travelers who plan their travel online now own a smartphone, and just under a third own a tablet. However, skiers and snowboarders are much more likely to own these devices than are general U.S. travelers (Phocuswright, 2013). Three quarters of day skiers own a smartphone, and nearly half own a tablet. Ski travelers are even more advanced in their digital adoption; eight in 10 own a smartphone, while more than half (55%) own a tablet (see Figure 8.4). This relatively high level of digital adoption among skiers reflects, in part, their higher income and spending levels compared to other travelers. But such high mobile device ownership affects the entire ski travel life cycle: ski travelers are more likely to research, shop for and share their ski travel experiences through their smartphones and tablets, and the ski and travel industries must be prepared to reach and influence these higher-spending travelers across mobile media.

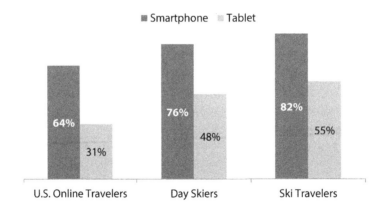

Figure 8.4: Smartphone and tablet ownership by traveler and skier type (Source: Phocuswright, 2013, p. 13)

Almost two thirds of skiers who own a smartphone or tablet have used the device to either connect with friends through social networks or post messages, photos or videos on social networks. Eleven per cent have not yet engaged in these social activities via mobile, but plan to do so in the next several years (see Figure 8.5). Mobile device usage is highest for activities such as checking the weather and email and getting maps and directions. Just one third of skiers who own a mobile device have used it to purchase lift tickets, but this activity has the highest future intent of all mobile-related activities with a large percentage (36%) planning to use their mobile device to buy lift tickets in the next few years.

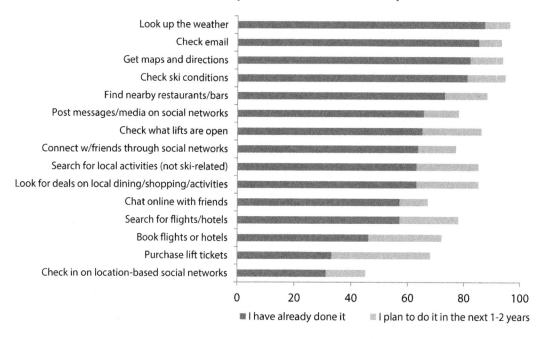

Figure 8.5: Previous and planned use of mobile services (Source: Phocuswright, 2013, p. 15)

The impact of technology on operations

As the above discussion suggests, skier demand for online (and especially mobile) services both before ski trips and on the slopes is substantial. In response, ski resorts are adopting new technologies that allow online booking capability for lift tickets and many more ski services (Phocuswright, 2013). Aspen Snowmass in Colorado, for example, uses radio-frequency identification chips in lift passes, so that skiers and boarders are clocked merely by walking through turnstile-type machines near the lifts. The same technology allows users to add additional days to their passes just by walking through the turnstile as the chip contains credit card information. The passes can also be used to buy meals and other services at the resort. This type of RFID technology has been used in Europe at ski lifts for many years. The technology – which includes the ability to keep track of which users have been up which lifts – was more of an immediate necessity in some ski resorts in Europe, where the land is split amongst many different owners. The tracking technology also assists in the area of safety, allowing resorts to search more efficiently for missing persons if they know the person's name. Many resort retail outlets now have online booking and electronic release forms for rentals.

At Marmot Basin in Alberta, Canada, for example, the My Marmot Card links to rentals, lessons, lift tickets, season passes and gift certificate purchases. In 35 resorts around Utah, California, Wyoming, Colorado and Canada, Ski Butlers brings equipment direct to hotels following online orders.

Other resorts (like Vail mentioned earlier) are developing mobile applications for their visitors. The app from Steamboat, Colorado puts snow reports, weather forecasts, discounts and deals, webcams, bus schedules and more at the users' fingertips. Steamboat also uses a technology called Mountainwatch that helps keep track of children in the busy ski schools, or assists ski patrollers to find a wayward skier or snowboarder. The app also provides a summary of the day's runs, and an increasing number of ski-related apps are offering similar functions. AlpineReplay in Australia, for example, measures speed, airtime, vertical, calories, distance and more.

The skiing and boarding experience has also been greatly enhanced by the evolution of lift technology. Detachable high-speed quads and 'six packs' provide easy loading, rapid transport and reduced lift lines. Surface conveyors (known as Magic Carpets) have replaced rope tows, resulting in a much more pleasant learning experience for children and other beginners. Some resorts are even offering heated ski lifts, such as the Orange Bubble Express at Canyons Resort, Utah, Gondola One in Vail, and the new $6.9 million six-pack heated chairlift at Okemo Mountain Resort in Vermont. Another was scheduled to open at Sunshine Village, near Banff, in the 2015/16 season. Others are experimenting with solar powered ski lifts. The tiny Swiss ski town of Tenna, for example, has built one of the world's first solar-powered ski lifts. Mayor Thomas Buchli, said: "When it was time to restore the old lift, we thought we could run it on solar power since we already have a lot of solar panels on the roofs of our stables" (Danigelis, 2012). The lift, which began operating in mid-December 2012, had to address a key challenge: there wasn't enough room on the lift station roof for all the solar panels they needed. To solve this, they designed a suspension bridge of solar panel 'wings' above the lift, which is nearly 500 yards long. The panels rotate to follow the sun and can be tilted to release snow if they start to get covered. On sunny days, the lift produces twice as much power as it consumes. In the springtime when the ski season ends, it becomes a mini solar power plant. The cost for the new lift was about $1.5 million, but it is expected to produce 90,000 kilowatt hours annually – well beyond the 21,000 kilowatt hours needed to run it during the season (Danigelis, 2012).

Snowmaking has also been influenced by technology. High-tech Whistler Blackcomb in Canada converts 15,000 gallons of water per minute into snow, while Heavenly Mountain Resort operators in California turn on snowmaking by iPhone. Responding to eco-concerns, resorts such as Breckenridge are investing in energy-efficient snow guns and upgraded compressors. In Canada, Fernie gets up to 47 feet of snow annually but still works on lessening environmental impact with energy-efficient nozzle and compressor technology for snowmaking in high-traffic areas. Scouting new terrain and identifying avalanche areas could be assisted in future by drone photography. Marmot Basin in Canada has been experimenting with this, giving aerial perspectives on snowmaking and grooming.

The impact of technology on clothing and equipment

Finally, technology has vastly improved clothing and equipment for winter sports enthusiasts over the years. Easier skis have emerged after a century of ski design innovations, with refinements in materials, size, shape and weight leading to today's rocker hybrids. The blend of rocker and traditional camber in Rossignol skis, for example, improves turn initiation and manoeuvrability in all-mountain versions and delivers maximum float in the 7 series freeride line. Honeycomb-like air tip technology reduces weight at extremities, keeping tips above snow effortlessly. Ski boots, traditionally a compromise between function-ality and comfort, are now custom-fitted. Specialized shops such as All In Skier Services, Fernie, mold and contour liners and shells to make high performance Nordica ski boots fit like slippers but perform in perfect harmony with skis. For off-the-shelf versatility, Lange's "choose your width" option suits all foot shapes. Boots like Rossignol's new Alltrack series for men and women feature new ski/hike technology and grippy rubber soles and arches for comfort and versatility.

Technical fabrics such as Thinsulate, Gore-tex, Spandex and polyesters are uti-lized in multi-layered skiwear to enhance waterproofing, windproofing, warmth and moisture-wicking. Created by nano-technology, Tencel - an eco-friendly fabric made from wood pulp cellulose with non-toxic solvents and nano-fibril structure to wick away moisture – is used by Nils Skiwear for base layers. Injury prevention technology is even appearing in ski underwear. Opedix Knee-tec leggings use 19 panels to enhance muscle and joint function, aligning joints to reduce the rate of fatigue and prevent injury. Heated clothing is now common, with rechargeable, lightweight battery heaters for vests and jackets (Volt); gloves and mitts (Seirus – see John Brice Profile in Chapter 7); boots (Therm-ic). And many manufacturers – including Nils Skiwear and Rossignol – have created hoods that fit over helmets to minimize windchill. Helmets, originally for racers, are now standard garb. Today's versions, such as Giro's Discord, have impact-absorbing dual density liners and lightweight, flexible but durable shells. Sixty years of research has led to Bolle's B-style ultra light polycarbonate shell with hypoallergenic foam liner, adjustable strap, removable ear-pads, and integrated audio kit.

Lastly, one of the biggest trends throughout sports today is the integration use of wearable technologies to monitor and track health and performance. A new technology called Trace from the makers of AlpineReplay, for example, provides skiers and snowboarders with real time data. The Trace sport tracker weighs just 1.4oz and clips easily onto skis and snowboards to measure speed, distance, turns, vertical, airtime, airs, calories burned, and more. The data accumulated allows athletes to track their progress and learn what areas of riding need to be improved on. Also included is Trace Cam, which syncs with all Bluetooth-enabled video devices, including GoPro, iPhone and Android and allows users to relive their experience instantaneously on the slopes through professional-quality highlight videos. Research group International Data Corp. said sales of wearable technology trebled in 2014 from a year before – and that the market could increase more than fivefold to more than 100 million units by 2018 (Hamlin, 2015).

Case study: Technology woven into the DNA at Vail Resorts

EpixMix app

In the old days of communicating customer service, something so insignificant as a ski lift pass would not really have provided managers with much opportunity. It used to be a scrap of paper, attached to a jacket with a metal or plastic clip, flapping in the wind and getting caught on tree branches and other obstacles, but needing to be visible to lift attendants. However, with modern 'smart card' technology, ski resorts all over the world now use lift passes for all manner of conveniences, including automatic access to ski lifts, keeping the pass inside a pocket, and doubling it up as a resort credit card.

An early adopter in the U.S. was Vail Resorts which has continued to investigate every nuance of smart card technology. "One of our biggest developments for the 2014-15 ski season was the introduction of Express Ticketing," says Robert Urwiler, Chief Information Officer for Vail Resorts. "Express Ticketing gives our guests the ability to buy tickets on their mobile device right up to the minute that they need them. If they already have ticket media, the product is loaded automatically. If not, we have express lanes set up at ticket windows where guests can quickly pick up their media by simply showing the confirmation bar code on their mobile phone." Benefits are two-fold. Firstly, it helps optimize ticket window lines by giving people the means to move themselves through the process very quickly. And, secondly, it provides more complete customer information than a resort might get through a traditional ticket window transaction. "In addition to Express Ticketing and other technology feature introductions and improvements across the resorts, we continue to make advancements in the sophistication and use of our CRM and Predictive Analytics capabilities," Urwiler adds. "The objective of these efforts is to drive more focused and targeted guest interaction across communication channels. We are constantly looking for better ways to engage our past, current, and future customers with targeted and relevant messages delivered at the appropriate time and place. Ultimately, this helps drive business."

The radio-frequency enabled Epicmix card is a hands-free season or day pass which can also be linked with a credit card to be used as resort charge for spending while on-mountain. The hard card media can be used year after year, rather than necessitating replacements every season. Furthermore, all hard card media can be linked to the free EpicMix ski app, enabling the user to capture on-mountain activity and share it with friends and family directly from the app on Facebook and Twitter. EpicMix allows guests to track their vertical feet, days skied, pins earned, Leaderboard status, photos taken by professional on-mountain photographers, race medals earned and even track progress in Ski and Snowboard School. Going a step further, EpicMix introduced two revolutionary brands during the 2014/2015 season – EpicMix Guide and EpicMix Challenges. EpicMix Guide provides customized run itineraries for guests based on location, ability level and desired duration while EpicMix Challenges allows guests to compete against themselves, friends and the community. "We've delivered six major releases of EpicMix to our guests including feature sets focused on stats/pins, photo, race, academy, guide, and, recently, challenges," Urwiler explains. "Challenges allows our guests to set goals for the day, vacation, or season and share the achievement of those goals socially."

Epicmixers can share accomplishments individually or chose to share a compilation of their day's achievements directly to social media from the free EpicMix iOS or Android app. The strategy behind all this has several advantages. "Overall, our business objective for EpicMix is to create an unobtrusive digital companion to our guests' skiing and riding experience with a focus on recording their on-mountain experiences," says Urwiler. "This gives our guests the ability to re-live their experiences digitally and to share those experiences socially. This, in essence, helps to create hundreds of thousands of brand advocates for Vail Resorts on social media while also helping to drive our CRM efforts through a better understanding of guest behavior."

Since the launch of EpicMix in 2010/2011, the innovative idea captured the attention of prominent travel and ski journalists resulting in many articles in magazines and newspapers including the prestigious travel section of the Los Angeles Times, *Skiing* magazine and Denver's *Huffington Post*. Furthermore, the app has secured Vail Resorts coverage in more unusual outlets for a ski company such as Mashable, CNET, Wired, Popular Mechanics, FastCompany, and other tech-focused publications. Stacey Pool, Sr. Director, Digital Experience for Vail Resorts, says that by far the most successful generation of EpicMix has been EpicMix photo, which resonates with every guest, both destination and local. "We're always watching the different social platforms where our guests seem to be engaging and trying to figure out a way for those guests to share EpicMix content in those platforms," she adds. Understanding the demographic, target market and appropriate content is crucial to the company's social media strategy. "We want the content to speak to our guests and inspire them to take action, whether that's engaging with us on these social platforms, sharing our content with others, or clicking through into our sites," says Pool. The predominant focus in 2015 was on Twitter, Facebook and Instagram. "As the different platforms evolve, and there starts to be real-time streaming within some of the new social platforms, we want to adapt our strategy to fill in any possible gaps along the customer journey," she explains.

With technology use now woven into the DNA of the company, Vail Resorts is recognized worldwide as a pioneer in the field of social media marketing, combining indirect marketing with customer service and added value. Ski resorts have traditionally charged for photographic services on the hill and usually don't provide any action shots. Vail Resorts saw the value in advertising spin-offs of providing photos for free in order to encourage skiers and snowboarders to send out more professional-looking tweets and Facebook photos of themselves. Vail Resorts was also the first ski hill to use its lift pass system as an app. They have created their own resort blogs about EpicMix with information as well as testimonials from consumers. "As a company we are very fortunate to have a tech-savvy CEO who has a real passion for leveraging technology to facilitate a better guest experience while driving our business," Urwiler concludes. "Our core values include striving to constantly re-imagine all aspects of our business through creative and innovative collaboration. With Rob (Katz) and our entire Executive Team as partners, we will continue to develop advanced CRM and Analytics capabilities, cross-platform digital experiences, and technology-enabled process improvements to ultimately help create an *Experience of a Lifetime* for every guest that we engage through every stage of the interaction lifecycle."

And, as Urwiler says, it is not just youthful skiers and riders who are taking advantage of EpicMix in Vail, Beaver Creek, Keystone, Breckenridge, Park City, Heavenly, Northstar, Kirkwood, Afton Alps and Mt Brighton. All age groups are enthralled with tracking stats, outdoing previous performances and crowing to their office-bound buddies back home about their skiing experiences. And it is attracting locals as well as tourists. The Epic Pass has also evolved into a very useful and affordable season pass. Offers for locals at Park City, for example, were as low as $579 if bought in advance for the 2015/16 season. The pass would pay for itself in just four days, the advertising said, and give access to nine Vail Resorts. New for the 2014/15 season was the Season Pass Auto Renewal Program, enabling automatic renewal every year while guaranteeing the following season's lowest price. The program takes a $49 down payment in the spring with the remainder charged in the fall.

Sources: Interviews with Robert Urwiler and Stacy Pool, April 2015

References

Adjei, M., Noble, S. and Noble, C. (2010) 'The influence of C2C communications in online brand communities on customer purchase behavior', *Journal of the Academy of Marketing Science*, **38**(5), 634-653.

Akhtar, O. (2014) 'How to market your brand on every social media channel', *The Hub*, accessed 12/19/2014 from http://www.thehubcomms.com/how-to-market-your-brand-on-every-social-media-channel/article/343604/

Algesheimer, R., Dholakia, U.M. and Herrmann, A. (2005) 'The social influence of brand community', *Journal of Marketing*, **69**, 19-34.

Aufreiter, N., Boudet, J. and Weng, V. (2014) 'Why marketers should keep sending you e-mails', *Insights & Publications*, McKinsey & Company, January, accessed 12/19/2014 from http://www.mckinsey.com/insights/marketing_sales/why_marketers_should_keep_sending_you_emails?cid=other-eml-ttn-mip-mck-oth-1412

Bagozzi, R. and Dholakia, U. (2006) 'Antecedents and purchase consequences of customer participation in small group brand communities', *International Journal of Research in Marketing*, **23**(1), 45-61.

Branislav, K. (2013) 'Online community marketing of ski resorts: An in-depth best practice study of aspen/snowmass and breckenridge ski resort', Masters Thesis, accessed 4/20/2015 from http://www.nb.no/idtjeneste/URN:NBN:no-bibsys_brage_46410

Court D., Elzinga, D. Mulder, S. and Vetvik, O.J. (2009) 'The Consumer Journey', *McKinsey Quarterly*, June, accessed 12/19/2014 from https://www.mckinseyquarterly.com/The_consumer_decision_journey_2373

Cruz, B. and Mendelsohn, J. (2010) 'Why social media matters to your business', Chadwick Martin Bailey, accessed 12/19/2014 from http://www.cmbinfo.com/cmb-cms/wp-content/uploads/2010/04/Why_Social_Media_Matters_2010.pdf

Danigelis, A. (2012) 'Solar 'wings' power Swiss ski lift', *Discovery News*, accessed 12/19/2014 from http://news.discovery.com/tech/worlds-first-solar-powered-ski-switzerland-120203.htm

Dholakia, U.M. and Durham. E. (2010) 'One café chain's Facebook experiment', *Harvard Business Review*, **88**(3), 26.

Divol, R., Edelman, D. and Sarrazin, H. (2012) 'Demistifying social media', *McKinsey Quarterly*, April, accessed 12/19/2014 from http://www.mckinseyquarterly.com

eBiz (2014) 'Top 15 most popular social networking sites', December 2014, accessed 12/19/2014 from http://www.ebizmba.com/articles/social-networking-websites

Edelman, D. (2010) 'Branding in the digital age', *Harvard Business Review*, **88**(12), 62-69.

Hamlin, K. (2015) 'The future is here, and it's wearable', *The Globe & Mail*, 2 January, B5.

Hertzfeld, E. (2015) 'Social media boosts hotel occupancy', *Hotel Management*, 24 March, accessed 26 March, 2015 from http://www.hotelmanagement.net/technology/social-media-boosts-hotel-occupancy-30683

8

Keller, K. (2009) 'Building strong brands in a modern marketing communications environment', *Journal of Marketing Communications*, **15**(2/3), 139-155.

Kim, J. and Hardin, A. (2010) 'The impact of virtual worlds on word-of-mouth: improving social networking and servicescape in the hospitality industry', *Journal of Hospitality Marketing & Management*, **19**(7), 735-753.

Lab42 (2012) 'Techie traveler. The behavior of today's tech-based travel aficionado', April, accessed 12/19/2014 from http://blog.lab42.com/techie-traveler

Lecinski, L. (2011) 'Winning the Zero Moment of Truth', *Knowledge@Wharton*, 11 May, accessed 12/19/2014 from http://knowledge.wharton.upenn.edu/article.cfm?articleid=2825

Lee, D., Kim, H. and Kim, J. (2011) 'The impact of online brand community type on consumer's community engagement behaviors: consumer-created vs. marketer-created online brand community in online social-networking web sites', *CyberPsychology, Behavior & Social Networking*, **14**(1/2), 59-63.

Mathieson, R. (2002) 'The future according to Spielberg: *Minority Report* and the world of ubiquitous computing', *Mpulse Magazine*, August, accessed 12/19/2014 from http://www.rickmathieson.com/articles/0802-minorityreport.html

Phocuswright (2013) *Ski Traveler Snapshot. U.S. Skier and Ski Traveler Report*, New York: Phocuswright Inc.

Regos, M. (2013) 'The social media ROI question as defined by Squaw Valley/Alpine Meadows', Out &About Marketing, 4 June, accessed 12/24/2014 from http://www.outandaboutmarketing.com/2013/06/04/best-of-ski-resort-marketing-201213-squaw-valley-alpine-meadows/

Rellihan, K. (2015) 'Travel trends for 2015', travelchannel.com, accessed 01/07/2015 from http://www.travelchannel.com/interests/hot-topics/articles/travel-trends-for-2015?refcd=n-def&nl=TCN_123114_featlink1&c32=c7e67d6b7c89533e9015acf696e3693075004d36

Roberti, J. (2011) 'Q&A', *Marketing Week*, 2 June, 29.

Scoop (2014) 'Ultimate selfies to hit South Island slopes', 23 July, accessed 12/19/2014 from http://www.scoop.co.nz/stories/CU1407/S00357/ultimate-selfies-to-hit-south-island-slopes.htm

Sullivan, E. (2010) 'A group effort', *Marketing News*, 28 February, 22-28.

tnooz (2014) 'Club Med crowdsources elements of latest ski resort in the French Alps', 18 February, accessed 12/19/2014 from http://www.tnooz.com/article/Club-Med-crowdsources-latest-ski-resort-in-French-Alps/#sthash.rWKo7nbd.dpuf

9 The Role of Events for Winter Sport Tourism

Darryl Joseph, member of the Jazz Ma Tazz Ski Club, New Orleans, enjoying the National Brotherhood of Skiers Annual Summit

The scene: a brand new on hill restaurant and après ski facility with Prosecco patio heated by trendy tabletop fire-pits. The clientele: exuberant skiers and snowboarders relaxing in designer gear, sampling appetizers, quaffing beer and Italian champers, dancing exuberantly to professional DJ music. Sounds like a chi-chi ski resort anywhere in the world, possibly Europe with such a heady level of animation. But it was actually Elk Camp at Aspen Snowmass in February 2013 when the National Brotherhood of Skiers (NBS) brought high-spirited African American attitude to the trendy town's newest venue.

The fun-loving fanfare was all to celebrate the 40th Anniversary Summit of the NBS, established back in 1973 when black skiing was truly a minority sport. Contradicting typical skiing ethnic demographics for the week, the 3,000-strong cohort of black skiers and snowboarders from all over America held court on the snow-deluged slopes of Snowmass, in the chic shops and in hotels, condominiums and private homes dotting the extensive ski in/out resort. Taking a sabbatical from Mammoth, Big Bear and Tahoe were 11 Californian clubs including the All Seasons Ski Club, Oakland; Camellia City Ski Club, Sacramento; Fire and Ice Ski from San José; Snowbusters from Pasadena; and Winter Fox and Bladerunners from Los Angeles.

Lenore Benoit, membership director for Winter Fox Ski Association based in LA, joined the club after moving from New York in 1990. "One of the ladies at my new company befriended me and told me about Winter Fox. She said it was a great way to meet people as well as learn to ski," said Benoit. She enjoys the club's year-round activities including camping, house boat trips, watersports, river rafting, concerts, wine tastings and, of course, several ski trips. "I've never been to Aspen so it is just an awesome experience to come here and see the beauty and the amazing runs," she said. The social scene is particularly important to her: "Each trip I get to see people I haven't seen for a while. They have become like family through the NBS. We meet skiing and then stay in touch, it's just a beautiful thing."

Fellow Fox, Ida Cochrane is a past president of the club and member since 1980. A veteran with the NBS, she has seen numbers fluctuate at yearly summits which reached a peak at Vail in 1993 when there were 4,000 registrants and another 2,000 hangers-on - every summit has its 'renegades', non-members who tag along for the party. Averaging 20 ski days per season, Cochrane meets up with friends from all over the States at NBS events including ski buddy, Georgia Odom who moved to Texarkana, Texas, but re-connects annually under the Winter Fox banner: "I have never missed a season, I'm afraid if I stop I'll never start again," she said at the mid-week picnic on the piste. "My motto is as long as I can walk, I can ski."

Odom has skied the Italian, French, Austrian and Swiss Alps as well as resorts from New Mexico to Canada. After taking instruction courses in North America, Italy and France, she is an accomplished skier who feels a resurgence of youth during every Summit. "I also join in with all the happy hours and really enjoy myself – you would think I was 30 years old," she said. After skiing Aspen Snowmass six times, it had become her firm favorite resort: "It's easy to get to and the lodging is mostly ski in/out. You don't need a car and everything is walkable. And the runs are wide open," she enthused.

The whole week of the NBS Summit, the party pulse was so persuasive that it made Snowmass locals and other tourists eager to join in the après action. "I worked security one night and saw so many non-members who wanted to join in all the fun," said Darryl Joseph, a member of the Jazz Ma Tazz ski club from New Orleans. "The resort staff were dancing more than us!" NBS sponsors Diageo had brought DJ Ike T and DJ B-Sharp from New Orleans to emcee the week's activities. Apart from the après ski, Joseph's main focus on NBS trips is the sport: "I am back on skis after surgery. I've been skiing three years and injury hasn't stopped me. I think Snowmass is wonderful, very welcoming, the mountain is great and the weather has been fantastic," he said. But it was the strength in numbers that was particularly gratifying for him. "When I ski outside the organization I don't see many African Americans. So it's great that once or twice a year I get to see so many African Americans enjoying skiing together," he said.

Original founders, Ben Finley and Arthur Clay were center stage that week, presiding over the opulent opening ceremony on the Westin Snowmass patio. Clay has been skiing since 1965 when he was often the only black skier on the slopes. Bringing together 350 skiers from 13 black ski clubs for the first NBS summit in Aspen, he has since helped develop the organization to encompass 60 clubs from 43 cities over 25 states. "It's a big family reunion," said Clay, who had to overcome considerable trial and tribulation to keep the NBS alive. "A lot of people have told me over the years you can't do this. But it is do-able although there's a lot of administration."

Featuring team colors and cheers, dances, prayers, national anthem, torchlight ski and fireworks, the opening ceremony heralded a host of diverse on and off snow activities throughout the week. As well as ski and snowboard races, piste picnics, happy hours, concerts and comedy, there were also special events for tag-along non-skiers including a movie screening, gospel fest and shopping spree.

So many people assume that African Americans don't ski and it's true they are still a minority in winter sports. But just like every other recreational and professional sport, as black populations climb the economic ladder, so black athletes are gradually infiltrating every winter sport discipline and it won't be too long before they are topping the podium at Olympic and World Cup events.

The NBS has already sent skiers to the U.S. National Championships, the Winter Paralympics and the Vancouver and Sochi Olympics. With over 3,000 members, the non-profit, volunteer-run association is one of the largest ski organizations within the industry. The Summit itself is the largest gathering of skiers and riders among all U.S. ski conventions. Although serious ski-related issues are addressed (such as introducing the sport to underprivileged inner city youth), it is all about skiing, snowboarding and socializing for most participants.

Sources: Both writers attended the 40th Anniversary Summit and interviewed the participants in February 2013

The growth of events

Events play a significant role in today's society, and for tourism destinations they are important due to their tourist, social and cultural functions (Getz, 2007), as well as their role in local and regional development (Wood, 2005). First and foremost, events are a great anchor for attracting tourism, providing tourists with a prime opportunity to get to know the local culture and experience the essence of the place. During an event, visitors have a unique chance to interact with the local community, gaining a deeper experience of the ambience, customs and local culture. Events can also help in improving a place's image, creating a window for positive media coverage. Finally, for the residents themselves, events are a unique occasion to celebrate the local culture and interact within the community – you can see examples of this in the opening Spotlight above.

According to Jackson (2013), three industries in particular are shaping the growth of the events sector (see Figure 9.1). Firstly, the hospitality industry - be it hotels, restaurants or venues - has viewed events as a way of encouraging new clientele or increasing the yield of existing customers. This is the case for the World Ski and Snowboard Festival held in Whistler, Canada every April in order to increase occupancy rates at the end of the winter season. Hotel rooms are fully booked during the event, which spans two weekends in order to maximize occupancy rates.

Secondly, tourism industry stakeholders, like DMOs, local authorities or trade associations, have turned to events as a means of either attracting tourists or enhancing the stay of visitors. Turkey is an interesting example of a country

9

planning to attract winter sports events in order to develop and promote its winter tourism product. "Turkey has more than 3,000 mountains, but we aren't using them to their full potential," said Erol Yarar, Chairman of the Turkish Ski Federation (TSF) (Mollman, 2014). In February 2015, one of Turkey's developed ski areas at Kayseri hosted the Snowboard European Cup. But Turkey is aiming for even more events and is willing to invest 48 billion Euros over the next 12 years to achieve its goals. The federation is planning to bid for the organization of the 2026 Winter Olympics, despite five failed Summer Olympic bids. The eastern province of Erzurum is the current superstar in the country's winter sport circuit having already hosted the 2011 Winter Universiade, as well as being named the official organizer of the Winter European Olympic Youth Festival in 2019. TSF Deputy Secretary, Necati Kaplan said: "Our goal is to have four million skiers in Turkey, either professional or recreational, within twelve years. This, and a boost in winter sports tourism, is going to happen organically, through the creation of facilities across the nation." (Mollman, 2014).

Finally, marketing and public relations practitioners are using events as an opportunity to achieve their objectives. The sponsorship activities of Red Bull, profiled later in this chapter, are a good example, and other brands associated with winter sports events mentioned in this chapter include Swatch, The North Face, ESPN and BMW.

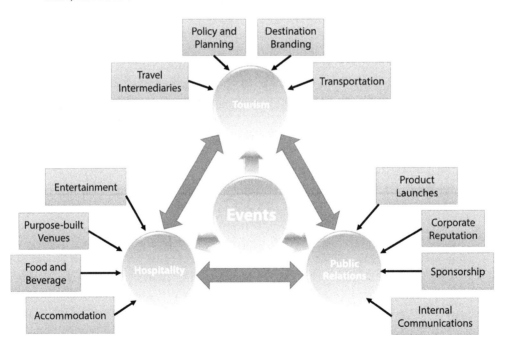

Figure 9.1: Three industries shaping the growth of events (Source: Adapted from Jackson, 2013, p. 7)

Types of events

Event sport tourism includes both elite and non-elite competitor events (Hinch & Higham, 2004). At an elite event, the body of spectators outweighs a small number of elite competitors, whereas at a non-elite competitor event, the number of competitors may be large, but the number of spectators negligible or non-existent. Exceptions to this general rule do exist where non-elite events attract large numbers of family and friends as spectators and, in some instances (such as a marathon), elite and non-elite competitors are accommodated in a single event.

An example of an elite winter sport tourism event is the Winter Olympic Games. The first Winter Games were held in Chamonix, France in 1924, with the original five sports (broken into nine disciplines) being bobsleigh, curling, ice hockey, Nordic skiing (consisting of the disciplines military patrol, cross-country skiing, Nordic combined, and ski jumping), and skating (consisting of the disciplines figure skating and speed skating). The Games were held every four years from 1924 until 1936, after which they were interrupted by World War II. The Olympics resumed in 1948 and was again held every four years. Until 1992, the Winter and Summer Olympic Games were held in the same years, but in accordance with a 1986 decision by the International Olympic Committee (IOC) to place the Summer and Winter Games on separate four-year cycles in alternating even-numbered years, the next Winter Olympics after 1992 was in 1994. The rise of television as a global medium for communication enhanced the profile of the Games, the 1960 Olympics at Squaw Valley being the first year that broadcasting rights were sold. This created an income stream that, along with advertising, has become lucrative for the IOC, and allowed outside interests, such as television companies and corporate sponsors, to exert influence.

The sports themselves have also evolved since the inception of the Winter Games. Sports and disciplines have been added and some of them, such as Alpine skiing, luge, short track speed skating, freestyle skiing, skeleton, and snowboarding, have earned a permanent spot on the Olympic program. Others (such as curling and bobsleigh) have been discontinued and later reintroduced, or have been permanently discontinued (such as military patrol, though the modern Winter Olympic sport of biathlon is descended from it). Table 9.1 lists the Winter Olympics sports that will be included in the 2018 Games to take place in Pyeongchang, South Korea (see Case Study at the end of this chapter). One of those sports is Freestyle skiing, which made its debut in the Sochi Winter Games in Russia in 2014. Freeskiing, once a rebellious departure from ski racing, has become widely popular, and will inevitably gain global recognition from being included in the Olympics.

As opposed to elite events like the Winter Olympics, non-elite competitor events attract far fewer spectators, although the number of competitors may be large. Many amateur events can be classified as non-elite winter sports events. An example is Empire State Winter Games held in Lake Placid, New York State. For

9

more than 34 years, these Games have provided athletes of all ages the opportunity to compete in the largest multi-sport amateur athletic winter sporting event in North America. Over 1,400 athletes participated in the 2014 fixture. The event was created in 1977 as a state-funded event, and is now a community-driven event, courtesy of a partnership between the Regional Office of Sustainable Tourism (ROOST), Towns of North Elba, Harrietstown, Brighton, Wilmington, Tupper Lake and Jay; Villages of Lake Placid, Tupper Lake and Saranac Lake; the counties of Essex and Franklin; the NY State Olympic Regional Development Authority, and State Senator Betty Little.

Ice sports	Alpine, skiing and snow-boarding events	Nordic events
Bobsled (Two-man, Two-women & Four-man) Luge Skeleton Figure skating (Men's and Women's singles, Pairs, Team and Ice Dancing) Speed skating Short track speed skating (500m, 1,000m, 1,500m and Relays) Curling	Alpine skiing (Downhill, Super G, Giant Slalom, Slalom, Super Combined) Freestyle skiing (Aerials, Moguls, Ski Cross, Ski Halfpipe, Ski Slopestyle) Snowboarding (Parallel Giant Slalom, Halfpipe and Snowboard Cross and Slopestyle)	Biathlon (combining cross-country skiing and target shooting: individual, sprint, pursuit, mass start and relay events) Cross-country skiing (individual and team sprint, freestyle, pursuit, classical and relays) Ski jumping Nordic combined (ski jumping and cross country skiing)

Table 9.1: Sports included in the Winter Olympic Games for 2018

Festivals, like events, also attract tourists to destinations, and many winter resorts play host to various types of festivals in order to engage, educate, and entertain both resorts guests and residents of local communities. Stowe Mountain Resort in Vermont, for example, regularly presents live and multimedia performances including theater, music, dance, variety, and film. In December 2014, five-time Grammy Award singer, James Taylor performed at a special concert to benefit the Spruce Peak Performing Art Center at Stowe. Some destinations may be known for just one festival. In the north of China, for example, Harbin is well known for its International Ice Festival held every January. Being one of the few tourism attractions in the city – an otherwise bleak industrial city of four million people where temperatures drop below – 30°C during winter – even an environmental disaster in 2005 did not deter the organizers from hosting the event. Water supplies were cut for over a week when toxic chemicals poured through the city's water supplies. The event went ahead as scheduled. Tens of thousands of visitors from around the country and the world travel to Harbin for the month-long festival, which is famous for its dazzling array of ice sculptures, including replicas of world historical monuments such as the Eiffel Tower, the Great Wall and Egyptian pyramids.

Conventions and exhibitions could also be considered part of the event market, and can be quite lucrative for destinations. This sector has experienced unparalleled growth during the past 20 years. High-quality convention and exhibition centers can be found in virtually every city around the world, and increasingly ski resorts are looking to conventions and exhibitions to smooth out seasonality. An example is the resort town of Gstaad in Switzerland (featured in the Profile in Chapter 3), that is betting on Les Arts Gstaad, a new $110 million vividly modern concert hall and exhibition space, to boost the resort's year-round economy (Eaton, 2014).

When it comes to numbers of international meetings, however, the U.S. remains in first place, according to the International Congress & Convention Association (ICCA). Colorado regularly plays host to SnowSports Industries America's (SIA) Snow Show. For more than 60 years, SIA has produced the non-profit and member-owned event that brings together nearly twenty thousand attendees from the industry. During the four-day trade show, over 1,000 brands present their collections for the following year. Representing over a $3.6 billion industry, more than 80 per cent of the industry's retail buying power attends to see product collections for the following snow sports season. Since its inception, the SIA Snow Show has been the largest global snow sports trade show. In addition to the trade show, the event includes a two-day On-Snow Demo/Ski-Ride Fest, where the industry gathers to ski and ride while retailers and media test the gear and accessories they saw at the Show, including ski, snowboard, backcountry and cross country products. The 2015 On-Snow Demo/Ski-Ride Fest was held at Copper Mountain Resort.

Finally, one new type of winter sports event is the 'virtual event.' The North Face Park and Pipe Open Series Virtual Competition is an excellent example, whereby halfpipe and slopestyle freeskiers anywhere can 'virtually' compete with one another by submitting videos of their dream park and pipe runs. Competition prizes in 2015 included the chance to film and ride with professional freeskier Tom Wallisch in his new project 'Good Company', a $10,000 cash purse, gear packages from The North Face and GoPro cameras. The videos that skiers submit can be edited to combine the skier's best tricks in the park or pipe, but it must flow like an actual competition run. The halfpipe may be any length or size, and the slopestyle entries must utilize eight features including four rails and four jumps. The same rail or jump may be used multiple times in the video edit.

After a public voting round, judges select finalist submissions based off a combination of public voting results and their own discretion. Judges analyze the entries similarly to a competition run and assign an overall impression score of 1-100. The final score determines the overall winners. Specialty awards are given out to best GoPro footage use, best trick, rail and air, biggest personality, viewer's choice and the Wallisch Select.

9

Profile: Crashed Ice

Tim Cimmer

Dynamic and dramatic, dangerous and daring, Ice Cross - alternatively named Ice Cross Down-hill - could be the next Olympic sport. A combination of skating and jumping on a fast obstacle course, the sport was christened 'Ice Cross' in 2014 by Tim Cimmer, a Canadian entrepreneur and Crashed Ice competitor.

Watching Red Bull's televised Crashed Ice events back in 2008, Cimmer dreamt of becoming an ice racer himself. When the chance to try out came four years later in Saskatoon, he was thrilled to make the squad for a Niagara Falls fixture. As the fastest skater on his hockey team and a daring motor cross racer, he assumed he was well set up for podium potential. "I thought that with the racing and skating experience I had I would be one of the best," says Cimmer. "But I found out that flat ice skating has nothing to do with it. My debut on the turbulent track, I felt like a two-year-old kid, skating on ice for the first time."

Despite this setback, Cimmer persevered with an intensive core training regime and, in 2013, became one of the first North Americans to qualify for a Red Bull Crashed Ice competition in Europe. "I made it through a qualifier in Airolo to go to Lausanne, Switzerland only to find the track started with a large jump called a spine. After finding out the hard way what a spine was, I was still determined to do this sport," Cimmer recalls.

A natural businessman, Cimmer began researching how to make the fledgling winter sport official. He consulted with another athlete and various business associates in March 2013, launching an innovative business plan to promote Ice Cross. "I knew it would be challenging and that making these courses affordable was a must," he says. He went on to create simple, fast and cost-efficient strategies for engineering both outdoor and inside tracks.

In 2014 he got the opportunity to put his new ideas to the test. Qualifying for a Red Bull contest in Jyväskylä, Finland, he met former world champion, Arttu Pihlainen, who was building a practice track at Laajis Laajavuori, a neighboring ski resort. Ground digging work and track planning had been going on since 2014 and snowmaking efforts and board structures were started in the fall. "We had weeks and several sleepless nights of ice building and icing," says Lasse Niivuori, General Director & Sales for Laajis Laajavuori. "This cannot come in one night, it's one of the most time-consuming and tedious tasks of the sport."

With just three weeks to go before Crashed Ice, Niivuori was open to Cimmer's suggestions to help finish the practice track. "We welcomed Tim with open arms with his competition format which he had in mind," he says. "The event was put up in record time - we basically had only two weeks of 'game time' to make it look like a spectacle. And Tim was the mastermind and engine behind this event." In order to save time and money, Cimmer had enlisted the help of the Laajis snowcat and groomer to carve the rollercoaster track and also to make obstacles. With added track length, plans evolved to make it into not just a practice area, but an event in its own right. "I think without Tim that Ice Cross as a sport would not have taken the leaps forward on the Riders Cup format in 2015. So from the bigger perspective, Tim is really the man giving true wings to this sport and making the Olympic dreams also a reality," says Niivuori.

The experience in Finland gave Cimmer – known as the Audacious Cowboy - the confidence to establish Ice Cross as a winter sport. "It was a huge success to all, young and old, with a crowd of over 5,000 spectators," Cimmer recalls. "Later that spring came the formation of the associations, international federation and the registrations of all that would be needed to formalize the sport of Ice Cross." Since Feb 2014, Cimmer has been founder, director, board member and owner of World Ice Cross Inc., which is dedicated to expanding the sport, educating participants and organizing events. Investing tens of thousands of dollars and countless man hours into the sport, he is also director and board member of both the Canadian and U.S. Ice Cross Associations and the International Ice Cross Sport Federation. Since 2014 he has been President and CEO of the World Ice Cross League.

Currently, four Crashed Ice events are held: in the USA (St Paul), Finland (Helsinki), Ireland (Belfast) and Canada (Edmonton). Four 'Rider Cups' were added to the schedule for the 2014/15 season - also in the USA, Austria, Finland, and Canada. A women's only division was launched in Canada in 2009. The last stop on the Crashed Ice Tour is at Edmonton each March, with the 2015 fixture marking its tenth year in Canada. The Edmonton city center track involves downhill skating with tight turns and dramatic drops over a fast-paced course, attracting hundreds of thousands of spectators. Red Bull says that each year the ice track is completely redesigned to challenge athletes' endurance, skills and nerve in exciting new ways. For 2015 there were nine turns over the 415m track with a 45m vertical drop. A 50-strong international crew worked for more than three weeks building the track and setting up audiovisuals for the massive production.

Going forward, Cimmer wants to take the sensational sport indoors, too, using NHL-scale arenas with existing flat ice both for events and practice. Plans for 2015 included opening up Ice Cross to additional global sponsors and international media in order to support and spotlight the next Olympic sport.

Sources: Interviews with Tim Cimmer and Lasse Niivuori March 2015

Planning and operating events

Event organizers face a number of unique issues and challenges, and these are summarized in Table 9.2. These challenges include the perishability of event capacity; if tickets or hospitality tents are not sold, the lost revenue cannot be made up later. Additionally, the need to be 'green' or environmentally responsible has become an important issue for event organizers.

Unique Operational Issues and Challenges for Events
Complex and risky event settings and programs
Crowd emotions and behavior
Lack of experience for one-time events
Peak demand periods and simultaneous entry or exit from venues
The perishability of event capacity
The need to be 'green'

Table 9.2: Unique operational issues and challenges for events (based on Getz, 2007, p. 275).

Unfortunately, there is little guidance in the literature for those wishing to set up new events. A number of researchers have attempted to assess the economic impacts of existing events (Dwyer, Forsyth & Spurr, 2006; Della Lucia, 2012; Andersson & Lundberg, 2013) or assess the viability of repeat visitors (Shani, Rivera & Hara, 2013). But there is a dearth of literature that focuses on the feasibility of new events and the need to measure potential demand for a new facility. One exception is the work of O'Toole (2011) who argues that events feasibility and development are the most rapidly growing areas of the industry (p. xvi). His text answers two fundamental questions faced by all events planners and organizers: "How do I justify this event to the client?" and "Why are we spending money on this event?"

One important consideration in the planning stage of events is human resource management. Events have unique human resource needs and challenges, especially because of their usual reliance on volunteers (Getz, 2007). Williams, Dossa and Tompkins (1995) examined the nature of volunteer motivations, behaviors, and perceptions associated with a winter sports event in Canada, and emphasized the importance of incorporating the needs and perspectives of volunteers into the planning and management of special events. Hanlon and Stewart (2006) conducted a study of staffing for a major sporting event. They concluded their study by making recommendations for tailored human resource practices, and these are summarized in Figure 9.2. The left-hand-side of the model has each of the five main human resource stages, and in the middle are nine special features of major sport event organizations. Tailored event mainstream human resource strategies were identified for each of the five human resource stages and these are listed on the right-hand side of Figure 9.2. The authors recommended that managers be provided with documented guidelines and procedures that reflect the tailored and sport-specific processes required to meet the challenges faced by sport event managers.

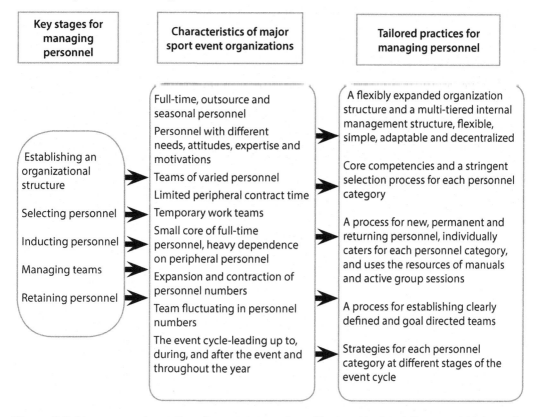

Figure 9.2: Management practices for event organizers (Source: Hanlon & Stewart, 2006, p. 83)

One important management function at most large events is corporate hospitality. Corporate hospitality can be defined as any event for the benefit of an organization entertaining clients or staff, or prospective clients, at the organization's expense (MDB, 2009). The activity can be an effective way of establishing networking opportunities and consolidating customer relationships. Often, an outside consultant will be used to organize corporate hospitality activities, especially for the larger events.

One of the biggest suppliers of hospitality for the Winter Olympics is Jet Set Sports. The U.S.-based company started with the 1984 Games in Sarajevo. Founder, Sead Dizdarevic, a Croatian native, saw an opportunity ahead of those Games to make the most of his language skills and knowledge of the region to create travel packages for U.S. Olympic sponsors. His new venture saw him entertaining 5,000 clients in Sarajevo, from a past generation of Olympic sponsors like Merrill Lynch, American Express, Sport Illustrated, Kraft and General Foods. Many Olympics later, Dizdarevic and Jet Set Sports counts more than 10 times that number of customers for its services that now include Summer and Winter Olympics. The corporate program Jet Set ran in Sochi in 2014, for example, catered for about 30,000 guests. In addition to arranging accommodations and transport for companies, Jet Set took over a restaurant in Sochi and brought in five Michelin-caliber chefs from around the world.

Marketing events

Hall (1997, p. 136) defines event marketing as "that function of event management that can keep in touch with the event's participants and visitors, read their needs and motivations, develop products that meet their needs, and build a communication program which expresses the event's purpose and objectives." There are certainly a number of components to event marketing, and Table 9.3 lists those activities and their purpose.

Marketing activity	Core event marketing purpose
Market research	Evaluate whether or not to put on an event Identify potential markets Evaluate communication methods used to attract participants and spectators Evaluate the success of the event
Marketing management	Create a marketing strategy Position an event relative to competition Construct and implement a marketing plan
Supply chain management	Identify how visitors will 'consume' the event via distribution/ticketing Manage venue, suppliers (technical and participants) and equipment Manage e-commerce
Brand management	Identify the corporate message an event wishes to portray Develop a mission statement, event logo and corporate image Dovetail sponsors' objectives within overall brand image
Marketing communication	Provide external communication to potential consumers Manage media coverage Generate sales leads Utilize digital marketing
Internal marketing	Communicate with staff and volunteers
Consumer relations	Construct mechanisms to understand consumer needs Develop standards and systems for meeting those needs Manage corporate hospitality and VIPs
Market and marketing evaluation	Construct evaluative measures Assess whether or not the event has met its objectives Learn, and suggest lessons for improvement

Table 9.3: The components of event marketing practice (Adapted from Jackson, 2013, p. 41)

Sporting events are often branded, one common approach being to use the resort or destination's name in conjunction with specification of the type of event. This was the original approach for Verbier Xtreme, a winter sports event held in Verbier, Switzerland, that has since morphed into Swatch Xtreme Verbier by The North Face. In fact, the event is now just one stop of the Freeride World Tour, an annually toured series of events in which the best freeskiers and snowboard freeriders compete for individual event wins, as well as the overall title of World Champion in their respective genders and disciplines. The events take place on what's commonly referred to as 'backcountry', 'big mountain' or 'extreme' terrain - essentially ungroomed powder snow on dangerously steep, mountainous slopes. The event in Verbier is now co-branded with Swatch and The North Face, and such co-branding is a common approach to the sponsorship of events.

Celebrities may also use their names as 'hosts', usually to promote a charitable event. An example is the Fairmont Banff Springs Sports Invitational, where Hollywood stars gather in the Canadian Rockies for an annual fundraiser in support of the Waterkeeper's Alliance, an umbrella organization for programs benefitting waterways affected by pollution. Hosted by Robert F. Kennedy Jr., the stars usually spend two days skiing and competing in fun events at Sunshine Village, and the fundraiser culminates with a gala in Banff that raises about $1 million for the organization every year. Among the celebrities attending the 2013 event were Lyle Lovett, Minnie Driver, Rachael Harris, Michael Keaton, Cheryl Hines, Susan Sarandon, and Pierce Brosnan.

Securing a title sponsor is critical for most major events. Title sponsorship is defined as "the right to share the official name of a property, event or activity in exchange for payment to the current property, event, or activity owner" (Clark, Cornwell & Pruitt, 2009, p. 170). In general, such sponsorship is expected to influence future cash flows as well as build image and awareness with consumers, improve employee morale, and promote goodwill. The Fédération Internationale de Bobsleigh et de Tobogganing (FIBT), has secured BMW as the title sponsor of the FIBT World Championships. In 2013/14, the FIBT World Cup competitions were broadcast into 17 countries and reached a cumulative audience of 497 million watching a total of 707 broadcast hours. TV viewership is strong across Germany, Russia, Switzerland, Canada, Latvia, the U.K. and others. As well as comprehensive advertising on banners in camera view and on athletes' helmets across all competitions, the package of rights for BMW includes logo placement on sleds for the FIBT World Championships. Furthermore, the logo is integrated on all communications materials and a hospitality contingent is provided which includes taxi bob rides on the World Cup track. At selected races, BMW provides cars for dedicated shuttle services.

As suggested above, an important marketing activity for event organizers is to gain media coverage for the event, and this will be much easier if the event is tied to a broadcaster. This is the case for the Winter X Games, an annual winter sports event that is controlled and arranged by American sports broadcaster, ESPN. It has been around since 1997, but 2002 was a big year for the X Games and ESPN as it was the first time that an X Games event was televised live. Viewership across the three networks that carried coverage of the event – ABC Sports, ESPN, and ESPN2 – exceeded 2001's household average by 30 per cent according to Nielsen Media Research. To accommodate the first-time live coverage, night-time competitions were added, resulting in record attendance for the Aspen/Snowmass venue. The most memorable incident of the 2002 Games was when the entire 2002 U.S. Olympic freestyle snowboarding team showed up to compete in the Winter X snowboard superpipe event, just weeks before the Salt Lake City Olympics. The Winter X Games are held in January or February (usually in January) and the location of the Winter X Games is in Aspen, Colorado through 2019 – see the Spotlight in Chapter 3 for more details.

Finally, when an event is over, it is important that organizers and marketers evaluate the success of the event. This may simply involve looking at the return on investment of the event although, increasingly, destinations are realizing that events can have significant long-term impacts, such as enhanced brand awareness, so the value of media exposure to the host destination should be calculated. There is also a growing recognition that events can have important social impacts (see Chapter 10), and there are established quality of life measures that can be employed to determine the influence of events on residents' quality of life. Unfortunately, low priority is usually given to post-events research with the emphasis given to planning and organization. Of course, many of these impacts are hard to measure, but it is important that money be set aside for such calculations.

Leveraging events

Event leveraging is a subtle but significant strategy for extending the range of tangible and intangible benefits from events. It involves using the power and momentum of event investments and developments to 'kick start' and/or accelerate the creation of additional tangible and intangible legacies (Faulkner & Tideswell, 1999). In recent years, policy-makers have become increasingly interested in using major sporting events as catalysts for generating beneficial economic, social and environmental legacies for host communities (Faulkner et al., 2000). For instance, the staging of mega sporting events has become a strategy for justifying a range of ancillary urban projects related to urban renewal and regeneration, place brand adjustment, as well as public and private sector investment in local businesses (Essex & Chalkley, 2004). Host destinations can leverage an event in three different ways to benefit the economy, society and the environment.

1) Economic leveraging

There are a number of opportunities for host communities to realize short and longer-term economic benefits from such mega-events (Chalip, 2004). For instance, opportunities exist to use events not only to increase spectator expenditures in the host destination, but also to extend the frequency and duration of visits to the area for leisure and other trade purposes. In the first year after Calgary's 1988 Winter Games, tourism revenues grew by about 12 per cent, and this was followed by average annual increases of about 3.25 per cent over the next five post-Olympic years (Ritchie & Smith, 1991). Most studies of mega-events, such as the Olympic Games, find a relatively small immediate impact on the cities that host them, and one reason for this is that the event displaces tourists who would otherwise have come to the city. One study by Leeds (2008), for example, found that expenditure at ski resorts in Colorado rose as a result of the 2002 Winter Olympic Games in Utah. Leeds suggests that cities and states that gain from such spill-over effect might want to support event bids by nearby destinations.

Events, especially mega-events, represent a significant opportunity to build or strengthen a destination's brand. In 2010, the Canadian Tourism Commission (CTC) worked closely with the Vancouver Winter Olympic Games Organizing Committee (VANOC) to leverage Olympic media-driven brand awareness during and after the Winter Games. It invested about $26 million into this Olympic leveraging strategy. An example of one of the CTC's leveraging tactics involved a partnership with VANOC in the pre-Games torch relay. In this event, 14 visual media clips of high profile actors, athletes, and dignitaries from countries from which Canada was hoping to lure tourists were repeatedly broadcast into specific target markets around the globe.

Events are often introduced to cope with seasonality and to boost tourism receipts during normally quiet times of year. For example, in 1995, Whistler held its first World Ski and Snowboard Festival in April in order to increase occupancy rates at the end of the winter season. Now the event is North America's largest snow-sport and music event, attracting thousands of enthusiasts from all over the world. In addition to ski and snowboard competitions, film events, parades and a lively club scene at night, more than 50 acts are booked for the Outdoor Concert Series. The concerts usually attract audiences of up to 10,000. According to an independent research study commissioned by the festival organizers, the 2006 event resulted in a CDN$37.7 million impact on the province, including nearly $21.3 million for the resort. Over 28,000 room nights were sold during the festival, with 86 per cent being driven by the World Ski and Snowboard Festival. The staging of major events in Whistler is not a new experience, and although the destination lost the World Cup skiing competition to Lake Louise, it was successful in its bid with Vancouver to be the host cities for the 2010 Olympic Winter Games. The estimated cost of the joint Vancouver/Whistler Olympic bid was about $20 million, but hosting the games generated $1.3 billion in revenue from ticket sales, sponsorships and television rights.

2) Social leveraging

Event planning that is sensitive to quality of life and equity outcomes is an essential ingredient of sustainable tourism, since hosts who are positively disposed to special events will enhance the tourists' experience and contribute to the destination's attractiveness (Madrigal, 1995). One of the most important perceived social benefits of a mega-event is the facilities created for the occasion but later used by locals (Gursoy & Kendall, 2006; Bramwell, 1997). However, some facilities used for Winter Olympic Games such as ski jumps and the bobsleigh/luge track, have limited use outside international competitions. The ski jump built for the Grenoble Games of 1968, for example, is now derelict because it is poorly situated and too expensive to operate (Essex & Chalkley, 2004). However, planning has improved over the years, and the 2010 Winter Games planners in Vancouver earmarked approximately $110 million as endowment or legacy funds to help the Olympic facilities remain financially sustainable. The Richmond speed-skating oval was converted after the Games into a much-needed community facility, and the Olympic curling venue in Vancouver's Hillcrest Park was built in partnership with the city and includes a new swimming pool, community centre, library and curling facility to replace an existing and out-dated rink.

Another way events can be leveraged for the benefit of residents is through community involvement in the hosting of sporting events – whether by organizing, watching, or participating in an event. Such involvement affects notions of community citizenship which, in the long-term, impacts tourism development (Misener & Mason, 2006). Criticisms are often raised that local community residents are left out of the organization and management of sporting events and that their needs are neglected. However, sport can foster localism, regionalism and nationalism (Bale, 2003), so it is important to create opportunities for citizen involvement at a local level in order to develop citizenship. In 2010, the Municipality of Whistler had in place a Volunteer Home Stay program that involved hosting Games volunteers in Whistler in order to build community connectedness. The Games also had an Adopt-an-Athlete program that supported international athletes in pre-Games training, as well as an Adopt-a-Family program that enabled the families of Canadian athletes to stay with a Whistler family during the Games.

A number of activities and projects can also be created around events to promote awareness about winter sports. For example, during the Sochi Winter Olympics of 2014, NBC Olympics, in partnership with the U.S. Olympic Committee and national governing bodies including the U.S. Ski and Snowboard Association (USSA), created the Olympic Gold Map to help newcomers take up Olympic sports and existing partners find competitive programs. The Gold Map helped viewers who were inspired by Olympic competition find out how to get started in their new favorite sports. Viewers could quickly click through NBCOlympics.com/GoldMap to learn about skiing and snowboarding, find a resort to try the sport, or locate a USSA competition club. The initiative was integrated into NBC's coverage of the Sochi Games.

3) Environmental leveraging

In the clamor to stage a successful event, in both economic and image terms, organizers often give lesser priority to environmental impacts (Essex & Chalkley, 2004). The economic justification is so compelling to decision-makers that other impacts are considered minor (Hiller, 1998). But policy-makers are increasingly concerned with the environmental as well as the economic impacts of events (Collins et al., 2007), and efforts are even being made to measure the environmental impacts of events (Collins, Jones & Munday, 2009). Because of intrusions into fragile mountain environments, awareness of the environmental impacts of the Winter Olympics has been more central to organizers for a longer period than for the Summer Games. Even as far back as the 1970s, Denver had to withdraw its candidacy for the 1976 Winter Games at short notice, partly because of concerns that the organizers were ignoring environmental considerations. Preparations for the 1994 Lillehammer Games for the first time embraced the principles of sustainable development. The approach influenced the IOC to add environmental commitment to its Charter and inspired Sydney, host of the 2000 Summer Games, to make sustainable development a core theme in its own preparations.

Although pressure is increasing on event organizers to be environmentally aware and friendly during an event, environmental leveraging requires a change in knowledge, attitudes and behaviors beyond the event itself. So the leveraging challenge is to determine how an event can foster such changes. Major events can serve as catalysts for bringing attention to environmental concerns and thus may preserve elements of the physical landscape and local heritage that would have otherwise been ignored (Deccio & Baloglu, 2002). Beijing's air quality has improved because of measures taken before and since the 2008 Summer Olympics – most notably by cleaning up heavy industry and restricting the number of cars allowed to drive in the capital during the week.

The event's use of environmentally friendly policies and procedures can have an impact on environmental stewardship. For example, the facilitation of travel to the event via public transportation could influence green behavior. The Vancouver Winter Olympic Games Organizing Committee (VANOC) neutralized all of the carbon emissions created by its organizations, which involved buying offsets for 110,000 tons of carbon. VANOC also worked to make reductions in its carbon footprint by constructing energy-efficient venues and worked out local plans for transportation for the Games that relied on public transit and charter buses rather than have people drive around in their cars. The public transportation system included the latest low and no emission technologies, and the Olympic fleet uses hybrid, electric and propane vehicles. Environment Canada also committed $13.4 million to support the 2010 Games by providing support to environmental sustainability. Part of this involves promoting best practices. Showcasing 'Green' buildings was an example, as LEED principles – Leadership in Energy and Environmental Designs – were applied to new facilities to ensure they use the least amount of energy possible.

Case study: Planning the South Korea 2018 Winter Olympics

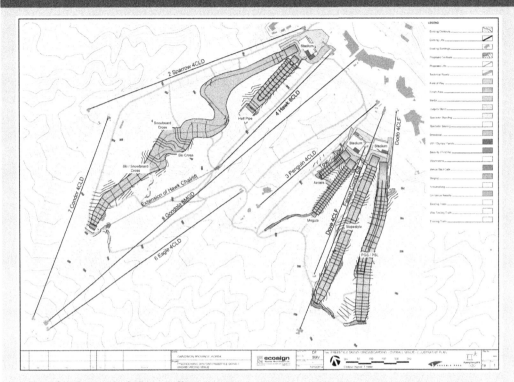

Plans for Phoenix Park, PyeongChang

Arguably the most prestigious event in winter sports is the Winter Olympic Games. From the initial bidding, building the competitive venues, constructing an Olympic village, hosting the world's top winter athletes and the media circus that goes with them - and somehow creating a lasting legacy to justify all the tax dollars spent on infrastructure - it is a mammoth task.

The Sochi 2014 Games cost a reported $51 billion. But was this huge investment worth it? Certainly many winter tourism destinations think so and the ski resort area of PyeongChang, South Korea was more than willing to take the risk. It made three attempts to bid successfully for the Winter Olympics, finally nabbing the elite event for 2018. It was all part of its aim to put South Korea's premier winter sports area firmly on the international ski map and challenge Japan for predominance in Asia. South Korea held the Summer Olympics in Seoul in 1988, co-hosted the football World Cup with Japan in 2002, and staged the Asian Games three times, including the 2014 event in Incheon. Each event was touted as a celebration of prosperity and the country's elevated international profile. However, public sentiment surrounding big sporting events is no longer unanimously positive because of growing worries over costs, including the burden of maintaining venues after the Olympic Games.

The indoor ice events for 2018 are planned for Gangneung, a northeastern coastal city with a population of around 230,000. But the international spotlight has been directed to the less densely populated county of PyeongChang, chosen for the mountain venues as well as the opening and closing ceremonies. The long-term legacy for PyeongChang is hoped to be a commercially viable, international ski center with new venues for training and competitive freestyle skiing and snowboarding events in the future.

Rather than compete with Sochi's extravagant facilities and expenditure, PyeongChang aimed to use many existing venues and create a lower key but more authentic atmosphere reminiscent of the 1994 Lillehammer Winter Olympics. Lillehammer's ski resorts are spread over five alpine centers: Skeikampen, Kvitfjell, Gålå and Sjusjøen. Incidentally, although Lillehammer may not have indulged in the huge financial outlay of Vancouver or Sochi, it is now the location for the award-winning TV drama series, *Lilyhammer*, starring Steven Van Zandt, which has given lasting marketing and advertising ROI to the quaint Norwegian mountain town. The Lillehammer Olympic ski jump was immortalized in one of the most iconic episodes.

Having worked on the 2010 Vancouver Olympics and the 2014 Sochi Winter Olympics, Paul Mathews' company, Ecosign was chosen to plan the Freestyle Skiing and Snowboarding venues for PyeongChang. Ecosign had already designed various ski resorts in South Korea including Konjiam Resort, Hyundai Sungwoo Resort at Tunnae Village and Yeongpyong Resort. "The job we are doing for POCOG, the Organizing Committee for the PyeongChang 2018 Olympic Winter Games has been to prepare an overall Venue Master Plan for Bokwang Phoenix Park Ski Area for Freestyle Skiing and Snowboarding," says Mathews. The master plan, formulated in 2013, also entailed detailed designs for construction.

The process of creating any Olympic venue is typically fraught with unexpected problems. In the case of PyeongChang, the original bid was based on fielding 12 Freestyle Ski and Snowboard sections. "In the summer of 2011, the IOC added eight competitions to Freestyle Skiing and Snowboarding so that the total for Sochi and PyeongChang was now 20 competitions; 10 for men and 10 for women," says Mathews, adding that the Korean budget had not initially allocated funds or terrain for these extra events.

Mathews says there have been other contentious issues. "They also had the 'impression' that Bokwang Phoenix Park was pretty well ready to host all Olympic competitions," he explains. "The truth is, Bokwang Phoenix Park had a moguls and aerial course and a halfpipe but none of those venues met the FIS Technical Requirements for Olympic Winter Games; there are different standards for Olympic Games, World Cup and then Europa Cup, Continental Cup, the local races, etc. Obviously, the Olympic Winter Games has the highest standards." Ecosign's new plans for Phoenix Park are pictured above.

Putting the venues in suitable places with lift access for athletes and workers, as well as technical roads and other infrastructure, turned out to be a much more complex undertaking than the Korean committee anticipated. "We then entered a competition to do the detailed design for construction of the six venues: aerials, moguls, ski/boarder cross, halfpipe, slopestyle and parallel giant slalom," Mathews recalls. "This work involves precise design and engineering of the competition fields of play within 20 cm accuracy to be built in soil but we had to forecast the final elevations in snow. This was becoming a very complex job but we have now finished this work and handed it over to a Korean engineering company which is making the final drawings for construction tendering for the summer of 2015."

9

The final price tag for the PyeongChang Olympics is expected to be about $10 billion – a pittance compared to the billions Russian President, Vladimir Putin spent turning summer into winter by the Black Sea. For the Koreans, PyeongChang will not be the 'coming-out party' as Seoul was, but more a ratification that their country now plays in the major leagues. "Thirty years ago, the world was seeing a developing nation," said Kim Jin Sun, organizing committee president and former governor of Gangwon, the nation's wintery province that will be heart of the Games. "One generation later, the world will be able to see a truly developed nation."

Sources: Interview with Paul Mathews, President of Ecosign, February 2015; Clarey (2014); Powers (2015); Tong-Hyun (2015)

References

Andersson, T.D. and Lundberg, E. (2013) 'Commensurability and sustainability: Triple impact assessments of a tourism event', *Tourism Management*, **37**, 99-109.

Bale, J. (2003) *Sports Geography* (2nd Ed), London: Routledge.

Bramwell, B. (1997) 'Strategic planning before and after a mega-event', *Tourism Management*, **18**(3), 167-176.

Chalip, L. (2004) 'Beyond impact: a general model for host community event leveraging', In B.W. Ritchie and D. Adair (Eds.), Sport tourism: Interrelationships, impacts and issues. Clevedon, pp. 226-252. U.K.: Channel View.

Clarey, C. (2014) 'For 2018 a different plan is in place', *New York Times*, 24 February, accessed 1/12/2015 from http://www.nytimes.com/2014/02/25/sports/olympics/south-korea-awaits-2018-games-with-a-different-plan.html?_r=0

Clark, J.M., Cornwell, T.B. and Pruitt, S.W. (2009) 'The impact of title event sponsorship announcements on shareholder wealth', *Market Lett*, **20**, 169-182.

Collins, A., Flynn, A., Munday, M. and Roberts, A. (2007) 'Assessing the environmental consequences of major sporting events: The 2003/04 FA Cup Final'. Urban Studies, **44**(3), 457-476.

Collins, A., Jones, C. and Munday, M. (2009) 'Assessing the environmental impacts of mega sporting events: Two options?', *Tourism Management*, **30**(6), 828-837.

Deccio, C. and Baloglu, S. (2002) 'Nonhost community resident reactions to the 2002 Winter Olympics: The spillover impacts', *Journal of Travel Research*, **41**(1), 46.

Della Lucia, M. (2012) 'Economic performance measurement systems for event planning and investment decision making', *Tourism Management*, **34**, 91-100.

Dwyer, L., Forsyth, P. and Spurr, R. (2006) 'Assessing the economic impacts of events: a computable general equilibrium approach', *Journal of Travel Research*, **4**, 59-66.

Eaton, P. (2014) 'Gstaad: The last resort', *TMagazine*, 31 October, accessed 1/24/2014 from http://tmagazine.blogs.nytimes.com/2014/10/31/gstaad-switzerland-hotels-resorts/?_r=0

Essex, S. and Chalkley, B. (2004) 'Mega-sporting events in urban and regional policy: A history of the Winter Olympics', *Planning Perspectives*, **19**(2), 201-204.

Faulkner, B., Chalip, L., Brown, G., Jago, L., March, R. and Woodside, A. (2000) 'Monitoring the tourism impacts of the Sydney 2000 Olympics', *Event Management*, **6**, 1-16.

Faulkner, B. and Tideswell, C. (1999) 'Leveraging tourism benefits from the Sydney 2000 Olympics', *Pacific Tourism Review*, **3**, 227-238.

Getz, D. (2007) *Event Studies. Theory, Research and Policy for Planned Events*, Oxford, UK: Butterworth-Heinemann.

Gursoy, D. and Kendall, K.W. (2006) 'Hosting mega events: Modeling locals' support', *Annals of Tourism Research*, **33**(3), 603-623.

Hall (1997) *Hallmark Tourist Events: Impacts, Management and Planning*, Chichester: John Wiley.

Hanlon, C. and Stewart, B. (2006) 'Managing personnel in major sport event organizations: What strategies are required?', *Event Management*, **10**(1), 77-88. DOI: http://dx.doi.org/10.3727/152599506779364624

Hiller, H. H. (1998) 'Assessing the impact of mage-events: A linkage model', *Current Issues in Tourism*, **1**(1), 47.

Hinch, T.D., and Higham, J.E.S. (2001) 'Sport tourism: A framework for research', *International Journal of Tourism Research*, **3**(1), 45-58.

Hinch, T.D., and Higham, J.E.S. (2004) *Sport Tourism Development*, Clevedon, UK: Channel View Publications.

Jackson, N. (2013) *Promoting and Marketing Events*, Oxon: Routledge.

Leeds, M.A. (2008) 'Do good Olympics make good neighbors?' *Contemporary Economic Policy: A Journal of Western Economic Association International*, **26**(3), 46-467.

Madrigal, R. (1995) 'Cognitive and affective determinants of fan satisfaction', *Journal of Leisure Research*, **27**(3), 205-228.

MDB (2009) UK Corporate Hospitality Market Research Report, February, Manchester: Market & Business Development Ltd.

Misener, L. and Mason, D.S. (2006) 'Creating community networks: Can sporting events offer meaningful sources of social capital?' *Managing Leisure*, **11**(1), 39-56.

Mollman, R. (2014) 'Turkey embraces slippery slope of winter sports events, investments', *Today's Zaman*, 13 December, accessed 1/20/2015 from http://www.todayszaman.com

O'Toole, W. (2011) *Events Feasibility and Development: From Strategy to Operations*, Oxford: Butterworth-Heinemann.

Powers, J. (2015) 'Pyeonchang ready to welcome 2018 Olympics', Boston Globe, accessed 3/26/2015 from http://www.pc2018.com/news/pyeonchang-ready-to-welcome-2018-olympics/

Ritchie, J.R.B. and Smith, B.H. (1991) 'The impact of a mega-event on host region awareness: A longitudinal study', *Journal of Travel Research*, 30(1), 3-10.

9

Shani, A., Rivera, M.A. and Hara, T. (2013) 'Assessing the viability of repeat visitors to cultural events: Evidence from the Zora! Festival', *Journal of Convention & Event Tourism,* **10**, 89-104.

Tong-Hyun, K. (2015) 'IOC urges Korean organizers to speed up work to be ready for Olympic test events', *The Canadian Press,* accessed 3/26/2015 March from http://www.squamishchief.com/sports/national/ioc-urges-korean-organizers-to-speed-up-work-to-be-ready-for-olympic-test-events-1.1797519

Williams, P.W., Dossa. K.B. and Tompkins, L. (1995) 'Volunteerism and special event management: a case study of Whistler's Men's World Cup of skiing', *Festival Management & Event Tourism,* **3**(3), 83-95.

Wood, E. (2005) 'Measuring the economic and social impact of local authority events', *The International Journal of Public Sector Management,* **18**(1), 37–53.

10 The Economic, Social and Environmental Impacts

Working for a heli-skiing operation would be a dream-come-true for many an avid backcountry skier. But faced with the challenging job of directing a heli-ski company's sustainability program, it may not be as cushy as it sounds. Dave Butler (RPF, RPBio) has the tough job of Director of Sustainability for Canadian Mountain Holidays (CMH) Heli-Skiing & Summer Adventures. He started his career as a Park Warden in Banff National Park, Canada, went on to work in government, handling adventure tourism tenures, and moved to CMH in 1997.

Heli-tourism represents one of the great dilemmas and conflicts between recreational enjoyment of the wilderness and the conservation of the fragile alpine and mountain areas. The question of responsibility towards the environment is one which tourism operators have generally been reluctant to accept but CMH has taken a more proactive approach to environmental issues.

Dave Butler

The Banff-based company operates in 11 mountain areas of South Eastern British Columbia, bringing in annual revenues of around CDN$60 million with a 70 per cent repeat-booking record. CMH holds license rights from the BC government to more than 14,000km² of remote territory in the Purcell, Cariboo, Selkirk and Monashee mountain ranges and is several times the size of its closest competitor in heli-ski visits. Its operations include up to 30 helicopters and eight remote lodges – many accessible in winter only by helicopter. There are three main strands to its business: heli-skiing, heli-hiking, and mountaineering.

As part of the senior leadership team, Butler heads up CMH's sustainability program including governance, implementation and reporting. "The company's efforts have been recognized with a range of provincial, national and international awards," Butler says. "I coordinate cross-functional teams and the integration of fiscal, environmental and human components of the business and I ensure the company's approaches are consistent with its long-term sustainability." Focusing on government and community relations, Butler deals with all land/resource tenures and regulatory issues. "And I supervise, and am accountable for, work of the Run Development Coordinator and Manager of Remote Fuel Operations – both seasonal positions," he adds.

As the grand-daddy of heli-skiing since its launch in 1965, CMH has demonstrated a commitment to the environment. "We look at environmental stewardship as one component, albeit a critical one, of our journey toward sustainability," Butler explains. The other vital ingredients are fiscal responsibility and social/cultural stewardship. "Our founder, Hans Gmoser, was committed to ensuring that we take good care of the special places that we share with our guests, and that commitment continues to today in what we do around wildlife, energy and waste management, fuel management, etc. In fact, Hans was the first in our industry to develop a specific set of wildlife procedures for guides and pilots," says Butler.

Over the years, CMH has trained its guides to keep a vigilant watch for wildlife. The guides plan their flying and skiing routes to avoid contact, and all wildlife sightings are provided annually to the BC Government for their overall management purposes. They use computer software to map wildlife sightings, and to maintain a sense, over time, about the areas where animals spend their time throughout the year. CMH also looks to external biologists to give them advice on how best to behave in these habitats.

One of the company goals is to increase energy efficiency in all aspects of the business. This helps alleviate costs as well as reduce CMH's overall footprint. "So, rather than paying money for off-sets, we use every dollar available to continue to look for ways to be more efficient in our energy use," Butler explains. "Examples include the way we light and heat the lodges, the ways in which we use helicopters, and the way we move our guests to/from our lodges."

Environmentalists typically raise concerns about the negative environmental impacts of heli-tourism on fish and wildlife, about waste and fuel storage areas, and about noise pollution. Vegetation, too, can be a contentious environmental issue. In the summer, existing hardy trails are used where possible, and use is dispersed throughout each operating area so that impacts on fragile alpine environments are minimized. CMH claims that the potential impact on the land in the winter is negligible because visitors leave only tracks in the snow. CMH guides are trained in the latest low-impact travel techniques for alpine areas, and they share these approaches with the visitors. CMH also works with local forestry companies coordinating efforts to harvest in ways that work best for skiers while reducing the visual impact of harvesting. Landing and pick-up locations are also placed in areas of minimum impact on the forest.

Waste reduction is also important to CMH. For example, in the Adamant Lodge in the Selkirk Mountains, food waste (that used to be consumed by lodge pigs before hoof-and-mouth scares) is eliminated by using a prototype composting system developed by maintenance manager, Duane Dukart. In 2002, CMH established the 'President's Award for Environmental Initiative', a program which empowers all staff to take a look at what they can change in their own jobs that will help the environment. Dukart received the first President's Award for his efforts to promote environmental stewardship. The same system is now used in the Bugaboo Lodge. The company also employs the latest technology in sewage treatment and uses only environmentally-friendly soaps and paper.

Helicopter fuelling locations use leading edge technology to prevent fuel spills from reaching the ground or the water. These systems include engineered containment berms and a state-of-the-art emergency spill response system. Use of helicopters is minimized wherever possible, as this is the greatest direct cost of operations. The fuel for the helicopters is stored at the lodges, and at remote fuel caches, using leading-edge storage facilities.

In order to communicate its strong sustainability standpoint CMH produces regular reports which are posted on its website. Sustainability and environmental policies are also used in marketing messages to potential and return guests. And staff members who interact with guests or media are trained in presenting CMH's environmental approaches, giving solid examples. "This includes media interviews, and special talks and presentations at colleges and universities, to special interest groups, and at tourism conferences," Butler adds.

In 2014 CMH created a new internal Sustainability Advisory Group: "a 'think tank' responsible for ensuring we keep looking for both low-hanging fruit, and larger company-changing ideas. This has only been in place since November. A very different approach than our old Second Nature team," says Butler.

Sources: Interview with Dave Butler, December 2014; www.canadianmountainholidays.com/

Impacts of winter sport tourism

The unprecedented expansion of tourism has given rise to a number of economic, environmental and social impacts that tend to be concentrated in destination areas (Wall & Mathieson, 2006). Tourism research has typically emphasized the economic impacts and yet there are increasing concerns about the effects of tourism on host societies and their environments. A number of techniques have been developed to monitor these impacts. Common analytical frameworks include an environmental audit, environmental impact analysis, carrying capacity, and community assessment techniques. It is beyond the scope of this book to cover these techniques in detail, but the tourism manager needs to have knowledge of the most current models. Managers must also have an understanding of the principles of sustainable tourism, described as "tourism which is developed and maintained in an area in such a manner and at such a scale that it remains viable over an indefinite period and does not degrade or alter the environment (human and physical) in which it exists to such a degree that it prohibits the successful development and well-being of other activities and processes" (Butler, 1993, p. 29). As shown in the Spotlight above, Canadian Mountain Holidays is a good example of this.

This increasing emphasis on sustainability has important implications for winter sport tourism, and this chapter focuses on the three pillars of sustainability – the economy, the environment and society. In the past, winter sport tourism was encouraged for its economic benefits with little consideration for the effects on the environment. But this is beginning to change. For tourism to be sustainable, it is vital that its impacts are understood, so that they can be incorporated into planning and management. Table 10.1 lists just some of the positive and negative impacts of winter sport tourism according to experts, many of which are covered in more detail throughout this chapter.

Advantages	Disadvantages
Employment and income benefits, both direct and indirect	Overdependence on tourism
Tax benefits to local, regional and national governments	Raises property prices beyond the reach of local young people
Attracts the higher-spending social groups	Leads to an increase in road traffic
Health benefits	Resident hostility towards tourists
Positive contribution to quality of life	Negative impact on wildlife
Catalyst for positive social change	Pollution
Increases local property values	Soil erosion
Quality of tourism increases	Displacement through land occupancy
Counteracts problems of seasonality	Heavy use of water for snow making
Improved recreation facilities for local communities	Creates pressures on land

Table 10.1: Positive and negative impacts of winter sport tourism

Economic impacts

As mentioned above, early tourism research focused mainly upon the economic aspects of the industry, with many early impact studies directed at international and national levels. However, there are an increasing number of studies that examine regional and local economic impacts, and this chapter contains several examples of these. Similarly, there are a growing number of studies that attempt to estimate the impacts of specific events. According to Wall and Mathieson (2006), four factors have contributed to both the emphasis on economic impact analysis and the quality of such studies.

Firstly, when compared with physical and social impacts, economic impacts are relatively easy to measure. There exist widely accepted methodologies for measuring economic impacts, but in social and environmental sciences these are still in the early stages of development. Secondly, large amounts of reliable and comparable data have been collected on economic aspects of tourism, often collected routinely by government agencies.

Thirdly, research has advanced the application of economic assessment tools in tourism research. Economists have traditionally used input-output (IO) analysis, but other methods such as linear programming, general equilibrium models and cost-benefit analysis have also been employed in recent years. Multiplier analysis is also popular with economists, whereby the money spent by tourists in the area will be re-spent by recipients, augmenting the total (see the Spotlight on The New Mexico True campaign in Chapter 6). The multiplier is the factor by which tourist spend is increased in this process. For example, research in Vermont has shown indirect benefits of skiing to be positive with a multiplier effect of 1.94 for every dollar spent (higher than that of the tourism sector in general at 1.69) (Lin et al., 1999). The final reason for the emphasis on the economics of tourism, especially its benefits, reflects the widespread belief among agency personnel that tourism can yield rapid and considerable returns on investments and be a positive force in remedying economic problems.

The impact of tourism goes far beyond enrichment in purely economic terms, helping to benefit the environment and culture and the fight to reduce poverty – especially in developing countries. Tourism can serve as a foothold for the development of a market economy where small and medium-sized enterprises can expand and flourish. And in poor rural areas, it often constitutes the only alternative to subsistence farming which is in decline. Big emerging markets (BEMs) like Brazil, India, Turkey and Vietnam, also see the potential of tourism as a powerful economic force. Winter sport tourism has an important role to play in this economic development. A number of emerging destinations are developing and diversifying their winter tourism products in an effort to lure strong foreign currency, and thus spur economic growth. The last chapter referred to Turkey's efforts to boost winter sport tourism through the creation of new facilities across the country and the hosting of major events. By allowing the building of infrastructure and the import of quality resort builders and operators, countries like Turkey are able to achieve economic growth by attracting foreign tourists.

Winter sport tourism today attracts millions of holidaymakers worldwide, contributing billions of dollars to the global economy. In the U.S. alone, the winter tourism industry is worth around $12.2 billion (NRDC, 2012), supporting over 200,000 jobs earning around $7 billion in salaries. In turn, this activity results in $1.4 billion in state and local taxes and $1.7 billion in federal taxes. Resort operations contribute the greatest amount of employment and value added to the economy, with 75,900 employed (36% of total winter tourism-related employment) and $2.9 billion in added economic value (23% total winter tourism-related economic value added). Dining (in bars and restaurants) is the second biggest source of income, contributing 31,600 jobs (15% of total winter tourism-related employment) and $942 million in added economic value (8% of total economic value added).

There are an increasing number of government agencies and individual states conducting economic impact studies of their own. A study by Ski New Hampshire, for example, found that winter resorts in the state generated $1.15 billion in direct and secondary sales for the 2012-13 season, stemming from visits by 3.26 million guests to the group's 33 member areas (Ski Area Management, 2014). Capital investment at these resorts has totalled more than $121 million in the last decade - $38.4 million in snowmaking equipment, $31.4 million in ski lifts, $22.2 million in new and improved lodges, $15.6 million in trail grooming equipment, $7.6 million in off season/summer facilities, and $5.9 million in trail improvements.

Another recent economic impact study found that the nine largest ski areas of Lake Tahoe contributed $564 million to the local economy (Morales, 2014). These ski areas represent more than 75 per cent of all visits to the area, and a total of 2.72 million visits. These visitors spent $427 million directly on skiing or ski-related activities, primarily on lift tickets, food and drinks, and hotel rooms. Indirect expenditures, such as purchases from food wholesalers by restaurants, brought the total economic impact to $564.5 million. That generated $33 million in tax revenue for state and local governments. The resorts themselves supported 8,290 full- and part-time jobs, spent $21 million on capital improvements and paid $5 million in property taxes. The study was conducted by Patrick Tierney from San Francisco State University.

It was mentioned in Chapter 1 that the ski industry is highly vulnerable not only to spending patterns, but also to poor snow conditions, which can have a devastating economic impact on ski resorts. A recent study by the Natural Resources Defense Council (NRDC) found that the ski industry in the U.S. lost over $1 billion in aggregate revenue because of poor snow seasons between 2000 and 2010 (NRDC, 2012). Tables 10.2 and 10.3 show model projections of national employment difference and national economic value added in good snow years versus bad snow years.

	2010 Employment	With Replacement Consumer Spending		Without Replacement Consumer Spending	
		Employment Difference (# of jobs)	Percent Change	Employment Difference (# of jobs)	Percent Change
Direct	125,300	-16,455	-13%	-16,455	-13%
Indirect	31,400	-3,775	-12%	-3,775	-12%
Induced	55,200	7,265	13%	-6,600	-12%
Total	211,900	-12,965	-6%	-26,830	-13%

Table 10.2: Model projections of national employment difference, good snow years vs. bad snow years (Source: Courtesy of NRDC, 2012, p. 15)

	2010 Value Added ($billions)	With Replacement Consumer Spending		Without Replacement Consumer Spending	
		Difference in Value Added ($ millions)	Percent Change	Difference in Value Added ($ millions)	Percent Change
Direct	$4.90	$(797)	-16%	$(797)	-16%
Indirect	$2.90	$(447)	-15%	$(447)	-15%
Induced	$4.40	$434	10%	$(690)	-16%
Total	$12.20	$(810)	-7%	$1,934	-16%

Table 10.3: Model projections of difference in national economic value added, good snow years vs. bad snow years (Source: Courtesy of NRDC, 2012, p. 15)

European ski resorts are also seeing a negative impact on revenues from warmer winters. The World Wildlife Fund has observed an 18.7 per cent reduction in snowfall in the Southern (i.e. Italian) side of the Alps. Future projections are not encouraging, as average global temperatures are expected to rise by at least two degrees Celsius by 2050. Higher temperatures and less snow result in fewer skiers. For instance, during the mild start of 2014-15 winter, a 30 per cent fall in skiers compared to the same period the year before, was observed in the badly hit Italian region of Friuli. In the long term, the effects of global warming will eventually affect most Alpine regions suggesting that the same loss can be expected throughout the Alps. This could entail a loss of as many as 36 million tourists, and result in devastating effects on the employment levels and economic state of the region (Affairs Today, 2014).

Social impacts

Social impacts of tourism are 'people' impacts, and are concerned with the tourist, the host, and tourist-host interrelationships. In contrast to the economic impact studies, such effects are often portrayed in the literature in a negative light (Wall & Mathieson, 2006). There are a few theoretical frameworks that are applicable to social impact research in tourism. The first was developed by Doxey (1976) who suggested that the existence of reciprocating impacts between outsiders and residents may be converted into varying degrees of resident irritation, depending on the destination. The late Jost Krippendorf (1994) blamed mass tourism in the Swiss Alps for the resident hostility towards tourists, particularly amongst the younger generation. He suggested that seasonal workers are over-saturated with interaction with tourists, and sooner or later the symptoms of overkill will come to the surface. The overstressed worker will then react in an irritated and aggressive way. Table 10.4 shows the levels of resident irritation over time according to Doxey.

Stages of Development	Residents Attitudes Towards Tourism
Euphoria	Initial phase of development, visitors and developers welcome, little planning or control mechanism.
Apathy	Visitors taken for granted, contacts between residents and outsiders more formal (commercial), planning concerned mostly with marketing
Annoyance	Saturation points approached, residents have misgivings about tourism industry, policymakers attempt solutions via increasing infrastructure rather than limiting growth.
Antagonism	Irritations openly expressed, visitors seen as cause of all problems, planning now remedial but promotion increased to offset deteriorating reputation of destination.

Table 10.4: Doxey's Index of Irritation (Source: Adapted from Doxey, 1976, p. 26)

Numerous situations provoke irritation or feelings of resentment towards tourists. The most intense feelings appear to develop from three particular conditions (Wall & Mathieson, 2006):

1   The physical presence of tourists in the destination area, especially if they are in large groups. Congestion is often mentioned as a problem.

2   The demonstration effect. Residents frequently resent apparent material superiority of visitors and may try to copy their behaviors or spending patterns.

3   Foreign ownership and employment. The employment of non-locals in managerial and professional occupations provokes resentment.

Many of the points above have been raised in arguments opposing winter sport tourism in some countries. Chapter 5, for example, referred to the controversy in France where the French have banned ski hosts employed by international operators. The French insist that all hosts must be fully qualified ski instructors certified by the notoriously tough French examining system. British tour operators are appealing against the ban on ski hosting, arguing that the decision is in breach of European law. The Swiss, too, are upsetting British tour operators, and Switzerland has experiencing a mass exodus of U.K. chalet operators in the last few years prompted by a change in Swiss employment law for hospitality workers that binds U.K. operators to the Swiss rather than U.K. minimum wage for its chalet staff. Chalet staff were previously employed under a U.K. contract, but the new law means they must be employed on a Swiss contract and paid a minimum wage of 3,407CHF ($3,790) a month, which, because of the way Switzerland calculates its salaries, amounts to about $51,000 per annum. The average U.K. salary is $40,300. Andy Perrin, CEO of Hotelplan U.K., which owns Inghams, Ski Total and Esprit Ski, said: "The current situation is commercially untenable. It's a lose-lose situation, for us and for the resorts. There are a lot of guests who are going to lose the opportunity to ski affordably in Switzerland" (Morris, 2014).

Another framework for analyzing the interaction of tourists and residents was presented by Wall and Mathieson (2006), based on the work of Bjorklund and

Philbrick (1975) who suggested that the attitudes and behavior of groups or individuals to tourism may be either positive or negative, and active or passive. The resulting combinations to tourism may take one or more forms in the diagram below (see Figure 10.1).

	Active	Passive
Positive	FAVORABLE. Aggressive promotion and support of tourist activity	FAVORABLE. Slight acceptance of and support for tourist activity
Negative	UNFAVORABLE: Aggressive opposition to tourist activity	UNFAVORABLE: Silent acceptance but opposition to tourist activity

(Attitude/behavior shown on vertical axis; Active/Passive on horizontal axis)

Figure 10.1: Host attitudinal/behavioral responses to tourist activity (Source: Adapted from Wall & Mathieson, 2006)

Within any community, all four forms may exist at any one time but the number of people in any category need not remain constant. For example, entrepreneurs who are financially involved in tourism are likely to be engaged in aggressive promotion while an often small but highly vocal group could lead aggressive opposition to such tourism development. Hudson and Miller (2005) discussed growing opposition to heli-skiing in Canada and how a small action group - EKES (East Kootenay Environmental Society) had emerged as a fierce opponent to tourism organizations who operate in British Columbia's (BC) backcountry. Claiming that BC's back-country was home to 75 per cent of the world's mountain goat population as well as being the last refuge for the endangered mountain caribou, EKES claimed that heli-skiing was seriously impacting their critical wildlife habitats and wild spaces.

Over in Alberta, Canada, environmentalists, skiers, policy-makers and ski operators have been debating for many years whether or not skiing is an appropriate use of Banff National Park (Hudson, 2002). The National Parks Act of 1930 placed the use and enjoyment of the park by the human population first and foremost, and this encouraged the first alpine ski resort in the area at Sunshine in 1932. By the late 1960s, Sunshine had been joined by the ski resorts of Lake Louise and Mount Norquay, as Banff became a playground for the masses. However, the environmental movement worldwide was gathering speed, and in 1996, the Minister of Canadian Heritage appointed the Banff–Bow Valley (BBV) Task Force to assess the cumulative environmental effects of development in the park. The task force for the Banff–Bow Valley Study made over 400 recommendations, including stricter limits to growth; creative visitor management programs; the refocusing and upgrading of the role of tourism; and improvements in education,

10

awareness, and interpretation programs for tourists and residents. For ski resorts, in particular, it recommended capping skier numbers and prohibiting night use of ski hills.

In response to the BBV report, Ottawa took a much more active role in the park's future. In 1998, the government imposed controversial limits on commercial development in the Banff town site. Then, in the spring of 2000, Sheila Copps, the heritage minister, introduced legislation in Parliament outlining new rules for restrictive development in Banff and other national parks. These new policies would cut back ski area operations, cap daily skier capacity, and restrict future expansions in Banff and Jasper National Parks. The new Act moves ecological integrity to the top of the park's management agenda. However, owners of the ski areas in the park are far from happy with this new legislation, and have pursued legal action against Parks Canada over these policies, saying that the government measures were taken without consulting them and without obtaining the environmental assessment required under the Canadian Environmental Assessment Act. They say that their 30-year leases allow them to build lifts, clear trees, and cut glades, but the government is now prohibiting them from doing so. The conflict is still on going.

At times, of course, opposing groups will come together to find solutions to social problems associated with tourism development. Mitsch Bush (2006) has written about collaborative efforts to preserve open and agricultural lands in Steamboat Springs, Colorado. She suggests that when groups in a community feel a common threat to the land and to the character of their town, they will put aside differences and come together to find solutions to common problems. In Steamboat, she found that all segments of community – ranchers, skiers, environmentalists, and tourism-related business leaders – shared a sense of place. This shared sense that it was important to preserve open space came from both the old ranching traditions and the culture of the ski area, as well as the identity of "Ski town USA". People felt that what they cherished about their home town was threatened, and so meeting around the table as equals to deal with such threats led to more lasting partnerships and consensus about preservation.

Loftin and Victor (2006) have examined the social implications of ski resort development in the French resort of Villard de Lans. Employing Heiddeger's (1971) concepts of 'dwelling' and 'modernity' as a reference frame, they portray how ski resorts' development and subsequent tourism brought change to the way of life and "sense of place" in the small mountain community. What the authors suggest is that the villagers, whilst embracing modernization, have realized that visitors (and they themselves) like the scale, character, and texture of the old medieval Villard de Lans, and that it is worth preserving. Both groups want a village, a valley, and a resort founded on the experience of 'dwelling'. Loftin and Victor suggest that recent requirements by the European Union regarding preservation of the existing landscape of the Alps have resulted in reviving a sense of pride in local inhabitants towards their heritage.

A number of researchers have considered the plight – a common one in many ski resorts – of people who find the local cost of occupancy in resort communities so severe that they are forced to move outside the community. Clark (2006), for example, suggests that the availability of affordable housing in exclusive mountain communities is a critical policy issue in rural regional development in many parts of North America. Krippendorf (1994) linked winter sport tourism with negative impacts on the housing market in mountain resorts. He referred to the 'unpaid social costs' for the host population associated with tourism development in the mountains (p. 49). First the locals sell off their land for building at low prices to non-residents, losing control of economic development. When land prices start to rise, the locals are left out in the cold, because it is others who make a profit. Ultimately, the locals can no longer afford to live, let alone build a house, in their own district because of high land prices and rents paid by non-residents. This kind of situation can be observed in various tourist districts in the Swiss mountain areas, but affordable housing problems also exist in many winter sport tourism destinations in North America.

But winter sports do have a number of positive impacts, and the limited studies on the impact of winter sport tourism to destinations, suggest that host populations consider that tourism brings to the destination more advantages than disadvantages (see Brida, Osti & Faccioli, 2011 for example). Certainly, the sport has health and recreational benefits for residents. The ski areas in Banff National Park, referred to above, are an important recreational resource for Alberta residents who make up half of the total number of visitors to the Alberta Rocky Mountain resorts. Visitors can also experience a significant contribution to quality of life from ski vacations, with several studies showing that vacations have a positive impact on travelers' physical and psychological wellbeing – benefits which they take back to the office. Previous research indicates that people who take vacations sleep better and are less likely to be tense or depressed. They are less prone to chronic diseases such as heart disease, hypertension and Type 2 diabetes. Travel stimulates the brain and promotes the growth of new synapses, heightens creativity, and may even help resist Alzheimer's disease. In addition, vacations are a primary source of family bonding and are good for marriages. We also know that vacations alleviate job stress and burnout, factors that cause absenteeism to rise – and this absenteeism results in a significant cost and source of disruption to businesses.

Fitness experts and researchers are finding that outdoor workouts in cold weather offer unexpected benefits. For example, increasing exposure to sunlight may help fend off seasonal affective disorder, or SAD, a type of depression linked to the change in seasons. A recent study from Finland found that working out in nature leads to greater emotional wellbeing and better sleep than exercising indoors (Howard, 2015). Downhill skiing burns on average 363 calories an hour, cross-country and snowshoeing 508, and ice skating 580 calories at more than 9mph. Certainly, ski areas can play an important role in providing opportunities for exercise, and some are proactive in pushing these benefits. For example,

Wachusett Mountain Ski Area in Massachusetts has partnered with Fallon Community Health Plans to allow members to use their fitness reimbursement ($400 in 2015) towards ski lift tickets and lessons.

Ski areas can also be catalysts for positive social change in their backyards. Corporate social responsibility has become an integral part of business for most large ski operators, with many dedicated to being charitable and being actively engaged with the local community (see Whistler Profile below). A good example is Vail Resorts, which announced in 2014 a gift of more than $1,300,000 in EpicPromise community grants, awarded to 30 non-profit organizations based in Summit and Wasatch counties. The grants support youth program and environmental initiatives that provide basic needs, connect children with the outdoors, rehabilitate popular trails and increase educational opportunities for all children. In addition to these programs, Vail Resorts is committed to connecting employees with the community. In 2013/14, employees gave more than 20,000 hours of company sponsored time.

Profile: Keeping Whistler wild

Since 1998, Whistler Blackcomb's sustainability programs have won 30 awards and its Environmental Fund has sponsored 46 local projects. Through its employee carpooling program it has reduced its emissions by 200 tons per year. It has saved 18 per cent of fuel per hour by purchasing new snow grooming fleets. And 4.5 million kilowatt hours of power is saved annually through its Power Smart partnership with BC Hydro. Around the resort 11,000 light bulbs have been changed to energy-efficient models.

Arthur de Jong

All of these eco projects have been spearheaded by Arthur de Jong who heads up Whistler Blackcomb's Environment Team. A team player, de Jong says he is only as good as the people surrounding him: "Allana Williams, our Energy manager, has been integral on many of these initiatives as she leads our energy conservation programs as well as the many staff at WB who help drive these initiatives. I am privileged to work with so many staff that are committed to driving our conservation culture."

Over more than 30 years at the British Columbia resort, his various roles have included Ski Patrol Manager and Mountain Operations Manager for Blackcomb, leading to a close rapport with the mountain terrain and a profound understanding of the mountain ecosystem. Pioneering work in environmental planning led to de Jong's current position as Mountain Planning and Environmental Resource Manager. "On climate change, we have considerable resilience here in Whistler but ultimately we will go as the global economy goes," says de Jong. "That is why we must demonstrate what a conservation culture is and compel the general economy to do the same." His everyday job is to develop sustainable planning techniques in order to improve guest experiences without compromising the natural environment.

In de Jong's introduction to his annual operating footprint report 2015, he said that Whistler Blackcomb's primary sustainability goal for mountain operations was as close to zero footprint as possible. "The business imperative is we become more cost efficient by operating with fewer inputs and outputs of fuel, hydroelectricity, and waste," he explained. "A direct benefit to the bottom-line." But there was also a moral imperative, he added: "Our general economy and society critically need examples of economic models that demonstrate sustainable growth especially targeted on the reduction of fossil fuels thereby addressing climate change."

He also explained that companies with the strongest brands place emphasis on actions that align with *both* imperatives, thereby adding value to the bottom line and also society in general. "Reducing our operating footprint clearly aligns with this," he concluded. An example of this is The Fitzsimmons Creek Renewable Energy Project which will return back to the power grid what Whistler Blackcomb consumes from the grid, leaving a zero footprint. This run-of-river project produces 33 gigawatt hours of hydroelectricity per year – enough to power the resort's winter and summer operations, including the 38 lifts, 270 snow guns and 17 restaurants. Involving more than six years of studies and planning, the Project is owned by Fitzsimmons Creek Hydro Limited Partnership in which Whistler Blackcomb is a strategic partner. This work led to the resort being awarded the Golden Eagle Award for Overall Environmental Excellence at the 2010 National Ski Areas Association National Convention and Tradeshow.

Another underlying theme of de Jong's philosophy is that building partnerships – with the community, NGOs and Government – is essential for sustainability success. As an active member of the Whistler community for three decades, de Jong believes that the key to effective planning is openness and community involvement. As well as belonging to numerous community social and environmental groups, he also dedicates volunteer time to crisis line counseling and international aid programs.

In respect to on-mountain development, he has learned not to change ecosystems for human use, but to build recreational experiences *inside* ecosystems. "That was the vision with the Symphony Chair expansion," he explained. This high-speed chairlift opened on December 16, 2006, bringing access to 1,000 acres of skiable terrain in the Symphony Amphitheatre, previous only accessed by arduous hiking. The design team included a black bear researcher and a professional forester along with planners and engineers, who had to manage a lift with a 2,400-hour capacity, while preserving the natural wildlife and fish ecosystems.

One of the ways the footprint was minimized included moving only those trees that were between tree islands or which presented a disease threat. Trees were removed via helicopter and all lift towers and assemblies were placed via helicopter. The selective forestry approach - called a "silviculture prescription" – actually enhanced lichen production for deer and berry production for black bears. Also, denning and wetlands areas were kept exempt from development. All lift foundations were built over the snow during April and May 2006, ensuring ground disturbance was reduced to the foundation site only. By utilizing many other environmental safeguards, the overall footprint – originally estimated at 40 per cent – was reduced to less than five per cent.

During de Jong's stewardship, Whistler Blackcomb has also developed programs for wide scale recycling, organic waste composting, reduction of single use cups, and garbage reduc-

10

tion in public and staff areas with signage to increase awareness. Through reduction, reuse and recycling, particularly in food and beverage, levels of waste have reduced 60 per cent since 1998. And building retrofits have saved more than 860 tons of emissions.

The Whistler Blackcomb staff culture helps perpetuate the resort's environmental goals. Involved in programs such as the Habitat Improvement Team, Operation Green Up and an annual Mountain Clean Up Day at the end of the ski season, employees are partners in environmental stewardship.

As a result of all these eco efforts, Whistler Blackcomb was named by Maclean's Magazine in 2009 as one of Canada's 30 Greenest Employers.

Sources: Interview with Arthur de Jong, March 2015; http://ww1.whistlerblackcomb.com/media/environment/department.asp

Environmental impacts

Conflicts between environmentalists and ski resort developers can be found in ski areas around the world although some – for instance, the Mt Buller and Mt Stirling ski area in Australia featured in the Case Study below – have tackled this in creative ways.

In the Alps, the mountains are among Europe's most threatened wilderness areas, with the rapid growth of skiing central to the crisis. Destruction has been caused by deforestation and altering the use of traditional Alpine land for construction of dams, skiing facilities and hotels and by the dumping of waste which has polluted nearby lakes (Hudson, 1995). There is a growing view that the landscapes of the western Alps in France, Switzerland and Austria are under serious threat from tourism, especially the development of higher resorts. Mountain Wilderness, Alp Action, the World Wild Life Fund (WWF), and the League Valaisan pour la Protection de Nature (LVPN), are just a few of the many organizations that have dedicated themselves to raising the awareness of environmental problems and the prevention of further damage. Ski resort developers are finding it increasingly difficult to expand due to opposition from these groups.

In Japan, the construction and enlargement of ski resorts has caused serious environmental problems (Tsuyazaki, 1994), but environmentalists have little power. Like Europe and North America in the 60s and 70s, the construction of new ski resorts in Japan today is for tourism rather than for the recreation of residents, and therefore the primary motivations are economic. Environmental deterioration according to Tsuyazaki includes landscape fragmentation, soil erosion, and noise and air pollution. Environmental considerations are often ignored during ski resort construction, and any regulation by law to restrict ski resort construction is not effective.

In North America, opposition to ski resort expansion and development has centered on environmental issues. Environmental protests against ski area developments date back to at least 1963, when Walt Disney tried (unsuccessfully) to build a ski resort at Mineral King, a high basin in the southern Sierra. Disney simply misunderstood the almost sacred character of the National Parks (Tejada-Flores, 1999). In the 70s, critics labeled ski area developers 'abominable snowmen' and charged that they cause soil erosion, water pollution and led to 'tacky pizza parlors, motels and gas stations' in formerly unspoiled mountain settings (Smith, 2013). Well-financed environmentalists are now battling ski resorts of all sizes. With a few exceptions, virtually every form of construction or expansion that is proposed for ski areas is being challenged. Even replacement lifts and improvements to on-mountain lodges are drawing intense opposition.

For the most part, the ski industry recognizes the potential for environmental impact that its activities may create (Todd & Williams, 1996). In June 2000, about 160 American ski areas signed the 'Sustainable Slopes' Charter. The Charter (now endorsed by 190 resorts) was developed with input from a variety of ski industry leaders; environmental groups; federal, state, county and local agencies; outdoor recreation groups; ski industry suppliers; and other stakeholders. The Charter is a voluntary set of guiding principles and tools that assist ski resorts in being able to effectively integrate environmental protection concepts into all aspects of design, maintenance and operation of ski resorts. It sets out dozens of rules for ski areas to follow in the management of their resorts and construction of new facilities. The Charter calls for: use of high-density development to cut back on sprawl; reductions in water consumed by snowmaking; and savings in the energy required for lodges, vehicles and ski lifts.

While ski resorts acknowledge that mistakes were made 20, 30 and 40 years ago, there are both a new management style and a new commitment to have skiing co-exist with the environment. Mair and Jago (2010) have proposed a conceptual model for corporate greening that could be applied to the ski sector. The model suggests that the organization (size, type, sector, etc.) provides the context for the process, and the organization is faced with a number of drivers (both internal and external) that exert pressure towards greening. The organization is also faced with a number of barriers (resources, for example) that may impede greening. Even once all the relevant drivers and barriers have been considered, the salience of the environment at a given time (affected by the extent and content of media coverage) may exert a positive or negative effect on the organization's intentions to become greener, leading to either a lower or higher degree of greening within the organization.

In the last few decades, ski resorts around the world have tried to tackle the problems linked to tourism and the environment, demonstrating that they are no longer necessarily looking for greater numbers of skiers, but are trying to consolidate and improve the quality of their existing facilities. The Aspen Skiing Company, for example, has taken a lead in showing ski destinations how to be environmentally conscious. The resort was the first to appoint an Environmental Affairs Director, and has won numerous awards for developing a green campaign. It was also the first ski resort to produce an Environmental Sustainability Report, and initiatives over the years have included the installation of a wind-powered surface lift; a state-of-the-art computer system that monitors and adjusts energy consumption among lifts and snowmaking pumps; the ski industry's first environmental website and intra-company environmental newsletter; and the banning of swordfish in restaurants so as not to contribute to the declining North Atlantic swordfish. Aspen's consciousness is reflected in virtually every one of their departments. Employees donate $1 a week to an Environment Foundation which was formed in 1999 as a way for employees to leverage corporate dollars to protect the environment. Their money is matched more than three times, by Aspen Community Foundation, Aspen Skiing Company's Family Fund, Keurig Green Mountain, Inc. (Keurig), and Swire Coca-Cola. In 17 years the foundation has donated almost $2.6 million to causes like clean energy legislation, trail maintenance, open space preservation and energy efficiency.

In Europe, there is no single ski resort that stands out for its commitment towards the environment. However, there is evidence of a new trend in environmental stewardship. At Klosters in Switzerland, following consultation with all interested parties – the lift companies, forest service, ski guides, hunters etc. – zones have been set aside in sensitive areas of the forest to protect flora and fauna. These are clearly marked and a brochure has been produced highlighting the location of the areas and informing skiers of the harmful effects of skiing in the forest. And, in order to regulate the amount of traffic, Lech in Austria now limits the number of ski lift passes available to day-trippers to 14,000. Signs on the motorway approaches from Germany indicate when the resort is full and advise drivers to try alternative resorts. Outside the village of Lech, a biomass heating plant provides energy and warm water for more than 100 hotels. It is run on sustainable wood from the surrounding forests.

The limited research on skiers and their environmental commitment has produced contradictory results. A Roper survey in the 90s discovered that skiers, more than many other groups of tourists, were especially worried about the environmental results of development and growth (NSAA, 1994). Also, SKI Magazine says it has conducted numerous independent surveys over the past decade that show skiers are more concerned about the environment than all other sportsmen (Castle, 1999). However, Fry (1995) found that skiers don't have strong views about the environment, and more experienced skiers actually favor expansion of ski areas. In an environmental awareness study in Austria, the majority of skiers (59%) were prepared to pay an 'environmental' tax if it would mean that something constructive would be done for the environment in their chosen holiday resort (Weiss et al., 1998). But although the skiers in the Austrian study showed a high degree of environmental awareness, they were not prepared to restrict their skiing to protect the countryside, and did not agree with limited sale of lift tickets. In a study of skiers in Banff, Hudson and Ritchie (2001) found a general lack of knowledge amongst skiers about environmental issues pertaining to skiing. The majority believe skiing and snowboarding to be environmentally friendly but say ski terrain should be limited because it disturbs wildlife habitat and migratory paths. Nearly half of the skiers agreed that skiing numbers in the National Park should be capped to protect the environment, but Canadian skiers (unlike US or British skiers) were not willing to pay extra for 'greener' ski areas.

The impact of climate change on winter sport tourism

Numerous studies have documented or discussed potential effects of climate change on tourism and outdoor recreation (Hall & Higham, 2005; Becken & Hay, 2007). Smith's (1990) seminal work on tourism and climate change predicted that tourism would experience a complex mix of winners and losers from climate change; more recent research suggests that these winners and losers could well be located in the same region (Brouder & Lundmark, 2011). Most of the research related to winter sport tourism and climate change has focused on potential 'losers'. Studies from Europe (Breiling & Charamza 1999; Burki et al., 2005; Elsasser & Burki, 2002), Canada (Scott, McBoyle & Minogue, 2007), the U.S. (Dawson & Scott, 2013; NRDC, 2012), and Australia (Pickering, 2011), have tended to highlight the major losers as a result of climate change – these losers are likely to be the low-altitude ski resorts in climatically and geographically disadvantaged regions (Brouder & Lundmark, 2011, Scott & Steiger, 2013).

However, Toglofer, Eigner and Prettenthaler (2011) argued that the negative effects of climate change have been ameliorated somewhat during the past 25 years, partly due to enhanced snowmaking technology. Similar findings were reported in the northeastern U.S. (Dawson, Scott & McBoyle, 2009). Their climate change analogue analysis showed that adaptions by ski businesses (such as snow-making), and diversification of year-round tourism products (such as golfing and cycling), appear to have reduced the negative impacts of increasingly warmer average winter temperatures. Pons-Pons et al. (2012) came to the same conclusion after studying climate change effects on the ski industry in Andorra, but they did warn that snowmaking should be considered only as a short-term adaptive strategy given the associated high costs and potential damage to the ecosystem.

A wide range of methodologies has been used to predict the effects of climate change on winter sports. To estimate the monetary loss for the Swedish skiing industry, for instance, Moen and Fredman (2007) combined regional projections of climate change with trends in alpine winter tourism and predicted effects on the number of skiing days. In Australia, Pickering (2011) obtained data on snow conditions and visitations for a six-year period in order to assess potential demand side responses to low levels of natural snow in the country. Toglofer et al. (2011) went further back in time, using air temperature and precipitation data to analyze the snow conditions for 185 ski areas over the last 34 winter seasons. Pons-Pons et al. (2012) presented a geo-referenced agent-based model to analyze climate change impacts on the ski industry in Andorra, Spain. This model took into account skiers' responses to snow conditions and the limited adaptive effect of

10

snowmaking on future season length. Finally, Scott and Steiger (2013) introduced a sensitivity analysis approach that utilized industry relevant indicators such as ski season length, snowmaking requirements, and the SkiSim 2™ ski operations model to facilitate inter-regional climate vulnerability comparisons across a wide range of potential climate futures in the USA and Austria.

Other researchers have questioned key stakeholders about their perceptions related to climate change in winter resorts to determine potential impacts on the industry. Brouder and Lundmark (2011), for example, questioned 63 entrepreneurs in Finland, finding that the general perception among businesses is that climate change will not drastically impact the tourism sector there during the next 10 years. Wolfsegger, Gossling and Scott (2008) and Wolfsegger (2005) found that most ski operators in low-elevation Austrian ski locations do not perceive climate change as a substantial threat, believing that adaptations such as snowmaking are effective in overcoming warming temperatures. Ghaderi, Khoshkam and Henderson (2013) found that stakeholders in the Iranian ski resort of Dizin were focusing on adaptive strategies to counteract climate change, such as developing other nature-based pursuits throughout the year as an alternative to skiing. More recently, Hopkins (2014) conducted a perceptual study of ski industry stakeholders in Queenstown, New Zealand and found a focus on short-term economic sustainability, with snowmaking central to addressing both current weather variability and medium/long term future climate change.

Regardless of ranking, it is clear that ski resorts can no longer ignore the threat of climate change. Dawson and Scott's (2013) climate change management decision-making flowchart for ski operators suggests that communities that lose ski tourism operations, revenues and related jobs will need to develop economic diversification strategies, if they have not already done so. Resorts that are potentially vulnerable will, at some point, need to determine if they want to invest heavily in adaptations, such as snowmaking and expanded facilities, or evolve into multi-season destinations, or ultimately terminate their businesses. It is not unheard of for a ski resort to cease operations because of a lack of reliable snow cover: Pigeon Mountain ski resort in Alberta, Canada, is one such example. There are others scattered across the landscape.

The ski industry, as a whole, is recognizing the need to strive toward adopting environmentally-friendly policies and practices. A number of individual tourism industry associations, such as the Banff Lake Louise Tourism Bureau, the Ontario Snow Resorts Association (Rutty et al., 2014), and individual ski resorts in Canada and the USA, have shown leadership on climate change by voluntarily adopting greenhouse gas (GHG) emission reduction targets. The industry, as a whole, has also engaged in public education campaigns on climate change and in support of government climate change legislation (United Nations World Tourism Organization, 2007). As noble as these policies and practices may be, the political will to address climate change amongst travel practitioners is questionable (Weaver, 2011; McKercher, Mak & Wong, 2014), and even then, their actions are likely to be insufficient to delay the projected rise in temperatures expected by 2050.

Other ski resorts in North America have signed up to the Sustainable Slopes Charter (adopted by the U.S. ski industry in 2000), which provides an overarching framework for ski areas regarding sustainability and enhanced environmental performance. As part of this Charter, the National Ski Areas Association has a voluntary climate challenge program dedicated to helping participating ski areas reduce GHG emissions and reap other benefits in their operations, such as reducing costs for energy use. Such initiatives may have a nominal effect on reducing GHGs and improving the bottom line of an individual ski resort, but the Natural Resources Defense Council (2012) argues that without any intervention, winter temperatures are projected to rise an additional four to 10 degrees Fahrenheit by the end of the century, with subsequent decreases in snowfall amounts and shorter ski seasons. Potentially, given the predicted and increasingly serious effects of climate change after the 2050s, ski tourism may become a niche product in the second half of the century (Steiger, 2013).

Case study: Recycling snow 'Down Under'

Snowmaking at Mt Buller, photo courtesy of Andrew Railton

The Mt Buller and Mt Stirling ski area in central Victoria, Australia has a strong background – and high ranking – in eco-tourism. But, like all ski regions threatened by global climate change, it has to address the tricky issue of producing artificial snow to bolster natural snowfalls.

Naturally, snowmaking requires large volumes of water which usually comes from nearby lakes and rivers. But as the resort's website says: "A priority of the Mt Buller and Mt Stirling Alpine Resort Management Board is protection of the high country streams and rivers which

10

originate from the snowfields and alpine slopes. The Delatite and Howqua Rivers ....sustain neighboring farm and town communities as well as provide lasting enjoyment to thousands of people including bushwalkers, canoeists, anglers and campers. Protection and preservation of water quality and quantity are of paramount importance to the wider community and a key objective of environmental management of the Resort."

So, while its snowmaking water was traditionally provided by Boggy Creek, a tributary of the Delatite River, the resort has spent considerable time and money looking elsewhere for supplies. Its Snowmaking and Wastewater Recycling Pilot Study investigated making snow from treated effluent (sewage!) from the local wastewater treatment plant run by the Mt Buller and Mt Stirling Alpine Resort Management Board. This would have two potential eco benefits: firstly, decreased volumes of effluent released into the environment and secondly, decreased extraction of water from Boggy Creek. Before using the wastewater for snowmaking, it had to be further purified both for health and environmental reasons to Class A standards (those required for human food crops and irrigation of parklands and golf courses).

Using ultra-filtration and ozonation via a $1 million filtering system, the resort was able to produce clean, pure water to pump through the snowmaking guns onto the slopes. Purifying around 800,000 liters of wastewater each day, the resort initially hoped to meet around 10 per cent of its needs over a three-year period from 2008. Since then, a new Class A Wastewater Treatment Plant can now provide up to two million liters of recycled water for snowmaking per day, increasing Mt Buller's capacity by 30 per cent. There is a fail-safe mechanism that ensures that the system automatically stops during a system malfunction to prevent any untreated water from entering Sun Valley Reservoir, the snowmaking dam. Requiring 24-hour monitoring for consistent water purity, the project has cost in the region of $3.43 million.

The Mt Buller and Mt Stirling Alpine Resort Management Board was recognized for this innovative work by the United Nations Association of Australia at the World Environment Day awards in 2002.

Mt Buller's Environmental Policy is designed to meet criteria outlined in AS/NZS ISO 14001:1996, the leading international standard on environmental management. The ski area is committed to an Environmental Management Plan which guarantees protection of the natural environment while ensuring the sustainability of resort activity and development. The plan incorporates flora and fauna, ecosystems, environmental values and useful information about climate and geography. As the resort is on Crown land, it encourages community input into management with an extensive committee established to address environmental matters.

With a resort entry fee instigated at Mirimbah, at the base of the mountain, some of the burden of funding environmental programs is shifted to the resort's guests. The fee – which grants access to both mountains – helps maintain essential infrastructure and services including roads and water treatment. Future aims include utilizing the recycled water for household use in new developments and for irrigating open spaces.

Sources: http://www.skiclub.co.uk/skiclub/skiresorts/greenresorts/resort.aspx/Mount-Buller#. VMeuW1uGhSU

References

Affairs Today (2014) 'The effects of global warming on the economy of the Alps', accessed 1/25/2015 from http://affairstoday.co.uk/effects-global-warming-economy-alps

Becken, S. and Hay, J. (2007) *Tourism and Climate Change: Risks and Opportunities*, Clevedon: Channel View Publications.

Bjorklund, E.M. and Philbrick, A.K. (1975) 'Spatial configurations of mental processes', pp. 57-75 in Belanger, M. and Janelle, D.G. (eds.) *Building Regions for the Future*, Notes et Documents de Recherche No. 6 Department de Geographie, Universite Laval, Laval, Quebec.

Breiling M. and Charamza, P. (1999) 'The impact of global warming on winter tourism and skiing: a regionalized model for Austrian snow conditions', *Regional Environmental Change*, **1**, 4-14.

Brida, J.G., Osti, L. and Faccioli, M. (2011) Residents' perception and attitudes towards tourism impacts, *Benchmarking: An International Journal*, **18**(3), 359-385.

Brouder, P. and Lundmark, L. (2011) 'Climate change in Northern Sweden: Intra-regional perceptions of vulnerability among winter-oriented tourism businesses', *Journal of Sustainable Tourism*, **19**, 919-933.

Bürki, R. Elsasser, H. and Abegg, B. (2003) *Climate change and winter sports: Environmental and economic threats. Proceedings of the 5th World Conference on Sport and Environment.* Turin, Italy, December 2-3, 2003.

Butler, R. (1993) 'Tourism - an evolutionary perspective', in Butler, R.W., Nelson, J.G., Wall, G. (Eds) *Tourism and Sustainable Development: Monitoring, Planning, Managing*. Department of Geography Publication 37, University of Waterloo, Waterloo, Chapter 2, pp. 29.

Castle, K. (1999) 'Skiing and the environment, Part 1: The battle lines are drawn', *Ski*, **64**(3), 118-128.

Clark, T. (2006) 'Paradise's closing door: Dynamics of residential exclusion in Mountain resort regions', in T. Clark, A. Gill and R. Hartmann (Eds.), *Mountain Resort Planning and Development in an Era of Globalization*, (pp. 127-147) New York: Cognizant Communication Corporation.

Dawson, J. and Scott, D. (2013) 'Managing for climate change in the alpine ski sector', *Tourism Management*, **35**, 244-254.

Dawson, J., Scott, D. and McBoyle, G. (2009) 'Climate change analogue analysis of ski tourism in the northeastern USA', *Climate Research*, **39**, 1-9.

Doxey, C.V. (1976) 'When enough's enough: The natives are restless in Old Niagara', *Heritage Canada*, **2**(2), 26-27.

Elsasser, H. and Bürki, R. (2002) 'Climate change as a threat to tourism in the Alps', *Climate Research*, **20**, 253-257.

Fry, J. (1995) 'Exactly what are their environmental attitudes?' *Ski Area Management*, **34**(6), 45-70.

Ghaderi, Z., Khoshkam, M. and Henderson, J.C. (2013) 'From snow skiing to grass skiing: Implications of climate change for the ski industry in Dizin, Iran', *Anatolia: An International Journal of Tourism and Hospitality Research*, **25**(1), 96-107.

Hall, C. M. and Higham, J. (eds.) (2005) *Tourism, Recreation and Climate Change*, Clevedon: Channel View Publications.

Heidegger, M. (1971) *Poetry, Language, Thought*. A. Hofstadter (Trans.), New York: Harper and Row.

Hopkins, D. (2014) 'The sustainability of climate change adaption strategies in New Zealand's ski industry: A range of stakeholder perceptions', *Journal of Sustainable Tourism*, **22**(1), 107-126.

Howard, B. (2015) 'Why winter is a great time to exercise...outside', *Wall Street Journal*, 19 January.

Hudson, S. (1995) 'Responsible tourism: A model for the greening of Alpine ski resorts', In Fleming et al., (eds), *Policy & politics in sport, physical education & leisure*. **55**, 239-256. LSA Publication.

Hudson, S. (2002) 'Environmental management in the Rockies: The dilemma of balancing National Park values while making provision for their enjoyment', *Journal of Case Research*, **22**(2), 1–14.

Hudson, S. and Miller, G. (2005) 'The responsible marketing of tourism: The case of Canadian Mountain Holidays', *Tourism Management*, **26**(2), 133-142.

Hudson, S. and Ritchie, J.R.B. (2001) 'Cross-cultural tourist behavior: An analysis of tourist attitudes towards the environment', *Journal of Travel and Tourism Marketing*, **10**(2/3).

Krippendorf, J. (1987) *The Holidaymakers*, London: Heinemann.

Lin, T., Halbrendt, C., Liang, C. and Wood, N. (1999) 'The impact of the tourism sector on the Vermont economy: The input-output analysis', paper presented at the American Agricultural Economics Association Annual Meeting, Nashville, Tennessee, Aug 8-11.

Loftin, L.K. and Victor, J.G. (2006) 'Villards de Lans: Global intervention and local resurgence,' In T. Clark, A. Gill and R. Hartmann (Eds.), *Mountain Resort Planning and Development in an Era of Globalization*, (pp. 53-64) New York: Cognizant Communication Corporation.

Mair, J., and Jago, L. (2010) 'The development of a conceptual model of greening in the business events sector', *Journal of Sustainable Tourism*, **18**(1), 77-94.

McKercher, B., Mak, B. and Wong, S. (2014) 'Does climate change matter to the travel trade?' *Journal of Sustainable Tourism*, Published online January 14.

Mitsch Bush, D.E. (2006) 'From collaboration to implementation in an era of globalization: Local policies to preserve agriculture, wildlife habitat, and open space in mountain resort towns of the Rocky Mountain West', in T. Clark, A. Gill and R. Hartmann (Eds.), *Mountain Resort Planning and Development in an Era of Globalization*, (pp. 202-220) New York: Cognizant Communication Corporation.

Moen, J. and Fredman, P. (2007) 'Effects of climate change on alpine skiing in Sweden', *Journal of Sustainable Tourism*, **15**, 418-437.

Morales, J. (2014) 'Ski industry lifts Tahoe economy by $564 million, study finds,' *SF State News*, 15 October, accessed 1/25/2015 from http://news.sfsu.edu/ski-industry-lifts-tahoe-economy-564-million-study-finds

Morris, H. (2014) 'Swiss law change sparks UK ski chalet closures', *Telegraph*, 22 August, accessed 1/25/2015 from http://www.telegraph.co.uk/travel/snowandski/skiing-news/11035026/Swiss-law-change-sparks-UK-ski-chalet-closures.html

Natural Resources Defense Council (2012) *Climate impacts on the winter tourism economy in the United States*. Elizabeth Burrows and Matthew Magnusson: New York: Natural Resources Defense Council.

National Ski Areas Association. (1994) 'Enhance ski areas' environmental image', *Ski Area Management*, **33**(1), 4.

Pickering, C. (2011) 'Changes in demand for tourism with climate change: A case study of visitation patterns to six ski resorts in Australia', *Journal of Sustainable Tourism*, **19**, 767-781.

Pons-Pons, M., Johnson, P.A., Rosas-Casals, M., Sureda, B. and Jover, E. (2012) 'Modeling climate change effects on winter tourism in Andorra', *Climate Research*, **54**, 197-207.

Rutty, M., Matthews, L., Scott, D. and Del Matto, T. (2013) 'Using vehicle monitoring technology and eco-driver training to reduce fuel use and emissions in tourism: A ski resort case study', *Journal of Sustainable Tourism*, Published online November 9.

Scott, D., McBoyle, G. and Minogue, A. (2007) 'Climate change and Quebec's ski industry', *Global Environmental change;* **17**, 181-190.

Scott, D. and Steiger, R. (2013) 'Vulnerability of the ski industry', *Climate Vulnerability,* **4**, 305-313.

Ski Area Management (2014) 'N.H. resorts tally $1.15 billion economic impact', *SAM Online*, 21 February, accessed 1/25/2015 from http://www.saminfo.com/news/nh-resorts-tally-115-billion-economic-impact

Smith, K. (1990) 'Tourism and climate change', *Land Use Policy*, **7**, 176-180.

Smith, M.S. (2013) *American Ski Resort. Architecture, Style, Experience*, Norman, OK: Oklahoma University Press.

Steiger, R. (2013) 'Scenarios for skiing tourism in Austria: Integrating demographics with an analysis of climate change', *Journal of Sustainable Tourism*, **20**, 867-882.

Tejada-Flores, L. (1999) 'Green vs growth', *Skiing: Winter adventure*, December, 149-157.

Todd, S.E. and Williams, P.W. (1996) 'From white to green: A proposed environmental management system for ski areas', *Journal of Sustainable Tourism*, **4**(3), 147-173.

Toglofer, C., Eigner, F. and Prettenthaler, F. (2011) 'Impacts of snow conditions on tourism demand in Austrian ski areas', *Climate Research*, **46**, 1-14.

Tsuyuzaki, S. (1994) 'Environmental deterioration resulting from ski-resort construction in Japan', *Environmental Conservation*, **21**(2), 121-125.

United Nations World Tourism Organization (2007) *Climate Change and Tourism: Responding to Global Challenges*, Advanced Summary, October.

10

Wall, G. and Mathieson, A. (2006) *Tourism. Change, Impacts and Opportunities,* Harlow, England: Pearson Education.

Weaver, D. (2011) 'Can sustainable tourism survive climate change?' *Journal of Sustainable Tourism,* **19**(1), 5-15.

Weiss, O., Norden, G., Hilscher, P. and Vanreusal, B. (1998) 'Ski tourism and environmental problems', *International Review for the Sociology of Sport,* **33**(4), 367-379.

Wolfsegger, C. (2005) *Perception and adaptation to climate change in low altitude ski resorts in Austria.* Unpublished Master degree, Lund University, Helsingborg, Sweden.

Wolfsegger, C., Gossling, S. and Scott, D. (2008) 'Climate change risk appraisal in the Austrian ski industry', *Tourism Review International,* **12**, 13-23.

11 Developing a Service Culture

Andrew Dunn - Photo Courtesy of Scott Dunn Travel

A British luxury travel company has spent over 25 years wowing its customers. From its first ski season when the owner personally drove to France with huge supplies of bacon to perfect its English breakfasts, Scott Dunn has gone the extra mile for service and for quality. 'From day one we wanted to be the best,' says founder Andrew Dunn. The company was established in 1986 initially as a ski chalet business, operating out of two chalets in Verbier, Switzerland. Despite first year losses, 22-year-old Dunn ploughed on, opening up chalets in neighboring resorts and differentiating on comforts such as down duvets and morning tea in bed. Launching his London office in 1988, he provided his own staff and British nannies for his Swiss and French properties, establishing a benchmark for Alpine chalet holidays with his emphasis on opulence and personal service. Up until then, most competitors had provided quaint but adequate accommodation, basic catering, and very low-budget wines.

When Giles Tonner joined the Scott Dunn team in the 1990s, worldwide tailor-made adventure holidays were added to the mix – this was soft adventure without compromising comfort. Seeing a bigger profit margin in high-end travel, Dunn also added long-haul luxury and Mediterranean villas with private chefs, hosts, nannies and exclusive children's clubs. He was following the advice of his grandmother who told him when he started his business: "Andrew, you never want to be selling the cheapest – people will always pay for the best."

A graduate in Psychology and Biology from Oxford Brookes University, Dunn has always been astute in consumer behavior. "I was acutely aware that a guest is not just a single purchase; they are a multiple purchase and there's potentially a lifetime journey with them." He looks to woo each customer early on and retain them through the different phases of their lives: marriage, parenthood and beyond. "It's a massive responsibility because if you screw up it's not just that booking you are going to lose; you've probably lost another six bookings over the next couple of years," he says. His education helped out with recruitment and training, too. "I've always had a knack for finding the right people to work for me. It's a question of whether I like an individual and a lot about chemistry. I need to know 'do they care' and 'do they want to give the guests the best experience possible' or do they just want to travel the globe," says Dunn. Unlike many travel companies, he retains a strong base of year-round staff in order to ensure consistency and high standards with a permanent management team in the U.K. and seasonal workers in resort – around a third of whom return year round.

"What makes us different is that nothing is too much trouble," explains Dunn. "That mantra is just as important today as it was 25 years ago. If you worry and you care and you want your guests to have a good time, then they will." The Scott Dunn website promises to craft something special for each customer. This type of one-on-one service has led to more than 70 per cent repeat business through loyalty and referral. The Scott Dunn service philosophy includes unexpected acts of kindness (UAKs) – a term Dunn coined – for guests, and there's a behind-scenes budget for this. The price tag of such extras is never questioned. "We obviously try to mitigate costs as much as we can but nothing that would affect a guest. If you're part of the DNA of the company, you understand the importance of the guest," Dunn asserts.

It has not been easy weathering two economic slumps during Scott Dunn's years in business. But, quick to react to external pressures, Dunn circumvented disaster early in his career when the 1992 recession compromised his company. He reached out to a dozen new investors by offering a one per cent share in the company as well as free holidays. Profits grew 20 per cent year-on-year between 1992 and 2008 and potential dangers from the 2008 recession were averted by cutting back on quantity rather than quality, reducing the amount of accommodation offered and securing more performance-linked contracts. By 2011 profits had soared again with sales of $40 million, zero debt and seven-figure profits from the 10,000 yearly holidaymakers who averaged more than $19,000 per booking. The business continued to grow, with Scott Dunn taking a majority stake in rival Imagine Travel in 2013. By 2014 revenues were up to about $100 million a year, with annual profits of around $9 million, attracting the interest of equity investors. That same year, Inflection Private Equity took a majority stake in the company, reportedly for over $100 million.

One thing in Dunn's favor, particularly during economic downturns, is that the high-spending clientele is relatively recession-proof: "When we're negotiating our rates (with chalets, hotel rooms), we explain to the resorts that they will want our guests rather than someone booking on Expedia, for example, as they are going to spend more and be more value. They're buying a caliber of guest who is not afraid to spend." When asked how Scott Dunn has outlived many competitors over the past quarter century, Dunn explains: "We've been consistent; we've always undersold and over-delivered and provided you do that, you manage people's expectations and they wax lyrical as you exceed their expectations. It's then all about having the right people working with you." He also thinks too many travel companies focus on the bottom line rather than on keeping customers: "they are too busy counting beans."

Despite changes in top management over the years, Dunn has remained the ideas person, focusing on guest loyalty and brand enhancement. In 2011 Scott Dunn was voted Favorite Specialist Tour Operator in Condé Nast Traveller Readers' Travel Awards. Scores were particularly high in relation to reliability, staff and service. "We call it guest service rather than customer service," insists Dunn. He thinks his style of exemplary service is why Scott Dunn has survived while other 'young pretenders' have failed. The company won the same award in 2014 along with the first 'baby&me Style Awards' for Best Family Tour Operator, and was voted runner up in the 'Best Luxury Tour Operator' category, by the readers of Ultratravel. Dunn says awards give the company "collateral for the next 12 months or so" for marketing, advertising and online clout. But he also rates highly the value of good press. "PR is very important for us, more so than advertising," he says. A recent coup was a three page feature story in *The Sunday Times* Saturday Travel section. "It helps us create that warm, fuzzy feeling," explains Dunn.

In a recent blog, Dunn discusses how the world of skiing has changed beyond recognition. "It's extraordinary to think back to when we started Scott Dunn in 1986, when ski chalets were often appalling: untrained chalet staff cooked stodgy staples served with poor quality wine, there was burnt porridge for breakfast, the blankets were itchy, the walls thin, the bathrooms shared. Owners had a boarding school mentality and would see how many beds they could cram in. And the worst thing was that no one minded because they didn't know any better." Dunn was determined to transform the world of chalet holidays. "With each property we halved the number of bedrooms, installed seriously smart bathrooms and offered the best service. Now, almost every room has its own bathroom and nearly half of our chalets have private pools."

Dunn also points to the importance of the family in today's marketplace. "The kids' market has really grown up in the past ten years and we're known and trusted for our kids' clubs. Many of our guests have grown up skiing with us, so now that they come back with their own children, we're meeting them full circle. They know we look after them – we call our guests 'guests' for a reason – and they've become so much more discerning than those skiers who endured the old chalets in the 1980s. More than a quarter of a century on from when we started, we're delighted about that."

Sources: Communication with Andrew Dunn, 2011 and 2015; O'Connell (2011); http://www.scottdunn.com; http://blog.scottdunn.com/the-dunn-thing; http://www.thesundaytimes.co.uk/sto/public/roadtorecovery/article661649.ece

11

Why service excellence is so critical

Service quality has been increasingly identified as a key factor in differentiating service products and building a competitive advantage in tourism. The process by which customers evaluate a purchase, thereby determining satisfaction and likelihood of repurchase, is important to all marketers, but especially to services marketers because, unlike their manufacturing counterparts, they have fewer objective measures of quality by which to judge their production. Service quality can be defined as customers' perceptions of the service component of a product, and these perceptions are said to be based on five dimensions: reliability, assurance, empathy, responsiveness, and tangibles (Parasuraman et al., 1988).

Many researchers believe that an outgrowth of service quality is customer satisfaction, measured as the difference between the service that a customer expects and the perceived quality of what is actually delivered (Reichheld & Sasser, 1990). Satisfying customers has always been a key component of the tourism industry, but never before has it been so critical. In these uncertain times, and with increased competition, knowing how to win and keep customers is the single most important business skill that anyone can learn. Customer satisfaction and loyalty are the keys to long-term profitability, and keeping the customer happy is everybody's business. Becoming customer-centered and exceeding customer expectations are requirements for business success.

Well-publicized research shows that companies can increase profits from 25 to 85 per cent by retaining just five per cent more of their customers (Reichheld & Sasser, 1990), and research indicates that merely 'satisfying' customers is no longer enough to ensure loyalty (Heskett et al., 1997). This means that it is not enough just to please customers. Each customer should become so delighted with all elements of their association with an organization that buying from someone else is unthinkable.

Consumers worldwide are willing to spend more on service excellence. One study found that seven in 10 Americans are willing to spend an average of 13 per cent more with companies they believe provide excellent customer service (AMEX, 2011). The same study found a similar willingness in other countries (Australia and Canada, 12%; Mexico, 11%; U.K., 10%; France, 9%; Italy, 9%; Germany, 8%; and Netherlands, 7%). In India, consumers would spend 22 per cent more for excellent customer service. Another recent study found that the value of great customer service in the U.S. economy is a staggering $267.8 billion per year (STELLA Service, 2010). This figure was calculated based on the average spend per person per year with each type of company. Value is the extra percentage that people are willing to spend if they know they will receive great service. If the consumers surveyed received great customer service, 70 per cent would use the same company again, and 50 per cent would make recommendations to family and friends. In the hospitality sector, the study found that consumers are willing to spend 11 per cent more for great service, higher than most other sectors.

The logic connecting employee satisfaction and loyalty to customer satisfaction and loyalty (and ultimately profits) is illustrated by the service profit chain (see Figure 11.1). The chain suggests there are critical linkages among internal service quality: employee satisfaction/ productivity; the value of services provided to the customer; and ultimately customer satisfaction, retention, and profits. The model implies that companies that exhibit high levels of success on the elements of the model will be more successful and profitable than those that do not.

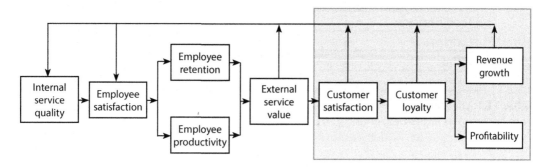

Figure 11.1: The service profit chain (Source: Adapted from Heskett et al., 1997).

The chain begins with internal service quality, where human labor is of critical importance to the tourism sector. Efforts need to be made internally to enhance the professional skills of employees and motivate them to satisfy the specific needs and wants of guests. The theory is that employee satisfaction will lead to increased productivity and higher retention levels, which will in turn increase the value of services for customers, resulting in satisfaction and loyalty. The resulting external value for customers comes in the form of exceptional service. Satisfied guests tend to make repeat visits and share their positive experiences with other potential guests, leading to greater profits. A high loyalty rate contributes to higher than average occupancy or return rates, and a healthy balance sheet, completing the profit chain.

To understand the financial value of building long-term relationships with customers, companies sometimes calculate lifetime values – as exemplified in the Andrew Dunn Spotlight above. The lifetime value of a customer is a calculation that considers customers from the point of view of their potential lifetime revenue and profitability contributions to a company. This value is influenced by the length of an average lifetime, the average revenues generated in that time period, and sales of additional products and services over time. For example, Snowsports Industries America (SIA) estimated in 2012 that each skier beginning at the age of 10 has a lifetime value to the industry of $72,758 (see Table 11.1).

11

Item	Retail price	Units/Year	Years	Total ($)
Skis	$358	0.2	35	$2,506
Boots	$283	0.2	35	$1,981
Bindings	$164	0.2	35	$1,148
Apparel	$218	0.1	35	$763
Accessories	$34	1	35	$1,190
Lifts tickets	$71	10	35	$24,850
Food/beverage	$34	10	35	$11,900
Lodging	$203	4	35	$28,420
TOTAL				$72,758
Avg/Year				$2,079

Table 11.1: Lifetime value of a skier/snowboarder starting at the age of 10 (Source: Adapted from Snowsports Industries America, 2012)

Creating a service culture

In order to provide top-notch customer service, winter sport tourism providers need to establish a strong service culture. A service culture is a culture that supports customer service through policies, procedures, reward systems, and actions. A services marketing program is doomed to failure if its organizational culture does not support servicing the customer. Such a program requires a strong commitment from management. If management expects employees to have a positive attitude toward customers, management must have a positive attitude toward the customer and the employees. All organizational leaders are crucial in transmitting and preserving the culture (Ford & Heaton, 2001). For companies without a strong service culture, the switch to a customer-oriented system may require changes in hiring, training, reward systems, and customer complaint resolution, as well as empowerment of employees. It requires that managers spend time talking to both customers and customer-contact employees.

Benchmark tourism and hospitality organizations spend considerable time and money teaching a culture value system so that when a situation with a customer arises that is not discussed in the training manual or can't be done by the book, the employee who has learned the culture will know how to do the right thing at that moment, will want to do the right thing, and will be empowered to do so by the organization (Ford & Heaton, 2001). At The Montage, Deer Valley in Utah, the unique service culture is instilled and maintained through intensive training. All 720 employees (called associates) go through multi-day education followed by a long training period called 'Montage Mores'. Dan Howard is Public Relations Manager for the hotel and says "No two Montage hotels look anything alike but they 'feel' identical - the same messaging, the same style of hospitality. Our goal is to provide comfortable luxury – I think this is uniquely American."

Certainly, establishing a service culture may be easier in some parts of the world. In Japan, for example, a high standard of customer service is the norm. The Japanese word for 'customer' translates as 'the invited' or 'guest', showing the status they give to their customers. Training for a service-oriented culture will also require more than a single program or class. Even before customer service training, new hires should have an initial training session that sets the tone for the employee's experience and begins to build a foundation for service. Once the value system is taught, training can be more specific. At the Broadmoor Resort in Colorado Springs, for example, every new restaurant employee attends a two-day orientation program, followed by a workshop series covering how to answer a phone, greet a guest, properly serve wine, bus a table, and so on. This is followed by specific customer service training. At the Broadmoor, there are 16 standards common to all employees based on five-star, five-diamond standards (Simons, 2005). These standards - such as 'use the guest's name', always say 'I will find out', never say 'I don't know', and 'walk a guest to his or her requested location' - specifically define what exceptional service means. These standards are reinforced through classes, contests and recognition programs.

Ritz Carlton employees are also trained based on certain specific standards. Each new recruit to the company receives a high level of continuous training and feedback, and is introduced to the Ritz Carlton Gold Standards. Printed on a card that every employee carries around, the Gold Standards illustrate the company's credo, the employee promise and rules for behavior towards guests and fellow members of staff. These rules explain, for example, the exact vocabulary that should be used to greet guests and guidance on personal appearance. Furthermore, they form a social contract between the institution and everyone that works there. The credo is summed up simply as 'We are ladies and gentlemen serving ladies and gentlemen.' Ritz Carlton tends to train internally, but some resorts and destinations may look externally for customer service training. In the case study at the end of the chapter, Steamboat Springs, a resort town in Colorado, brought in a consultant to give the whole town customer-service training!

Converting guests into apostles

As mentioned before, well-publicized research shows that businesses can increase profits from 25 to 85 per cent by retaining just five per cent more of their customers, but merely 'satisfying' customers is no longer enough to ensure loyalty. There is little or no correlation between satisfied (versus highly satisfied) customers and customer retention. This means that it is not sufficient just to please customers. Each customer should become so delighted with all elements of their association with a company that using a competitor is unthinkable. In a sense these customers become 'apostles' for their favorite brands. A popular model that explains these behavioral consequences of customer service is the *Apostle Model*, developed at the Harvard Business School. Based on satisfaction and loyalty, this approach segments customers into four quadrants: *Loyalists*, *Hostages*, *Mercenaries*, and *Defectors* (see Figure 11.2 below).

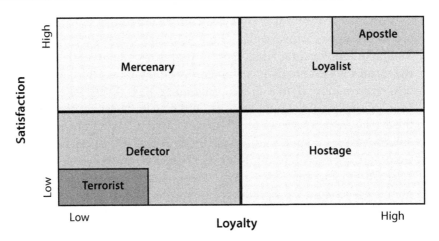

Figure 11.2: The Apostle Model (Source: Adapted from Jones & Sasser, 1995).

Defectors are those who have low satisfaction and low loyalty. A sub-segment comprises the *Terrorists*, with the lowest satisfaction and loyalty scores. In addition to the costs associated with losing them, these customers are so unhappy that they speak out against a brand at every opportunity. *Hostages* are customers who have low satisfaction, but still report high loyalty. This typically is due to lack of competition or high switching costs. Customers in this category feel 'trapped.' Tourism brands in this category often win business simply due to their location (when no suitable alternatives are nearby) or because of the strength of their loyalty club. However, these customers exhibit 'false loyalty' – acting loyal even when they are just waiting for a chance to jump ship. *Mercenaries* are those who have high satisfaction, but low loyalty. These customers are often price-sensitive and will switch easily when they have the opportunity.

Loyalists are customers who have high satisfaction and high loyalty. Sub-segments of loyalists are *Apostles*, who have the highest satisfaction and loyalty scores. Some 80 per cent of Starbucks' revenues come from *Apostles* who visit their stores an average of 18 times a month. These customers are loyal because they love a business. But how do those in the ski industry create apostles? The key seems to lie with customization. In the travel industry in general, requests for customized and personalized vacations are rising sharply, aided by technology and increasingly expectant and discerning consumers. So, leading resorts and hotels are attempting to customize the experience for guests to make individual customers feel unique and to make them believe that the hotel has singled them out for special attention.

In Colorado, Vail Resorts is always looking for ways to exceed expectations and drive loyalty. "We have a program called Epic Wishes," says Ashley Lowe, Senior Manager of Communications. "Staff are empowered to seek out guests who mention on social media that they're coming to visit, and we find a unique experience to offer them to enhance their Epic Vacation. Examples include providing birthday cake, giving rides in grooming cats to kids, and offering a woman who injured herself on her first day of skiing a free spa treatment and dinner." Lowe acknowledges that these initiatives need to come from the top. She points to one General Manager, Jonathan Fillman, of Mountain Thunder Lodge in Breckenridge, who routinely writes hand written notes to his guests, and encourages his staff to as well. When a recent guest commented on TripAdvisor that it was his seventh stay at Mountain Thunder Lodge and he loved it, Jonathan sought him out, discovered he was still staying at the property, and asked him how he could make his stay better. "The gentleman said he was going to hike a 14'er the next day and asked Jonathan if he knew how to get there. Jonathan replied, 'Do I know how to get there? I'll take you there!' Jonathan picked the guest up at 4am the next morning and did the full hike with him."

In Utah, hotelier Dan Howard, Director of Public Relations at Montage Deer Valley (mentioned above) also believes that delivering highly personalized service is critical to retaining customers. "We collect information on our guest preferences so that we are able to customize their stays," he says. Even children receive a personalized experience. "Our Paintbox department invites guests ages five – 12 for half-day and full-day enrichment activities – 'science day', 'arts day', 'culinary day', etc. – and all children receive a personalized, painted Paintbox sign welcoming them by name when they check into their rooms. They also are asked to select a native Utah stuffed animal out of a sleigh so they will have a new 'friend' that they can take home with them as a memento of Montage Deer Valley," Howard explains. The Montage's culinary teams also collect copious notes on dietary restrictions so that associates can address the guests in advance of their orders when they come to the tables, helping reassure guests that they are recognized and that their dietary needs are being taken to heart in preparing their meals. "We consider every meal custom to order," says Howard.

Similarly, Spa Montage has a signature treatment called SURRENDER in which the first 45 minutes of the treatment is a conversation between a dedicated therapist and the guest to review health, exercise, diet and hereditary factors prior to being prescribed with a very specific spa 'diagnosis regimen' that is personalized for the guest. All of the notes are maintained in the Spa Montage database so that guests traveling to other Montage properties can continue their Spa Montage regimen without needing to repeat themselves or start from the beginning. "These types of actions in the culinary and spa departments provide such a highly personalized level of service that guests are most eager to return to a hotel where they are known and recognized and where their needs are anticipated," says Howard.

Just along the road, at the Stein Eriksen Lodge, Deer Valley, the staff use every bit of personal information they can as an opportunity to create a memorable experience for guests. "Every guest receives a personal escort to their room", says Hotel Manager, Dan Bullert. "And this enables the staff to develop a personal contact with the guest and possibly obtain information for which the hotel can then take the experience a step further. For instance, a guest made reference to

11

their favorite TV show, *Downton Abbey*; the team then felt inclined to put together a nice card in reference to the show along with the times and where to find it on the channel line-up. Along with the card was a chips/salsa amenity to enjoy while watching the show."

Finally, at the Alta Lodge at the foot of Alta Ski Area, CEO Marcus Dippo takes guest loyalty to heart, and encourages employees to make every effort to place an emphasis on personal attention from the time a guest arrives until he or she departs. Just like Southern Lakes Heliski profiled below, making visitors feel like friends is one of niceties that keep hotel guests returning to Alta Lodge. The lodge has one 88-year-old female guest who has been coming every year with her family, children and grandchildren since 1951. Another guest comes from Santa Barbara for one week every month, and for him the lodge will throw a birthday party once a year.

But is such customization enough to create 'apostle-type' guests who are so satisfied that they want to convert others to share their experiences? One company in Canada (see the Spotlight in Chapter 10) Canadian Mountain Holidays (CMH), operator of eight remote 44-bed lodges, believes that its greatest marketing vehicle is 'encouraged word of mouth'. Ninety per cent of the marketing budget is spent on customer service, in order to encourage repeat bookings, and loyalty runs at about 65 per cent. CMH does very little advertising, although an important ingredient of CMH's marketing strategy is social media, according to former Media Manager, Sarah Pearson: "This is an increasingly integral and important factor in our marketing strategy. The more we can drive traffic to our website and convert those viewers into active leads, the more successful our marketing strategy is. Engaging both our potential and existing guests through social media is a very powerful tool for increasing referrals, retaining guest connections, and spreading the culture of CMH."

CMH also hosts marketing events called 'An Evening with CMH' throughout North America, Europe, Japan, and Australia. These are invitation-only evenings at which CMH staff and guides entertain and provide information to past guests and their friends. These events are very successful, generating high conversion rates. Pearson feels these events are well worth the investment: "It's hard to track the conversion rate to bookings right away as that really spans a two year period. But we feel it is very worth doing as it builds customer loyalty in the markets we're going into and we see an immediate pick up on bookings from those regions. Over time, where we put a lot of energy into events, they continue to grow and we get more names in the system and more people in the marketing funnel."

On the other side of the world, another heli-skiing operation firmly focused on customer service is Southern Lakes Heliski featured below. Here the high price tag attracts clients with big expectations.

Profile: Customer service 'Kiwi-style'

Southern Lakes Heliski

Customer service has to be key in heli-skiing operations. It is a potentially dangerous sport, skiers need professional guidelines and reassurance, and there needs to be a close rapport between staff and customer. Southern Lakes Heliski has been operating in New Zealand for 30 years and has over 8500sq/km of untouched terrain spread across 11 mountain ranges, boasting more than 600 runs. Their domain stretches across the Southern Lakes Region from Makarora, Wanaka, Glenorchy, Queenstown and down to Kingston.

Elysia Gibb is the Manager for Southern Lakes Heliski (SLHS). The company offers both daily heli-skiing trips and a range of weekly vacations. "We provide a number of different options to our customers with our main product being daily heli-skiing," says Gibb. "It's one of the cheapest places in the world to do a day of heli-sking and SLHS offers either a three, four, six, or eight run option. We also offer private charters and weekly packages."

Attracting male skiers, in particular, the company gets most of its clients from Australia. "Our target markets are either wealthy men over 40 or younger men with no commitments and money to burn," says Gibb. The company promotes itself via social media, PR articles and advertising in target magazines. "We also have a lot of word of mouth and thus we get repeat customers. I'm not sure of the exact numbers but I'd say approximately 30 per cent are repeats," she adds.

After safety, customer satisfaction is top of the list. "We try to be as customer service orientated as we can from the moment the customer walks up to the sales desk to the moment they return from a fantastic day's heli," says Gibb. This starts with relaying correct and comprehensive information and continues throughout the guest's experience. "This information allows us to group people into groups of similar ability and then they are put with a guide who works with them to give them the best day of their life," she explains. The company established offices in both Queenstown (24 hours) and Wanaka to facilitate customer convenience.

11

Choosing well-trained guides with the right personality is also important. "We always get guides who are top of their game and because of this we have had an excellent safety record and a lot of happy customers," says Gibb. One of the guides is Japanese, an extra encouragement and convenience for Japanese visitors, who make up around 10 per cent of the company's clientele.

Southern Lakes' Head Guide is Tarn Pilkington, an IFMGA guide - the highest certification in the industry - with Avalanche Management Level 2. Responsible also for many background operations, Pilkington oversees the heli-ski guiding program. He has worked in snow safety positions since 1986. With over 16 years ski patrolling in N.Z., USA and Switzerland and over 10 seasons heli-ski guiding in N.Z. and Canada, he is a year round mountain guide.

Customers on weekly packages are allocated one guide to be their point of call for the whole week. Each heli-ski group consists of one guide to four guests, a very small ratio guaranteeing a personalized service. With guests ranging from intermediate to expert, each group is ability-graded.

SLHS offers a number of different weekly packages to cater to all budgets and abilities, one option being the Unlimited Package where clients are met at Queenstown Airport and transported to their luxury accommodation and heli-staging posts. They are guaranteed 36 heli runs and are refunded for any runs not completed during the week - an effective service recovery solution. On inclement days, they are offered a range of alternate guided activities. The aim of this trip is for the clients to arrive and not have to lift a finger except to have fun. Everything is included as well as a gourmet chef cooking local dishes using local produce.

Accommodation is unique with one option staying on a Luxury Superyacht on Lake Wakatipu. The boat can move to different locations around the lake depending on what terrain area has the best conditions. It's a great way to experience how dramatic Queenstown's scenery is and also to ski multiple different areas.

It's a personal service from the get-go. "Guides ring all their clients in the morning to let them know if we are flying," says Gibb. "They then pick up their clients from their accommodation and take them to the heli-staging area. Here safety equipment is issued and a guide allocated to four guests." Following safety training, the guide goes on to assess each guest's needs and work out how to incorporate them into the day's ski plan. "Every client has expectations and because they are spending around NZD$1,000 for the experience their expectations are a lot higher," Gibb acknowledges. "The guides do an amazing job at keeping everyone safe but also exceeding client expectations. At the end of the day you'll often find the guides having a beer with their clients as they debrief the day. Clients become friends not clients."

After each guest's visit, the company sends out a follow up email, thanking them for coming, offering enticements for return visits and enabling access and feedback via Tripadvisor, Facebook and the company's informative newsletter.

Sources: Interview with Elysia Gibb and Tarn Pilkington, March 2015

Managing service promises

A major cause of poorly perceived service is the difference between what a firm promises about a service, and what it actually delivers. To avoid broken promises companies must manage all communications to customers, so that inflated promises do not lead to overly high expectations. This difference between what is promised and what is delivered can cause customer frustration, perhaps driving the customer to the competition. As Jim Knight, Senior Director of Training for Hard Rock International says: "The worst mistake a business can make is to over-promise and under-deliver."

Zeithaml et al (2007) suggest that there are four strategies that are effective in managing service promises (see Figure 11.3).

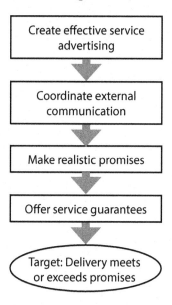

Figure 11.3: Four strategies that are effective in managing service promises (Source: Adapted from Zeithaml et al., 2007)

How to create effective advertising is discussed in Chapter 6, but a second important, yet challenging, aspect of managing brand image is the unification of all marketing communications tools, as well as corporate and brand messages, so they send a consistent, persuasive message to target audiences. These marketing communications tools include print advertising, websites, sales promotions, public relations, direct marketing and personal selling. When Westin Hotels partnered with New Balance to lend fitness gear to guests, they used a variety of communication materials to promote the new service. The campaign, run by the New York office of Bartle Bogle Hegarty, included print ads, billboards, and in-hotel marketing materials on key cards and on mirrors in guest rooms. A commercial was also shown online, on seat back video screens on Delta airplanes

11

and in about 10,000 elevators in office buildings through the Captivate Network, a Gannett company. The ads were introduced in travel trade journals such as *Meetings & Conventions* and *Successful Meetings*, and also appeared in many publications including *The Wall Street Journal*, *The New York Times* and *Runner's World*.

The Internet is increasingly used by hospitality marketers to set expectations. British luxury travel company Scott Dunn, for example (see Spotlight above), has an attractive website that promises to craft something special for each customer. This type of one-on-one service has led to more than 70 per cent repeat business through loyalty and referral. "If you're part of the DNA of the company, you understand the importance of the guest," says Chairman, Andrew Dunn. He looks to woo each customer early on and retain them through marriage, parenthood and beyond. "What makes us different is that nothing is too much trouble," explains Dunn. "We've always undersold and over-delivered and provided you do that, you manage people's expectations and they wax lyrical as you exceed their expectations. It's then all about having the right people working with you."

Companies must also make realistic promises. To be appropriate and effective, marketing communications about customer service must accurately reflect what customers will actually receive in service encounters. Customer expectations can be influenced by explicit and implicit promises from the service provider, and if expectations are not met then customers will become frustrated and are likely to complain. Therefore it is important for marketers to understand the actual levels of service delivery in an organization before making any promises.

Making realistic promises means there needs to be effective internal communication in an organization. Managers need to pay significant attention to the communication of marketing strategies and objectives to employees, so that they understand their own role and importance in the implementation of the strategies and in the achievement of the objectives. Because service advertising promises what people *do*, frequent and effective communication across functions—horizontal communication—is critical. If internal communication is poor, perceived service quality is at risk. If company advertising and other promises are developed without input from operations, contact personnel may not be able to deliver service that matches the image portrayed in marketing efforts.

Communication mechanisms may come in the form of company meetings, training sessions, newsletters, emails, annual reports, or videotapes. Fairmont Hotels & Resorts distributes a bi-monthly newsletter in each hotel as well as a company-wide newsletter to keep staff up to date on new company procedures. Southwest Airlines created a 'Culture Committee' whose responsibility is to perpetuate the Southwest spirit. Committee members promote the company's unique, caring culture to fellow employees and they can appear anywhere, at any time, to lend a helping hand. Southwest also has a blog called 'Nuts about Southwest' which addresses employees concerns, relays information about changes in the company, and tries to boost employee moral.

Finally, a growing number of organizations are offering customers a service guarantee, promising that if service delivery fails to meet pre-defined standards, the customer will be entitled to one or more forms of compensation, such as an easy-to-claim replacement, a refund or a credit. They are finding that effective service guarantees can complement the company's service recovery strategy. One of the reasons for having a service guarantee is to build marketing muscle, and research has shown that providing a guarantee in advertising materials significantly enhances consumers' intentions to buy. Research has also found that a guarantee has a positive, long-term effect on both employee motivation and customer intention to return, although there are suggestions that organizations need to make better use of the information and knowledge gained from invocations of a service guarantee. From the customer's perspective, the primary function of service guarantees is to lower the perceived risks associated with purchase.

In response to customer concerns over lack of snow, many ski resorts now offer some type of snow guarantee. Solitude in Utah offers a 'Snow Guarantee' at the Inn at Solitude as well as the Village Condos. If the mountain is less than 50 per cent open due to inadequate snowfall, the resort offers a full refund of a deposit up to 48 hours before arrival. Confident in the quality of its snow cover, Val Thorens in France offers a limited type of snow guarantee. Under the terms of the guarantee, if skiers find a European ski resort with more open connected runs, Val Thorens offers a free skiing day. During the 2014-15 season, Snowshoe in Virginia guaranteed to have more skiable terrain open than any other ski mountain in the Southeast. If they didn't, they would offer a free day of skiing like Val Thorens. In Australia, the snow guarantee provided by Mt Buller is a money-back guarantee on all prepaid accommodation, lift ticket, rental and lesson packages. It applies if insufficient snow cover means they don't have at least four of their 'Snow Guarantee' lifts operating in the two days before a scheduled arrival.

Service recovery

Service delivery failure is likely to occur at some point in time for organizations in the ski industry. Though it is unlikely that businesses can eliminate all service failures, they can learn to respond effectively to failures once they do occur. This response is often referred to as service recovery, defined as the process by which a company attempts to rectify a service delivery failure. One study of hotel customers found that their level of satisfaction and lasting impression of a hotel is based first and foremost on what happens when something goes wrong (Johnston, 2004). Mostly, customers accept that mistakes happen; the problem begins when there is no strategy in place to rectify the situation easily.

Despite the significance of the tourism sector both economically and as a source of customer complaints, there has been little research that explicitly addresses complaining behavior and service recovery. Research that does exist is relatively recent and still evolving. In the hospitality industry, Lewis and McCann

11

(2004) focused on service failure and recovery in the U.K. hotel industry, finding that guests who were satisfied with the hotel's response to their problems were much more likely to return than those who were not satisfied with recovery efforts. Leong, Kim and Ham (2002) studied the impact of critical incidents of service failures and recovery efforts in a hotel, finding that only complete resolution results in repeat patronage, while partial resolution and unresolved service failures served as a deterrent to the guest's return patronage. O'Neill and Mattila (2004) presented findings from a survey of 613 hotel guests indicating that guests' overall satisfaction and intention to re-visit were much higher when they believed that service failure was unstable and recovery was stable. Finally, the influence of service recovery on satisfaction and re-visit intention was also stressed by the study of Yavas et al. (2004).

In the restaurant sector, Hoffman, Kelley and Rotalsky (1995) examined service failures and recovery strategies commonly occurring in the industry, and Leong and Kim (2002) focused on recovery efforts in fast-food restaurants, finding that reasonable care in providing a service failure resolution that meets the customer's expectation may influence customer loyalty. Lastly, Sundaram, Jurowski and Webster (1997) investigated the impacts of four types of service failure recovery efforts in restaurant service consumption situations that differ in the degree of criticality. They argued that the importance of the situation to the consumer plays a significant role in their responses to service failure recovery efforts.

The service recovery paradox

Some researchers have suggested that customers who are dissatisfied, but experience a high level of excellent service recovery, may ultimately be even more satisfied and more likely to re-purchase than those who were satisfied in the first place (Hart, Heskett & Sasser, 1990; McCollough & Bharadwaj, 1992). This idea has become known as the service recovery paradox (see Figure 11.4). There are somewhat mixed opinions on whether a recovery paradox exists, but customer complaints about defective services may represent an opportunity for the company to improve its image and perceived quality since it permits the company to make a positive correction or to resolve the complaint (Albrecht & Zemke, 1985; Grönroos, 1990; Heskett, Sasser & Hart, 1990).

McCollough, Berry and Yadav (2000) tested the service recovery paradox for airline passengers, finding that customer satisfaction was lower after service failure and recovery than in the case of error-free service. Hudson and Moreno-Gil (2006), however, found that hotel customers in Spain who had experienced a recovery encounter, perceived a higher level of service quality for intangible attributes (assurance, trust, reliability, responsiveness, and empathy) than non-complaining customers - supporting, to some extent, the service recovery paradox. The results showed that resolving customer problems related to intangible aspects of the service in a hotel has a strong impact on perceived service quality and thus customer satisfaction. Sousa and Voss (2009) studied service recovery in an e-commerce setting and also found a recovery paradox effect but only for a small proportion of 'delighted' customers: those who perceived an outstanding recovery. They concluded that despite not being a viable strategy in general, delighting customers in the recovery may make sense for profitable customers.

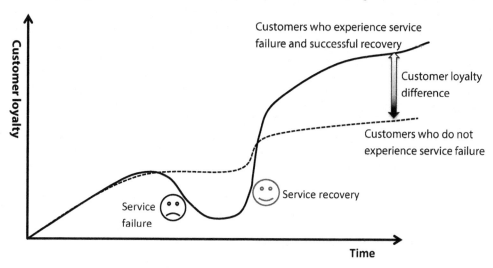

Figure 11.4: The service recovery paradox (Source: Adapted from Schindlholzer, 2008)

But given the mixed opinions on the extent to which the recovery paradox exists, 'doing it right the first time' is still the best and safest strategy in the long run.

The service recovery process

Every tourism and hospitality organization should have a systematic plan for winning back customers who have been disappointed by some facet of service delivery. One such plan – a five-step procedure – was proposed by Zemke and Schaaf (1989).

1. Apology

The process of service recovery begins with an apology. As Isadore Sharp from the Four Seasons says: "Whatever the issue, making it right starts with a sincere apology" (Sharp, 2009, p. 232). Once an organization accepts that failure sometimes occurs, it can instil in its employees the necessity of extending a genuine apology when a customer is disappointed. This simple act can go a long way to framing the customer's perception of his value to the organization and helps pave the path for subsequent steps to regain goodwill (Fisk, Grove & John, 2000). One restaurant study found that recovery strategies that included personal service interaction with customers were more successful than strategies that included monetary compensation (Silber et al., 2009). When contact employees treat customers with respect and courteousness during a service recovery, customers will report significantly higher satisfaction levels (Swanson & Hsu, 2009).

11

2. Urgent reinstatement

The next step is to do something to remove the source of customer disappointment. Urgent means the action is taken quickly; reinstatement means making an effort to correct the problem. If an organization is slow to address customer dissatisfaction or fails to present evidence that it is taking some action, the customer is likely to perceive that his or her problems are not important, and may well defect at this point. Customers who complain and have their problems resolved quickly are much more likely to re-purchase than those whose complaints are not resolved. In fact, research by TARP (1986) showed that if complaints are resolved quickly, 82 per cent of customers will re-purchase. However, if complaints are resolved, but not necessarily quickly, only 52 per cent of customers will return. Urgency is therefore the key, and employees must therefore be empowered to solve problems as they occur.

Sandy Best, former Director of Public Relations for Lake Louise in Canada, helped implement a new 'service with no boundaries' system for employees to deal with service issues. Staff are empowered to solve problems and also compensate for them: "For example, if a washroom has no toilet paper, the staff solve the issue but if, as the customer, you are still really pissed off, the staff member offers you lunch in return. We train them to do that," says Best. He has found that employees feel good about their work when they are empowered in this way. The extra money spent is well worth the good PR that service recovery engenders. In the era of instant communication through all the far-reaching tentacles of social media, Best deems it cheaper to solve a problem instantly than to let it escalate into something more serious by leaving it until a guest gets home. Despite initial concerns from 'the money people', Best says that the 'service with no boundaries' system is working well. It is monitored weekly, he adds, as a learning tool for management: "If the bottom of the totem pole rots out, the management hit the ground hard and fast because they fall from higher up", he explains.

3. Empathy

Empathy means making the effort to understand why the customer was disappointed with the organization. If service employees can put themselves in the shoes of the customers, they may be able to grasp the disappointment felt by the customer, and successfully display that understanding. An important part of the service recovery process is not economic reimbursement, but empathy and responsiveness of employees (Liden & Skalen, 2003). The payoff of empathy is the customer's realization that the organization is in fact sensitive to the service failure. Tax and Brown (1998) have suggested that customers are looking for three specific types of justice following their complaints: outcome fairness, procedural fairness, and interactional fairness. Outcome fairness concerns the results that customers receive from their complaints; procedural fairness refers to the policies, rules and timeliness of the complaint process; and interactional fairness focuses on the interpersonal treatment received during the complaint process.

4. Symbolic atonement

The next step in the recovery process is to make amends in some tangible way for the organization's failure, and this may take the form of a room upgrade, a free dessert, or a ticket for a future flight. This step is called symbolic atonement because the gesture is designed not to replace the service, but to communicate to the customer that the organization takes responsibility for the disappointment caused and is willing to pay the price for its failure. At this point, it is important for service organizations to determine customers' thresholds of acceptability. In order to calculate how much compensation a firm should offer after service breakdown, Lovelock and Wirtz (2007) suggest that managers need to consider the positioning of the firm, the severity of the service failure, and who the affected customer is. But the overall rule of thumb for compensation for service failures should be 'well-dosed generosity'. In fact, Timm (2008) believes that companies should go beyond symbolic atonement and always go the extra mile in the eyes of the complaining customer.

5. Follow-up

By following up to see if the gesture of symbolic atonement was well received, an organization can gauge how well it placated the customer's dissatisfaction. The follow-up can take many forms depending on the service type and recovery situation. Follow-up gives an organization a chance to evaluate the recovery plan and identify where improvements are necessary. A study of service recovery in the hotel sector found that many hotels did not follow-up and were thus missing out on an effective way of satisfying guests and informing themselves of the adequacy of their recovery strategies (Lewis & McCann, 2004). The final encounter in a service interaction is critical in determining overall satisfaction, so service providers should ensure that encounters end on a good note.

The consequences of an effective recovery process

Research has shown that resolving customer problems effectively has a strong impact on customer satisfaction, quality and bottom-line performance: Heskett et al., 1990; Berry & Parasuraman, 1993; Kelley, Hoffman & Davis, 1993; Tax, Brown & Chandrashenkaran, 1998; Tax & Brown, 1998. An effective recovery will retain customer loyalty regardless of the type of failure. In one study, customer retention exceeded 70 per cent for those customers who perceived effective recovery efforts (Kelley, Hoffman & Davis, 1993). Retained customers are much more profitable than new ones because they purchase more and they purchase more frequently, while at the same time requiring lower operating costs. British Airways calculates that service recovery efforts return $2 for every dollar invested. In fact, the company finds that 'recovered' customers give the airline more of their business after they have been won back.

An effective recovery process may also lead to positive word of mouth, or at least diminish the negative word of mouth typically associated with poor recovery efforts. One study reported that customers who experienced a service failure told nine or 10 individuals about their poor service experience, whereas satisfied customers told only four or five individuals about their satisfactory experience (Collier, 1995).

In fact, research by U.S. firm TARP back in 1979 shows that for every 26 unhappy business to business customers, only one will lodge a formal complaint with management. Instead, on average, each unhappy customer will tell 10 people, who in turn will tell five others. Therefore, an average of 1,300 people will hear about at least one of these unhappy customers' experiences. This 'Customer Complaint Iceberg' is illustrated in Figure 11.5. Furthermore, repeated service failures can aggravate employees. The cost in employee morale is an often overlooked cost of not having an effective service recovery program.

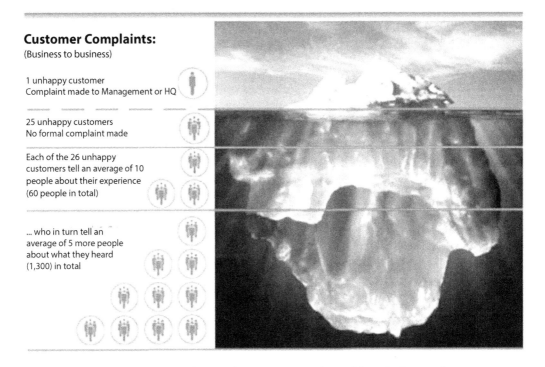

Customer Complaints:
(Business to business)

1 unhappy customer
Complaint made to Management or HQ

25 unhappy customers
No formal complaint made

Each of the 26 unhappy customers tell an average of 10 people about their experience (60 people in total)

... who in turn tell an average of 5 more people about what they heard (1,300) in total

Figure 11.5: The Customer Complaint Iceberg (Source: Adapted from TARP, 1979)

The service recovery process can be used to improve the overall quality of service delivery as the service occurs. This is possible if the customer provides feedback during the service experience, which allows the organization to refine its service process. Keeping track of sources of dissatisfaction that create a need for recovery can also help the organization. Careful collection and storage of information regarding the incidents may produce a rich database of information on service quality. In analyzing this data, patterns may emerge that specify particularly troublesome aspects of its service delivery system.

Case study: Customer-centric service at Steamboat Springs

Ed Eppley

It's most unusual for a town to train the whole community in customer service techniques. But this is exactly what Steamboat Springs, Colorado decided to do in 2014. The innovative plan was hatched by management consultant, Ed Eppley in conjunction with the Steamboat Springs Chamber Resort Association and also the Steamboat Ski and Resort Company (SSRC). Pivotal in planning and implementation were Jim Clark, Executive Director of the Chamber, and Rob Perlman, Senior VP of Sales & Marketing for SSRC.

Steamboat has long been known for its Western-style, family-friendly atmosphere, so focusing on service isn't new, according to Perlman. "The new part is how we approach service," he says. "The Service Excellence program at Steamboat is really a derivative of a sales conversion initiative through our call center operations at Steamboat Central Reservations that we started back in 2010. This whole thing began as an exercise to convert more sales leads into Steamboat vacations. During that process, we really moved the needle with a consultative selling style that connected with customers in a way that isn't possible through traditional product sales. This approach of building relationships with our guests quickly spread to other departments and Service Excellence was born."

According to Eppley, owner of Ohio-based company ProspeX at the time, it was all about exceeding customers' expectations. The impetus for the dramatic move came after the town of Steamboat Springs witnessed the resort achieve two years of industry leading guest service results from their Service Excellence program while comparing those results with the town's visitor survey in 2013 which revealed a significant decrease in responders saying they would recommend Steamboat Springs to friends and colleagues. The town's survey showed a seven point drop from a previous 2010 study.

Several years before, the Steamboat Ski & Resort Corporation had engaged ProspeX to improve the conversion rate for incoming sales enquiries. "This work resulted in SSRC raising their Net Promoter Scores with external customers to be the highest in their competitive set," Eppley recalls. "It also produced a 20 per cent plus increase in their bookings conversion rate through their call center."

The idea of training the whole town as well as the ski resort was the brainchild of the Steamboat Chamber CEO and SSRC's COO, Chris Diamond, who was also on the Chamber Board of Directors. "They felt it was important that someone who comes to Steamboat have exceptional experiences, whether they were on the mountain or in the nearby town," Eppley explains.

11

He went on to custom design a pilot training program, initially involving four four-hour sessions over the space of a month, teaching the very latest in customer service culture and using many Disney examples of 'going the extra mile'. His course included techniques such as the 'connection stack': finding common ground with customers and then using that more intimate relationship to gain their confidence and loyalty to the destination.

From summer 2014, the Chamber worked with leaders in government, lodging, restaurants and retail to enlist top customer service providers from within these sectors to help train others within the community. Eppley taught a pilot group and those participants then went back and disseminated the new information and tactics among their own staff. "We've trained key thought leaders in the community to become semi-subject matter experts in delivering what we call Service Excellence," he explains. "They go into businesses that ask for the training and present the concepts to their staff."

Eppley says that the first requirement is for the owner or executive management of each company to embrace the idea that exceptional customer service is important, and that it comes as much from the culture of the company as any external program or training. "Second, we teach the staff that directly interacts with the guest a simple, quick method to 'connect' with the guest," he explains. "The process of teaching them the connecting method tends to build confidence in the staff to actually use the tool right away. Finally, for the companies who want to change their culture to support Service Excellence, we teach their managers an approach to managing and leading that makes it easier for people to behave the right way."

At SSRC, the following guidelines were identified by Eppley and Perlman:

1) *Find out why you want to do this.*

2) *Clear focus on what you want (or need) to achieve. How will we know if we are successful?*

3) *Passionate internal champions at all levels of the organization. 'Street Cred' is critical.*

4) *Persistence – this will take years to gain full traction. It's been said you'll need one full year for every layer of management.*

5) *You'll need a doctrine to make your own. For Steamboat, that's our culture and Service Excellence.*

6) *Determination – when challenged, use your decision-making to reinforce your commitment to Service Excellence. Don't undermine it.*

Not everyone in Steamboat Springs is on board yet, however. Eppley says, as with any broad initiative, it is a 'bell curve': "There are certain businesses that feel they don't need help. At the other end of the spectrum are companies that are hungry for the help. The companies that have embraced the concepts feel like they have really benefited from doing so. When asked, most of their staff feels like it has helped them. And they also feel like it makes their interaction with their guests more fun."

Results are measured quantitatively via the town's Net Promoter Scores, although instant increases were not anticipated since only 15-20 per cent of the town's businesses had gone through the program by early 2015. "As of February, Net Promoter Scores for the town have not moved in any significant way and were not expected to do so," Eppley acknowledges. At the ski resort, however, every employee receives an introduction to Service Excellence and results have already proved its worth. "At SSRC, the real movement came starting in the second year and third year," Eppley says. "It wasn't until the Christmas and New Year's weeks this season, that SSRC had their highest scores to date." He adds that those were the two busiest weeks of the entire season – a time when customer service scores might logically be expected to decrease. In March 2015, the resort recorded a 91 per cent Net Promoter Score as a result of which they offered 90 randomly selected staff members with prizes.

Qualitative results had already started to show around town with one multi-unit restaurant owner recording improved guest satisfaction scores and asking for more training for his management team. A condominium owner also noticed significant increases in bookings. "Another good indicator is unsolicited comments from guests to Steamboat Springs. Those appear to be moving up," Eppley confirms.

Improving customer service is definitely a trend in ski resorts world over. In a recent survey of businesses, over 60 per cent said they wanted to make customer service a competitive advantage by 2016, Eppley says. "Saying you want to create customer service experiences that are greater than your competitors is easy," says Eppley. "Creating a culture that supports that and rewards your people for doing so takes a tremendous effort. SSRC has been doing this now for four plus years. I also know that customers of all kinds, retail, B2B, etc., have higher demands and expectations than ever before. It may be that delivering exceptional customer experiences won't be a competitive advantage, it may be what's required to stay in business."

Sources: Interviews with Ed Eppley and Rob Perlman, March 2015; Mount (2014); Franz (2014)

References

Albrecht, K. and Zemke, R. (1985) *Service America*, Homewood: Dow Jones-Irwin.

AMEX (2011) 'AMEX Global Service Barometer 2011 Press Release', accessed 9/1/2011 from http://www.thetrainingbank.com

Berry L.L., Zeithaml, V.A. and Parasuraman, A. (1990) 'Five imperatives for improving service quality', *Sloan Management Review*, **31**(4), 29-38.

Berry, L. and Parasuraman, A. (1993) 'Marketing de los servicios: La calidad como meta', Paramón ediciones, S.A. Madrid.

Collier, D. A. (1995) 'Modeling the relationships between process quality errors and overall service process performance', *Journal of Service Industry Management*, **64**(4), 4-19.

Fisk, R.P., Grove, S.J. and John, J. (2000) *Interactive Services Marketing*, Boston: Houghton Mifflin Company.

Ford, R.C. and Heaton, C.P. (2001) 'Lessons from hospitality that can serve anyone', *Organizational Dynamics*, **30**(1), 30-47.

Franz, S. (2014) 'New customer service training in Steamboat aims to help turn summer visitors into raving fans', *Steamboat Today*, 6 Feb, accessed 2/1/2015 from www.steamboattoday.com/news/2014/feb/06/new-customer-service-training-steamboat-aims-turn-/

11

Grönroos, C. (1990) *Service Management and Marketing*, Lexington, Mass: Lexington Books.

Hart, C.W.L. (1990) 'The power of unconditional service guarantees', *Harvard Business Review*, **68**, 54-62.

Hart, C.W.L., Heskett, J.L. and Sasser, Jr., W.E. (1990) 'The profitable art of service recovery', *Harvard Business Review*, **68**(4), 148-156.

Heskett, J., Sasser, W. and Hart, C. (1990) *Service Breakthroughs: Changing the Rules of the Game*, New York: The Free Press.

Heskett, J. L., Sasser, W. E., Jr. and Schlesinger, L. A. (1997) *The Service Profit Chain: How Leading Companies Link Profit and Growth to Loyalty, Satisfaction, and Value*, New York: Free Press, 83.

Hoffman, K.D., Kelley, S.W. and Rotalsky, H.M. (1995) 'Tracking service failures and employee recovery efforts', *Journal of Services Marketing*, **9**(2), 49-61.

Hudson, S. and Moreno-Gil, S. (2006) 'The influence of service recovery and loyalty on perceived service quality: A study of hotel customers in Spain', *Journal of Hospitality & Leisure Marketing*, **14**(2), 45-66.

Johnston, R. (2004) 'Towards a better understanding of service excellence', *Managing Service Quality*, **14**(2/3), 129-133.

Kelley, S. W., Hoffman, K. D. and Davis, M. A. (1993) 'A typology of retail failures and recoveries', *Journal of Retailing,* **69**(4), 429-452.

Leong, J.K. and Kim, W.G. (2002) 'Service recovery efforts in fast food restaurants to enhance repeat patronage', *Journal of Travel & Tourism Marketing*, **12**(2/3), 65-93.

Leong, J.K., Kim, W.G. and Ham, S. (2002) 'The effects of service recovery on repeat patronage', *Journal of Quality Assurance in Hospitality & Tourism*, **3**(1/2), 69-94.

Lewis, B.R. and McCann, P. (2004) 'Service failure and recovery: Evidence from the hotel industry', *International Journal of Contemporary Hospitality Management*, **16**(1), 6-17.

Liden, S.B. and Skalen, P. (2003) 'The effect of service guarantees on service recovery', *International Journal of Service Industry Management*, **14**(1), 36-58.

Lovelock, C. and Wirtz, J. (2007) *Services Marketing: People, Technology, Strategy*, 6th edition, New Jersey, USA; Prentice Hall International.

McCollough, M.A., Berry, L.L. and Yadav, M.S. (2000) 'An empirical investigation of customer satisfaction after service failure and recovery', *Journal of Service Research*, **3**(2), 121-137.

Mount, I. (2014) 'A Whole Town in Colorado Pushes to Improve Its Customer Service', *New York Times*, 15 October, accessed 1/2/2015 from: http://www.nytimes.com/2014/10/16/business/smallbusiness/a-whole-town-tries-to-improve-its-customer-service-how-could-we-be-a-70.html?_r=0

O'Neill, J.W. and Mattila, A.S. (2004) 'Towards the development of a lodging service recovery strategy', *Journal of Hospitality & Leisure Marketing*, **11**(1), 51-64.

Parasuraman, A., Zeithaml, V. A. and Berry, L. L. (1988) 'SERVQUAL: a multiple item scale for measuring consumer perceptions of service quality', *Journal of Retailing,* **64**, 12-20.

Reichheld, F. F. and Sasser, W. S., Jr. (1990) 'Zero defections: Quality comes to services', *Harvard Business Review,* **68**, 105-111.

Silber, I., Israeli, A., Bustin, A. and Zvi, O.B. (2009) 'Recovery strategies for service failures: The case of restaurants', *Journal of Hospitality Marketing & Management*, **18**, 730-740.

Simons, K. (2005) 'Exceptional customer service requires training all employees', *H&MM*, 20 June, 10 & 17.

Snowsports Industries America (2012) 'Revisiting growing the snowsports industry', accessed 3/12/2014 from http://issuu.com/siasnowsports/docs/growing_the_industry_2011_revisited

Sousa, R. and Voss, C.A. (2009) 'The effects of service failures and recovery on customer loyalty in e-services', *International Journals of Operations & Product Management*, **29**(8), 834-864.

STELLA Service (2010) *The Value of Great Customer Service: The Economic Impact for Online Retail and Other Consumer Categories*, accessed 9/7/2011 from http://media.stellaservice.com/public/pdf/Value_of_Great_Customer_Service.pdf

Sundaram, D.S., Jurowski, C. and Webster, C. (1997) 'Service failure recovery efforts in restaurant dining: The role of criticality of service consumption', *Hospitality Research Journal*, **20**(3), 137-149.

Swanson, S.R. and Hsu, M.K. (2009) 'Critical incidents in tourism: Failure, recovery, customer switching, and word-of-mouth behaviors', *Journal of Travel & Tourism Marketing*, **26**, 180-194.

Tax, S.S. and Brown, S.W. (1998) 'Recovering and learning from service failure', *Sloan Management Review*, **40**(1), 75-80.

Tax, S.S., Brown, S.W. and Chandrashenkaran, M. (1998) 'Consumer evaluation of service complaint experiences: Implications for relationship marketing', *Journal of Marketing*, **62**(2), 60-76.

Technical Assistance Research Program (TARP) (1979) *Consumer Complaint Handling in America: A Final Report.* Washington, DC: White House Office of Consumer Affairs.

Timm, P.R. (2008) *Customer service. Career Success Through Customer Loyalty*, Upper Saddle River, NJ: Pearson Prentice Hall.

Zeithaml, V. A., Bitner, M. J., Gremler, D., Mahaffey, T. and Hiltz, B. (2007) *Services Marketing: Integrating Customer Focus Across the Firm*, Canadian Edition, New York: McGraw-Hill.

Zemke, R. and Schaaf, D. (1989) *The Service Edge*, New York: Plume.

11

12 The Future of the Winter Sport Tourism Industry

Tina Maze

Slovenia's skiing has been put into the international spotlight by Tina Maze, the most successful female ski racer in Slovenian history. Multi-tasking Maze is one of the few winter athletes who competes - and regularly wins on the international level - in all five skiing disciplines: Slalom, Giant Slalom, Super G, Downhill and Combination.

In her own country, Maze is a superstar: five-time winner of best Slovenian athlete, a fabulous fashion model and a pop star with Slovenia's most watched You Tube music video. Born in 1983, Maze grew up in Crna na Koroskem in northern Slovenia, less than two hours drive from the country's top ski resort, Kranjska Gora which hosts the men's World Cup Slalom events every March.

Tourists come to Kranjska Gora from all over Slovenia, Germany, Croatia, Italy and also Great Britain. According to Kranjska Gora Tourist Board Director, Mirjam Žerjav, out of a total of 177,398 overnight stays in the resort during the 2013/14 season, domestic visitors accounted for 81,429 and foreign visitors 95,969. Of the international visitors, the majority was from Croatia (21,117) followed by Italy (17,416), Britain (13,997) and Germany (3,634).

British ski operator Inghams has been bringing skiers to family-focused Kranjska Gora on and off over the past 20 years. Their numbers have ranged considerably from year to year, from a maximum of around 3,000 down to around 300 predicted for the 2014/15 season. This is in line with national ski visitation numbers which reached a peak in 2008/9 at 207,790 but were reduced to just 128,296 skiers in 2013/14 - reflecting the slow recovery in the European economy since the recession.

Compared to typical ski holidays in Switzerland and France, prices are low in Kranjska Gora. During the 2014/15 season, for example, a week's stay with Inghams in a four-star hotel in February cost around £579 per person (including flight, resort transfer, accommodation, breakfast and dinner) and was discounted to £429 by the end of January.

In the past two decades, there has been considerable investment in hotels, new apartments and sports facilities, says Žerjav: "All the lifts are practically new - the investment in the past 10 years was over 20 million EUR. And all hotels have been renovated, an investment of around 50 million EUR." Hotel beds have increased from 1,384 in 2006 to 1,905 in 2013 and apartment beds have risen from 1,384 in 2006 to 3,054 in 2013.

Set near the Italian and Austrian borders with the spectacular Julian Alps as a backdrop, the affordable ski resort with 30km of skiable slopes appeals particularly to novice and intermediate skiers. As the most forested country in mainland Europe, the scenery is also highly rated. With a good variety of ski trails and the challenging World Cup run at Podkoren, this is one of Slovenia's most popular ski resort for families, says Zuber Sameja, Inghams' product manager for Slovenia. Snow cannons, producing more than 500,000 m3 of artificial snow, supplement precipitation on 85 per cent of the ski terrain.

Factors which encourage skiers to try Kranjska Gora include family facilities, novelty, affordable skiing, good value après ski, the blend of Austrian and Italian cuisine in traditional inns, and the friendliness of local people. "Skiers want to try something else and also Kranjska Gora holds the World Slalom and Giant Slalom Cup every year," Zuber adds. The town of Kranjska Gora, set in the Zgornjesavska Valley is picturesque, attracting domestic and international visitors summer and winter due to its mountain and lakes appeal.

As well as the ski hill, winter amenities include a snow park, cross country trails, ice climbing, night skiing, sledding, snowshoeing, ski touring, and kids' activities. Hotels are equipped with triple and quad rooms, most with door-to-slope skiing. There are many family-friendly events throughout the winter, including in December a live nativity scene which is constructed in the Ice Kingdom. As well as the Vitranc Cup (part of the World Cup series), the Planica World Cup Finals, a ski jumping event, is held each March.

The national profile of Slovenia's ski industry received a boost when ski racer Tina Maze burst onto the World Cup scene around 10 years ago, winning in all five alpine disciplines, as well as nabbing two Olympic gold medals at Sochi. Awarded best female athlete of the year for 2005, 2010, 2011, 2013 and 2014, she is a Slovenian national heroine. "We've yet to see internationally but certainly she is a great ambassador for ski Slovenia and she is present at many U.K. events hosted by Spirit Slovenia," says Zuber. "Slovenia Tourism is working very hard and, as a frequent visitor, I have seen many changes that are positive - especially new German ownership of the main airport of Ljubljana, quite a few gateways from Croatian airports, too, so more possibility of improving numbers."

Sources: Interview with Zuber Sameja, January 2015

The future for the ski industry

The opening Spotlight focuses on Slovenia's emerging ski industry, and Eastern Europe is one of the few parts of the world where the ski industry is growing. Countries like Bulgaria, Russia and Poland, have joined Slovenia in taking advantage of the increased interest in winter sports following the 2014 Winter Olympic Games held in Sochi. China, too, is rapidly expanding its ski industry (see the Case Study in Chapter 1), with plans to open up 250 new ski centers in Heilongjiang province alone in the next decade. Ski resorts are certainly popping up in some unlikely places. In 2014, the Masikryong Ski Resort in North Korea opened up, to the delight of young dictator Kim Jong Un. The winter wonderland is just one of Mr. Kim's tourism projects, as he has instructed state companies to boost numbers of foreign tourists from 200,000 a year to 1 million by 2016 (*The Economist*, 2014). The 1,400-hectare Masikryong resort sits at an altitude of 768m, and is said to have cost the regime $35 million. The resort says it wants to attract 5,000 people daily, which might be a challenge, given that barely a few thousand North Koreans know how to ski.

In North America, the industry remains in a phase of maturity, characterized by increased consolidation and diversification. But looking back on the last few decades, there have been some significant changes in the industry in that part of the world. Table 12.1 puts a spotlight on the U.S. winter sport tourism environment in the years 1994 and 2014, showing that while overall skier/rider visits have not changed in 20 years, the composition of those on the slopes has. The number of downhill skiers on the slopes has dropped, while that of snowboarders has more than doubled. More females are participating in both activities, and participants tend to be older than they were 20 years ago. Perhaps of concern is a substantial drop in the number of lessons being taken today compared to 20 years ago, implying there might be fewer beginners taking to the slopes. Certainly, in the U.K. there are concerns that the poor performance of the schools market will have a negative impact on the number of new entrants to the sport.

12

	Snowboard 1994	Snowboard 2014	Downhill Ski 1994	Downhill Ski 2014
Number of participants (participated 2 times+)	2,061,000	5,991,000	10,620,000	8,337,000
Gender mix M/F	82 to 18	67 to 33	59 to 41	61 to 39
Frequency of participation				
Core= 9+ days	695,000	2,132,000	4,248,000	2,396,000
Casual 2 to 9 days	1,366,000	3,859,000	6,372,000	5,942,000
Age distribution				
Under 18	52.00%	30.00%	25.00%	25.00%
18 to 34 Years	39.00%	51.00%	49.00%	36.00%
35 to 54 Years	4.00%	18.00%	24.00%	33.00%
55+	3.00%	1.00%	3.00%	6.00%
Ethnic diversity				
White	NA	67.1	NA	67.3
Asian/Pacific Islander	NA	10.4	NA	11.6
Hispanic	8.00%	9.10%	7.80%	7.80%
Black	0.00%	10.20%	0.20%	9.60%

Notable Themes	1994	2014
Skiers' and Snowboarders' concerns	Expense, Lack of time, Nobody to go with, risk of injury, don't know how to start	Expense, Lack of time, Nobody to go with, climate change, risk of injury, don't know how to start
Business	Fed raises interest rates 6 times to curb inflationary pressure. Economy hurt by Northridge earthquake. Aerospace and defense industries cut spending/cost. House and commercial construction on the weak side.	Cyber security at the forefront of retail business concerns. Chinese middle class balloons, low cost production to Vietnam and Bangladesh. Smart phones used to research and purchase products. Apple introduces Apple Pay mobile wallet technology.
Number of ski/ride areas	516	478
Number of skier/rider visits	56,540,000	56,700,000
AVG number of beginner lessons	7,684	6,189
AVG number of lessons all levels	26,237	20,629
AVG days open (areas)	118	125
AVG % of snowboarder visits	10.80%	29.50%

Table 12.1: Comparing 1994 to 2014 for the U.S. ski industry (Source: Adapted from Snowsports Industries America, 2014b, p. 5)

However, some experts suggest that the greatest opportunity for ski resorts lies in persuading people who have already adopted skiing/snowboarding to do it more – or persuading those who are lapsed skiers/boarders to take it up again – rather than convincing people who have never skied/boarded before, that they should begin this new sport (SIA, 2014a). In America, for example, there are 10.5 million people who consider themselves skiers or snowboarders but have lapsed due to increased family obligations, nobody to ski or ride with, and other issues that keep them from participating.

Table 12.1 also shows that the ethnic diversity of participants is improving, but it still doesn't match the diversity found in the general population. Income and education levels are more predictive of snow sports participation than ethnicity. Certainly more could be done to attract a more diverse participant base to snow sports. In fact, a recent report from Snowsports Industries America (2014b, p. 2) said that "future efforts to grow snow sports must break old paradigms in order to have significant impacts." This could include courting the accessible tourism market. The potential size of the accessible tourism sector is estimated at between 600 and 900 million people worldwide (ITB, 2012), suggesting that roughly 10 per cent of travelers are looking for barrier-free or accessible travel. With an ageing population this percentage will continue to grow, and there is an increasing recognition that this is no longer a niche market. In the U.S. alone, adults with impairments spend $13.6 billion on travel every year.

However, the travel industry needs to improve on every level to create better conditions for disabled travelers before the gap between the potential customer base and the actual number of travelers can be reduced. In Germany, for example, about 37 per cent of disabled travelers have decided not to travel in the past due to a lack of accessible facilities. Yet 48 per cent would travel more frequently if these were available, and 60 per cent would be willing to pay higher travel costs for improved accessibility (ITB, 2012). Some ski resorts, like Sun Peaks in Canada (see Profile below) are positioning themselves well for this growing market.

The LGBT tourism (lesbian, gay, bisexual and transgender) market is another segment that is growing in significance for the ski industry. The annual economic impact of LGBT travelers is over U.S.$100 billion per year in the U.S. alone (CMI, 2014). Twenty nine per cent of LGBT participants are frequent leisure travelers, taking five or more leisure trips per year, with 10 or more leisure hotel room nights per year. Whistler in Canada is one ski resort catering to this market, hosting the Whistler Pride and Ski Festival, one of the biggest gay and lesbian weeks in North America. The event features eight days of skiing, snowboarding, parties, comedy nights and social events. Other North American resorts hosting gay ski events include Aspen and Telluride in Colorado, Stowe in Vermont, and Park City in Utah. Elsewhere, European Gay Ski Week and European Snow Pride are held each year in the French Alps, whilst Gay Snowhappening is held in Solden in Austria.

12

Finally, Table 12.1 shows a fall in the number of resorts across America from 516 to 478 in the last two decades. Bill Jensen, a ski-industry expert, believes this number could get even smaller. He separates resorts into five tiers: Uber, Alpha, Status Quo, Survivor and Sunset (Glendenning, 2015). The 10 Uber and 35 Alpha resorts account for 40 per cent of ski business, while 125 Status Quo resorts with flat annual revenues tick by, and another 150 or so Survivor resorts just survive. The remaining 150-plus so-called Sunset resorts he believes will not survive. According to Jensen, new realities for success have to include sufficient hospitality infrastructure, a re-invigoration of winter sports culture, resort alliances and partnerships, and continued capital investment in snowmaking and other infrastructure.

As mentioned several times already in this book, diversification is also essential for ski resort survival. A recent report on ski trends from Wyndham Vacations, found that one in five people who take a ski vacation do not actually ski or snowboard. Those travelers are looking for alternative activities to enjoy, from dining and shopping to other unique mountain experiences like dog sledding (Wyndham Vacations, 2015). As mentioned in Chapter 10, ski resorts can no longer ignore the threat of climate change, and as they lose ski tourism operations, revenues and related jobs, they will need to develop economic diversification strategies, if they have not already done so (Dawson & Scott, 2013). Snowfall was down 28 per cent in the U.S. over the 2014-15 winter season, resulting in a five per cent drop in ski visits to 53.6 million.

Profile: From fear to fearlessness – Adaptive skiing

Skiing is scary enough for able-bodied participants but most people can only imagine how difficult and challenging it is for those with disabilities. Inspired in part by the evolution of the Para-Olympics, an increasing number of ski resorts are encouraging disabled kids and adults to get into winter sports.

Para Alpine Skier and Para Track Cyclist, Mel Pemble was born with Cerebral Palsy affecting the right side of her body. "At school I was different and felt frustrated in sports as I did not have the dexterity or strength to compete," Pemble says. "I hated team sports as I always felt I was letting the team down." Born in the U.K., her first taste of skiing was at age seven in France where a fall initially put her off the sport. "The experience left me with a twisted knee and a great fear of skiing, I never wanted to ski again," she remembers.

Moving to Canada with her family two years later, she next encountered skiing at Mount Washington, British Columbia, where her parents encouraged her to try one more time, explaining her situation to resort staff and asking for their best private ski instructor. "Dave Brown was that ski instructor and had I not met him I would not be skiing today," says Pemble, who skis with one pole. Her disability affects balance, depth perception and steering and she also wears orthotics in her ski boots to address a collapsed arch and pronation. Despite a limp, improper heel strike, blistering and poor circulation, Pemble says that skiing makes her forget her disability: "It just does not exist and it's a wonderful feeling."

Mel Pemble

Gaining confidence and expertise with Brown as her regular instructor, Pemble was gradually introduced to the idea that she could not only ski but she was a very fast skier. Thrilled by her aptitude, the family decided to move to Mount Washington for the winter season 2011/12 and enrol her in the Podium of Life Ski Academy. "You do academics in the morning, skiing in the afternoon. It's the coolest school in the world," says Pemble. Making the Adaptive Snow Sports Team by January 2012, she entered her first Provincial Adaptive race in February, after just seven days of training, and qualified for the Provincial Adaptive Championships at Cypress Mountain March 2012. "My first race was Giant Slalom. It was such a buzz," she says. "I was bib number 70 and second to go and to my relief I made all the gates, got lots of adrenaline and got gold!"

With lofty dreams of qualifying for the 2018 Paralympics, Pemble continued to work hard on speed and technique after her dazzling downhill debut. Next season she competed in the British Columbia Alpine Provincial Championships, won two golds at the 2013 Western Canadian Para-Alpine Championships and was named Vancouver Island Adaptive Snowsports Athlete of the Year. Having got into track cycling in 2013, she added road cycling to her regime in summer 2014, making the Dr. Walker Cycling Team. By winter 2014/15 she became one of five top British Columbia 'athletes to watch' in the Canada Winter Games, winning a gold in Giant Slalom and a silver in Slalom for Team BC. She also won four gold medals in the Western Championships and was invited to a Skills Assessment Camp with the Canadian National Team at Sunshine Village, Banff.

In order to further her ambitions to compete in the 2018 Paralympics, Pemble and her family now spend winters in Sun Peaks BC. Designed by Paul Mathews for ease of access to the slopes, Sun Peaks is very well set up for disabled athletes. During winter 2014/15 Pemble lived with her parents in an apartment in Hearthstone Lodge literally a stone's throw from the resort base, making it relatively easy for the necessary to-ing and fro-ing each day. The

12

condominium's outdoor hot tubs and gym are also useful facilities to enhance her training. With the slopes set in an arc around the resort, all the accommodation at Sun Peaks is ski in/out and Main Street is a wide, snowy thoroughfare where visitors and residents can ski down to all the lifts and services.

From its office on Main Street, Adaptive Sports at Sun Peaks (ASSP) runs low cost learn-to-ski programs for locals and pro-rated lessons for visitors. It is run by volunteers and sustained by fundraising. Pat McKimmon, President of ASSP, says that ski racing, however, is prohibitively expensive for the program – potential para athletes have to seek their own funding. "In terms of race development we envision providing some training for those students whose skills have developed to the ceiling of our program and who want to go further," says McKimmon. "We see this more as preparation for the racing circuit but once students reach that level we cannot offer the support or finances they need."

Pemble's mother, Rachael Chubb-Higgins took the adaptive training program and also volunteered with the ASSP. "The high quality programs are continually being developed as the organization invests heavily in instructor training in CADS, CSIA & CASI certifications," she says. "Instructors are encouraged to up their skill set. They continually strive to raise funds and awareness for ASSP. To improve in the future, they are focusing on increasing the number of instructors and encouraging more students and also training people with disabilities to become instructors." The ASSP offers sit-skiing, 3-track skiing, 4-track skiing, visually-impaired skiing, snowboard adaptations, snow limousine and facilities for autism and intellectual disabilities.

Pemble's rigorous training program at Sun Peaks involves six days on snow per week, coached by Bill Rublee from Sun Peaks Alpine Club. As well as its Adaptive Sports facilities, the family chose Sun Peaks because of its great onhill community and family atmosphere. Other pluses for Pemble are the resort school and swimming pool. "And Bolacco's café has fantastic home baking," she says. Plans for 2015/16 season were to return to Sun Peaks for training and hopefully progress to the provincial and national team.

Sources: Interview with Mel Pemble and Rachael Chubb-Higgins at Sun Peaks, March 2015

Ten consumer trends influencing winter sport tourism

The final section of this chapter takes a closer look at consumer behavior and highlights ten consumer trends that will influence the future of winter sport tourism.

1. Learning and enrichment

One of the major trends in tourism today is the desire of the tourist to have a learning experience as a part of the vacation. A recent survey found that half of North American travelers want to visit art, architectural, or historic sites on vacations, while one-third would like to learn a new skill or activity. Today's travelers are seeking experiences that provide them with a greater insight, increased understanding, and a personal connection to the people and places they visit (see the final Case Study at the end of this chapter). Learning and enrichment travel refers to vacations that provide opportunities for authentic, hands-on, or interactive learning experiences, featuring themes such as adventure, agriculture, anthropology, archaeology, arts, culture, cuisine, education, forestry, gardening, language, maritime culture, mining, nature, science, spirituality, sports, wine, and wildlife – to name only a few!

The ski industry is responding to this trend by offering a number of programs that combine winter sports and learning opportunities. A good example is The Learning Curve Institute in Europe that offers Snowboard & Ski Language Camps for students from all over the world to meet new friends through skiing or snowboarding whilst also becoming fluent in a foreign language. Students are fully immersed in either French or Spanish for the duration of the camp, which takes place in Les Deux Alpes, France, and they receive daily ski and snowboard tuition in the language they are learning. The ethos of the camps is 'learning, safety and fun' with an emphasis being put equally on each of these three core aspects.

2. Ethical consumption

In the last few decades, responsible tourism has emerged as a significant trend in the western world, as wider consumer market trends towards lifestyle marketing and ethical consumption have spread to tourism. Tourism organizations are beginning to realize that promoting their ethical stance can be good business as it potentially enhances a company's profits, management effectiveness, public image and employee relations.

International leisure travelers are also increasingly motivated to select a destination for the quality of its environmental health and the diversity and integrity of its natural and cultural resources. Studies indicate that environmental considerations are now a significant aspect of travelers' destination-choosing process. According to a travel study in 2012, the 'green' travel trend is gaining momentum, as 71 per cent of travelers surveyed said they planned to make more eco-friendly choices in the ensuing 12 months compared to 65 per cent the previous year (TripAdvisor, 2012).

In response to these trends, the ski industry as a whole is recognizing the need to strive toward adopting environmentally-friendly policies and practices. A number of individual tourism industry associations, such as the Banff Lake Louise Tourism Bureau, the Ontario Snow Resorts Association (Rutty et al., 2014), and individual ski resorts in Canada and the USA, have shown leadership on climate change by voluntarily adopting greenhouse gas (GHG) emission reduction targets. Other ski resorts in North America have signed up to the Sustainable Slopes Charter (adopted by the USA ski industry in 2000), which provides an overarching framework for ski areas regarding sustainability and enhanced environmental performance. Chapter 10 covers this topic in more detail.

12

3. Health-consciousness

Consumers are increasingly health-conscious, and in the U.S., the market segment that is focused on health and fitness, has been labeled the LOHAS segment. LOHAS is an acronym for Lifestyles of Health and Sustainability, and describes an estimated $290 billion marketplace for goods and services focused on health, the environment, social justice, personal development and sustainable living (French & Rogers, 2010). Research shows that one in four adult Americans is part of this group – nearly 41 million people. A more health-conscious society is often attributed to the influence of the baby boomer. Baby boomers are generally healthier, financially better off, better educated, and more interested in novelty, escape, and authentic experiences than were previous cohorts of older people. But younger generations, too, are health and wellness focused. Millennials, for example, are dieting less frequently than other generations, but consuming fewer calories daily. They spend money on gym memberships, running gear and energy bars and seek out specific health foods like whole grain breads, nuts and seeds, and quinoa (Forbes Consulting Group, 2012). This generation is also driving the demand for self-tracking technologies (Ericksson Consumer Lab, 2013).

The tourism sector is responding to this health-conscious trend with health and wellness centers springing up in many destinations. Mountain resorts, for example, are combining alternative health and wellness services with winter sport tourism. As mentioned in Chapter 11, The Montage, Deer Valley has a signature spa treatment called SURRENDER that creates a customized regimen for each guest which is transferable to other Montage properties. The Montage is also responding to the demand for healthier foods. Culinary teams collect copious notes on dietary restrictions of customers so that associates can address the guests in advance of their orders when they come to the tables, helping reassure guests that they are recognized and that their dietary needs are being taken to heart in preparing their meals. "We consider every meal custom to order," says Howard.

In keeping with this trend, ski resorts in general have been improving their restaurant and café offerings over the past decade, adding vegetarian, vegan, gluten- and dairy-free options, emphasizing local and fresh ingredients. There has been a gradual movement away from the more typical fast food fare in North American ski resorts, towards the fine dining that has traditionally characterized European resorts.

4. Customization

Consumers are increasingly looking for customized solutions that fit their specific needs, becoming more engaged with product creation (BDC, 2013). In the travel industry, requests for customized and personalized vacations are rising sharply, and both agents and traditional tour operators are changing their businesses to meet that demand. In addition to booking air and hotel reservations, agents and outfitters today are arranging customized wine tastings, visits to artisan workshops, and private after-hours tours of attractions such as the British crown jewels and the Vatican. Destinations attracting winter sport tourists are responding to this trend. At the Grand America in Salt Lake City, for example, Director of Guest Experience, Annie Fitzgerald says: "We ensure all employees are empowered to make each guest's stay exceptional and a personalized experience. If our employees learn something about our guests that will enhance their stay, we will recognize and deliver. For example, if we learn upon arrival that a couple is celebrating an anniversary, we will deliver a cake and card wishing them a Happy Anniversary, likewise with honeymoon couples who receive chocolate covered strawberries and a card. We recognize birthdays and we love taking care of guests who bring their children. We often provide balloons or small welcome toys for the little ones."

The Grand America also has a 'Grand Ambassador' whose role is to ensure that all repeat guests are recognized appropriately. "Our operating system will track all of our guest preferences, and our Ambassador then reviews all reservations and prepares for these requests," says Fitzgerald. Requests can range from a preference for a special room or view, to the type of linens a guest requires to be comfortable. "All of these things make the Grand America truly a home away from home and ensure the retention of our guests".

5. Convenience and speed

The increasing desire for convenience and speed is having a great impact on various sectors of the tourism industry. In the restaurant sector, drive-through sales are on the rise; in transportation, self check-in terminals are increasingly popular; and in accommodation, business travelers are seeking convenient rooms for shorter stays. An example of the latter is the hotel concept introduced at Heathrow and Gatwick Airports in the U.K. Owing much to Japanese 'capsule hotels', Yotel cabins are a cross between a hotel and a first-class airline seat. Each self-contained cabin has a double rotating bed, and facilities include an ensuite bathroom with shower, a flat-screen television and a pull-down desk.

There is also the suggestion that travel in the future will be geo-local, meaning that people will travel much closer to their home – more within their homeland and continent, and less outside it. A survey by the European Commission found that E.U. residents generally stay in their home country during their time off – 57 per cent of people in the E.U. last year took a trip within their own country. When they do leave their home country, most E.U. residents head south, as shown in Figure 12.1. Some 15 per cent of all E.U. residents spent time on holiday in Spain in 2013, the most popular destination ahead of France (11%) and Italy (10%), according to the survey (Karaian & Yanofsky, 2014).

This desire for convenience and speed has also influenced the services on offer in ski resorts. A good example is the Ski Butlers service that makes renting ski and snowboard equipment convenient and hassle-free all for the same price or less than most resort ski shops. Founded in 2004 in Park City, Utah, Ski Butlers now serves over 30 North American resorts in Colorado, California, Utah, Wyoming and British Columbia, Canada. The key to Ski Butlers' success and growth is customer service, according to president and founder, Bryn Carey. "Ski Butlers was founded on customer service and today thrives on customer service. Taking the hassle out of renting skis, hiring exceptional team members, and offering the highest level of equipment, all for an affordable price, is a different model than most ski rental shops. We like to have the Starbucks feel to our service," said Carey. "Customers can expect the same exceptional service, with new Rossignol equipment, at all locations. Customers can also save their info online so new reservations take only a few moments. These are the benefit you don't see from other ski shops."

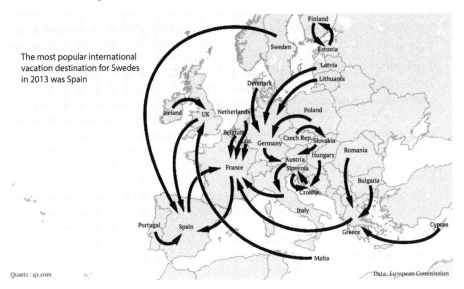

Figure 12.1: The Top International Vacation Destinations for Europeans (Karaian & Yanofsky, 2014: Courtesy of Quartz.com)

6. Spiritual enlightenment

The desire for spiritual enlightenment on a vacation has led to a boom in religious tourism. Even monks are taking advantage of this growing trend. Monasteries and temples provide the perfect backdrop for peaceful periods of mediation, prayer and reflection for world-weary business men and women. Often set in beautiful scenery, more religious institutions are jumping on the tourism bandwagon and opening their facilities for one- to three-day stays. South Koreans, for example, have around 36 different Buddhist temples to choose from for their retreats from everyday life. The notion of combining religion and tourism is also gaining momentum in other countries, notably Japan, where the Wakayama region is attracting daytrippers from Kyoto and Nara. Visitors can also stay overnight in rooms ranging from simple to luxurious. With views of the Pacific from ancient forest trails, tourists learn about Shinto and Buddhist theory by day. By night, accompanying their vegetarian meals served by the monks, guests can also enjoy sake and beer.

Winter sports resorts are responding to this demand for spiritual enlightenment on a vacation. Sundance in Utah, for example, has several spiritual learning classes for visitors including a Mindfulness Meditation class that, according to the resort, "will show you how to discover the nature of our mind and begin to actualize its extraordinary potential for lasting happiness through the joyful and heart-opening path of compassion and wisdom. This 30-minute class is designed to strengthen your body, quiet your mind and bring your body, mind and spirit in harmony." Another Morning Yoga at Sundance class combines the most useful elements of Beginning and Advanced Hatha, Vinyasa and Ashtanga Yoga, "leaving you feeling empowered and awake." Sundance also offers a Nature Walk whereby a "knowledgeable and caring expert will guide you along your unique path to greater peace, balance and awareness using practices from Native American traditions as well as introduce you to the legend of Mount Timpanogos." The website encourages participants by promising "a physical and spiritual uplifting, the chirping of birds, the sound of the snow crunching under your snowshoes, a beauty of a fresh morning air, calm environment."

7. Service quality

As discussed in Chapter 11, service quality has been identified as a key factor in differentiating service products and building a competitive advantage. Becoming customer-centered and exceeding customer expectations are now requirements for business success; research shows that consumers worldwide are willing to spend more on service excellence, and that they are more likely to remain loyal to service providers that focus on customer service. In order to provide top-notch customer service, winter sport tourism providers need to establish a strong service culture, a culture that supports customer service through policies, procedures, reward systems, and actions. This book has provided numerous examples of organizations that have created such a culture and who are responding to the demands for exceptional customer service. These include Lake Louise Ski Resort, Vail Resorts, Steamboat Springs, the Montage Deer Valley, Canadian Mountain Holidays, and Scott Dunn Travel. All these companies understand the financial implications of exceeding customer expectations.

8. Engagement and connectivity

As discussed in Chapter 8, the Internet has upended how consumers engage with ski resorts. After visiting, they often enter into an open-ended relationship with the resort, sharing their experiences online through social media. The Case Study on Vail's EpicMix in Chapter 8 is a great example of such engagement. Tourists are also demanding constant connectivity, and resorts are responding to this with

12

places like Alpendorf and Sölden in Austria (featured in Chapter 7) installing free Wi-Fi access points within their entire ski areas. Alpendorf's website boasts "with over 300 Wi-Fi hotspots in the Ski amadé you will be able to access the internet no matter where you are." Val Thorens in France also offers free Wi-Fi through Aerohive Wi-Fi terminals. "We want to offer our users quality optimal service in order to improve their stay in the resort. We anticipate their needs by providing them with Wi-Fi access in our ski lifts," says Eric Bonnel, SETAM ski lift company's sales and marketing manager (Val Thorens United, 2014).

We are witnessing a new mobile lifestyle (Roberti, 2011) that is revolutionizing where, when, and how we communicate personally and with businesses. Skiers and snowboarders are much more likely to own mobile devices than are general U.S. travelers, and such high mobile device ownership affects the entire ski travel life cycle: ski travelers are more likely to research, shop for and share their ski travel experiences through their smartphones and tablets, and the ski and travel industries must be prepared to reach and influence these higher-spending travelers across mobile media.

9. The blurring of business and leisure travel

The lines between business and leisure travel are becoming increasingly blurred. A recent Expedia study found that 56 per cent of Millennials expand their business trips into leisure trips (Newcombe, 2014). Mobile devices are having a profound effect on the traditionally defined silos between managed and unmanaged travel. A recent study found that 43 per cent of international travelers always take their mobile professional devices with them on holiday or on weekend trips (Ali et al., 2013). This presents new opportunities for airlines, hotels and destinations alike, all of which have to configure their services to be flexible. Conference and meeting planners also have to be cognizant of these changes, ensuring that they incorporate an element of leisure when they plan their meetings. An example is a conference organized by research specialists, Qualtrics, in Salt Lake City in February 2015, that one of the authors attended. This included a day's skiing in Park City as part of the conference.

Ski resorts are recognizing this trend and are aggressively targeting business travelers. The Edelweiss Hotel at the foot of the Alberg in Austria, for example, promotes itself as the ideal conference or business incentive destination. Promotional material promises seminars and incentives in the Arlberg that "will leave an unforgettable impression on all participants. Enhance motivation, loyalty and team spirit in an Incentive in the Arlberg: While skiing, while dining together and while relaxing and celebrating in the bars and lounges." Ski destinations are also equipping themselves to satisfy the technology demands of business travelers. Tour operators, too, are catering for travelers who want to combine business with time on the snow. Travelplan Ski Holidays, based in Australia, for example, offers a range of conferences for professionals in some of the world's best ski resorts. Over the years Travelplan has offered a variety of specially designed conferences at ski resorts such as Aspen, Fernie, Whistler-Blackcomb, Sun Peaks and Steamboat "that ensure you maximize your skiing time whilst you learn".

10. Experiences

A key innovation in today's business is experiences. Firms across a variety of industries from health care to airlines to automobiles are developing strategies around providing meaningful customer experiences (Schmitt, 2003). The 'experience economy' was a term coined by Pine and Gilmore (1999) to describe the business of selling experiences. They described experiences as a fourth economic offer, one that is distinctly different from the traditional commodities, goods and services that drive economic growth. Using a theatrical analogy, they describe 'services' as the stage used to create experiences and 'goods' as the props that are used in planning and sequencing a series of memorable events. Pine and Gilmore provide examples of how large companies like Walt Disney welcome guests, engage visitors, and provide an endless array of interactive experiences.

In an environment of ever more sophisticated consumers, those who deliver memorable customer experiences consistently create superior value and competitive advantage (Voss, 2003). Some of the benefits of delivering experiences are happy customers, repeat business, increased sales, enhanced brand identity, free marketing via word of mouth referrals and the creation of an emotional bond with customers. The benefits of creating experiences for customers is gaining momentum and demonstrating its business value in the tourism industry. In 2002, the World Tourism Organization reported a shift from active holidays to holidays as an experience (Klancnik, 2002). A survey sponsored by American Express found that the number one ranked 'most-memorable experience' for consumers was connected to a holiday (Buhasz & Bisby, 2005). Demand is growing for authentic travel that engages the senses, stimulates the mind, includes unique activities, and connects in personal ways with travelers in an emotional, physical, spiritual or intellectual level. A related trend is 'experience caching' whereby consumers continually collect, store and display their experiences for private use, or for friends, family, even the entire world to peruse.

The ski industry is responding to these demands, as it is naturally keen to attract new customers, repeat guests, and meet the needs of niche and mainstream markets interested in experiential travel. These companies are experience providers who sequence and stage carefully choreographed activities, personal encounters, and authentic experiences, designed to create long lasting memories, engaging travel, and increased customer loyalty. A good example can be found at the Washington School House in Park City Utah, mentioned earlier in the book. Apart from winter sports, the hip town's newest luxury boutique hotel, offers guests one of the most unusual winter activities with yoga deep inside a 10,000-year-old crater at The Homestead Resort. The instructor demonstrates yoga poses from the dock while guests move and bend on paddleboards that float

12

in the 90-plus-degree natural therapeutic pool. And to satisfy demand for 'experience caching', the hotel produces a motion picture for guests with a snapshot of their entire trip. A videographer snaps photos and films a day's worth of live footage, and following the visit, guests receive their very own edited feature film and photo book.

The final Case Study of the book once again features Lake Louise in Canada, where the forward-thinking family owners are encompassing all ten of the top consumer trends in winter sport tourism.

Case study: The Locke ladies

The Locke family

What could be more enviable than growing up at Lake Louise and being heirs to one of the world's top ski resorts? Imagine being Princesses of the Pistes with a powder playground as your back yard. This is the legacy for the Lake Louise ladies, the second generation of Lockes – Robin and Kimberley – who are being groomed to take over the family business when parents Charlie and Louise relinquish the reins.

"Kim and I are 'officially' co-Vice Presidents of the company," says Robin Locke. "Our business cards say 'Vice President of Strategy and Corporate Affairs'. This being said, our titles, we feel, are a bit arbitrary and really are for very official capacities only, such as for our bankers, for example. We are more 'Jills of all trades' - at least we aspire to be."

Of course it's not just the ultimate ski bum dream for the Lockes. With any ski resort comes huge responsibility, a full year-round work schedule and the need for a forward-thinking blue-print, constantly evolving with new inspirations in order to keep abreast and ahead of the competition and in sync with the clientele. "We are leveraging our extensive and complemen-tary experiences outside the ski industry and we are working, we feel, very well together as partners with an eye to learning everything that Charlie does – both for Lake Louise Ski Resort (LLSR) and his other companies," Locke explains. Dad's business interests range from ranching to oil to property and finance.

Since Robin Locke started working full time for LLSR in 2010, she and Kimberley have been immersed in the business both from "the top down and from the bottom up". Tasks range from annual business planning, and capital expenditure-related decision-making, to front-of-house experience learning about every department. They get involved in lodging, dining, bathroom renos, creating design concepts and hiring contractors. And, at the busy Christmas Holiday season, the family puts up the dazzling decorations and helps with selling tickets, flipping burgers and greeting customers in order to facilitate seamless flow for peak period crowds.

As well as learning the routine ropes, the Locke ladies have to keep an eye on constantly mor-phing trends in the winter sports industry. One of the subjects under scrutiny is the average age of skiers. "The global ski industry, and the Canadian one in particular, is a mature one, and thus we have all been keenly interested - especially recently - in skier demographics," Robin Locke says. "Challenges relate to an aging skier population - and an increasingly dynamic, evolving and competitive landscape - but the industry is responding. For example, LLSR has a super senior pass for $20, and we sell many more of these than you'd think." Lake Louise also promotes nostalgia with its interpretive heritage photos around lodges, retro events, a growing seniors club, and Throwback Thursdays, a retrospective of photos and videos posted on social media.

In order to mitigate the aging skier trend, she says, operators are diversifying, offering myriad activities rather than depending on just ski tickets to ensure a sustainable year round busi-ness model. "Investments are directed toward making ski areas more attractive to skiers/ snowboarders, certainly, as well as making our areas attractive to non-skier counterparts. To be sure, the vacationing family is demanding a fuller menu of possible activities. LLSR is par-ticipating and reacting to the extent possible given the regulatory constraints of being in a Canadian National Park."

Industry-wide, however, there is a drive to create new skiers, says Locke: "One market we will be focusing on going forward is 'new Canadians', who are 'lower hanging fruit'. Emerg-ing markets are excellent opportunities to tap into as well, and we are working on attracting these with our regional, provincial and federal partners. Finally, we pride ourselves on being a family-friendly resort; we have amazing programs, services and ambiences for kids, and we see our efforts to this regard working – we do seem to have a very young market, in the last year or two especially, whom we hope will become lifetime LLSR loyalists."

A more sophisticated indoor product is also in demand nowadays, with guests wanting higher quality day lodges, finer and healthier culinary experiences, modern washrooms, etc. "In the

12

last two years, for example, we have refreshed the two day lodges at the resort which were the most outdated – Whitehorn Lodge and Whiskey Jack Lodge," Locke says. "We have similar investment projects scheduled every year for the next five, and beyond that – during what we call the jumping off period to our 'Long Range Plans' – we aspire to significantly alter the experience at Lake Louise in keeping with evolving trends and guest expectations."

With skiers requiring a quick, easy and convenient experience from home to hill, eliminating hassles is also a priority for Lake Louise which works closely with the village community as well as the Bow Valley area and the province to coordinate travel, transport and lodging. Another plus for Lake Louise is its commodious topography which means no annoying flats or uphill slogs for skiers and snowboarders. "The entire design of the ski area is predicated on principles of convenience, speed and ease of access," Locke explains. "The base area is ultra-convenient and user-friendly, with all facilities readily apparent and accessible in one central location. Access from local hotels is extremely quick and easy, with 'lobby-to-lift' times typically averaging about 10 minutes. 'Parking-lot-to-peak' time is also unrivalled – with no access lifts to contend with, and with main lifts' lower terminals just steps from the lodges, another frustrating bottleneck more common to other areas is eliminated."

Lake Louise is also up to date with technology, boasting direct-to-lift cards, debit-loadable passes, efficient IT systems for purchasing and rentals, as well as Wi-Fi, recharging stations for phones, and computer terminals – all vital in the era of social media. In fact, since the advent of social media, customers have become important marketers, says Locke. The resort is focusing on improving guest experience in order to encourage positive word of mouth: "When an unhappy customer can broadcast his or her negative experience to hundreds or thousands in a second – or vice versa they will boast the quality of our products and their happy experience, here, in real time to their networks with similar urgency – what we offer, and our service, becomes that much more important than ever before."

The Lockes deem marketing and social media the most dynamic challenges for the ski industry: "The jobs of our marketers are that much more difficult, too, in this dynamic, digital world where customer purchasing habits and expectations are constantly changing and more demanding – for example, direct online booking is more pervasive, therefore SEO, content marketing and social media are more integral," says Robin Locke. This makes marketing and sales more challenging, with real time response the fundamental key to success.

There are many more mediums to juggle, too. While grassroots and guerrilla marketing-type endeavors still resonate, traditional PR and media relations remain important, says Locke. "It's not yet appropriate to totally abandon traditional advertising, and the constantly evolving online and analytical world is of course now paramount as is social media, which itself is constantly changing and one of the best places to reach and hear from (i.e. engage with) current and potential customers." Lake Louise was an early adopter of social media and in the 2014/15 season one of the first resorts on Snapchat. They employed a dedicated social media guru to keep up with the latest trends online and useful platforms. They are also exploring sophisticated methods of tracking progress and benchmarking online platforms where skiers and snowboarders are interacting and making purchase decisions.

Learning something new is an increasingly important part of vacations nowadays. As part of a commitment to education and enrichment, Lake Louise creates educational programs and installations in order to deliver key conservation and heritage tourism messages to visitors to Banff National Park. LLSR also invests in and supports Go International, an international exchange program focusing on culture, nature and conservation. There are Avalanche Awareness, Outdoor Education and Backcountry Skiing courses. In winter, they offer Ski Friends Winter Heritage tours (free of charge) and snowshoe tours which combine activity with tidbits on the area, animals, geography and history. And in summer there are interpretive hikes and a Junior Ranger Program as well as an Interpretive Centre.

In terms of ethical consumption and sustainability, Lake Louise is in a unique position with more stringent practices required than at most ski resorts. "Operating within Banff National Park UNESCO World Heritage Site is a special privilege that demands the highest levels of environmental accountability," says Locke. "The Lake Louise Ski Area was the first ski area in the Canadian Rockies to introduce an Environmental Management Department, which oversees 'green' operations and projects, including cutting-edge water conservation, waste management and energy-saving endeavors, delivery of interpretive programs and the supporting of staff in graduate level research." Other initiatives include green groomers, eco-upgrades to snowmaking, water and energy conservation in lodges, efficient lighting and heating, recycling, community clean-ups and an established Corporate Social Responsibility Program. Future plans include improving public transit, lower-emission chairlifts, more eco-efficient snowmaking and resort-wide energy consumption.

Health-consciousness is another important thread to the resort's future planning: "Going forward we are certainly cognizant of the fact that our demographic is more and more health conscious, and in recognition of same and to appeal to that, we have been working with our partners on related ideas such as the upcoming ski and yoga retreat and we have also been discussing various other ideas such as yoga/health and wellness retreats at Skoki Lodge," Locke explains. Already the resort promotes health among personnel with its staff gym, offers discount days to encourage locals into sport, donating proceeds to athletic scholarships, supports the village ice hockey rink, and is continually upgrading mountain food service to include healthy, vegan and gluten-free offerings.

LLSR has put diversification front and foremost with its new desk in the main daylodge as well as a large outlet in the village mall. Entitled 'Experience Lake Louise' the service provides booking and information for activities such as snowmobile tours, heli-hiking tours, heli-snowshoeing, heli-skiing, cat skiing, dog sledding, tubing, guided snowshoe tours and sleigh rides, complete with customization options.

Sources: Interview with Robin Locke, January 2015

12

References

Ali, R., Clampet, J., Schaal, D. and Shankman, S. (2013) '14 global trends that will define travel in 2014', accessed 4/10/2015 from http://www.fairtrade.travel/uploads/files/Skift_Trends_2014.pdf

BBMG, GlobeScan and SustainAbility (2013) *2013 Aspirational Consumer Index*, accessed 10/22/2014 from http://www.globescan.com/98-press-releases-2013/291-two-and-a-half-billion-aspirational-consumers-mark-shift-in-sustainable-consumption.html

BDC (2013) 'Mapping Your Future. Five Game-Changing Consumer Trends', Business Development Bank of Canada, October, accessed 12/9/2014 from http://www.bdc.ca/Resources%20Manager/study_2013/consumer_trends_BDC_report.pdf

Buhasz, L. and Bisby, A. (2005) 'Canadians dream of unique trips', *The Globe and Mail*, 17 September, T4.

CMI (2014) *LGBT Tourism Demographic Profile,* accessed 3/22/2015 from http://www.communitymarketinginc.com/gay-lesbian-marketing-tools-for-tourism-hospitality/gay-lesbian-tourism-demographic-profile-gay-demographics/

Dawson, J. and Scott, D. (2013) 'Managing for climate change in the alpine ski sector', *Tourism Management*, **35**, 244-254.

Ericksson Consumer Lab (2013) '10 Hot Consumer trends 2014', accessed 10/22/2014 from http://www.ericsson.com/res/docs/2013/consumerlab/10-hot-consumer-trends-report-2014.pdf

Forbes Consulting Group (2012) 'Millennials', Insight Series, accessed 10/22/2014 from http://www.forbesconsulting.com

French, S. and Rogers, G. (2010) 'Understanding the LOHAS consumer: The rise of ethical consumerism. A strategic market research update from the Natural Marketing Institute (NMI)', accessed 10/22/2014 from http://www.lohas.com/Lohas-Consumer

Glendenning, L. (2015) 'In Denver, ski industry experts ponder business uncertainties', *The Aspen Times*, 29 January, accessed 3/3/2015 from http://www.aspentimes.com/news/14828670-113/in-denver-ski-industry-experts-ponder-business-uncertainties

ITB (2012) *ITB World Travel Trends Report*, IPK International, Germany, accessed 10/22/2014 from www.itb-berlin.de/media/itbk/itbk_media/itbk_pdf/WTTR_Report_2013_web.pdf

Karaian, J. and Yanofsky, D. (2014) 'Where Europeans go on vacation, once they leave their country', *Quartz.com,* 14 February, accessed 10/22/2014 from

http://qz.com/177366/where-europeans-go-on-vacation-not-so-far-from-home/

Klancnik, R. (2002) 'A year after 9-11: Climbing towards recovery', The World Tourism Organization, accessed 10/22/2014 from http://www.hospitalitynet.org/news/4013195.html

Newcombe, T. (2014) 'Expedia CEO: Business and leisure becoming blurred', *Buying Business Travel*, 4 February, accessed 10/22/2014 from http://buyingbusinesstravel.com/news/0422001-expedia-ceo-business-and-leisure-becoming-'blurred'

Pine, J. and Gilmore, J. (1999) *The Experience Economy: Work is Theatre and Every Business a Stage*, Boston: Harvard Business School.

Roberti, J. (2011) 'Q&A', *Marketing Week*, 2 June, 29.

Rutty, M., Matthews, L., Scott, D. and Del Matto, T. (2014) 'Using vehicle monitoring technology and eco-driver training to reduce fuel use and emissions in tourism: A ski resort case study', *Journal of Sustainable Tourism*, ??(5), 787-800.

Schmitt, B.H. (2003) *Customer Experience Management*, Hoboken, NJ: John Wiley & Sons.

Snowsports Industries America (2014a) *Revisiting Growing the Snow Sports Industry*, accessed 9/12/2014 from http://www.snowsports.org/portals/0/documents/Revisiting%20Growing%20the%20Snow%20Sports%20Industry.pdf

Snowsports Industries America (2014b) *2014 SIA Downhill Consumer Intelligence Report. Phase I – The Discovery Phase*, accessed 7/11/2014 from http://www.snowsports.org/SuppliersServiceProviders/ResearchSurveys/DownhillConsumerIntelligenceProject

The Economist (2014) 'Skiing in North Korea. Mounting problems', *The Economist*, 14 February accessed 11/23/2014 from http://www.economist.com/blogs/banyan/2014/02/skiing-north-korea

TripAdvisor (2012) 'TripAdvisor survey reveals travelers growing greener', accessed 10/22/2014 from http://www.http://www.tripadvisor.com/PressCenter-i5154-c1-Press_Releases.html, 7 April.

Val Thorens United (2014) 'Wi-Fi on the ski area', accessed 10/22/2014 from

http://www.valthorens.com/winter-en/val-thorens/live/news/news-detail/wi-fi-on-the-ski-area.378.a624.html, 7 April.

Voss, C. (2003) 'The experience profit cycle', A Research Report published by the London Business School, Centre for Operations and Technology Management, pp. 2.

Wyndham Vacations (2015) Wyndham Vacation Rentals 2014-15 Ski Trends Research Report, accessed 3/22/2015 from http://digital.turn-page.com/t/159494-2014-15-ski-trends-research

12

Index

ABC Sports, 41, 18
accessibility - site, 65, 96
accessible tourism, 253
Adamant Lodge, 201
Adaptive Ski Bash, 138
Adaptive Sports at Sun Peaks (ASSP), 256
advertising, 6, 21, 42, 59, 72, 103, 105-110, 113-115, 117,
    132-136, 140, 141, 145, 146, 149, 155, 161, 174, 181,
    189, 195, 225, 232-237, 266
AFP World Tour, 42
agency decisions, 109, 110
Alberta Rocky Mountain resorts, 209
alliances, 123, 124, 125, 254
All Mountain Mamas, 159, 163
All Seasons Ski Club, 177
Alp Action, 212
Alpe d'Huez, 79, 93
Alpine Meadows, 165, 166
Alpine Partners, 68
Alta Ski Area, 140, 232
Altay Mountains of China, 7
American Express, 187, 263
American Natural Resources Defense Council, 15, 204
Andermatt, 78, 81, 82, 83
Apostles, 229, 230
après ski, 3, 12, 32, 33, 50, 52, 57, 67, 88, 98, 101, 111,
    120, 136, 143, 177,178, 250
Arizona Snowbowl, 143
Arosa, 63, 68
Aspen Community Foundation, 214
Aspen Highlands, 167
Aspen/Pitkin County Housing Authority, 80
Aspen's Buttermilk, 41
Aspen Skiing Company, 67, 167, 213, 214
Aspen Skiing Company's Family Fund, 214
Aspen Snowmass, 115, 116, 120, 162, 164, 169, 177, 178,
    190
Association of Freeskiing Professionals, 41, 42
Atomic, 10, 42

Baby Boomers, 44, 45, 51, 143, 165, 167, 258
Badgastein Austria, 87

Banff, 2, 4, 30, 78, 80, 123, 125, 126, 139, 170, 189, 199,
    207-209, 214, 216, 255, 257, 266, 267
Banff–Bow Valley, 207, 208
Banff Lake Louise Tourism Bureau, 216, 257
Banff National Park, 139, 199, 207, 209, 216, 266, 267
Bartle Bogle Hegarty Global, 235
Bavaria, 8, 70
Beaver Creek, 30, 73, 160, 174
Bell Martin, 136
Bergbahnen Sölden Lift Company, 149
Berry, Michael, 92
Best, Sandy, 240
big emerging markets, 203
Big White Ski Resort, 68, 69
Blacktail Mountain Ski Area, 124
Bladerunners, 177
BMW, 180, 189
Bokwang Phoenix Park, 195
Bond James, 148, 150
Bonnel Eric, 262
Boyne Resorts, 30
branding, 107, 108, 138, 155
Branson, Richard, 12, 141
Breckenridge, 30, 73, 160, 164, 170, 231
Brent Harley & Associates, 64, 68, 69
Brice, John, 142, 144, 146
Brighton Ski Resort, 15, 68, 182
British Association of Snowsport Instructors, 93
British Columbia, 2, 23, 25, 62, 64, 65, 68, 69, 79, 87, 89,
    99, 123, 154, 157, 199, 210 154, 255, 260
Broadmoor Resort, 229
Bruchez, Patrick, 10, 12, 13
BUMPS FOR BOOMERS, 135, 162, 165, 166, 167
Burton Snowboards, 37, 92
Butler, Dave, 199-201

Calgary Winter Olympics, 62
Camelback Mountain Resort, 93
Campaign evaluation, 109, 113
Canadian Environmental Assessment Act, 208
Canadian Mountain Holidays, 71, 139, 199, 202, 232,
    261, 24

Canadian Ski Hall of Fame, 88
Canadian Tourism Commission, 16, 17, 124, 191
canopy tours, 32
Canyons Resort, 33, 63, 67, 69, 72, 74, 170
Cardrona Alpine Resort, 162
cause-related marketing, 137
celebrity endorsement, 89, 141
Chamonix, 8, 70, 71, 181
Charity Ski Weeks, 137
Charlie Locke, 1, 2, 4, 10, 95, 264, 265
China, 7, 10, 14, 15, 16, 17, 24, 34, 62, 66, 182, 251
Christiana, 7
Cimmer, Tim, 184, 185
Cine Tirol Film Commission, 149, 150
Club Med, 164
Club Ski, 126
CNET, 173
Colorado High Country, 72
Condé Nast Traveller, 140
Condé Nast Traveller Readers' Travel Awards, 225
Conversion Cup Challenge, 93
Copper Mountain Resort, 136, 183
Coronet Peak, 162
Cougar Mountain, 33
Crashed Ice, 5, 184, 185
Crested Butte Mountain Resort, 33, 67
Crystal Ski Holidays, 48, 49, 118, 119, 120
customer complaint iceberg, 242
customization, 230, 232, 258, 267
Cypress Hills Eco-Adventures Ltd, 32

Daily Mail Ski & Snowboard Shows, 118
De Jong, Arthur, 210-212
Deer Valley Resort, 91, 129
Digital Marketing Communications, 156
Diamond, Chris, 243
direct mail, 106, 115, 116, 120, 135, 156
direct marketing, 106, 110, 113, 114, 115, 157, 160, 174, 235
direct response television, 115
Disney, Walt, 213, 244, 263
diversification, 10, 26, 30, 75, 78, 215, 251, 254, 267
Doppelmayr, 62
DreamSki Adventures, 125, 126,127
Dunn, Andrew, 140, 223, 224, 225, 227, 236

Eaglecreast Ski Area, 93
Eagle Point, 143
East Kootenay Environmental Society, 207
Ecosign, 38, 62, 63, 64, 82, 195, 196
Edelweiss Hotel, 262
ethical consumption, 257, 267
Elevate Women's Ski Camp, 57, 59

Elk Camp, 177
empathy, 226, 238, 240
English, Susie, 129, 131, 139
environmental impacts, 6, 7, 192, 193, 199, 200, 212
environmental leveraging, 192, 193
EpicMix, 160, 161, 173, 174, 261
ESPN, 41, 180, 189
European Gay Ski Week, 253
European Snow Pride, 253
event marketing, 188
event leveraging, 190
Extreme Freeskiing Championships, 136
experiences, 9, 27, 31, 49, 52, 62, 73, 92, 108, 111,126, 134, 136, 139, 154, 161- 164, 167, 168, 173, 174, 210, 211, 227, 232, 243, 245, 254, 257, 258, 261-263, 265

Fairmont Banff Springs Sports Invitational, 139, 189
Fairmont Hotels & Resorts, 236
familiarization trip (Fam trip), 106, 133
Fédération Internationale de Bobsleigh et de Tobogganing (FIBT), 189
FIBT World Championships, 189
Fire and Ice Ski, 177
First Choice Holidays, 119
Fitzsimmons Creek, 33, 211
Fondueland, 52
Food Network Magazine, 103
Four Seasons, 35, 37, 88, 239
Four Valleys, 13
Freeride World Tour, 188
freestyle, 16, 22, 63, 96, 136, 181, 182, 190, 195
Friends of Stowe Adaptive Sports, 138

Garmisch-Partenkirchen, 8
Gauthier, Andrew, 41-42
Generation X, 44
Generation Y, 44,51
Giant Slalom Cup, 250
Gmoser, Hans, 24, 200
Go International, 266
Golden Eagle Awards for Environmental Excellence, 140
GoPro cameras, 183
Grand America, 259
Greene, Nancy, 87, 89
Grouse Mountain, 32
Grünwald Resort 149
Gstaad, 44, 51, 52, 53, 183
Gstaad Saanenland Tourismus, 51, 52, 53
Gunstock Mountain, 33

Habitat Improvement Team, 212
Hamilton Lodge, 53

Hard Rock International, 34, 235
Harveys World Travel, 133
Haute Savoie, 8
Hearthstone Lodge, 255
Heavenly, 30, 73, 145, 160, 170, 174
heli-hiking, 200, 267
heli-skiing, 23 27, 71, 125, 139, 199-200, 207, 232, 233, 267
heli snowshoeing, 267
heli-tourism, 199
Hollywood Bowl, 143
Homestead Resort, 263
hostages, 229, 230
Hotel de Verbier, 12, 13
Hotelplan, 13, 123, 206
Howard, Dan, 112, 228, 231, 258
Hunter, Ian, 21, 22
Hyatt, 16, 143
Hyundai Sungwoo Resort, 195

IBISWorld, 14, 29, 30, 31, 48
Ice Cross Downhill, 184
Ice Kingdom, 250
Imagine Travel, 224
IMAX, 142
Inghams, 12, 13, 119, 123, 206, 250
Inn at Solitude, 237
integrated marketing communications, 105, 107, 114
intermediaries, 6, 7, 103, 105, 120, 122, 123, 135
International Alpine Design, 64
International Congress & Convention Association, 183
International Ice Cross Sport Federation, 185
International Olympic Committee, 16, 38, 63, 181
International Ski Federation, 10
Intrawest, 14, 30, 70, 71, 96, 97
iSKI Swiss, 52
Island Lake Catskiing, 25
ISTD qualifications, 93

Jackson Hole, 57, 58, 72
Japan, 10, 14, 16, 23, 24, 28, 62, 67, 80, 97, 99- 101, 121, 125, 126, 128, 133, 194, 212, 229, 232, 234, 259, 260
Japanese National Tourism Organization, 100, 101
Jasper National Parks, 208
Jay Peak Resort, 67
Jazz Ma Tazz Ski Club, 177, 178
Jet Set Sports, 187
Jiminy Peaks, 92
Jong de, Arthur, 210, 211, 212
Joseph, Darryl, 177, 178
Jumbo Glacier Resort, 64, 65, 66

K-Bar, 57
K2, 37

Ketchum Global Research & Analytics, 146
Keurig Green Mountain, Inc., 214
Keystone Resort, 30, 73, 160, 174
Kia Motors, 136
Kicking Horse Mountain Resort, 124, 153
Killington, 30
Kim, Jin Sun, 196
Kim, Jong Un, 251
Kirk, Jori, 32, 33
Kirkwood, 41, 73, 145, 174
Konjiam Resort, 195
Kootenay Rockies, 123, 124
Kranjska Gora, 250
Krippendorf, Jost, 76, 205, 209
Klout, 147, 154
Knight, Jim, 235
Knudsen, Earl, 68

Laax, 63
Lake Louise Ski Resorts, 265, 266, 267
Lake Tahoe Visitors Authority), 133
Lange, 37, 171
Langevin, Alexandre, 125
Larch Mountain, 3
Last Vegas, 142
Lauberhorn drag-lift, 8
Lauterbrunnen-Murren railway line, 8
League Valaisan pour la Protection de Nature, 212
Learn to Ski and Snowboard Month, 144
LEED, 70, 193
Le Ski, 96
Les Belleville, 70, 71
Les Menuires, 30, 78
Les Portes du Soleil, 69
Les Trois Vallees, 69
Lewis Kyle, 159, 237
LGBT tourism, 253
Liberty Mountain Resort, 93
Lifestyles of Health and Sustainability, 258
Ligety, Ted, 129
Lillehammer Winter Olympics, 195
Lilyhammer, 195
Locke, Robin, 264, 265
Loyalists, 229, 230, 265

MacGillivray Freeman Films, 142
Maclean's Magazine, 212
Mammoth Mountain, 177, 194
Managing service promise, 235
Mancuso, Julia, 59, 129
market diversification, 75, 78
marketing communications, 105, 107, 108, 114, 137, 155, 156, 235, 236

Marriott, 143
Marshall, Debbie, 119, 120
Masikryong Ski Resort, 251
master development plans, 64
Mathews, Paul, 38, 39, 61, 62, 63, 195, 196, 255
Maze, Tina, 141, 249
McKinsey & Company, 160
McMillan, Jess, 57
measurability, 114
Media Q, 147, 148
media selection, 113
Megève, 8
Methodikal, Inc, 159
Mendes, Sam, 148, 149
merchandising, 106, 135
Méribel, 9, 30, 69, 78
Merrill Lynch, 187
message strategy, 106, 110
MGM's Aria Hotel, 142
Miller, Andy, 73, 74
Millennials, 51, 52, 53, 258, 262, 44
Miller, Warren, 24, 59, 100
Monarch Airlines, 157
Montage Deer Valley, 112, 228, 231, 258, 261
Mosteller, Matt, 124,153,155
motivation, 46-49, 57, 143, 186-188, 212, 237, 262
Mount Norquay, 207
Mount Washington, 61, 254, 255
Mount Zao, 63
Mountain Creek Resort, 93
Mountain Collective Pass, 124
Mountain Thunder Lodge, 231
Mountainlands Community Trust, 80
Mountain Talks Theatre, 136
Mountain Wilderness, 212
Mt Bachelor, 93, 137
Mt Baker, 87
Mt Brighton, 174
Mt Buller, 212, 217, 218, 237
Mt Cook, 162
Mt Hutt, 162
Mt Seymour, 87
Mt Stirling, 212, 217, 218

Nancy Greene Ski League, 89
Nancy Greene's Cahilty Lodge, 89
National Brotherhood of Skiers, 177
National Forest System, 64
National Parks Act of 1930, 207
National Safety Month, 92
National Ski Areas Association, 77, 92
National Ski Areas Association National Convention

and Tradeshow, 211
National Ski Patrol, 91
NBC Olympics, 192
NBS, 177, 178,1 79
Nevin, Joe, 135, 162, 165, 166, 167
New Balance, 235
New Mexico Tourism Department, 103
Nippon Cable, 62
Niseko Annupuri, 100
Niseko Promotion Board, 100
Niseko United, 67, 97, 100, 101
North Lake Tahoe, 41,136
Northstar at Tahoe, 15, 30, 93
Now Generation, 44, 51, 143
Okanagan Ski Areas, 88
Okemo Mountain Resort, 170
Ontario Snow Resorts Association, 216, 257
Oslo, 7
Outside Magazine, 104
Owl Bar, 98

Palms Casino Resort, 147
Paradiski, 69
Park City Chamber, 130
Park City Mountain Resort, 27, 30, 67, 69, 72, 73, 74,
Parks Canada, 2, 208
Perrin, Andy, 206
PEAK 2 PEAK Gondola, 89
Peak Walk, 52
Pemble, Mel, 254,255
personalization, 114
personal selling, 106, 132, 135, 235
Planica World Cup Finals, 250
Powder Alliance Pass, 124,
Powderbird, 162
Powder Highway, 123,124
Powderkeg Lounge, 3
Powder Magazine, 162
POWDR Corporation, 30
Precision targeting, 114
press conferences, 133
press release, 73, 74, 130, 133, 149, 245
Pretty Faces, 57, 59, 111
privacy, 13,114
product differentiation, 30
product diversification, 30, 75, 78
product improvement, 30, 75, 77
promotions, 105-107,114,117,132,135,235
public relations, 52, 53, 106, 110, 129, 130-151, 180, 228, 231, 235, 240,
PyeongChang Organizing Committee for the 2018 Olympic Winter Games, 195

Quasar Expeditions, 47

Raine, Al, 87, 89, 97
Red Bull, 180, 184, 185,
Redford, Robert, 98
Red River, 103
Regional Office of Sustainable Tourism, 182
Republican National Convention in San Diego, 142
Resorts of the Canadian Rockies, 2
return on investment, 105, 108, 165
Revelstoke Mountain Resort, 124
Ritz Carlton, 229
road shows, 135
Rosa Khutor, 30, 38, 39, 63, 65
Rossignol Ski Company, 130
Roundtop Mountain Resort, 9
Ruby Mountains Heli-Experience, 143
Ruhfass, Christina, 149
Runner's World, 236
Russia, 7, 24, 30, 37-39, 61, 63-66, 82, 128, 181, 196, 251
Ryan Solutions, 48

Saanerslochgrat, 52
Saanewald Lodge, 53
Sales promotions, 107, 117, 132, 135, 235
Salomon Freeski TV, 42
Sandia Peak, 103
Savognin, 63
Sawyer's Nook, 3
SBC Skier, 42
Schmuck, Jeff, 42
Schee & Mehr, 52
Schuster, Chris, 41, 42
Scott Dunn, 140, 223, 224, 225, 236, 261
Selkirk Wilderness Skiing, 25
Seirus Innovation, 143
Serre Chevalier, 93, 94, 95
service culture, 223-243
service excellence, 154, 226, 243, 244, 245, 261
service recovery, 234, 237, 238, 239, 240, 241, 242
service quality, 226, 227, 236, 238, 240, 261
Sharp, Isadore, 239
Sheen, Martin, 139
Shinto, 261
Sidecut Extreme, 9
Sierra Nevada College, 41, 42
Silver Travel Advisor, 120
Sipapu, 103
Site feasibility, 64, 65
Ski and Snowboard Schools of Aspen, 166
Ski apps, 93, 94, 95, 173
Ski Area Management, 112, 204
Ski Big 3, 126

Ski Butlers, 170, 259, 260
Ski Club of Great Britain, 12,157
Ski Dubai, 34
Skiline, 52
Ski Lift Lodge, 143
Ski Magazine, 140, 143, 214
Ski Santa Fe, 103
Ski School App, 94, 95
Ski Sunday, 118
Ski Total, 123, 206
Ski Utah, 112, 129, 130, 131
Ski Vermont, 159, 163
Skoki Lodge, 267
Snowbasin, 124
Snowbird, 68, 130, 162
Snowcat, 28, 91, 185
Snowboarder Magazine, 162
Snowboard and Ski Language Camps, 257, 204, 213-215
Snowland, 34
snowmaking, 2, 4, 9, 63, 69, 72, 73, 77, 82, 90, 170, 171, 185, 217, 218, 254, 267
snow-trains, 8
snowshoeing, 3, 25, 26, 27, 46, 50, 88, 101, 103, 155, 209, 250, 267
Snowsports Industries America, 49, 55, 135, 183, 227
Sochi Winter Olympics, 63, 192, 195
social impacts, 190, 201, 202, 205
Solden, Austria, 148
Southern Lakes Heliski, 233
Spectre, 148,149,150
Spirit Slovenia, 251
Spiritual enlightenment, 260,261
Spitzhorn, 53
Squaw Valley, 41, 165, 181
St Moritz, 8, 13, 74, 81
staffing, 98, 186,
Starbucks, 3, 230, 260
Steamboat, 30, 97, 170, 208, 229, 243, 244, 245, 261, 263
Stein Eriksen Lodge, 111, 231
Stowe Mountain Resort, 138, 182
Sugar Bowl Resort, 117, 165
Summer X Games, 41
Sundance Mountain Resort, 97, 98, 261
Sun Peaks Resort, 87, 89
Sunshine Village, 170, 189, 255
Superpass, 52, 124
Sustainable Slopes, 213, 217, 257
Swatch, 12, 180, 188
Switzerland, 8, 11-13, 23-24, 28, 52, 68-70, 74-75, 88, 94, 183-184, 188-189, 206, 212, 214, 223, 234, 250
symbolic atonement, 241

Tamarack, 31, 78, 145
Tamworth Snowdome, 34
Taos Ski Valley, 103
TARP, 240, 242
Telegraph Ski and Snowboard Show, 136
Telemark, 7, 25, 26, 106, 115, 135
telemarketing, 106, 115, 135
Telluride, 253
Teton Mountain Lodge & Spa, 57
The North Face, 42, 162, 180, 183, 188
The North Face Park and Pipe Open Series Virtual
    Competition, 183
The Travel Foundation, 139
Thomas Cook, 121
Thomson Holidays, 119
Thomson Ski, 123
Thompson Rivers University, 89
Thyon, 13
Tignes, 9, 30, 77
Tirol Werbung GmbH, 149
Travelplan Ski Holidays, 262
TripAdvisor, 165, 231, 234, 257
Toboganning, 26
Travel Alberta, 139
Travel exhibitions, 106, 135
Turkish Ski Federation , 180
Turner, Darren, 93, 94, 95

Uber, 254
Union Pacific, 8
United Nations Association of Australia, 218
United Nations Educational, Scientific and Cultural
    Organization (UNESCO), 1, 267
Urwiler, Robert, 172, 174
U.S. Forest Service, 64
U.S. Olympic Committee, 192
U.S. Ski and Snowboard Team, 192
U.S. Ski Team, 130
Utah Office of Tourism, 130, 142

Vail Resorts, 14, 30, 67, 69, 72-74, 97, 124, 131, 138, 141,
    160, 161, 163, 172-174, 210, 230, 261
Val d'Isere, 30, 77, 79
Val Thorens, 30, 69, 78, 164, 237, 262
Vancouver Winter Olympic, 191, 193
Venue Master Plan, 38, 63, 195
Verbier, 11, 12, 13, 188, 189, 223
Verbier Xtreme, 188
Veysonnaz, 13
Viceroy Snowmass, 98
Villard de Lans, 208
Virgin Atlantic Airways, 141
Visit California, 142

Visit Ogden, 130
Visit Salt Lake, 130
Vitranc Cup, 250
Vonn, Lindsey, 141

Wachusett Mountain in Massachusetts Ski Area, 113
Waldorf Astoria, 73
Wallisch, Tom, 83
Walt Disney Company, 263
Wanda group, 34
Warren Smith Ski Academy, 136
Wasatch Benefit, 131
Washington School House, 26, 263
Waterkeeper's Alliance, 139,189
Westin Hotels, 235
Whiskey Jack Lodge, 265
Whistler Blackcomb, 16-17, 33, 97, 125, 170, 210-212, 263
Whitehorn Lodge, 3,265
White Mountain SuperPass, 124
Whitetail Resort, 93
Whitewater Ski Resort, 123
Wiegele, Mike, 24
Wieringa Onno, 140
World Tourism Organization (UNWTO), 75
World Wildlife Fund, 205
Winchester, Gerry, 122,125
Wine Spectator Award of Excellence, 98
Winter Alpenglow Mountain Festival, 136
Winter Fox Ski Association, 177
Winter Olympic Games, 8, 37, 181, 182, 191-194, 251
Winter Park Resorts, 30
Winterstart World Cup, 1
Winter Universiade, 180
Winter X Games, 42, 44, 162, 189, 190
World Ice Cross Inc., 185
World Slalom, 250
World Ski Awards, 1
World Ski and Snowboard Festival, 75, 79, 179, 191
Wright, Crystal, 57, 58, 59
Wyndham Vacations, 254
X-games, 5, 41, 162

Yarar, Erol, 180
Yeongpyong Resort, 194
Yield management, 75, 79
Yotel cabins, 259
Zermatt, 12, 13, 28, 81
Žerjav, Mirjam, 250
Zero Moment of Truth (ZMOT), 159
Zip-lining, 32, 67
Ziptrek Ecotours, 33